Thatcher's Grandchildren?

Palgrave Studies in the History of Childhood

Series Editors: George Rousseau, University of Oxford, Lawrence Brockliss, University of Oxford

Palgrave Studies in the History of Childhood is the first of its kind to historicise childhood in the English-speaking world; at present no historical series on children/ childhood exists, despite burgeoning areas within Child Studies. The series aims to act both as a forum for publishing works in the history of childhood and a mechanism for consolidating the identity and attraction of the new discipline

Editorial Board: Jo Boyden, University of Oxford, Matthew Grenby, Newcastle University, Heather Montgomery, Open University, Nicholas Orme, Exeter University, Lyndal Roper, University of Oxford, Sally Shuttleworth, University of Oxford Lindsay Smith, Sussex University, Nando Sigona, Birmingham University

Titles include:

Hilary Marland
HEALTH AND GIRLHOOD IN BRITAIN, 1874–1920

George Rousseau
CHILDREN AND SEXUALITY
From the Greeks to the Great War

Stephen Wagg, Jane Pilcher
THATCHER'S GRANDCHILDREN?
Politics and Childhood in the Twenty-First Century

Palgrave Studies in the History of Childhood
Series Standing Order ISBN 978–1–137–30555–8 (Hardback)
(*outside North America only*)

You can receive future titles in this series as they are published by placing a standing order. Please contact your bookseller or, in case of difficulty, write to us at the address below with your name and address, the title of the series and the ISBNs quoted above.

Customer Services Department, Macmillan Distribution Ltd, Houndmills, Basingstoke, Hampshire RG21 6XS, England

Thatcher's Grandchildren?

Politics and Childhood in the Twenty-First Century

Edited by

Stephen Wagg
Professor, Leeds Metropolitan University, UK

and

Jane Pilcher
Senior Lecturer, University of Leicester, UK

Editorial matter, introduction and selection © Stephen Wagg and Jane Pilcher 2014

Remaining chapters © Respective authors 2014

Softcover reprint of the hardcover 1st edition 2014 978-1-137-28154-8

All rights reserved. No reproduction, copy or transmission of this publication may be made without written permission.

No portion of this publication may be reproduced, copied or transmitted save with written permission or in accordance with the provisions of the Copyright, Designs and Patents Act 1988, or under the terms of any licence permitting limited copying issued by the Copyright Licensing Agency, Saffron House, 6–10 Kirby Street, London EC1N 8TS.

Any person who does any unauthorized act in relation to this publication may be liable to criminal prosecution and civil claims for damages.

The authors have asserted their right to be identified as the authors of this work in accordance with the Copyright, Designs and Patents Act 1988.

First published 2014 by
PALGRAVE MACMILLAN

Palgrave Macmillan in the UK is an imprint of Macmillan Publishers Limited, registered in England, company number 785998, of Houndmills, Basingstoke, Hampshire RG21 6XS.

Palgrave Macmillan in the US is a division of St Martin's Press LLC, 175 Fifth Avenue, New York, NY 10010.

Palgrave Macmillan is the global academic imprint of the above companies and has companies and representatives throughout the world.

Palgrave® and Macmillan® are registered trademarks in the United States, the United Kingdom, Europe and other countries.

ISBN 978-1-349-44821-0   ISBN 978-1-137-28155-5 (eBook)
DOI 10.1057/9781137281555

This book is printed on paper suitable for recycling and made from fully managed and sustained forest sources. Logging, pulping and manufacturing processes are expected to conform to the environmental regulations of the country of origin.

A catalogue record for this book is available from the British Library.

A catalog record for this book is available from the Library of Congress.

Typeset by MPS Limited, Chennai, India.

Transferred to Digital Printing in 2014

Contents

List of Figures and Table vii

Notes on Contributors viii

Introduction x

Acknowledgements xvii

1 'Kill a kid and get a house': Rationality versus Retribution in the Case of Robert Thompson and Jon Venables, 1993–2001   1
Julian Petley

2 Citizen Journalists or Cyber Bigots? Child Abuse, the Media and the Possibilities for Public Conversation: The Case of Baby P   27
Bob Franklin

3 The Changing Politics and Practice of Child Protection and Safeguarding in England   45
Nigel Parton

4 Child Trafficking: Known Unknowns and Unknown Knowns   69
Julia O'Connell Davidson

5 'What have the Romans ever done for us?' Child Poverty and the Legacy of 'New' Labour   89
Danny Dorling

6 'When I give food to the poor ...' Some Thoughts on Charity, Childhood and the Media   101
Stephen Wagg

7 A Coming or Going of Age? Children's Literature at the Turn of the Twenty-First Century   118
David Rudd

8 Punishment, Populism and Performance Management: 'New' Labour, Youth, Crime and Justice   140
Tim Newburn

9 Children's Rights Since Margaret Thatcher   160
Marc Cornock and Heather Montgomery

10 Whiteboard Jungle: Schooling, Culture War and the Market at the Turn of the Twenty-First Century   179
Stephen Wagg

vi Contents

11 Troubling Families: Parenting and the Politics of
    Early Intervention   204
    Val Gillies

12 Recolonising the Digital Natives: The Politics of Childhood
    and Technology from Blair to Gove   225
    Keri Facer

13 Kids for Sale? Childhood and Consumer Culture   242
    David Buckingham

14 The Politics of Children's Clothing   258
    Jane Pilcher

15 Children's Rights or Employers' Rights? The 'Destigmatisation'
    of Child Labour   275
    Steve Cunningham and Michael Lavalette

16 Saving the Children? Pornography, Childhood and the Internet 301
    David Buckingham and Despina Chronaki

Index   318

List of Figures and Table

Figures

3.1 *Every Child Matters*: categorising children 49
3.2 *Every Child Matters*: Targeted services within a universal context 50
3.3 Processes and tools to support children and families 52
8.1 Reduction in proven offences by young people, 2001/2 to 2011/12 144
8.2 First-time entrants into the youth justice system, 2001/2 to 2011/12 145
8.3 Average custodial population (under 18), 2000/1 to 2012/13 146
8.4 Trends in the use of ASBOs for young people, 2001–11 148
8.5 Trends in reprimands, final warnings and conditional cautions 149
8.6 Trends in penalty notices for disorder (PNDs) for young people, 2005/6 to 2011/12 150
8.7 Stops and searches under PACE 1984 and other legislation, 2001–8 154

Table

8.1 Young people sentenced for all offences, by type of sentence, 2001/2 to 2010/11 (%) 145

Notes on Contributors

David Buckingham is Professor of Communication and Media Studies at Loughborough University in the UK. He also teaches at the Norwegian Centre for Child Research, NTNU Trondheim. His latest book is *The Material Child: Growing Up in Consumer Culture* (2011).

Despina Chronaki did doctoral research on children, the media and sexual material at Loughborough University and was awarded her doctorate in 2014.

Marc Cornock lectures in law at the Open University and has written widely on the legal aspects of children's rights.

Steve Cunningham is a Senior Lecturer in the School of Social Work at the University of Central Lancashire in the UK. He has written on child labour and children's rights, and has a more general interest in the sociology of welfare. He is the co-author of *Sociology and Social Work* (2008) and *Social Policy and Social Work: An Introduction* (2012).

Danny Dorling is Halford Mackinder Professor of Human Geography at the University of Oxford in the UK. He is the author of *The No Nonsense Guide to Equality* (2012) and, with Bethan Thomas, of *Bankrupt Britain: An Atlas of Social Change* (2012).

Keri Facer is Professor of Educational and Social Futures at the University of Bristol in the UK. Her personal blog, with a full list of previous projects, publications and talks is available at http://kerifacer.wordpress.com/.

Bob Franklin is Professor of Journalism Studies at the Cardiff School of Journalism, Media and Cultural studies. He is the editor of *The Rights of Children* (1986), *The New Handbook of Children's Rights* (2001) and, with Nigel Parton, *Social Work, the Media and Public Relations* (1991).

Val Gillies is Professor of Social Research and a co-director of the Families and Social Capital Research Group at London South Bank University. With Jane Ribbens McCarthy and Carol-Ann Hooper she recently co-edited *Family Troubles? Exploring Changes and Challenges in the Family Lives of Children and Young People* (2013).

Michael Lavalette is Professor in Social Work and Social Policy at Liverpool Hope University in the UK and national coordinator of the Social Work Action Network. He is author of *Voices from the West Bank* (2010), which looks at Palestinian young people's experiences of life under occupation.

Heather Montgomery is Reader in the Anthropology of Childhood at the Open University in the UK. She is the author of *Modern Babylon? Prostituting Children in Thailand* (2001) and *An Introduction to Childhood: Anthropological Perspectives on Children's Lives* (2008). She has edited *Local Childhoods, Global Issues* (2013) and co-edited, with Laurence Brockliss, *Childhood and Violence in the Western Tradition* (2010).

Tim Newburn is Professor of Criminology and Social Policy at the London School of Economics. He is currently Official Historian of Criminal Justice (with David Downes and Paul Rock). He recently edited *Criminology* (2013) and is writing a history of postwar policing.

Julia O'Connell Davidson is Professor of Sociology at the University of Nottingham in the UK and author of *Children in the Global Sex Trade* (2005).

Nigel Parton is Professor of Applied Childhood Studies at the University of Huddersfield in the UK. He is currently writing a book on the politics of child protection, to be published by Palgrave Macmillan in 2014.

Julian Petley is Professor of Screen Media at Brunel University in London and a freelance journalist. His most recent book is *Moral Panics in the Contemporary World* (2013, with Chas Critcher, Jason Hughes and Amanda Rohloff).

Jane Pilcher is Senior Lecturer in Sociology at the University of Leicester in the UK. Her books include *Age and Generation in Modern Britain* (1995) and *Young People in Transition: Becoming Citizens* (co-editor with C. Pole and J. Williams, 2005). Jane has also published a number of articles on historical constructions of childhood in relation to health and sex education, and on children's consumption of clothing.

David Rudd is Professor of Children's Literature at the University of Bolton in the UK. He recently published *Reading the Child in Children's Literature: An Heretical Approach* (2013) and edited *The Routledge Companion to Children's Literature* (2010).

Stephen Wagg is a professor in the Carnegie Faculty of Leeds Metropolitan University in the UK and, with Jane Pilcher, edited *Thatcher's Children?* (1996). He also writes regularly on the politics of sport and leisure. With Helen Lenskyj, he edited *The Palgrave Handbook of Olympic Studies* (2012) and, with Brett Lashua and Karl Spracklen, is the editor of *Sounds and the City: Music, Place and Globalisation* (Palgrave, 2014).

Introduction: Sociology, Politics and Childhood – the Contemporary Landscape

Thatcher's Grandchildren? is not a second edition of *Thatcher's Children?* (Pilcher and Wagg 1996); it is a sequel to it. It does, however, seek to provide a much needed update to many of the accounts provided in that volume, by exploring political controversies about childhood that have emerged, nationally and internationally, since the late 1990s. Whilst some of the contributors to *Thatcher's Children?* appear again in *Thatcher's Grandchildren?*, developing their original work, others have contributed chapters on new topics. In *Thatcher's Grandchildren?* we also have several new authors, covering sociological and political issues that have become increasingly significant in the twenty-first century.

In the introduction to *Thatcher's Children?* (Pilcher and Wagg 1996), we remarked on how the social study of childhood had undergone considerable change. The new paradigm, set out most effectively by Prout and James (1990), had challenged notions of the universal character of childhood and the disproportionate focus in the study of children on issues of socialisation. The new social studies of childhood established childhood as a social and cultural institution which represented the ways, varying across history and culture and embedded in discourse, that the physiological and psychological immaturity of children was understood and made meaningful. Children were recognised not simply as passive recipients of socialisation, but as social actors who were themselves engaged in constructing and reconstructing childhood.

Move forwards 15 or so years since the publication of *Thatcher's Children?*, and the new social studies of childhood have burgeoned. As Wyness (2006) points out, there is now great depth and breadth in theoretical and conceptual work on children and childhood, and in empirical studies of children. One feature of the newer social study of childhood builds on a claim we made in *Thatcher's Children?*: that, whilst children must be recognised as active, reactive and creative beings, their agency is not practised under circumstances of their own choosing or control. James and James (2004), for example, focus on how children and childhood are shaped and controlled by adults in key areas of their social lives, including in schools, families and in the criminal justice system. Alanen (2001) and Mayall (2002) have developed the notion of childhood as a 'generational space' within the social order. In one sense, 'Childhood is a universally present, structural feature of societies' (Qvortrup 1994). Yet, childhood is also something which is serially and temporarily occupied by different generations of children over time. This approach reconceptualises the social study of childhood as essentially being the study of child–adult relations, temporally located in history and culture, and ways in which these relations take place in and through various social institutions, relationships and processes.

A second feature of the newer social studies of childhood relates to a concern with analytical distinctions and recognising 'difference' when discussing children and childhood. For James and James (2004), 'childhood' is the structural site or cultural space occupied by 'children', as a collectivity. 'A child' is a member of the category 'children' whose unique agency is exercised within 'childhood'. Use of the term 'the child' is unwarranted because it implies that children are all the same, whereas in the newer social studies of childhood, differences *between* children are increasingly recognised as significant. Social class, gender, ethnicity and so on are argued to make childhood a differentiated rather than a uniformly experienced stage of the life course. We might, therefore, more accurately speak of 'childhoods' rather than childhood.

The impetus within the new social studies of childhood to establish children as having agency, as being differentiated individuals, and as embedded in a generational space which is temporally and culturally variable and powerfully shaped by adult–child relations, comes at a period when theorists of late modernity are arguing strongly for the dissipation of structurally determined social identities amongst (adult) individuals (Lee 2001). This point brings us to a third feature of the newer social studies of childhood: the increasing emphasis that has been placed on the ways that the study of children and childhood has the potential to impact upon sociology and social science more broadly. To paraphrase Cook (2008), giving proper recognition to the importance of children/childhood means that dominant conceptualisations within existing social theory, including those around individualisation, may become undermined, and thus require revising.

This book explores the contemporary politics of childhood in the light of these considerations, ever mindful, as observed earlier, that while children make their own childhoods, they do not do so in circumstances chosen by themselves. Although the title of the book, like its predecessor, invokes the name of a particular politician, it does so simply to identify a political landscape, and not to imply that that landscape was solely or even largely the creation of the politician herself. Indeed, the sociologist Peter Golding referred as early as 1983 to 'what we now, in absurd flattery of its heroine, call Thatcherism' as having characterised a section of the British Conservative Party since the 1930s (Golding 1983). Nowadays academics and other commentators refer to it as 'neoliberalism' (see, for example, Harvey 2007) – the broad nature of which (marketisation, privatisation, a renewed rhetorical stress on individual responsibility and 'enterprise') is widely known. Politically, in Britain in the decades either side of the year

2000, the flagship for neoliberalism was the 'New' Labour Party and its chief advocate was Tony Blair, Labour leader between 1994 and 2007 and Prime Minister for the last ten of those years. It is a political quip widely aired since her death in 2013 that 'New' Labour was Margaret Thatcher's greatest political achievement (see, for example, Conservative Home 2008) and, broadly speaking, although 'New' Labour's public pronouncements may have differed from what was styled as Thatcherism, its policies, in the view of many analysts, did not. Moreover, in keeping with this routinely personality-oriented rendition of politics, a number of the Conservative politicians prominent in the Conservative–Liberal Democrat Coalition government that took office in 2010 have made known their admiration for Blair. These are said to include Prime Minister David Cameron, Chancellor of the Exchequer George Osborne and influential Education Secretary Michael Gove (see, for instance, Glover 2010). Blair, Cameron, Gove and others can all be seen in the ensuing pages as cheerleaders for what is, in essence, a neoliberal politics of childhood.

Thus, the period 1995 to 2013 saw many enactments and debates which touched crucially upon childhood: for example, 'New' Labour spokespeople on several occasions vowed to end child poverty; 'New' Labour administrations continued existing policies of restructuring the English school system; there were arguments over the sexualisation of children and the inappropriateness of children's clothes and literature – for example, the children's author Philip Pullman was accused of attacking Christianity in his trilogy *His Dark Materials* (1995–2000); the growing influence of the tabloid press was seen in 2000 when the *News of the World*, following the murder of a young girl called Sarah Payne, campaigned for 'Sarah's Law', under which the public would have access to the Sex Offenders' Register; the word 'paedo' – short for 'paedophile' – became common currency in the popular press; in 2009, following the death two years earlier of 17-month-old Peter Connelly as a result of abuse by his mother and others, a media campaign led to the dismissal of the head of Haringey child protection services; there were periodic panics over child pornography, as, for instance, in 2009 when a worker at the Little Ted's nursery in Plymouth was charged with taking indecent photographs of her young charges; similarly, there was regular allusion to the supposed threats to children of adult pornography, carried principally by the Internet; from time to time the public were alerted to the fact that their favourite sportswear or Primark bargains had been assembled by child workers earning next to nothing; in August of 2011, in the wake of the summer's urban rioting and looting, British Prime Minister David Cameron located the source of the disturbances not in the social deprivation that prevailed in certain inner-city areas, but in the childhoods of the rioters, citing 'a complete lack of responsibility, a lack of proper parenting, a lack of proper upbringing, a lack of proper ethics, a lack of proper morals' (see, for example, Porter 2011); and so on. All these issues are taken up in this book.

The chapters

In Chapter 1, in what is effectively a sequel to the chapter he wrote with Bob Franklin for *Thatcher's Children?*, Julian Petley charts an important period in British legal and press history, wherein the case of Robert Thompson and Jon Venables, convicted as boys of the killing of the Liverpool infant James Bulger, was taken up by tabloid newspapers. These papers, whose initiatives carried much apparent weight with successive home secretaries, campaigned seemingly not only against the pair's release, but against the twin notions of children as not fully criminally responsible and of rehabilitative justice itself. The judiciary, both in Britain and in the European Commission, resisted this campaign.

Chapter 2, by Bob Franklin, is similarly concerned with the idea of retribution. Written specifically to test the now widely canvassed argument that the proliferation of social media will lead to more democratic and enlightened public conversation about crime and punishment, the chapter offers a detailed analysis of YouTube representations on the case of Peter Connelly ('Baby P'), a one-year-old child killed in north London in 2007 by his mother and her partner. The analysis yields many starkly retributive judgements on the offenders in this case and little ground for optimism as to the possibilities of humane public dialogue via the social media in question.

In Chapter 3, Nigel Parton, another contributor to *Thatcher's Children?*, looks at recent developments in child protection, judging in particular the impact on policy both of high-profile child deaths, such as that of Baby P, and of growing poverty as a result of successive reductions in public expenditure on social care. He also charts the rise of what he sees as an increasingly authoritarian, neoliberal social policy, with a greater proportion of social care provision now in private hands.

The next chapter is about child trafficking, about which, as Julia O'Connell Davidson demonstrates, there is much public alarm but comparatively little reliable knowledge. The chapter uses Donald Rumsfeld's infamous formulation of 'known knowns, known unknowns and unknown unknowns' to decipher contemporary political discourse on child trafficking which, the author argues, combines two key sources of anxiety in Western societies in the twenty-first century – perceived threats to childhood and the spectre of migrants.

Chapters 5 and 6 are essentially companion pieces. In Chapter 5, Danny Dorling shows why, despite solemn promises and heart-warming political rhetoric, the 'New' Labour administrations of Tony Blair and Gordon Brown (2007–10) did not bring an end to child poverty. In Chapter 6, Stephen Wagg provides a political analysis of the celebrity child poverty initiatives that have burgeoned since Live Aid in 1985. (Chapter 15, on child labour, clearly supplements some of the arguments made here.)

The theme of child-based moral panic recurs in the following chapter, in which David Rudd gives an analytical overview of trends in children's

xiv *Introduction*

literature at the turn of the twenty-first century. Writers seem increasingly to be addressing child readers as young people with a capacity for discrimination and the digestion of complex social issues. The popular press, meanwhile, has been wont to sound the alarm and to claim that, through access to what is claimed to be 'adult' material, young minds are being polluted and young fears aroused.

Chapter 8 is by Tim Newburn and gives an overview of 'New' Labour policy on juvenile justice, in which, like Julian Petley (whose chapter is, to a degree, a companion to this one), he identifies a clear strain of punitive populism, but also a strong element of managerialism, bringing with it a culture of the now apparently ubiquitous performance indication. He also takes account of the urban riots in Britain in the summer of 2011, research on which revealed increasingly fractious relations between young people and the police.

In Chapter 9, Marc Cornock and Heather Montgomery give a detailed account of the progress of children's rights, in the UK and beyond, in the years since 1991 when the British government ratified the United Nations Convention on the Rights of the Child. (This chapter can usefully be read in conjunction with Chapters 12 and 15.)

Chapter 10, in which Stephen Wagg discusses the contemporary politics of schooling, is another to draw on the notion of moral panic. In this case, successive government spokespeople strove to promote the idea of a menace to many schoolchildren posed by teachers who were either 'incompetent' or harbouring 'low expectations' of their young charges. This (plainly ideological) campaign seemed calculated to furnish a pretext for privatising state schools, a policy already in train since the early 1990s.

In Chapter 11, Val Gillies also deconstructs a contemporary moral panic, this time about parenting. She surveys and analyses successive government attempts to lay the blame for escalating social problems at the door of (invariably working-class) mothers and fathers allegedly ill equipped to be parents.

To use her own words, Keri Facer's work in the next chapter, on children's relationship to technology, 'explores how adult–child relations are being constructed in media and political discourses in two key fields: first, in the debates over children's online safety; and secondly, in the use of digital technologies in schools'. She suggests that strategies of surveillance now being concocted, partly as a response to media-promoted fears of the Internet, pose a real danger to children's rights.

Chapters 13 and 14 may also be seen as companion pieces. In the first, David Buckingham discusses the latest manifestations of an old-established fear in relation to childhood: that childhood is being sullied by the commercial blandishments of unscrupulous marketers, and children, in effect, thus robbed of their childhood by being obliged too early to assume the role of consumer. He argues (as we noted that sociologists are now increasingly inclined to do) that this ignores the *agency* of the child and his/her capacity to judge and to choose. He also questions why excessive commercialisation – a fact of life under neoliberalism – should be a problem for children and not for adults. In the second of the chapters, Jane Pilcher attends to the parallel panic over children's clothing and the insistence, on the part of sections of the popular press and conservative pressure groups, that children are once again being denied a proper childhood, this time by the marketing to youngsters of overly sexualised clothing. Drawing on her own research, and once again giving a voice to actual children, she argues that children are themselves quite capable of judging what is too sexy and what isn't.

Chapter 15 returns to the issue of children's rights, this time in relation to child labour, an issue more pressing in poorer countries, which are routinely trawled by Western corporations in their search for inexpensive labour. Here Steve Cunningham and Michael Lavalette show how the debate over child labour and children's rights is being skewed in favour of the employers. This is done, firstly, by the suggestion by right-wing lobbyists that the employment of children (a factor, after all, in the industrialisation of Western societies) is a necessary (if regrettable) stage to be passed through on the road to economic growth and, secondly, that to deny children the opportunity to work (and thus support their families in impoverished circumstances) is to infringe their rights. The neoliberal policies adopted by global financial institutions, whereby developing countries must privatise as a condition of receiving loans, do nothing to alleviate this situation.

Finally, in Chapter 16, David Buckingham and Despina Chronaki take a dispassionate look at yet another ongoing moral panic about childhood, namely that today's children are in moral and emotional danger from sexual material that is easily available via modern media, particularly the Internet. The chapter provides a clear and dispassionate discussion of the place – legally, socially and politically – of pornography in human societies and then draws on Chronaki's own research with young adults, reflecting on their own experiences of explicit sexual material as children. Once again, the evidence points, first, to an over-heated and often misleading public account of this 'problem' and, second, to the capacity of children to deal with graphic sexual imagery without suffering emotional distress.

References

Alanen, L. (2001). 'Explorations in Generational Analysis'. In L. Alanen and B. Mayall (eds), *Conceptualising Adult–Child Relations*. London: Routledge.
Conservative Home. (2008). 'Margaret Thatcher's Greatest Achievement: New Labour'. Conservative Home blog. http://conservativehome.blogs.com/centreright/2008/04/making-history.html (accessed 27 June 2013).
Cook, D. (2008). 'The Missing Child in Consumption Theory'. *Journal of Consumer Culture* 8(2): 219–43.

Glover, S. (2010). 'A duplicitous warmonger in thrall to the rich ... so why DO the Tories want to be heirs to Blair?'. *MailOnline*, 18 March. http://www.dailymail.co.uk/debate/article-1258774/Why-DO-Tories-want-heirs-Tony-Blair.html (accessed 27 June 2013).

Golding, P. (1983). 'Rethinking Commonsense about Social Policy'. In D. Bull and P. Wilding (eds), *Thatcherism and the Poor*. London: Child Poverty Action Group.

Harvey, D. (2007). *A Brief History of Neoliberalism*. Oxford: Oxford University Press.

James, A. and James, A. (2004). *Constructing Childhood: Theory, Policy and Social Practice*. Basingstoke: Palgrave Macmillan.

Lee, N. (2001). *Childhood and Society: Growing Up in an Age of Uncertainty*. Buckingham: Open University Press.

Mayall, B. (2002). *Towards a Sociology of Childhood: Thinking from Children's Lives*. Buckingham: Open University Press.

Pilcher, J. and Wagg, S. (eds). (1996). *Thatcher's Children? Childhood, Politics and Society in the 1980s and 1990s*. London: Falmer.

Porter, A. (2011). 'London riots: water cannons to be used on sick society'. *The Telegraph*, 10 August. http://www.telegraph.co.uk/news/uknews/crime/8694401/London-riots-water-cannons-to-be-used-on-sick-society.html (accessed 16 June 2013).

Prout, A. and James, A. (1990). 'A New Paradigm for the Sociology of Childhood? Provenance, Promise and Problems'. In A. James and A. Prout (eds), *Constructing and Reconstructing Childhood* (2nd edn). London: Falmer.

Qvortrup, J. (1994). 'Childhood Matters: An Introduction'. In J. Qvortrup (ed.), *Childhood Matters*. Aldershot: Avebury.

Wyness, M. (2006). *Childhood and Society: An Introduction to the Sociology of Childhood*. Basingstoke: Palgrave Macmillan.

Acknowledgements

Our thanks go to:

Julian Petley, for suggesting a sequel to *Thatcher's Children?*
All the people who, whether they were able to accept it or not, responded so warmly to our invitation to write for this book.
Heather Montgomery and David Buckingham for their help in putting the book together.
Laurence Brockliss for his interest in the project.
Patrick Kingsley, Phil Coomes, Sarah Goodall, Megan Thomas and Jadeane Francis for their support and cooperation in procuring the cover image.
Brett Lashua for moral and technical support and friendship.

Stephen would like to thank his granddaughters Evangeline Squaletti (b.2008) and Genevieve Squaletti (b.2011) for countless insights into the contemporary politics of childhood. His work for this book is dedicated to them.

1
'Kill a kid and get a house'
Rationality versus Retribution in the Case of Robert Thompson and Jon Venables, 1993–2001

Julian Petley

Introduction

On 24 November 1993, at the conclusion of the trial of Robert Thompson and Jon Venables for the murder of James Bulger, Mr Justice Morland sentenced them to be detained at Her Majesty's pleasure, the child's equivalent of a mandatory life sentence for murder. He stated that they would 'be detained for very, very many years until the Home Secretary is satisfied that you have matured and are fully rehabilitated and are no longer a danger to others'. On 29 November he submitted to the Home Secretary, Michael Howard, his assessment of the 'tariff' (the proportion of the sentence that reflects retribution and deterrence, as opposed to the protective element of the sentence that reflects the risk posed by the offender to society). This he set at eight years, to be reviewed after five. He sent his recommendation to the Lord Chief Justice, Lord Taylor of Gosforth, who ordered that the boys should serve a minimum of ten years, with review at seven. Both agreed that the boys would not serve the latter part of their sentence in an adult prison, mainly to avoid revenge attacks. Under the system then in operation for mandatory adult life sentences, he then passed his recommendation to Howard for a final ruling.

In many quarters, not least in large sections of the British press, there was considerable surprise, not to say anger and disappointment, at the length of the original tariff. According to David James Smith (1995: 244), the ranks of the angry and disappointed included Howard himself, who had been considering a tariff of 20 to 25 years. In January 1994 Lord Taylor's recommendations were passed to the boys in confidence, but they became public, and the Bulger family immediately launched a campaign to persuade Howard that they should never be released. This was supported vociferously by the tabloid press, and in particular by the *Sun*, which published a coupon that read: 'I agree with Ralph and Denise Bulger that the two boys who killed their son James should stay in jail for LIFE', and over 21,281 of these were sent by readers to Howard. The Bulger family also organised a petition demanding life sentences, and this attracted more than 278,300 signatures. Additionally, Gerald Howarth, the Conservative MP for Knowsley North, handed in a petition, this one demanding a 25-year sentence, which was signed by 5,900 people.

In July 1994, Howard announced that the boys would remain in custody for a minimum of 15 years, thus preventing review for 12 years and ensuring that both boys would be in adult prisons by the time any initial assessments took place. He openly admitted that he had taken note of the coupons, emphasising the 'need to maintain public confidence in the system of criminal justice'. The popular press was duly satisfied, but, appearing the following year on *Panorama*, Lord Donaldson, a former Master of the Rolls, spoke for the bulk of legal opinion when he accused Howard of 'institutionalised vengeance' and complained that 'one can't have a politician playing to the gallery at the expense of a convicted person. That's not justice in my book' (quoted in *The Times*, 10 October 1995).

This chapter examines the processes which led from here to Thompson's and Venables' release on licence in 2001. It is a story from which the English legal system emerges as generally rational and humane; and it also underlines the fundamental importance of the European Convention on Human Rights, which was incorporated into UK law by the Human Rights Act 1998. It is a story from which politicians, and especially home secretaries Michael Howard and Jack Straw, emerge with considerably less credit, and the narrative needs to be read against the background in which 'New' Labour and the Tories contended to see who could out-tough the other on law-and-order issues. Indeed, the Bulger case played a very important role in this process. Just six days after the murder, on 19 February 1993, Tony Blair, then shadow Home Secretary, made a speech in which he warned that:

> The news bulletins of the last week have been like hammer blows struck against the sleeping conscience of the country, urging us to wake up and look unflinchingly at what we see ... Solution to this disintegration doesn't simply lie in legislation. It must come from the rediscovery of a sense of direction as a country and most of all from being unafraid to start talking again about the values and principles we believe in and what they mean for us, not just as individuals but as a community. We cannot exist in a moral vacuum. If we do not learn and then teach the value of what is right and wrong, then the result is simply moral chaos which engulfs us all. (Quoted in Rentoul 2001: 200)

As Blair's biographer John Rentoul put it: 'His speech was of no direct relevance to the Bulger case, but touched a national mood of anxiety over the break-up of morals and families. It was like a Conservative politician's speech, responding to a moral panic induced by an atypical case by condemning a general moral decline' (ibid.). Rentoul notes that Blair's office was subsequently 'flooded with letters of approval and support' and argues that it played a major role in his acceding to the leadership of the party after John Smith's death in 1994. As Matthew Parris pointed out in *The Times* on 2 October 1994:

> Tony Blair has parked his tanks on Michael Howard's lawn. When a toddler was abducted and murdered earlier this year, with suspicion falling on two other boys, the killing inspired a moral panic across Britain. John Major announced a 'crusade against crime', and the numbers who told MORI they were worried about law and order doubled within a month. Sensing an electoral opportunity, both parties revamped their message … [Tony Blair's] slogan 'tough on crime, tough on the causes of crime' has already entered the political lexicon. This week in Brighton [at the Labour Party conference], he discovered that his words carried a resonance even with a progressive, activist audience. When he cheekily proclaimed that Labour was now the party of law and order he won healthy applause; and, using language more often heard at a Tory party conference, he declared that 'hooligans', 'muggers', 'perverted' rapists and 'racist thugs' should be kept out of society 'until they learn to behave like human beings'.

The effect of this political and ideological volte-face on the part of 'New' Labour meant that, at the parliamentary level, an authoritarian-populist consensus had rapidly coalesced around the Bulger case, and thence around law-and-order issues in general, one which left virtually no space for counter-discourses of any kind. Whether 'New' Labour's punitive turn stemmed from Blair's and Straw's 'communitarian' convictions, or whether it was rather more opportunistic in origin, or both, is a moot point, but one thing is absolutely certain: it chimed perfectly with the profoundly illiberal stance taken by the vast bulk of the English daily and Sunday newspapers on social issues. These are the third set of actors in our story. In the narrative that follows I have attempted to give an indication of how the key events described were reported by the press. In the space available it is difficult to give an impression of the sheer volume of reportage, and quite impossible to analyse it all, but I have attempted to isolate the main themes. Because I am particularly concerned to show the pressures to which the courts and politicians were being subjected by newspapers, I have concentrated on those (the majority) which were clamouring to keep Thompson and Venables locked up, preferably for good, but I have also quoted on occasion from those which took a more liberal line, partly in order to show that press coverage of this issue was not homogeneous, but, more particularly, in order to demonstrate that there is a trenchant critique of journalism that emanates from within journalism itself rather than simply from within academia. Furthermore, whilst the case has given rise to some of the worst journalism I have ever seen, it has also given rise to some of the best – for example Andrew O'Hagan (1993) and the two *Independent on Sunday* articles included in Sereny (1995).

The story presented here could be read as one in which reason and a belief in rehabilitation triumph, ultimately, over populist demagoguery and a crude desire for revenge. But, unfortunately, this would be to ignore the wider context in which the events took place, and, in particular, the passing of the Criminal Justice and Public Order Act 1994 and the Crime and Disorder Act 1998. The latter, with its provision for antisocial behaviour orders (ASBOs), parenting orders, child safety orders, local child curfews, detention and training orders, and abolition of *doli incapax* (which meant that a child under 14 could be held criminally accountable only if the prosecution could prove that they knew at the time that what they were doing was seriously wrong), had the effect of massively increasing the possibilities for the criminalisation of young people. This topic is unfortunately beyond the scope of this chapter (but see Tim Newburn's chapter in this book).

'Who are you deterring?'

On 7 November 1994 leave was granted to Thompson and Venables for a judicial review of Howard's actions. And the following November, in a case which was seen as having important repercussions for the boys, Mr Justice Turner stated that the Home Secretary had 'failed to live up to the required standard of fairness' when he increased from 15 to 20 years the tariff fixed by a judge on double killer John Pierson (quoted in the *Guardian*, 11 November 1995). Pierson's QC, Edward Fitzgerald, revealed to the court that the Home Office was handing out longer terms to life prisoners than those recommended by the trial judge in 60 per cent of cases.

The judicial review of Howard's actions in the Bulger case was heard in April 1996 in the High Court. Edward Fitzgerald, QC for Venables, argued that Howard was wrong to conclude that there was no difference between a sentence of detention during Her Majesty's pleasure imposed on juveniles and a mandatory life sentence imposed on adult murderers, pointing out that 'that not only flies in the face of common sense and the principle in every civilised penal code that children should be treated differently from adults, but is also contrary to both domestic and European law. No other country would have a situation where a child as young as ten can have a punitive sentence imposed by a politician'. He also argued that Howard had failed to take into account mitigating circumstances and rehabilitative needs, and that the deterrent aspect of the sentence was entirely inappropriate, given the nature of the crime. 'Who are you deterring?,' he enquired, 'Other children of ten?' (quoted in the *Guardian*, 18 April 1996).

On 2 May the High Court ruled Howard's actions unlawful, in that he had treated Thompson and Venables as if they were adult murderers, as opposed to children who 'change beyond recognition during the running of the tariff period'. Lord Justice Pill pointed out that the central imperative of detaining a young person during Her Majesty's pleasure was to keep the need for detention under regular review, and that 'it is inconsistent with the requirement to keep under review to fix a fifteen-year tariff at the beginning of a sentence on a child of eleven' (quoted in *The Times*, 3 May 1996). Howard retorted that 'the power I exercised was given to me by Parliament in the last century and updated three times since then. If Parliament had wanted a change it could have used any of the six Criminal Justice Bills of the past ten years' (quoted in ibid.). He also pointed out that the power had been exercised 400 times without challenge since 1983. The former Master of the Rolls, Lord Donaldson, described these comments as breathtaking, disturbing and a 'novel constitutional doctrine' which amounted to 'dictatorship by permission'. He continued: 'The Home Secretary says that because Parliament has chosen not to change the law, then it must be the will of Parliament that they do not wish any change in the law.' The whole basis of government was that ministers exercised their powers within the law. If they went beyond those powers, they were acting unlawfully. 'But Mr Howard seems to suggest ministers can act unlawfully and if anybody objects, then they can change the law' (quoted in ibid.). The decision had implications for the other 230 young murderers detained at Her Majesty's pleasure.

Howard appealed, unsuccessfully, to the Divisional Court in July 1996. The majority ruling again centred on the contradiction in setting a tariff whilst maintaining the duty to keep the children's progress under review. The judges also argued that Howard had acted unfairly in making his decision on a summary of the case by a judge, without seeking psychiatric or social reports, and without disclosing to Thompson's and Venables' lawyers the material on which he was basing his decision, thus making it impossible for them to make any representations about this material. Lord Woolf, the Master of the Rolls, and one of the judges in the case, made it clear that Howard should never have taken the coupons and petitions into account, stating that:

> A court would regard it as quite improper for this type of material to be put before it, and to run a campaign designed to increase the punishment in a particular case would amount to interference with the due administration of justice. This being the position as to the courts, I find it difficult to see the justification for the Home Secretary taking a different view. I can only describe the approach in these cases as perfunctory and as falling far below the standards that a court would adopt if contemplating sentencing a child for a period of fifteen years. (Quoted in *The Times*, 31 July 1996)

Undaunted, Howard appealed to the Lords in January 1997. In June the Lords dismissed the appeal and the 15-year tariff was quashed. Lord

Browne-Wilkinson argued that the policy applied by Howard 'precludes any regard being had to how the child has progressed and matured during ... detention until the tariff originally fixed has expired'. Thus throughout the tariff period, 'appropriate weight to the circumstances directly relevant to an assessment of the child's welfare' could not be given, and hence the essential prerequisite of flexibility in dealing with the welfare of the child had been denied. Similarly Lord Hope expressed the view that a sentencing policy 'which ignores at any stage the child's development and progress while in custody as a factor relevant to his eventual release date is an unlawful policy'. In addition, he argued that Howard had failed to demonstrate an appropriate 'measure of detachment from the pressure of public opinion', while Lord Steyn dismissed the petitions and coupons as 'worthless' and 'irrelevant' and stated that the Home Secretary should act 'with the same dispassionate sense of fairness as a sentencing judge'. (All quotations taken from Haydon and Scraton 2000: 434–5).

This was a pretty damning judgment all round. But it needs to be stressed that the Lords did not actually declare illegal the setting of fixed penal tariffs by home secretaries. Thus the ruling did not stop the imposition of a 15-year – or indeed longer – provisional tariff in the future, as long as it was clear that the minister was prepared to recognise that a child's development whilst in detention might call for a rethink. The judgment also left open the question of when the first review of the detention should take place, and the new regime set out by the Lords fell short of the annual reviews of detention recommended by many penal experts. Still less did the Lords consider raising the age of criminality to 14, or, failing that, banning public trials for under-14s.

Struck down in Strasbourg

By this time, Jack Straw had become Home Secretary, and so it was left to him to fix a new tariff. However, the judgment obliged him and his successors to treat Thompson and Venables, and other children in the same situation, differently from adult lifers and, in particular, to review regularly their progress towards rehabilitation, with a view to their eventual release. The final decision on their release would be taken by the Parole Board, but the Home Secretary would determine the earliest date at which the case would be referred to the Board. Straw decided to wait until after the judgment of the European Commission/Court of Human Rights, which, as we shall see, had also been examining the fate of Thompson and Venables.

Dominic Lloyd, the solicitor for Thompson, had stated in May 1994 that an application had been lodged with the European Commission on Human Rights with the intention of challenging both the way that child defendants were tried in England and Wales and the power given to home secretaries in determining sentences in serious cases. Britain was the only country, apart from the Irish Republic, where a politician – as opposed to a judge – could fix the sentence in such cases. And only France and Holland had indeterminate sentences for juveniles. Lloyd was also concerned that Howard had already made it clear that he intended to take 'public opinion' into account when deciding on this case – and indeed on others too. The child law specialist, Alan Levy QC, warned that Howard would be vulnerable on this point:

> It's very strongly arguable that public opinion is irrelevant, that he is taking account of something he shouldn't. That renders the decision challengeable and, I think, void. Also, it's very difficult to gauge public opinion. The petition may have been signed by 270,000 people but there's a population of 55 million. The public would not be aware of all the circumstances. It's a matter for the professionals – the judiciary and the parole board. Leaving it to the executive goes against the whole trend in Europe and I think it would be struck down in Strasbourg. (Quoted in the *Guardian*, 26 July 1994)

And indeed, in December 1994, the European Commission on Human Rights decided that the Home Secretary's role in deciding when young murderers were released, once they had served their tariff, violated the European Convention on Human Rights (ECHR), and that their release dates should be determined by an independent, court-like body. The case in question had been brought by Prem Singh and Abed Hussain, then in their thirties but still detained at Her Majesty's pleasure for murders they had committed as 15- and 16-year-olds respectively. Hussain was sentenced to indeterminate imprisonment, and the Home Secretary had twice refused to release him, in spite of being recommended by the Parole Board to do so.[1]

The European Court of Human Rights upheld the Commission's ruling in February 1996. This left the government no option but to change the law to give prisoners detained at Her Majesty's pleasure for murders committed while under 18 the right to challenge their detention before a judicial body, thus taking the final decision out of the Home Secretary's hands. The ruling did not affect the Home Secretary's right actually to set the tariff in the case of juvenile murderers, but it did abolish his right to decide when a prisoner should be released once the tariff had expired. The relevance of this judgment to the Thompson and Venables case was abundantly clear, and inevitably the ruling brought forth calls from the usual quarters for the UK to withdraw from the ECHR – even though two all-party parliamentary committees had recommended removing politicians from sentencing, the House of Lords had attached (unsuccessfully) an amendment to this effect to the most recent Criminal Justice Bill, and the judiciary was united on the issue. As Melanie Phillips put it the *Observer* (25 February 1996):

> The fact remains that we signed up to the Human Rights Declaration in 1950 and it is no use whingeing when it is applied as it should be.

8 *Julian Petley*

We signed up because we thought we were so civilised it was not necessary for us, only for other countries which needed a boot up their undemocratic backsides. Well, since we have been behaving like some tinpot banana republic we have been getting it in the neck, and rightly so. The answer is that we should stop behaving like a tinpot banana republic, not blame the judges of the Court of Human Rights for pulling us up when we flout those conventions we purport to uphold.

In March 1999 the European Commission on Human Rights announced that Thompson and Venables had won the right to have their case – namely that their trial was unfair and amounted to 'inhuman and degrading treatment', and that their term in detention should not have been fixed by the Home Secretary – heard before the European Court of Human Rights. The Commission ruled by 14 votes to 5 that the trial had breached Article 6 (right to a fair trial) of the ECHR, although it did not agree that it had amounted to 'inhumane and degrading treatment' (which would have infringed Article 3). But it did criticise the 'highly charged' atmosphere in which the trial had taken place, and the 'formal panoply of the adult criminal trial involving judge and counsel in wigs and gowns', concluding that all this amounted to a 'severely intimidating procedure', and one which 'must have seriously impinged on [the boys'] ability to participate in the proceedings in any meaningful manner'. According to the Commission: 'In these circumstances, the primary purpose of the proceedings, the establishment of the facts of the case and the allocation of responsibility were impaired', and the trial risked 'presenting the appearance of an exercise in the vindication of public outrage'. It also upheld by 18 votes to 1 the complaint over the way in which the boys' sentences had been increased by a politician as opposed to an 'independent and impartial tribunal'.

This decision brought forth an early attack on human rights of the kind which has now become an almost daily occurrence in most of the British press. This was by Roger Scruton in *The Times*, 16 March 1999. According to Scruton: 'British justice, and the English law in which it is based, have enjoyed the confidence not only of the British people but of the entire civilised world'. On the basis of this highly questionable assertion he then goes on to lament that:

> All that is changing. First, our native sense of justice, derived from a law that places duty before right and precedent before innovation, is being overridden by the rights-based law of the European courts: a law invented by ideologues and activists, with no roots in the customs and feelings of the people. We see an illustration of this in the James Bulger case, in which our justice system delivered a verdict that brought some peace to our troubled hearts, only to be subjected to mad litigation directed through the European Court of Human Rights, whose only interest is in the 'rights' of those who committed this terrible crime.

On 16 December 1999 the Court ruled that Thompson and Venables had not received a fair trial, and that Howard had breached their human rights when he increased their sentences. Thompson was awarded £15,000 costs and Venables £29,000. Noting that, read as a whole, Article 6 of the ECHR guarantees the right of the accused to participate effectively in their criminal trial, the Court concluded that the children had been denied a fair trial on the following grounds:

> The formality and ritual of the crown court must at times have seemed incomprehensible and intimidating for a child of eleven, and there is evidence that certain of the modifications to the court room, in particular the raised dock which was designed to enable the applicants to see what was going on, had the effect of increasing their sense of discomfort during the trial since they felt exposed to the scrutiny of the press and public.
>
> There was psychiatric evidence that, at the time of the trial, both applicants were suffering from post-traumatic stress disorder as a result of what they had done to the two-year-old, and that they found it impossible to discuss the offence with their lawyers. They had found the trial distressing and frightening and had not been able to concentrate during it.
>
> In such circumstances the court did not consider that it was sufficient for the purposes of Article 6 (1) that the applicants were represented by skilled and experienced lawyers. Although their legal representatives were seated, as the Government put it, 'within whispering distance', it was highly unlikely that either applicant would have felt sufficiently uninhibited, in the tense court room and under public scrutiny, to have consulted with them during the trial or, indeed, that, given their immaturity and disturbed emotional state, they would have been capable outside the court room of co-operating with their lawyers and giving them information for the purposes of their defence.

Article 6 lays down, inter alia, that in the determination of any criminal charge, including the matter of sentencing, everyone is entitled to a fair and public hearing by an 'independent and impartial tribunal established by law'. As the House of Lords recognised on the occasion of Howard's appeal to it in June 1997, the fixing of the tariff amounted to a sentencing exercise. Since Howard, as a politician, did not constitute a court or tribunal independent of the executive, and since no judicial supervision was incorporated into the fixing of the tariff, Article 6 had been breached. Furthermore, since their conviction in November 1993, the boys had not had their continuing detention reviewed by a judicial body, thus there had been a violation of their rights under Article 5 (4), which lays down that 'everyone who is deprived of his liberty by arrest or detention shall be entitled to take proceedings by which the lawfulness of his detention shall be decided speedily by a court and his release ordered if the detention is not lawful'.

Five judges specified significant issues which together amounted to a 'substantial level of mental and physical suffering'. In their view, 'bringing the whole weight of the adult processes to bear on children ... is a relic of times where the effect of the trial process and sentencing on a child's physical and psychological condition and development ... was scarcely considered, if at all'. It was a prosecution brought for 'retribution, rather than humiliation', but vengeance, particularly against children, 'is not a form of justice ... and should be excluded'. The indefinite sentence imposed upon the boys represented a denial of their status as children and, as such, 'must be qualified as inhuman'.[2]

'A bunch of foreigners'

The European Court thus reinforced the Lords' judgment that the Home Secretary could have no say in when children convicted of murder should be freed. Essentially, the judgment meant that Britain would be forced to change the way in which children who kill are tried and sentenced. Straw's room for manoeuvre was distinctly limited: he could either accept the original judge's eight-year tariff, or the ten-year one set by the Lord Chief Justice, or ask the new holder of the post, Lord Bingham, to set a new one. In the meantime, of course, he was left in no doubt by significant sections of the British press about how they viewed the whole matter. Thus the *Sun* (17 December 1999) demanded: 'Who gave a bunch of European lawyers, from countries with much less satisfactory and mature legal systems than ours, the right to dictate how British courts and elected British politicians should deal with child murderers?'; while for the same day's *Daily Mail*, the ruling amounted to 'an outside court interfering in long-standing judicial and political procedures which have been democratically established and accepted by the British people'. With remarkable obtuseness it also entirely missed the point of the UK and European judgments by arguing that 'surely it is the job of democratic politicians to take account of public feeling'. Nor were these sentiments confined to the tabloid press. Thus in the same day's *Telegraph* Minette Marrin complained that 'there is something rather monstrous ... about a bunch of foreigners telling us what is right. And what a gallimaufry of foreigners they are too', whilst an editorial argued that 'revulsion from extraordinarily wicked crimes is still entitled to expression in sentencing ... Jack Straw is better placed to judge that entirely proper outrage than a gaggle of lawyers in Strasbourg'.

True to form, the British government did the absolute minimum to comply with the European Court's judgment. Thus on 13 March 2000

Straw announced that children accused of murder would still be tried in the Crown Court but that Lord Auld, then reviewing the workings of the criminal courts, would be asked to consider changes that could be made to avoid an 'unnecessarily overbearing atmosphere'. He noted that he had already consulted with the new Lord Chief Justice, Lord Bingham, on how Crown Courts could be made less intimidating for children, and that on 16 February he (Lord Bingham) had issued a practice direction to judges on this matter. As reported in *The Times* (17 February 2000), measures included limiting admission to the public and the media, discouraging the wearing of robes and wigs, and banning any 'recognisable police presence' unless for good reason. Anyone responsible for a young defendant who was in custody should not wear a uniform. The trial process should not expose children to 'avoidable intimidation, humiliation or distress', and when attending court as defendants, children should not be exposed to 'intimidation, vilification or abuse' either inside or outside the court, especially in high-profile cases. In this respect, judges should be ready to make orders banning identification of a child defendant. All participants in the trial should be on the same or almost the same physical level, and children should be free to sit with members of their family in a place which permitted easy communication with their lawyers. Lord Bingham also stated that 'all possible steps should be taken to assist the young defendant to understand and participate in the proceedings. The ordinary trial process should so far as necessary be adapted to meet those ends', and that, as far as was practicable, the trial should be 'conducted in language which the young defendant can understand'. The trial should also be conducted according to a timetable which took full account of a young defendant's inability to concentrate for long periods, so that there should be frequent and regular breaks.

Straw also announced on 13 March that the new Criminal Justice Bill and Court Services Bill would require tariffs to be set by the trial judge in open court, 'ensuring that the views of victims and their relatives are better taken into account'. The tariffs would be open to challenge by either the defendant or the Attorney General, but neither the Lord Chief Justice nor the Home Secretary would have the power to overturn them. Those already in detention would have their tariffs reviewed. The numbers involved, as reported in *The Times* (14 March 2000) were startling. Thus, at that time, about 250 people sentenced while children were detained at Her Majesty's pleasure; 75 of these were entitled to a Parole Board hearing to decide if they could be released, and 20 had not at that time been given a minimum gaol sentence. Of the remainder, who could now make representations about their minimum terms, 25 had had a sentence set by a Home Secretary that was higher than the Lord Chief Justice had recommended. Seventeen of these cases had been sent to the Parole Board, leaving eight still to be sent.

'Victims of the system'

On the same day, Straw also revealed that he would ask Lord Bingham to set a new tariff for Thompson and Venables. He also made it clear that they would be freed only if the Parole Board was convinced that they were no longer a danger to the public. The shadow Home Secretary, Ann Widdecombe, responded that 'it is not in the interests of the perpetrators to regard themselves as victims of the system. Instead they should be regarding themselves as perpetrators of an unthinkable crime and one that they should come to terms with rather than being encouraged to think they have received unfair treatment' (quoted in *The Times*, 14 March 2000). And an indignant Michael Howard asked Straw: 'Will you renew the efforts made by the previous government to increase the respect shown by the European Court of Human Rights for national courts so as to ensure that they intervene much less often in the decisions of those national courts?' (quoted in the *Independent*, 14 March 2000). In legal circles it was generally thought that Lord Bingham would order the boys' release in 2003, after they had served the original ten-year tariff. The Home Secretary would be bound to accept his ruling.

Again, a ringing condemnation of the way in which Thompson and Venables had been treated by politicians in thrall to populist newspapers came from an unexpected source:

> I detest the retributive theory of punishment. In this case, the idea that we need to take extraordinary retaliation against two children to express society's collective abhorrence of crime is a descent into barbarism. We do not need to wreck a child's life to tell Britain that a child killing a child is wrong. We do not need to exact punishment to console a victim's parents in their grief. It is medieval to express sympathy in the guise of revenge. But we do expect politicians to support judges in the difficult task of handling children who have done wrong. We also expect them to restrain the lynch law instincts of the mob ...
>
> The idea of putting all such misfits away at 'Her Majesty's pleasure' gained ground under the last government. No Tory centralisation was as politically appealing as the desire to 'play judge' in removing discretion from courts, prison and probation services. It was seized to the ministerial bosom. Power was shifted from those best qualified and those best placed to meet the surge in child criminality. It passed to politicians in thrall to the press and public opinion. This move was bad. The fight against crime exchanged reason for spasm. It brought closer the day of plebiscitary justice, of sentencing by referendum, of newspapers as jurors and of a return to corporal and capital punishment. Open this gate and the path leads only to hell. We owe a vote of thanks to the European Court of Human Rights.

Thus spoke Simon Jenkins, in *The Times* (15 March 2000).

'A corrosive atmosphere'

The unenviable task of setting a new tariff passed to Lord Woolf, who became Lord Chief Justice in June 2000. That month, the Home Office announced that the young men would remain in local authority secure units until they were 19, as opposed to being transferred at 18 to a Young Offender Institution run by the prison service. If still in custody at 19, they would be transferred to a Young Offender Institution, and would then be transferred to an adult prison on reaching 21. Significantly, when in October 1999 Sir David Ramsbotham, the Chief Inspector of Prisons, said of Thompson and Venables in an interview with the *New Statesman* that 'I would not wish them to go to some of the institutions I have seen', he was forced to explain to a furious Jack Straw why he 'went beyond his terms of reference', following which he 'apologised unreservedly for speaking publicly on matters outside his responsibilities and, specifically, in relation to cases in which the Home Secretary acts in a quasi-judicial role' (quoted in the *Independent*, 3 November 1999). In March 2000 it was made abundantly clear to him by the Home Office that his contract would finish when it came up for renewal the following December, and Straw eventually announced that Ramsbotham would be retiring in July 2001.

The injunctions preventing publicising of the young men's whereabouts, their progress whilst in custody and their present-day appearance would cease when they became 18. However, in July 2000, as four newspaper groups went to court to clarify what would happen after that date, the injunctions were extended by an interim injunction given by Dame Elizabeth Butler-Sloss, President of the High Court Family Division. Thompson's and Venables' lawyers also made it clear that they were planning to ask the courts to extend the injunctions permanently. In so doing they would be greatly aided by the coming into force of the Human Rights Act in October 2000.

On 26 October 2000 Lord Woolf recommended that the tariff be reduced from ten to eight years, arguing that 'further detention would serve no constructive purpose' as 'they have done all that is open to them to redeem themselves'. In spite of the drubbing recently suffered by the unfortunate Sir David Ramsbotham, he also criticised the 'corrosive atmosphere' of Young Offender Institutions, pointing out that incarceration in such an atmosphere would very probably destroy the good work put into their rehabilitation (*Guardian*, 27 October 2000). His recommendation then went to the Parole Board, which would decide if and when they should be released. In February 2001 they would have served eight years.

Inevitably, much of the press was incensed, its coverage leading the then *Guardian* press commentator, former *Daily Mirror* editor and now leading journalism professor, Roy Greenslade, to denounce the journalists concerned as 'mob orators leading a hue and cry demanding lynch law' and to condemn a form of journalism based largely on the desire for commercial gain: 'Guiding people towards a more benevolent view of the human condition might just threaten sales. It is safer to put the more simplistic viewpoint, to demonise individuals, to reinforce the notion that evil exists independently of society. It is, of course, truly barbaric' (*Guardian*, 30 October 2000). But what those responsible for this raging stream of bile seem to have been too driven or simply too stupid to realise was that their hate-filled and demagogic coverage was making the case for a permanent injunction ever clearer and more urgent with every day that passed, although the more cynical among them may have counted on the granting of such an injunction serving as a useful means of adding further fuel to the populist fire which they were so assiduously stoking.

'A serious desire for revenge'

On 13 November 2000 Thompson's and Venables' lawyers appeared at the High Court before Dame Elizabeth Butler-Sloss, requesting a permanent injunction banning the media from disclosing any information about their clients, on the grounds that the disclosing of such information would not only compromise their right to life (Article 2 of the ECHR) and to freedom from inhuman and degrading treatment (Article 3) but also expose them to 'serious physical risk and serious psychological fear and the likelihood of harassment'. Four national newspaper groups (led by News Group Newspapers, and joined by the Mirror Group, the Telegraph Group and Associated Newspapers) contested the action (incidentally employing two sets of counsel to present identical arguments), whilst the Home Secretary, the Official Solicitor and the Attorney General supported it.

On 8 January 2001 an injunction was granted *contra mundum* under the common law right of confidence and Articles 2 and 3 of the ECHR. As Dame Butler-Sloss explained:

> I have been provided with a wealth of information from Home Office evidence, press reports, judicial observations, and other information that has convinced me that these young men are uniquely notorious and are at serious risk of attacks from members of the public as well as from relatives and friends of the murdered child.
>
> Threats to injure and to kill them have been set out in the evidence presented to me and have been reported in the press. I am satisfied that, although there has been balanced discussion in press articles in recent months, the sense of moral outrage has not diminished and there remains among some members of the public a serious desire for revenge if the two young men are living in the community ... I am therefore convinced that their lives are genuinely at risk as well as their physical safety if their new identities and whereabouts became public knowledge.

I also read a number of press reports and editorials both from the time of the trial and later litigation and recently, and have come to the conclusion that certain sections of the press would not wish the two young men to remain anonymous and would wish to have them identified and if information about them became available, there was a real possibility it would be published.

In my judgment, if any section of the media decided to give information leading to the identification of either young man, such publication would put his life at risk. In the exceptional circumstances of this case and applying English domestic law and the right to life enshrined in Article 2 of the European Convention, I have come to the conclusion that I am compelled to take steps in the almost unique circumstances of this case to protect their lives and well-being. (*Guardian*, 9 January 2001)

The response of much of the press to this judgment served only to confirm why such action was necessary in the first place. Thus, for example, a *Sun* editorial (9 January 2001) announced that it would take advantage of the fact that Dame Butler-Sloss had not banned publication of details of their lives over the previous eight years 'to inform our readers how a very large amount of public money has been spent, some of it on keeping the killers in a life of comparative luxury. People will be able to judge whether the punishment of Thompson and Venables has fitted the crime'. The same day's paper duly included an article headed 'Luxury Life of Bulger Killers', which complained that taxpayers have 'footed the bill for plush rooms with VIDEOS and TRIPS to the seaside – as well as for the finest EDUCATION money can buy'. (It is, incidentally, impossible to read press coverage of this matter without coming to the conclusion that, for most papers, Thompson's and Venables' second worst crime was to have received a good education.)

The other line followed by much of the press was that the judgment set a dangerous precedent. Here it was very clearly haunted by the spectre of Myra Hindley being treated in a similar fashion to the young men. Thus in an editorial entitled 'A Decision That Mocks Justice', the *Daily Mail* (9 January 2001) raged: 'It is a most extraordinary decision, sending out a profoundly disturbing message', arguing that Dame Butler-Sloss 'has said in effect that the more heinous the crime the greater the courts' indulgence towards the perpetrators' and thus 'turned logic on its head'. The same line was taken by the same day's *Times*, which claimed that 'the High Court's message is that the more revolting the crime and the greater the public anger it arouses, the more the State will coddle the criminal', whilst the *Telegraph* argued that 'injunctions to protect adult offenders (as Thompson and Venables now are) could also be claimed by any notorious killer or paedophile. James Bulger's killers may have little hope of a normal life without new identities, but the same might be argued, say, of Myra Hindley …' However, the problem with this argument is that it entirely ignores the role

16 *Julian Petley*

played by newspapers in stoking 'public anger' and making certain criminals 'notorious' in the first place. It is thus disingenuous (to put it mildly) for the *Telegraph* to argue that it contested the injunction not because of any 'vindictive desire to hunt down the pair after their release'. This is beside the point, as Roy Greenslade noted in the *Guardian* (11 January 2001), in a malediction aptly entitled 'Filthy Rags':

> It is newspapers who provide the information that would lead to the risk that others would take the law into their own hands. That, surely, is the key point. These papers are not neutral purveyors of information. While proclaiming the public interest, they are inciting the mob, both feeding off the understandable grief of the Bulger family and taking every opportunity to stoke the embers of hatred.

The obvious retort to such newspapers (although one that is rarely made) is that if they reported crime in a less emotive and punitive fashion, injunctions such as this might not be necessary.

Various papers also flew the flag for press freedom, the *Telegraph* making the point that 'freedom of expression is vital in a democracy, and threats by vigilantes are not best dealt with by curtailing newspapers', whilst *The Times* similarly condemned what it saw as 'an unjustifiable encroachment on press freedom', and the *Mail* argued that the judgment 'clearly affronts the principle of press freedom and the public's right to know'. But this, too, is a threadbare argument, as the *Independent* (9 January 2001) noted in a leader revealingly headed 'Pity the Country Where Anonymity Is Necessary for Rehabilitated Children'. Excoriating a tabloid press 'whose cant, hypocrisy and vengefulness have few equals anywhere', it noted:

> So when the inevitable pious complaints pour forth about how the freedom of the press has been violated, let us ask ourselves, which freedom? The freedom of healthy criticism that underpins a democracy and helps ensure that public money is spent wisely – or the freedom to conduct witch-hunts without end, pander to the baser instincts of readers and propagate a prurient right-to-know culture without end?

A similar line was taken by Greenslade, who argued that:

> The scream of rage from various newspapers at the court decision to grant the killers of James Bulger lifetime anonymity was utterly disgraceful. Raising the banner of press freedom and shouting slogans about the people's right to know, these papers sought to gloss their bloodthirsty cries of vengeance by casting themselves as champions of the public interest. In reality, their attempt to lift injunctions against publication of details

about the youths Jon Venables and Robert Thompson showed a streak of venality, even barbarism, which besmirches Britain's press.

Such comments, unfortunately all too rare, and especially from journalists, are particularly resonant at the time of writing, in the wake of the Leveson Inquiry, given the way in which the notion of press freedom has been deployed by most newspapers in a strident and self-interested campaign to ward off any form of effective and meaningful press self-regulation which would act in the public interest (as opposed to the owners' political and economic interests masquerading as the 'public interest').

The press intervenes directly

However, nothing daunted, sections of the press simply redoubled their efforts to try to ensure that Thompson and Venables would, like Myra Hindley, never be released. But now, instead of simply baying from the sidelines, they began to intervene directly in the process on which they were reporting, and thus became key players in the story itself. This they did by concocting stories aimed fairly and squarely at persuading the Parole Board not to release the young men.

The *Sunday People* (14 January 2001) ran a lengthy interview with James Bulger's father, headlined 'Dancing on James' Grave'. Apart from rehearsing the original details of the crime in particularly graphic detail, it reports that he is 'furious at the soft life that the killers, now 18, have had during their eight years in a special institution' and quotes him to the effect that 'they have been given everything possible to make life easy and privileged for them ... These boys have had a private education, holidays, outings, computers and opportunities that they would never have had if they had not killed James'. From the very start, the allegedly easy life led by the boys whilst detained was, along with the fact that they were simply 'evil', the key plank in the press campaign against them (Franklin and Petley 1996) and would remain so even after they were released on licence. But now an additional tactic was employed. Thus, in a separate article, the paper claimed that 'evil Robert Thompson has made a cold-blooded and calculating attempt to strangle another boy at the care home where he has been locked up'. The paper made no secret of why it was running this story: 'This savage attack – confirmed to the *Sunday People* by the latest victim's solicitor – makes a mockery of claims by lawyers, psychiatrists and social workers that Thompson, 18, is rehabilitated and ready for freedom ... Thompson's chilling behaviour is a complete contradiction of the glowing terms used by Lord Woolf to describe one of Britain's most notorious child killers'. The paper also gloated that 'our disturbing revelation WILL have an effect on the well-oiled legal machinery which is preparing Thompson for early and secret release. For the family of the boy he tried to strangle are now planning legal action against their son's attacker'. There follows a long interview with a 'pal of the victim', and a shorter one with the mother of the alleged victim, who claims that in 1999 Robert Thompson had tried to strangle a fellow inmate after the 15-year-old had taunted him about the murder.

The following week the *People* (21 January 2001) published a second article, headlined 'Bulger Killer in Attack No.2: He Battered Newcomer over "Top Murder" Boast'. This alleged that Thompson had had a 'ferocious bare-knuckle fight with another teenager' over who had committed the worst crime. The paper commented: 'Our revelations make the Lord Chief Justice Woolf's statement that Thompson had not shown "any aggression or propensity for violence" at the unit look increasingly bizarre', and it also claimed that it had been shown 'secret documents' concerning the fight. It further alleged that the fight had been reported to the Home Office 'but incredibly no action was taken'. Former Tory cabinet member David Mellor, in his Man of the People column under the heading 'Bulger Silence a Disgrace', stated that the story 'totally undermines the case for letting him out'.

In February, the boys attended preliminary parole hearings. Immediately the *People* (4 February 2001) published an interview with the boy who claimed to have been strangled, headed 'Killer Will Do It Again: Exclusive: Boy, 17, Attacked by Bulger Murderer Breaks Silence'. He is quoted as saying: 'The only reason why I am putting myself through all this is so that people know what Thompson is really like and hopefully the truth will make the Parole Board think again about releasing him. I am convinced Thompson wanted to kill me. I could see the evil in his eyes. It is that look which makes me certain if he is released he could kill again.'

The following week (11 February 2001), under the headline 'Bulger: The Proof: Official Documents Show Killer Thompson Was Involved in "Danger" Fight', the paper published 'sensational proof that James Bulger's killer Robert Thompson DID have a violent brawl with another boy in their top security unit – despite top-level efforts to sweep it under the carpet'. The paper claimed that it had obtained 'secret documents confirming a "dangerous" fist fight', and that 'the two official report forms make it clear that Home Office civil servants were told about the punch-up more than FOUR YEARS ago. And it raises yet more serious doubts about Thompson's fitness to be set free'. The paper also opines that 'there are disturbing signs that Thompson's violent behaviour is being ignored in the headlong rush to free him', and concludes: 'The pressure to give Thompson and Venables a cushy existence continues to anger most decent people in Britain. Now, following our latest revelations, they will be asking: Why are the authorities so keen to give Robert Thompson and Jon Venables the opportunities James Bulger will never have?'

On 15 February 2001 lawyers acting for Ralph Bulger, who was attempting to get Lord Woolf's decision judicially reviewed, argued that Woolf had given disproportionate weight to the matter of rehabilitation and had set the tariff correspondingly low; and they also claimed that the Home Secretary had fettered his discretion and merely rubber-stamped Lord Woolf's recommendation. The 'evidence' gathered by the *People* played an important role in their case, but in the course of the hearing, David Pannick, QC for the Home Secretary, stated that the second 'fight' had never occurred at all and was in fact 'a complete fabrication'. Indeed, the other boy was actually in court when the incident was alleged to have happened, as was confirmed by the logbook of the unit in which the two young men were detained. Furthermore, the two boys were actually friends, and the supposed victim had contacted the unit on the day the story was published to say that he had been 'deeply upset' by it. Pannick argued that 'what appears to have happened is that someone obtained a blank form, which they filled in and supplied to the *Sunday People*'. The other incident, the alleged 'strangling', was relatively minor and the staff had not felt it worth commenting on to Lord Woolf – furthermore, the other boy was in fact the protagonist and Thompson was 'the subject of prolonged provocation' involving verbal abuse and physical violence. (All quotations taken from the *Guardian*, 16 February 2001.)

On 16 February Ralph Bulger was refused leave to appeal against Lord Woolf's decision. The court also made it clear that the matter of the forged forms would be referred to the Director of Public Prosecutions for a possible criminal investigation. Nothing daunted, the *People* (18 February 2001) ran another lengthy interview with Ralph Bulger headed 'Bulger: the Whitewash: Tragic Tot's Angry Father Says Judges and Politicians Have Blood on Their Hands'. In another article ('Bulger: Riddle of Papers That Lawyers Branded Fakes'), the paper stated that it was 'carrying out an in-depth inquiry' and quoted a spokesman who said that 'we are baffled by what possible motive there could be for anyone to carry out such an elaborate forgery', although three possible reasons immediately spring to mind: keeping Thompson under lock and key, financial gain on the part of the forger, and circulation boosting on the part of the paper. In his column David Mellor lashed out at the judges in the case as 'a dictatorship of bewigged fools'.

A state of denial

By now, the paper was in a state of complete denial about the evidence based on its reports which had been presented at the judicial review. On 25 February it published a long open letter to Jack Straw from Ralph Bulger headed 'Just How Much More Evidence Do You Need Mr Straw?', demanding that he 'launch an independent inquiry to investigate all the claims that have come to light before it is too late'. The Voice of the People column, headed 'Public Wants the Facts, Not Theories', argued that 'it is in the public interest that all the evidence we have uncovered should be put before the

Parole Board'. Claiming that 'The *Sunday People* has led the way in getting at the truth', it complained that 'every step of the way the authorities have attempted to thwart us. And liberal do-gooders have heaped a mountain of abuse on this newspaper'. In the same edition David Mellor stated that the paper 'blazed a brave and lonely trail proving that Thompson isn't a reformed character at all'. The fact that it proved no such thing makes it all the more disturbing that at that time its editor, Neil Wallis, was not only on the Code Committee of the Press Complaints Commission but also on its main body.

Not to be outdone, the *Sun* (20 February 2001) ran a series of articles ('Sick Boast of Bulger Killer', 'Murderer "Obsessed" with Tots' and 'Serious Matter for Concern') based on an interview with Leon McEwan, who was in the same secure unit as Thompson in 1998–9. McEwan, who had served five years for arson, alleged that Thompson had told him: 'You could have killed someone and only got eight', adding: 'He was joking about it. He didn't seem to be sorry for what he'd done', and concluding: 'He's just evil and I don't think he should be let out – full stop. He should be locked up in a proper jail.' Much is made of Thompson having watched *The Silence of the Lambs* and played the video game *Silent Hill* which, the paper helpfully adds, 'is reckoned to be one of the most frightening available. Its plot features the sinister disappearance of a seven-year-old girl'. But the articles themselves also contain a number of details which contradict the 'evil' image being constructed here, namely that Thompson liked to protect the younger boys in the unit, and that he took an interest in the progress of expectant women on the unit's staff. However, much of the copy is taken up with yet another disapproving recital of the supposedly luxurious conditions in which Thompson had lived, although much of the 'evidence' is surely vitiated by being based on the testimony of somebody who was clearly resentful because he thought that a fellow inmate had received better treatment than he himself had been given. Thus 'Leon blasted':

> His family used to visit once a day and the staff would pick them up and bring them to the unit and then take them home again. But my mum had to save up to pay to come and see me. I do feel as if he got special treatment. There is no way Bobby will be reformed in there because there is nothing hard or frightening about it. He was well fed, he got educated, had his own room and bathroom, it's luxury really .... Bobby used to call it the five-star holiday home. He's probably right. It seemed like he had preferential treatment for visits. When he was in front of the social workers he was a creep, that's why he got the special treatment. But we all knew what he was really like. He was himself in front of us.

And just in case its readers didn't get the message, the *Sun* also published a leading article in which it says of its interview with McEwan: 'The picture that emerges of Thompson is NOT that of a totally reformed character. He still shows violent signs ... REAL questions need to be asked of the authorities that have housed Thompson – and the process that allows him to go free so soon.'

The story also ran in the same day's *Times* ('Thompson "Boasted of Leniency" over Bulger'), which additionally quotes McEwan as saying that 'I was moved to prison when I turned 16 and that terrified me – it was dreadful, really frightening. My year in prison is the reason I wouldn't go back to crime again, not my time in the secure unit – that was like a home-from-home. For many it was probably better than home.' The story was covered in the same day's *Express* ('Bulger Killer "Taunted Me over His Light Sentence"') and the next day's *Times* ('Thompson "Violence" May Affect Parole').

On 21 February the *Sun* ('Battle to Keep Bulger Killer', 'Parole Board Must See Letters') claimed that 'a batch of menacing letters ... said to have been written' by Thompson to McEwan had 'come to light'. It also noted that the Bulgers' lawyers would pass these to the Parole Board and added, clearly in a spirit of hope, that 'if his [Leon's] story can be verified, Thompson's imminent release from the secure unit could be called off'. The paper claims that 'several contain threats of violence to fellow inmates', but all that is contained in the published extracts are youthful bravado and laddish boasting of exactly the kind that one would expect to find in such an institution. A leading article claims that 'if some, or all, of the letters apparently written by one of James Bulger's killers are genuine, they are of great concern'. It continued: 'We suspect that Thompson is not as reformed as has been claimed. We're not convinced that the Parole Board saw all the evidence. Or the right kind of evidence.' It should be noted from the quotes above that the *Sun* did allow for the possibility that the letters were fakes, but the story was nonetheless picked up by the same day's *Express* ('He Visited Shopping Mall Like One Where He Snatched James, Says Former Inmate') and *Mail* ('Bulger Killer Wanted to Harm Other Inmates Says Teenager'). On 22 February the *Sun* ran an article headed 'A Very Nasty Person Wrote These Words'. This was the conclusion of Erik Rees, a 'top handwriting expert' and chairman of the British Institute of Graphologists, to whom the paper had showed the letters. The paper explains that 'in his analysis, Erik picks out personality traits which would worry any parole board considering the release of someone who had tortured to death a two-year-old like James'. However, most of Rees's comments could equally well apply to the overt content of the published letters as to any insights gained from an analysis of the handwriting. The paper claims that it did not reveal the identity of the writer until Rees had completed his analysis, but when it did so, Rees apparently (and certainly conveniently) stated that 'on the basis of what I have seen, I do not believe he should be let out'. The letters were also covered in the same day's *Mail* ('Sex, Shopping, Sport, Sunbathing and £30 a Week Pay. Easy Life in "Five-star Hotel" Secure Unit').

Thompson's solicitor denied that the letters were genuine (as did Thompson himself) and described their publication as 'another step in a concerted campaign to vilify my client' (quoted in the *Guardian*, 22 February 2001). The *Observer* (25 February 2001) published an article in which the *Sun*'s editor, David Yelland, stated that should the letters purportedly from Thompson turn out to be fakes, then 'on a Richter scale of one to ten of cock-ups, this would be about a three', which is surely remarkably low considering that what was at stake was a young man's future. He also states that 'the more information that is revealed about Thompson and Venables, the further it trashes any concept that justice has been served. It's a scandal'.

'We shall do all in our power to watch over them'

In the week beginning 18 June 2001, after a six-month review, the Parole Board held two separate hearings into the release of the boys. The Board comprised a judge, a psychiatrist and a lay member; a representative of the Home Office attended, as did lawyers, probation officers and security officers. The Board heard evidence from Thompson and Venables, their lawyers and expert witnesses. Among written reports were documents from lawyers representing James Bulger's parents, written statements by the boys, and reports from their secure units and probation officers. The main questions concerned how much remorse the boys had shown, how successfully they had responded to treatment, how well they were likely to cooperate with the rehabilitation scheme lined up for them, and whether they posed a risk to the public.

On 23 June the Board announced that the boys were no longer a threat to public safety and that they could be released on lifelong licence, as their minimum tariff had expired in February. The Home Secretary, David Blunkett, approved the decision on the same day, and they were released a few weeks later on lifelong licence. Both had already been given new identities and they were moved to secret locations – in the first instance, semi-secure halfway houses. The terms of their release meant that they were not allowed to contact each other or the Bulger family, nor could they visit Merseyside (except with the prior written consent of those supervising them). A senior probation officer would supervise each of them on a daily basis and they would also have regular appointments with psychologists and psychiatrists in order to monitor their progress. If they breached any of the rules governing their freedom or were deemed to be a risk to the public in any way, they could be returned to prison immediately. Ministers would be provided with regular reports on their progress.

By this time, most of the press seemed to have resigned itself to the inevitable. However, by way of a coda, a number of comments are worth noting.

The *News of the World* (24 June 2001), still flush from the 'success' of its anti-paedophile 'naming and shaming' campaign which it had launched in

July 2000, devoted a good deal of its leader column to the by now achingly over-familiar complaints about the young men's 'sickeningly premature release' and 'ludicrously brief sentences', their 'unique, astonishing protection', and the way that they had been 'cossetted' and given 'the kind of privileged education usually unavailable to decent youngsters'. However, as a harbinger of future events, the key part of the article is its conclusion:

> The *News of the World* has a long and honourable tradition of fighting for its great family of readers. Today we make this pledge. Though we will NOT breach the injunction, we WILL monitor this evil pair closely. Whether they are at college, with girlfriends, perhaps working with unwitting colleagues, we shall do all in our power to watch over them. And, at the very first hint of a breach of their parole licences, we shall do everything legally possible to tell you, our readers, exactly what is going on. That is the very least that a law-abiding society deserves.

David Mellor's final comment on this matter in the *Sunday People* (24 June 2001) marks one of those moments when popular journalism in Britain plumbs new depths. The news that John Venables' family had been rehoused at public expense elicits the exquisitely tasteful response: 'The moral of little James' murder is clear: Kill a kid and get a house.' Mellor then berates those responsible for the young men's release:

> They [the Parole Board members] have been chosen for being good Yes Men, guaranteed to sign up to the politically-correct view that we must pity these nasty little runts as victims, not criminals. And anyway, the Parole Board people will all be middle-class types who won't have to live anywhere near the Venables and the Thompsons, or whatever they now call themselves, so why should they care if their little social experiment goes wrong and some other child gets done? This whole sorry mess reveals once again the breathtaking arrogance of the judges, especially Chief Justice Woolf. Woolf is a bleeding-heart liberal, with no background in criminal matters. He has no involvement with ordinary people, and no understanding of how the rest of us think outside of his own self-satisfied, back-scratching, tiny community. He doesn't care that millions of good, honest people are disgusted by what he has done in letting these thugs out so soon. He will wear it as a badge of courage, facing down what he will regard as the ignorant opinions of trash like you and me.

As a textbook example of populism (as befitting, of course, a 'man of the people'), and particularly of its anti-juridical aspect, this takes some beating. It is pointless to argue that the costs involved in trying to ensure the anonymity of Thompson, Venables and their families were at least partly the result of having to protect them from the consequences of years of hate-filled journalism such as this; this is not the realm of rational argument, but of demagoguery pure and simple. As Roy Greenslade put it in the *Guardian* (2 July 2001), elements of the press 'have incited the mob ever since the trial of Venables and Thompson' and 'have created a climate in which it has become impossible to have a rational, compassionate, sensitive debate'. Worse still, he argued, 'the papers have created the conditions for a tragedy to occur', singling out the *News of the World* article quoted for particular criticism, noting with withering irony that:

> Of course, it doesn't believe that its scandalous leader last Sunday with its awful threats and encouragement to the public to seek out the boys' new identities will engender violence against them. It has merely handed its readers the matches. It cannot possibly be responsible for what they do with them. It has simply been acting, like its tabloid rivals, entirely in the public interest.

That a tragedy has not yet occurred is little short of a miracle. Anyone who has taken a close interest in this case knows that, from the moment that the boys were convicted, journalists began to cultivate contacts in the police and in the secure units in which they were held. With large sums of money on offer, and not a few officials sharing the tabloids' view of the boys, there was certainly no shortage of leaked stories. And, before the young men's release, at least one paper had dozens of pictures of them, taken on outings from their respective units.

Significantly, the very first prosecution arising from Operation Elveden, set up in the wake of the phone-hacking scandal to investigate illegal newsgathering, was of a former operational support officer at a high-security prison near Milton Keynes, who, in March 2013, received a 16-month prison sentence for passing on details about Jon Venables whilst he was in prison, having breached the terms of his licence. The officer, Richard Trunkfield, pleaded guilty to receiving £3,450 between 2 March and 30 April 2010 for giving the *Sun* confidential details of where Venables was held and about his regime, and the fact that he was isolated. As the *Guardian* reported (28 March 2013):

> The *Sun*'s internal accounts system record four sets of payments for £750 for 'Bulger killer's cover blown', 'Jon Venables back in custody', 'Armed cops grab Bulger killer' and an 'Exclusive on Jon Venables case'. He received another £350 for the story 'Jon Venables snubbed by family' and £100 for a tip that led to a story headlined 'Five minutes to pack: Cops whisk him away'.

Talk to any journalist who has taken an interest in the Bulger affair and they will tell you that this case represents but the tip of an iceberg. Indeed, it would be truly remarkable if it does not feature again, and frequently, in Operation Elveden.

That sections of the British press have not revealed the new identities and whereabouts of Robert Thompson and Jon Venables (in spite of everything, in the case of the latter) is simply because they cannot do so, and it is significant (and most welcome) that the current Attorney General, Dominic Grieve, has made it clear that the injunction that has thus far successfully protected the young men applies, globally, to all forms of new media as well. At the time that the injunction was granted there was a good deal of hopeful speculation and snide comment in sections of the press to the effect that it would be increasingly unenforceable in the age of the Internet, but, as is becoming more obvious by the day, the Internet is not in fact a regulation-free zone. On 26 April 2013, Neil Harkins and Dean Liddle, who published photographs on Twitter and Facebook said to show recent pictures of the young men, received 15-month suspended jail sentences, even though they had taken down the pictures within hours of putting them up.

In spite of the anti-juridical sentiments which daily disfigure large swathes of the British press (and no more so than in this case, as we have seen), newspapers employ large numbers of expensive lawyers to ensure that their stories stay on the right side of the law – even if only just, in many cases. But we are all publishers now, and those who attempt online to ape the standards of the worst of British journalism, or indeed to go where even the most *enragé* of popular papers fear to tread, should seriously consider the possible consequences of their actions, both for themselves and the targets of their wrath.

Notes

1. Singh was released on licence in 1990, but recalled the following year after being arrested for alleged offences of deception and threatening behaviour. The charges were dismissed in 1992 but his licence was revoked and he was returned to prison. In 1994 the Parole Board recommended his release but Howard refused to accept the recommendation. In both cases, the tariffs had expired.
2. The full judgment may be found at http://hudoc.echr.coe.int/sites/eng/pages/search.aspx?i=001-58593#{%22itemid%22:[%22001-58593%22]} (accessed 17 June 2013).

References

Franklin, B. and Petley, J. (1996). 'Killing the Age of Innocence: Newspaper Reporting of the Death of James Bulger'. In J. Pilcher and S. Wagg (eds), *Thatcher's Children? Politics, Childhood and Society in the 1980s and 1990s*. London: Falmer Press.

Haydon, D. and Scraton, P. (2000). '"Condemn a little more, understand a little less": The Political Context and Rights Implications of the Domestic and European Rulings in the Venables–Thompson Case'. *Law and Society* 27(3): 416–48.

O'Hagan, A. (1993). 'Diary'. *London Review of Books* 15(5), 11 March, p. 21.
Rentoul, J. (2001). *Tony Blair: Prime Minister*. London: Little, Brown and Company.
Sereny, G. (1995). *The Case of Mary Bell: A Portrait of a Child Who Murdered*. London: Pimlico.
Smith, D. J. (1995). *The Sleep of Reason: The James Bulger Case*. London: Arrow Books.

2
Citizen Journalists or Cyber Bigots?
Child Abuse, the Media and the Possibilities for Public Conversation: The Case of Baby P

Bob Franklin

Introduction

The paradox at the heart of newspaper and broadcast media reports of child abuse is that they have tended to offer only scant attention to the child who should be at the centre of the coverage. Instead, journalists have preferred to fabricate and focus on two oppositional portrayals of social welfare professionals. Both stereotypes have been highly unflattering, have influenced social work practice, hindered recruitment to the profession, but also helped to inform and shape public conversations about the appropriate policy response to such cases. Across 40 years of press coverage ranging from Maria Colwell (1973) to the Peter ('Baby P') Connelly tragedy (2007), journalists have presented social workers as either ineffectual wimps incapable of protecting children who were suffering physical or sexual abuse or, alternatively, as bullies whose unjustifiable interventions in the private affairs of families have resulted in their precocious break-up (Franklin 1998a, 1998b, 1999; Franklin and Parton 1991). This chapter explores a distinctive approach which places social media at the heart of its concerns by examining YouTube representations and reactions to the death of Peter Connelly in Haringey in 2007. It analyses the public conversation about the death of this child by conducting a qualitative analysis of a sample of the most popular videos (by viewing) uploaded to YouTube and viewers' postings in response to them. The research ambition informing this chapter is to compare recent social media – especially YouTube – conversations about child abuse, with earlier journalistic accounts.

The analysis of videos and postings reveals a wide range of responses (distinguished by format and content) to the Peter Connelly case by 'ordinary people' who, because of their engagement with social media and their role in actively constructing a public conversation about significant issues such as the death of this 17-month-old child, have come to be known as 'participant' or 'citizen' journalists. These terms are hotly contested, but Dan Gillmor is among numerous academics who have welcomed participant journalists' engagement with the world of news production and distribution. 'For the first time,' Gillmor claims, 'people at the edges of the network have the ability to create their own news entities' (Gillmor cited in Lasica 2007). In this way, citizens cease to be simply passive recipients of news handed down by journalists who claim authority for their views. By contrast, digital media enable them to participate actively in news production and even to contest journalistic accounts (Bruns 2008), a process Bruns describes as a shift from news production to 'produsage', signifying that previous users of news are now also producers (Bruns 2008). Similarly, for Jay Rosen, citizen journalism is simply what happens 'when the people formerly known as the audience employ the press tools in their possession to inform one another'.[1] This move to citizen journalism, then, is seen essentially as a transition in power relationships between the press and the public, with considerable implications for the improvement of open and democratic debate.

The designations 'citizen' or 'participant' journalist also reflect the fact that, unlike their professional counterparts, there is no requirement for any formal professional training or experience in journalism. Perhaps unsurprisingly, certain features in this new 'reportage' are strikingly different to the reports filed by traditional print journalists. First, and most evident, is the fact that the content of the YouTube videos typically centres on the interests and rights of the children concerned, especially the children's evident need for protection. Second, the videos and postings reveal an untypical focus (compared to press reports) on the perpetrators, combined with alarmingly punitive measures proposed as suitable punishment for their abusive behaviour. Professional journalists' protocols designed to separate factual coverage from opinionated commentary, an emphasis on objective coverage and the use of wide-ranging news sources to 'stand up' their story are largely absent from the contributions of participatory journalism.

Third, social workers barely feature in the dramatis personae of the new social media reporting, although they continue to dominate print journalism accounts in what have come to be termed 'legacy media'. A former editor, for example, described newspaper reporting of social workers in the Peter Connelly case as 'vindictive', 'simplistic', 'guilty of demonising individual social workers and maintaining "the myth" that it is possible to design a system that never lets a child die' (Pugh 2011), while press criticism of social workers and Sharon Shoesmith, Director of Children's Services at Haringey, bizarrely outstripped the negative coverage given to Tracey Connelly who was actually convicted of causing the death of her son (McKay 2009: 3).

This chapter is in three parts. The first reviews the key features of newspaper reporting of child protection across the 40 years since the Maria Colwell case. The second describes the qualitative approach which informs the investigation into the construction of the public conversation around the Peter Connelly case and presents findings from the analysis of YouTube videos and postings. In the final section, questions are raised concerning the value of many of the contributions to online discussion and their suitability for inclusion and consideration in any public debate with policy consequences. My suggestion is that the optimism of those who envisage social media facilitating a more pluralistic, democratic and productive citizen conversation about policy in a revitalised public sphere is perhaps undermined by the threatening and intemperate language in which too many contributions are couched.

Newspaper reporting of social work and child protection: a review

'Sexual intercourse,' according to Philip Larkin's poem 'Annus Mirabilis', 'began / In nineteen sixty-three ... / Between the end of the *Chatterley* ban and the Beatles' first LP' (Larkin 1974: 34). The public 'discovery' of child physical and sexual abuse began a decade later, triggered by the extensive media coverage and public discussion about the death of Maria Colwell, a young child who at the time of her death was in the care of a local authority social services department. Media reporting of the case constituted nothing less than a feeding frenzy (Sabato 1991), but a review of press coverage of child abuse prior to the Colwell case discovered only nine articles between 1968 and 1972. By the time of the Cleveland case (1987–8) press interest had grown apace, with the public relations officer for the (now defunct) county of Cleveland claiming that the first five weeks of newspaper reporting generated 9,000 press cuttings, 'while mentions on national television news were an everyday occurrence' (Treacher 1988: 15). A succession of child abuse tragedies followed across the late 1980s and 1990s, with each being afforded high news salience by newspaper editors, manifest in 'white on black' headlines and a picture story on the front page. The roll call of the children involved is unforgettably imprinted on society's collective memory. The mere mention of Maria Colwell, Tyra Henry, Jasmine Beckford, Kimberley Carlisle, Victoria Climbié and Peter Connelly, or the infamous cases of child sexual abuse in Cleveland, Rochdale and the Orkneys, is sufficient to trigger public outrage and an alarmingly uniform and hostile view of the social workers involved, who were readily denounced as the culpable 'folk devils' in this seemingly endless and contemporary moral panic.

What is particularly curious, given the prominence and persistence of child abuse as a press concern, is the absence of virtually any academic studies of press coverage, although notable exceptions are worthy of mention (Aldridge 1994; Ayre 2001; Elsley 2010; Gaber 2011; and Warner 2013a, 2013b). There is a similar scholarly neglect of the more recent cases and the impact of digital media – especially social media and video sharing sites like YouTube and Flickr – on the reporting of child abuse. Again, this seems curious given that such new media are radically reshaping 'every aspect of the gathering, reporting and reception of news' (Franklin 2012; see also

Kennedy 2010). The purpose here, at least in part, is to contribute to making good this particular instance of child 'neglect'.

The most detailed and evidence-based study of national newspaper reporting of child protection is *Hard Pressed*, which examined press coverage of social work and social services in nine national newspapers – the *Daily Mail*, the *Daily Telegraph*, the *Guardian*, the *Independent*, the *Mail on Sunday*, the *Mirror*, the *Observer*, the *Sun* and the *Sunday Mirror* – between 1 July 1997 and 30 June 1998 (Franklin 1998b). Commissioned by the magazine *Community Care*, the study analysed 1,958 news reports, measuring 97,932 column centimetres, to assess the subject focus of coverage, but also journalists' attitudes towards social work and social workers, whether positive/beneficial, neutral or adverse/critical. Reporting of social work and social services was extremely negative in all newspapers (tabloid and broadsheet), although the *Daily Mail* and its sister paper the *Mail on Sunday* were by far the most critical. The ratio of negative to positive reporting of social issues in the *Mail* across the sample period was 29:1, while in the *Mail on Sunday* the outpouring of editorial opprobrium achieved the remarkable ratio of 38:1 (Franklin 1998b: 13). Interestingly, readers' letters provided the only overwhelmingly positive view of social work (Franklin 1998b: 5).

When newspapers' coverage of social work was separated from the reporting of the broader areas of social services and social issues, the journalistic bile became particularly acrid and corrosive of any notion of editorial balance, measure or even-handedness. The study identified the *Mail on Sunday*, the *Sun*, the *Daily Telegraph* and the *Daily Mail* as the most critical of social workers, with at least 75 per cent of each newspaper's coverage rated as 'adverse or critical'. But the reports in the *Mail on Sunday* offered a uniquely oppositional profile, with 95 per cent of published items about social work rated as 'adverse', only 3.6 per cent as 'neutral', with a mere 1.2 per cent rated as positive (Franklin 1998: 15). By contrast, only 33 per cent of reports in the *Guardian* and 14 per cent in the *Sunday Mirror* were 'adverse'.

Journalists routinely explored a small number of highly critical themes in their coverage of social workers, repetitively employing the same pejorative words and phrases to fix a by now well-known litany of sins in the readers' minds. The ten most frequent phrases (from a list of 45), accounted for 70 per cent of all newspaper descriptions of social workers and included: 'abusing trust' (16.8 per cent), 'negative' (9.6 per cent), 'incompetent' (7.2 per cent), 'negligent' (6.3 per cent), 'failed' (6.2 per cent), 'ineffective' (5.5 per cent), 'suspended' (4.3 per cent), 'misguided' (3.9 per cent) and 'wasteful' (3.8 per cent). Only five descriptions among the 30 most popular terms in the journalistic lexicon were positive or beneficial, but all were located well down the rankings and included: 'socially useful' (16th), 'caring' (21st), 'effective' (23rd), 'effective use of funding' (24th) and 'helpful' (27th) (Franklin 1998b: 18).

This narrow range of terms to describe social workers constructs two broad, but antithetical stereotypes in press accounts. The 'wimp' portrays social workers as too soft, as ineffectual, inexperienced, professionally incompetent and lacking in the common sense sufficient to intervene to protect children when the circumstances clearly demand it – in short, the stereotype so evident in press reports at the time of the deaths of Colwell, Beckford, Climbié and Connelly. Little wonder, perhaps, that some client groups direct dramatic accusations at social services such as, 'Do you come from the Council that kills babies?' (Kitchen 1980).

The emergence of the Cleveland case in 1987 witnessed the arrival of a different representation of social workers: as 'bullies' and authoritarians who allegedly 'seize children in the middle of the night', who 'break up families' with little regard for privacy or civil liberties. The press complaint here is less that social workers fail to intervene to protect children but that they intervene too readily and, in so doing, injure the interests of children and their carers. To cite a diagnosis of the social worker's professional dilemma which has long since become a cliché, social workers are 'damned if they do' but also 'damned if they don't'. The *Sunday People* drew inspiration from both stereotypes when it described social workers as being 'like the SAS in Cardies and Hush Puppies' (*Sunday People*, 10 March 1991).

Here are some of the many negative descriptions of social workers in national newspaper reports identified by the *Hard Pressed* research study. Social workers were variously described as 'bunglers' and 'incompetents' (*Sun*, 15 October 1997), 'blundering' (*Mail*, 24 February 1998) and 'politically correct' (*Mail*, 23 December 1997). They 'fail to intervene' (*Observer*, 10 August 1997) or 'intervene ineffectually and help to create a costly dependency culture' (*Mail*, 28 March 1998). They are the 'faceless cohort of unjudgemental social workers' (*Telegraph*, 13 August 1997); they lack 'common sense values' (*Guardian*, 23 December 1997). But social workers are also 'negligent' and 'take your kids away' (*Sun*, 19 Janaury 1998). They 'sexually abuse youngsters in their care' (*Mail*, 5 December 1997), they 'physically abuse clients' (*Independent*, 30 October 1997) and refuse to foster children with couples who are 'too old, too overweight or because they smoke' (*Mail*, 13 April 1998). They also 'suffer from the pernicious doctrine of political correctness' (*Telegraph*, 27 March 1998). Finding his journalistic voice, ex-Cabinet Minister Norman Tebbit in his usual dyspeptic tones denounced social workers as the 'great blunderbuss (and blunder is the right word) of the social services' (*Mail on Sunday*, 28 September 1997). Their work with children is 'haphazard and inconsistent' (*Independent*, 25 June 1998), they are 'child stealers' engaged in 'legalised kidnap and baby snatching' (*Mail on Sunday*, 7 April 1991); on occasion, parents have only been able to 'watch in horror and disbelief as their weeping children were dragged from their beds by "care" workers in frightening dawn raids' (*Mail on Sunday*, 1 February 1998). In short, social services have 'taken over' (*Sun*, 25 February 1998) and become 'another organisation with the initials SS' (*Mirror*, 30 June 1987). But if social workers complain about such negative misrepresentations in media accounts, they are told to 'stop whingeing' and are rebuked for defining 'themselves as victims rather than presenting reasoned explanations for their actions' (*Guardian*, 30 April 1998).

The triggers for such coverage are readily identified. Newspapers are driven by the need to retain, if not build, their circulation, which feeds an editorial appetite for dramatic, if not sensational, 'bad news' stories. In Nick Davies' phrase, journalists are driven by the rules of 'Churnalism', especially rule 8, which demands that journalists 'Give them [the readers] what they want to believe in', and rule 9, 'Go with the moral panic' (Davies 2008: 141–5). On all these counts, social work and child abuse offer considerable prospect for 'good copy, a circulation spike and enhanced profitability'. But there are other drivers at work here. Newspapers like the *Mail* and the *Sun* are ideologically hostile to the institution of social work, founded on notions of welfare communitarianism and collectivism expressing a postwar policy consensus, which has shifted subsequently and now sits uncomfortably with the market-inspired ideological narratives of Thatcherism and New Labour (Franklin and Parton 1991: 39–44). In this sense, 'middle England is less a geographical location than a set of political and cultural values', and the popularity of knocking copy about social workers seems guaranteed when the 'great majority of *Daily Mail* readers reside there' (Franklin 1998b: 22). (It is, perhaps, worth adding that the social-worker-as-bully/intruder stereotype was introduced into press discourse amid the hue and cry over Cleveland, when the parents under suspicion were themselves from 'Middle England', the *Mail*'s natural constituency.)

Newspaper reporting of the Peter Connelly case exemplified these longstanding traditions of journalistic framing of child abuse stories outlined above. First, there was a good deal of high-profile reporting in both tabloid and broadsheet/compact newspapers. A research study using the Lexus Library database identified 2,823 items of coverage in the sample period from 1 November 2008 to 1 November 2009, with the *Sun* setting the agenda with 848 published items while the *Guardian* published 228 items related to the case. A similar study by the Children's Rights Alliance England (CREA) across a six-month sample period, from October 2007 to March 2008, identified 2,642 articles, with the *Sun* again publishing the largest number of items (409) for any single newspaper and with tabloids (57.6 per cent) offering the story greater news salience than the broadsheets (CREA 2009).

Second, newspaper coverage was highly derogatory concerning the professional groups involved, with social workers in Haringey 'viewed as being culpable in their failure to protect Baby P' (Elsley 2010: 2). The *Independent*, for example, claimed there were 'systemic deficiencies' (12 November 2008) while the *Sun* argued that 'NO-ONE realised the danger he [Baby Peter] was in. And NO-ONE saved him' (*Sun*, 12 November 2008) (Elsley 2010: 5).

Third, when mainstream newspapers used their online editions to report the Peter Connelly case, they framed the story in ways which replicated coverage in their print editions; online, the predominant frame remained that of social worker incompetence, neglect and culpability. If anything, journalists used the potential offered by certain features of digital media to engage with readers and emphasise their particular narrative about events. Consequently, the *Sun* organised an online petition demanding the sacking of Sharon Shoesmith, Director of Children's Services at Haringey, as well as two social workers, which secured a million and a quarter signatures in two weeks and was forwarded to the Prime Minister. Interestingly, the social work profession responded and employed the new access to readers delivered by the Web, blogs and social media to promote a distinctive and alternative agenda about the Peter Connelly story, and launched their own 'counter' petition to call for an end 'to the witch hunt of social workers' (Hunt 2008).

YouTube and public conversation about the Peter Connelly case

This chapter now turns its focus to the ways in which new media, especially the video sharing website YouTube, have contributed to the public conversation about child abuse; an analysis of videos relating to the death of Peter Connelly will be used as a case study. Two broad questions form the basis for the inquiry here. First, what kinds of videos were uploaded to YouTube to generate the discussion in the subsequent reader postings? Second, how did YouTube viewers respond to these videos? What key themes in the Peter Connelly case did they address and how might their responses be assessed as contributions to a public conversation about child abuse with possible policy consequences and prescriptions? In exploring these questions I found Kennedy's analysis of the 'Maddie McCann phenomenon' on YouTube very helpful (Kennedy 2010: 225–42). YouTube's search engine was used to establish the number of uploaded videos, as well as the number of viewings and postings. Repeated viewings enabled distinctive themes to emerge from the video content, which were then employed to construct a modified version of Kennedy's classification of particular types or categories of videos (Kennedy 2010: 228). To address the second concern, conversational threads in the postings of selected videos were examined.

But perhaps the first question to address is why social media might be significant to this discussion. The brief answer is that social media, especially Facebook, Twitter and YouTube, have recently become significant and widely cited sources of news while simultaneously assuming the role of being among the major drivers of audiences to news sites (Franklin 2012: 663; Phillips 2012: 669–79). The number of uploads to the site and number of viewers it can boast gives YouTube massive audience reach and makes it a significant shaper, contributor and distributer of popular narratives, public conversations and news about social issues such as child abuse. Statistics concerning site operations defy credibility.

34 Bob Franklin

So far as audience reach is concerned, YouTube has 300 million accounts and attracts 800 million unique users each month who watch 4 billion hours of video across the four weeks; there are 92 billion page views per month. In 2011, the site enjoyed more than one trillion views or approximately 140 views for every person on Earth. YouTube is localised in 43 countries, content is carried in 60 languages, 70 per cent of traffic is outside of the United States and traffic on mobile devices expanded threefold in 2011. The network connections between social media are significant, with 500 years' worth of YouTube watched on Facebook every day and 700 YouTube videos consumed on Twitter every minute. Seventy-two hours of video are uploaded every minute with three hours uploaded every minute from mobile devices.[2] These data signal the potential of YouTube videos for constructing networks and conversations about public issues by a range of groups. But the sheer scale of YouTube traffic also signals the problems in establishing ways to investigate its contribution to public debate. Typing the search parameters "Baby Peter" into the YouTube search engine delivers 874,000 results, with 4,140,000 for "Baby P" and 3,630 for "Peter Connelly". This study uses videos accessed in April 2013 at the following URL: http://www.youtube.com/results?search_query=baby+P&oq=baby+P&gs_l=youtube. 12...33290.37770.0.40760.20.12.0.0.0.0.918.4711.7j6-5.12.0...0.0...1ac.1.97 TQQGnAFDM. Consequently, the scale of operation makes a quantitative study of YouTube extremely complex, labour intensive and time consuming. The preferred option here is to adopt a qualitative approach which, while it 'does not provide us with easy answers, simple truths or precise measurements', can, moreover, 'be controversial, contradictory and ambiguous', but significantly can also be 'insightful, enlightening, emancipatory and fascinating' (Brennen 2013: 1).

Classifying YouTube videos

Kennedy's study of YouTube videos relating to the Madeleine McCann case identified 13 distinctive video styles, which she labelled: (1) tribute (created as a tribute to the missing child); (2) hostility (anger directed exclusively towards the parents); (3) mass media (extracts from media coverage); (4) original music (music composed specifically in response to the case); (5) forensic (a focus on forensic aspects of the case); (6) psychic/religious (a focus on these aspects of the case); (7) humour (jokes/satire); (8) official (posted by official organisations); (9) support (support for the McCanns); (10) missing kids (a general focus on missing children); (11) mediation (a focus on mediation of the McCann case); (12) art (concerned with format and a 'cinematic creative approach'); and (13) competition ('promoting competitions around user generated content in response to the case') (Kennedy 2010: 228).

The typology of videos presented here, which is inspired by Kennedy's study, involves six more broadly defined categories: (1) *tributes*; (2) *critical*;

(3) *hostile/angry*; (4) *social work/charity responses*; (5) *government responses*; and (6) *remediation* (of materials produced by and for distribution on other media platforms).

Tribute videos express a wide variety of formats and contents but typically, as Kennedy discovered, they are 'produced on standard home-editing software' and present a 'montage of images of [Peter Connelly] ... taken from mainstream media sources' with 'background music from poignant popular songs" (2010). They constitute by far the most viewed form of uploaded video. The most popular Connelly video exemplifies this format and content, achieves 1,030,971 viewings and 2,214 'likes', but all viewer comments are currently disabled. In 'The Peter Connelly Story',[3] the opening shot of a sunset on a peaceful coastline provides the backcloth for the message 'Peter Connelly came to this world on March 1st 2006, Went to heaven August 3rd 2007'. A succession of shots of the young child is shown as the video text unravels the narrative timeline of the tragic events of the case. Another video, 'A Song for Baby P',[4] offers a further example of this 'genre'. Sarah McLachlan singing 'Angel' provides the background music for a number of images of the child uploaded from mainstream media. Eric Clapton's 'Tears in Heaven', written in remembrance of his young son who died in an accident, is quite widely used as a backing track for tribute videos. As with the analysis of the McCann videos, the tribute video is by far the most popular category used to present and discuss the Connelly case.

Critical videos focus on the allegedly irresponsible and incompetent behaviour of two professional communities: social workers and hospital staff. A video titled 'Disgusting Torture and Murder of Baby P. READ THE INFO'[5] discusses 'a catalogue of missed opportunities' by Haringey Social Services and the local hospital to prevent injuries to the child and ultimately save his life. The sacking of Sharon Shoesmith and her subsequent reinstatement provided more focused opportunities for the discussion of the role of social services, which typically were critical – for example, the Press Association video 'Shoesmith Wins Baby P Sacking Case'.[6]

Hostile videos differ from critical videos by the intensity with which the expressed views seem to be held, the targets for those very hostile and often angry views (typically the perpetrators rather than hospital or social services' staff) and the language used to articulate those views. Hostile videos are characterised by their extensive use of swear words to express very powerful hostility to Tracey Connelly and Baby Peter's stepfather Steven Barker, which can involve threats of physical violence and even torture and death. In 'RAW and EMOTIONAL',[7] for example, a young woman speaks directly to a camera which seems to be located in her kitchen; she is close to tears, deeply distressed and her voice is wavering. She describes the events leading to the death of Peter Connelly, which she has watched on a YouTube video, as 'fucking disgusting'. Her anger with the parents is evident. 'They should rot in hell for the rest of their fucking lives. They deserve a hell of a lot more than that, I say a shotgun to the temple, but what do I know?' She calls Barker 'a sick fuck'. It is a very powerful and deeply disturbing video.

A fourth category of YouTube video represents the *social work response*. The video 'Baby P – NSPCC Campaign Action Group to Protect All Children'[8] deploys the effective and dramatic graphic device of a succession of white 'headlines' on an otherwise black screen to convey a series of messages about child protection, such as 'Every 10 days a child dies at the hands of its parents in England and Wales', and to pose a number of questions like 'How could anyone kill this lovely little boy?' and 'How many more Baby Ps are there?'

Government response videos offer precisely that: the government's response to child protection. The video 'The Munro Review to Look at Children's Social Work and Frontline Child Protection'[9] features then children and families' minister Tim Loughton, presenting a 'piece to camera' about the launch of the Eileen Munro review into the future of safeguarding children from abuse. It is more professional in its production values, factual rather than editorialising in its commentary, and, in accordance with government guidelines, concerned to convey information to viewers rather than persuade them to a particular viewpoint.

The final category is concerned with what might be termed *remediation* videos, which feature sections of – or even entire – television programmes with relevance for the Connelly case and issues arising from it. 'Baby P The Whole Truth Part 1',[10] for example, represents a seven-minute section from a BBC *Panorama* programme about Peter Connelly. Predictably, the video retains the production values of a professionally produced piece of work and the objectivity and rounded appraisal of issues that might be anticipated from a public service broadcaster. Interestingly, while these remediations of video derived from other media enjoy large viewings (in this case 29,294), they do not seem to attract large numbers of postings. A second remediated video, titled 'Baby P The 17 Month Old Baby Tortured',[11] extracted the opening story from a BBC news bulletin which features newsreader George Alagiah announcing: 'The social worker who wanted Baby P taken into care. A BBC investigation finds she was overruled by her bosses. The police also wanted the child taken away; instead he was sent back to his mother and her violent boyfriend.' This last example illustrates clearly how some videos may straddle at least two of the identified categories; in this case *remediation* and *critical*.

Conversational threads and YouTube postings: 'sentimentalists' and 'retributivists'

It is important to make at least three observations about the relationship between the various types of videos detailed above and the postings of viewers which they trigger. First, there is no evident connection between the number of viewings a video enjoys and the extent of viewer responses to it. To illustrate this lack of 'connect', a video entitled 'A Song for Baby P', achieved 218,165 viewings and generated 1,120 comments, while another video, 'Baby Peter Connelly, Before and After', listed considerably more viewings (265,179) but fewer postings (987).

Second, there seems to be a correlation between the 'quality' of the video (measured by traditional broadcast criteria) and the number of comments posted, which suggests that postings diminish as the quality increases. The remediation videos (for example), which include segments of high quality public service programmes extracted from well-known news and current affairs brands such as *Panorama* and Sky News, attract derisory viewer appraisals. A video extract from the *Panorama* programme 'The Whole Truth, Part 1', for example, generates a miserly 45 comments despite achieving well in excess of 29,000 viewings, while a Press Association video titled 'Shoesmith Wins Baby P Sacking Case' failed to attract a single comment.

Third, there may be considerable dissonance between the tone and content of the readers' comments and the style and content of the associated video. The most cursory glance at comments posted at many of the tribute videos, for example, reveals themes, sentiments and a use of language which connect unequivocally with the key elements and defining characteristics of the hostility video. The video 'Baby P in Memory X',[12] offers a classic example of the tribute genre. The blue screen opening shot provides the background for the title text, 'In memory of Baby P. R.I.P. Little man xx'. Images of the young child are intercut with pictures of a blue teddy bear and informational text slides. The first of these slides presents a poem which reads: 'If tears could build a stairway and memories a lane ..., / I'd walk right up to heaven and bring you back again'. The final shot features a montage of this 'stairway to heaven' and slow-fades to the caption 'RIP Baby Peter. You will never be forgotten by the people who truly love you xx'. But the unalloyed sentimentality of this tribute video sits uncomfortably with the violent and retributive comments posted below. Consider the following extracts from viewers' (47) comments.[13]

> R.I.P baby p bless yhoo ... you dident disurve that the knobs who did it they shud die there selfs !!!

> I just wish we could do 3–50000000x the damage they did!!! fucking cunts!!!! it's a shame for me really coz by the time the release of prison for them is up they will be dead and i wont be able to beat the fucking shit out of them!!! i dont usually swear but fucking hell ... WHY!!!!!!! its a fucking defenceless kid! fucking wankers!!! i swear if i ever get to anywhere near them i will make them suffer!!

Repeated readings of viewers' postings signal that their responses to videos, as well as their subsequent contributions to public conversation, range across a spectrum which is defined and delimited at one end by a cluster of attitudes and responses to the Baby Peter case which might be termed 'caring sentimentality' and, at the other, by 'violent retributivism'.

The caring sentimentalists' prime concerns are for the child. Their postings are typically warm, emotional and empathetic. Like the related videos, their comments articulate a mawkish sentimentality combined with an unsophisticated religiosity that is unquestioningly accepting about the existence of an afterlife as a place of sanctuary from abuse. References to Connelly as 'my little angel' or 'my little man', along with the suggestions that he is now 'safe in heaven' or 'playing with the angels', are commonplace. Sentimentalists remain reactive to the events in the child's life rather than articulating any strong policy views about how to resolve the problem of child abuse, but they are evidently and overwhelmingly concerned with the safety of children and any offered proposals are concerned with how that safety might be enhanced.

By contrast, retributivists are angry, vindictive and vengeful; the content of their postings is often bigoted in its articulation. Their response to abusive behaviour against children – and, in the case of Peter Connelly, to child murder – is to advocate an almost identical (if not worse) treatment for the perpetrators. Moreover, their suggestion that the perpetrators of violence against children should be killed, tortured or suffer unlimited violence clearly strikes them as uncontentious. The focus of their comments is squarely on the abuser rather than social workers; their suggestions for 'appropriate' dispositions to deal with abusers are essentially retributivist. The unalloyed sentimentality and religiosity of the caring sentimentalists is replaced by very explicitly violent sentiments and language, which advocate punishments that are alarming because of their severity and the fact that on occasion they seem to have been considered at length and in great detail.

The examples of viewers' postings below illustrate these two responses to YouTube video representations of the Peter Connelly case. The listing begins with a successive thread of comments which unravel the retributivist position more fully; they are taken from the comments posted to the video titled 'Baby Peter':[14]

- baby p's parent should be tortured slowly and painfully.
- Even this isnt enough! Man even the electric chair is not enough for them !
- Maybe drowning them?
- That wouldn't be enough!
- Hang them publicly, just like the good ole' days.
- i hope they put them in a really small isolatin cell where they will spend another 60 years in and give them shit for food … that autta teach'em. oh and lash them 20 times a day

Two further comments illustrate how alarming and systematically violent some of the suggestions for revenge can become. The first example is posted under the video 'Justice 4 Baby P',[15] which has received 86,000 viewings to date. Because of the evident time and energy devoted to establishing the most painful torture imaginable (at least by this particular poster of comment) for child abusers, this posting is reminiscent of the House of Commons' Committee tasked to decide the most painful and slow death for Guy Fawkes, following his placing of explosives in the cellars of the English Parliament. To suggest it is distasteful risks the challenge of understatement.

> I would give those people a Colombian Necktie until they bled out. Revive them just so they can feel the pain all over again. Lay them on a table and have bamboo grow through their limbs and hit then in the knees with an ax and make them walk up the stairs of the empire state building.

And finally this comment from 'Baby P Tribute':[16]

> their ugly faces should be burnt by acid and nails should be ripped off and their heads should be continously beaten by hammer. Every one in this world cried by horrific death of baby p. Its so sad that his murderers are still alive.

Despite the extremity of the views expressed here, they are not exceptional. But the absence of any quantitative data means it is not possible to identify the percentage of total comments which this style of posting represents. However, these are worrying texts given the violent severity of their expressed views, the extensive audience reach they achieve (based on viewing figures for videos and attached postings) and the ready and easy access to these views by anyone who wishes to consult them.

The caring sentimentalist position is more closely focused on the impact of events on the child and even the rights of the child, especially rights to societal protection. But what is very striking when postings are clustered together, as below, is the presence of religious references in viewers' responses. God is typically seen as the ultimate, if not only, protector of children. Heaven is a sanctuary and the afterlife is a compensation for a troubled life on earth. Many of the comments express a very sincere empathy and concern for the child; some are deeply moving. None seem morally concerning.

- These children have no protection, they have no rights. Do you care? I dare you to watch this and and share.
- omg i crying now just from watching this video and god i hope peter is happy and feels safer up there with u everyone loves u peter rip baby.
- God, make baby p fell better in heaven.
- Why do people keep kids if they don't want them? Who does this to a beautiful innocent baby that loves them? I wish I could do something

for kids like this. Makes me just want to pick them up hold them tight and tell them I love you. As for the terrible people why? Breaking a babys back? bruising him so badly you have to cover his mouth with chocolate? What goes through these peoples heads? I would vote they should never be able to have a another child in there care again. Poor child. RIP.

Postings selected from the video 'A Song for Baby P'[17] reveal similar sentiments:

- Happy Birthday Baby P. Today, March 1 2010 you would have been 4 years if you lived. As long as I live I will always remember you and you will always be in my heart
- Poor Baby Peter ... I will never forget you. I am writing a book about your short horrific life so no child will ever be hurt like you were. May God give you the peace and love you never knew on earth. May the angels sing you lullabys that you didn't get to hear. May all of us report any sign of child abuse so no other child will have to die. Play in Heaven's clouds.
- R.I.P. baby p. i miss u. i pray for u everyday. i cry my eyes out when i think of you u beautiful angelic little boy. I LOVE U God Bless You ♥♥♥♥♥

Discussion

This brief consideration of representations of child abuse in print journalism and YouTube across the 40 years since the death of Maria Colwell has addressed two broad questions. First, what is the character of public conversation about child abuse, especially the Baby Peter Connelly case, emerging from the analysis of YouTube videos and the readers' postings responding to them? Second, how do these more contemporary social media accounts compare to earlier newspaper accounts of child abuse?

The argument here is that YouTube offers an extraordinarily wide range of divergent responses to the death of Peter Connelly, with readers' postings representing a sort of 'electronic readers' letters page'. The comments posted certainly lack the detachment, objectivity, wide sourcing and fact checking which characterise professional journalistic writing. Moreover, they are not regulated by a letters' page editor – or, more worryingly, by anyone else. But the number of active contributors to the public conversation about child abuse has undoubtedly grown, and immeasurably so. Tens of thousands of viewers of YouTube videos respond to the uploaded videos with comments that are read potentially by the millions who view those same videos. The varied responses to the Baby P videos extend across a spectrum which is limited at each end by two groupings, identified as 'caring sentimentalists' and 'violent retributivists'; the views of each group are marked by areas of convergence and divergence, although they illustrate an extensive overlapping of concerns.

So, how does this recent discussion about child abuse on YouTube compare to press accounts? Three marked differences were suggested at the beginning of this chapter, which seem to be supported by the subsequent analysis of newspaper and new media contributions to public debate. First, YouTube accounts offer a much clearer focus on the welfare of the child, especially the requirement for protection, although this is more evident in the postings of the caring sentimentalists. Second, the abuser has superseded the social worker as the villain of this particular drama and has become the prime target for criticism and blame, although this is perhaps more apparent in the comments of retributivists. Third, social workers and other welfare and medical actors have become considerably more marginalised in mediated reports and community conversation about child abuse. But despite these differences, social media discussions of child abuse illustrate certain continuities with newspapers' accounts. The YouTube discussion, for example, undoubtedly continues to influence and shape public opinion and policy agendas about the issue of child abuse along with the best ways to prevent further cases like Baby Peter Connelly.

Rather than comparing the representations of child abuse offered by print and social media, perhaps we need to acknowledge that in certain ways they are complementary. YouTube delivers a more pluralist conversation by allowing greater numbers of voices into the debate, and voices which explore the more emotional and opinionated responses to child abuse. But the hyperbole and invective that characterises some of the YouTube postings cited above raises doubts about their value as contributions to a productive public debate about child abuse or policies to eradicate or at least reduce this social problem. Many of the comments posted online seem to fit journalist Andrew Marr's pessimistic and caricatured description of citizen journalism as 'the spewings and rantings of very drunk people late at night ... [which] ... is fantastic at times but it is not going to replace journalism. ... [It] ... is too angry, too abusive. Terrible things are said online because they are anonymous. People say things online that they wouldn't dream of saying in person' (Marr, cited in Plunkett 2010). Marr's resort to stereotypes, however, risks falling foul of the difficulties he identifies with online conversation, but the final couple of sentences identify a possibly important relationship which helps to explain the extensive use of intemperate, abusive and even violent language online.

Perhaps the question which must be addressed is: How might the quality of YouTube public conversation about child abuse be improved? And maybe one solution involves withdrawing the anonymity that YouTube allows to those who post comments. Scholarly research in the field of journalism studies is beginning to address precisely this question: How does anonymity relate to what might be termed 'the "civility" of postings?' (Santana forthcoming). The widespread use of violent and aggressive language in online postings has prompted increasing comment from journalists, lawyers and scholars of journalism studies, with Christopher Wolf, an attorney with the Anti-Defamation League, writing to the editor of *The New York Times* to argue that 'People who are able to post anonymously (or pseudonymously) are far more likely to say awful things, sometimes with awful consequences' (cited in Santana forthcoming). A recent US study of online comments attached to articles discussing the highly contentious issue of immigration compared postings in selected online newspapers, which allow posters anonymity, with online newspapers, which do not. The study found a very close and unequivocal effect for anonymity on the degree of civility which characterised the conversational exchanges between those who posted comments. Santana concluded: 'In measuring civility in online newspaper commenting forums, anonymity matters. The ways people express themselves online is significantly dependent on whether their true identity is intact' (Santana forthcoming). So perhaps something as simple as requiring those who post comments to YouTube videos to shed the veil of anonymity, which seemingly encourages a lack of civility and protects posters from its consequences, could enhance the quality of public conversation about a significant social and welfare issue such as child abuse. Reforming posting conditions to YouTube obviously raises important issues around regulation, if not – some will claim – censorship, so there must a serious and public debate and one informed by more quantitative data than this study has presented. But if the removal of anonymity would improve the quality of debate, we should do so immediately.

Notes

1. J. Rosen, 'The Definition of Citizen Journalism': http://www.youtube.com/watch?v=QcYSmRZuep4. All URLs in this chapter were accessed for verification on 21 November 2013.
2. YouTube, YouTube Statistics: www.YouTube.com/t/press_statistics.
3. 'The Peter Connelly Story': http://www.youtube.com/watch?v=0E1rKYrP_DY.
4. 'A Song For Baby P': http://www.youtube.com/watch?v=yGZuhqvKbt0.
5. 'Disgusting Torture and Murder of Baby P. READ THE INFO': http://www.youtube.com/watch?v=Ea9-0qBx6QE&list=PLwqXGZ1C66SZARjRe_0pTQlgg_EARFWc.
6. 'Shoesmith wins Baby P Sacking Case': http://www.youtube.com/watch?v=N1RW92d2A8o&playnext=1&list=PLwqXGZ1C66SZARjRe_0pTQlgg_EARFWc.
7. 'RAW and EMOTIONAL': http://www.youtube.com/watch?v=CzsuY-Kkaqw.
8. 'Baby P – NSPCC Campaign Action Group to Protect All Children': http://www.youtube.com/watch?v=Oba80Hr8qrI.
9. 'The Munro Review to Look at Children's Social Work and Frontline Child Protection': http://www.youtube.com/watch?v=IBznWUQNtAY.
10. 'Baby P The Whole Truth Part 1': http://www.youtube.com/watch?v=nhLURjB99D0.'
11. Baby P The 17 Month Old Baby Tortured': http://www.youtube.com/watch?v=bwNXvROJaNU&list=PLwqXGZ1C66SZARjRe._0pTQlgg_EARFWc
12. 'Baby P in Memory X': http://www.youtube.com/watch?v=94EVGou3Fsc&list=PL788AC6E751D38CC7.

13. These postings are typical for their uses of (a) 'text talk' writing conventions, (b) swear words and (c) misspellings, which signal fairly low levels of literacy. Citations from YouTube have not been corrected or altered in any way. They are reproduced here exactly as the authors produced them.
14. 'Baby Peter': http://www.youtube.com/watch?v=Ea9-0qBx6QE&list=PLwqXGZ1C 66SZARjRe_0pTQlgg_EARFWc.
15. 'Justice 4 Baby P': http://www.youtube.com/watch?v=_s1BaQE3-s4.
16. 'Baby P Tribute': http://www.youtube.com/watch?v=_CrZ8YTgoac.
17. 'A Song for Baby P': http://www.youtube.com/watch?v=yGZuhqvKbt0.

References

'A Song for Baby P'. http://www.youtube.com/watch?v=yGZuhqvKbt0 (accessed 21 November 2013).
Aldridge, M. (1994). *Making Social Work News*. London: Routledge.
Ayre, P. (2001). 'Child Protection and the Media: Lessons from the Last Three Decades'. *British Journal of Social Work* 31(6): 887–901.
'Baby P – NSPCC Campaign Action Group to Protect All Children'. http://www.youtube.com/watch?v=Oba80Hr8qrI (accessed 21 November 2013).
'Baby P The 17 Month Old Baby Tortured'. http://www.youtube.com/watch?v=bwNXvR OJaNU&list=PLwqXGZ1C66SZARjRe_0pTQlgg_EARFWc (accessed 21 November 2013).
'Baby P The Whole Truth Part 1'. http://www.youtube.com/watch?v=nhLURjB99D0 (accessed 21 November 2013).
'Baby P Tribute'. http://www.youtube.com/watch?v=_CrZ8YTgoac (accessed 21 November 2013).
Brennen, B. (2013). *Qualitative Research Methods for Media Studies*. New York and London: Routledge.
Bruns, A. (2008). *Blogs, Wikipedia, Second Life and Beyond: From Production to Produsage*. New York: Peter Lang.
CREA (Children's Rights Alliance England). (2009). Children's Rights and Equality in the Newspapers. http://www.partnershipforyounglondon.org.uk/data/files/Participation/childrens_rights_and_equality_in_the_newspapers_crae_may_2009.pdf (accessed 13 January 2014).
Davies, N. 2008. *Flat Earth News*. London: Vintage Books.
'Disgusting Torture and Murder of Baby P. READ THE INFO'. http://www.youtube.com/watch?v=Ea9-0qBx6QE&list=PLwqXGZ1C66SZARjRe_0pTQlgg_EARFWc (accessed 21 November 2013).
Elsley, S. (2010). *Media Coverage of Child Deaths in the UK: The Impact of Baby P: A Case for Influence?* Edinburgh: University of Edinburgh.
Franklin, B. (1998a). 'The SAS in Cardies …'. *Community Care* (10–16 December): 30–1.
Franklin, B. (1998b). *Hard Pressed: National Newspaper Reporting of Social Work and Social Services*. London: Reed Business Services.
Franklin, B. (1999). 'Education … Education and Please, Less Prejudice'. *British Journalism Review* 10(1): 41–9.
Franklin, B. (2012). 'The Future of Journalism; Developments and Debates'. *Journalism Studies* 13(5–6): 663–81.
Franklin, B. and Parton, N. (eds) (1991). *Social Work, the Media and Public Relations*. London: Routledge.
Gaber, I. (2011). 'That's a Great Story! The Media, Social Work and Child Abuse'. *British Journalism Review* 23(3): 57–63.

Hunt, L. (2008). 'Baby P: Social Work Campaigners Launch "Anti Witch Hunt" Petition'. *Community Care* (17 November). http://www.communitycare.co.uk/articles/17/11/2008/110000/baby-p-social-work-campaigners-launch-anti-witch-hunt-petition.htm.

'Justice 4 Baby P'. http://www.youtube.com/watch?v=_s1BaQE3-s4 (accessed 21 November 2013).

Kennedy, J. (2010). 'Don't You Forget About Me; An Exploration of the 'Maddie' Phenomenon on YouTube'. *Journalism Studies* 11(2): 225–42.

Kitchen, M. (1980). 'What the Client Thinks of You'. *Social Work Today* (June).

Larkin, P. (1974). 'Annus Mirabilis'. In *High Windows*. London: Faber & Faber.

Lasica J. D. (2007). 'What is Participatory Journalism?' *Online Journalism Review*. http://www.ojr.org/ojr/workplace/1060217106.php (accessed 13 January 2014).

McKay, H. (2009). 'Child Abuse, Social Work and the Press; Baby P.' Unpublished MA dissertation, London Metropolitan University.

Phillips, A. (2012). 'Sociability, Speed and Quality in the Changing News Environment'. *Journalism Practice* 6(5–6): 669–79.

Plunkett, J. (2010). 'Andrew Marr says bloggers are "inadequate, pimpled and single"'. *Guardian*, 11 October. http://www.guardian.co.uk/media/2010/oct/11/andrew-marr-bloggers (accessed 13 January 2014).

Pugh, A. (2011). 'Child protection reporting "vindictive" and "simplistic" in community care'. http://www.pressgazette.co.uk/node/47228 (accessed 10 December 2012).

'RAW and EMOTIONAL'. http://www.youtube.com/watch?v=CzsuY-Kkaqw (accessed 21 November 2013).

Rosen, J. 'The Definition of Citizen Journalism'. http://www.youtube.com/watch?v=QcYSmRZuep4 (accessed 21 November 2013).

Sabato, L. J. (1991). *Feeding Frenzy: How Attack Journalism Has Transformed American Politics*. Michigan: Free Press.

Santana, A. D. (Forthcoming). 'Virtuous or Vitriolic: The Effect of Anonymity on Civility in Online Newspaper Reader Comment Boards'. *Journalism Practice*.

'Shoesmith Wins Baby P Sacking Case'. http://www.youtube.com/watch?v=N1RW 92d2A8o&playnext=1&list=PLwqXGZ1C66SZARjRe_0pTQlgg_EARFWc_ (accessed 21 November 2013).

'The Munro Review to Look at Children's Social Work and Frontline Child Protection'. http://www.youtube.com/watch?v=IBznWUQNtAY (accessed 21 November 2013).

'The Peter Connelly Story'. http://www.youtube.com/watch?v=0E1rKYrP_DY (accessed 21 November 2013).

Treacher, R. (1988). 'The Problem with Being on the Media Map'. *Local Government Chronicle* (22 July): 15.

Warner, J. (2013a). '"Heads must roll"? Emotional Politics, the Press, and the Death of Baby P'. *British Journal of Social Work* (published online 4 March). DOI: 10.1093/bjsw/bct039.

Warner, J. (2013b). 'Social Work, Class Politics and Risk in the Moral Panic over Baby P'. *Health, Risk and Society* (published online 1 March). DOI:10.1080/13698575.20 13.776018.

YouTube. YouTube Statistics. www.YouTube.com/t/press_statistics (accessed 21 November 2013).

3
The Changing Politics and Practice of Child Protection and Safeguarding in England

Nigel Parton

The purpose of this chapter is to provide a critical analysis of the changes in child protection policy and practice in England since the publication of my original chapter in *Thatcher's Children?* in 1996 (Parton 1996). In doing so, I will be drawing on a number of articles and books which have been published in the intervening 20 years (for example, Parton 1997, 2006, 2008a, 2008b, 2009, 2010, 2011, 2012, 2014).

I will argue that the period from the mid-1990s until 2008 saw policy change in significant ways. In particular the state developed a much broader focus of concern about what caused harm to children and what the role of professionals and official agencies should be in relation to this. The object of concern was increasingly upon 'safeguarding and promoting the welfare of the child'. In the process we witnessed an important change in the relationships between children, families and the state. Underlying such developments were new and sometimes competing ideas about risk to children and the best ways of addressing these. Such developments were implemented in the context of the introduction of a range of new systems of information communication technology (ICT), and a heavy reliance was placed upon top-down forms of performance management.

However, the period from late 2008, following huge social reaction to the tragic death of Baby Peter Connelly, saw policy and practice move in new directions. Not only was 'child protection' rediscovered as an issue of significant political and policy concern, but policy and practice began to be reconfigured in quite new ways. Such developments were given a major impetus following the election of the Conservative/Liberal Democrat Coalition government in May 2010, and we can see the emergence of what I call an authoritarian neoliberal approach to child protection and child welfare more generally.

The last 40 years have witnessed a considerable growth in concern about child abuse and the failures of professionals to intervene appropriately to protect children. As I argued in the 1996 chapter (Parton 1996), following high-profile and very public criticisms of social workers and other health and welfare professionals in cases of child abuse in the 1970s and 1980s (Parton 1985; Butler and Drakeford 2011), the long-established state child welfare services in England came under increasing pressure and came to be dominated by a narrow, legalistic and forensically orientated focus on child protection. Similar developments were evident in the other nations in the UK, as well as North America and Australia (Gilbert 1997; Waldfogel 1998; Lonne et al. 2009). By the early 1990s, the child protection and child welfare systems could be characterised in terms of the need to identify 'high risk' cases so that these could be differentiated from the rest. Thereby children could be protected from abuse while ensuring that family privacy was not undermined and scarce resources could be directed to where, in theory, they were most needed (Parton 1991; Parton, Thorpe and Wattam 1997). 'High risk' was conceptualised in terms of 'dangerousness', for it was the small minority of 'dangerous families' (Dale et al. 1986; Parton and Parton 1989), subject to extreme family dysfunctions and violent personalities, who were seen as the primary cause of child abuse and which therefore needed to be identified so that children could be protected.

This was clear in the official government guidance at the time – *Working Together Under the Children Act 1989: A Guide to Arrangements for Inter-Agency Cooperation for the Protection of Children from Abuse* (Home Office et al. 1991) – where the focus of attention was explicitly stated as 'the protection of children from abuse'. This was reinforced further in the only official guide on the purpose and content of professional assessments, *Protecting Children: A Guide for Social Workers Undertaking a Comprehensive Assessment* (Department of Health 1988). The guide was specifically designed for social workers in cases where abuse was either substantiated or highly suspected and was concerned with how to carry out a comprehensive assessment for 'long-term planning in child protection' cases. At the time Pithers commented that 'The guide addressed the key issue of whether a family is considered safe for a child, or whether it can be made safe, or whether it is so potentially dangerous that alternatives have to be found' (Pithers 1989: 18).

New Labour and the move to safeguarding

However, during the mid-1990s a major debate opened up about how policies and practices in relation to child protection integrated with and were supported by policies and practices concerned with family support and child welfare more generally (Audit Commission 1994; Department of Health 1995). Rather than simply be concerned with a narrow, forensically driven focus on child protection, it was argued that there needed to be a 'rebalancing' or 'refocusing' of the work, such that the essential principles of a child welfare approach should dominate (Parton 1997). Policy and practice should be driven by an emphasis on partnership, participation, prevention and family support. The priority should be on *helping* parents and children in the community in a supportive way and should keep notions of policing and coercive intervention to a minimum. This change in thinking was evident in the official guidance published at the end of the decade, *Working Together to Safeguard Children: A Guide to Inter-agency Working to Safeguard and Promote the Welfare of Children* (Department of Health et al. 1999). The words 'protection' and 'abuse' were dropped from the title, which was framed in terms of the general duty placed on local authorities by Section 17(1) of the Children Act 1989 'to safeguard and promote the welfare of children in their area who are in need'. The guidance underlined the fact that local authority social services had wider responsibilities than simply responding to concerns about 'significant harm' and identifying child abuse and was explicitly located in the much wider agenda for children's services being promulgated by the New Labour government, associated with social exclusion (Frost and Parton 2009). The *Framework for the Assessment of Children in Need and Their Families* (Department of Health et al. 2000), published at the same time as the 1999 *Working Together*, attempted to move the focus from the forensic assessment of the risk of child abuse and 'significant harm' (Department of Health 2001) to one which was much more concerned with the broader idea of the impairment to a child's overall development in the context of their family and community environment.

We can thus identify an important change in the nature of the risk which policy and practice was expected to respond to. The object of concern was no longer simply children at risk of abuse and 'significant harm'. Effective measures to safeguard children were seen as those which also promoted their welfare, and should not be seen in isolation from the wider range of support and services provided to meet the needs of all children and families. There was a broadening of concerns from 'child protection' to 'safeguarding', or, as I have argued elsewhere (Parton 2010), from 'dangerousness' to 'risk'.

This is not to say, however, that child protection disappeared; rather it was located in the wider concerns about 'safeguarding and promoting the welfare of children'. This was defined for the first time in *Working Together* published in 2006, where it was stated that:

Safeguarding and promoting the welfare of children is defined for the purposes of this guidance as:

- protecting children from maltreatment;
- preventing impairment of children's health or development; and
- ensuring that children are growing up in circumstances consistent with the provision of safe and effective care; and undertaking that role so as to enable those children to have optimum life chances and enter adulthood successfully. (HM Government 2006: para.1.18, original emphasis)

Child protection continued to be specifically concerned with assessment and intervention in situations where children were 'suffering, or likely to suffer, significant harm'. While the focus of both assessment and intervention had thus broadened between 1991 and 2006, the forensic investigation of possible 'significant harm' continued to inhabit the core of the system and it was local authority children's social workers who had the clear statutory responsibility in this regard.

Risk and *Every Child Matters: Change for Children* programme

The 2006 *Working Together* guidance (HM Government 2006) was published at a time of major change in children's services in England. The government had launched its *Every Child Matters: Change for Children* (ECM) programme (Department for Education and Skills 2004a), where the overriding vision was to bring about 'a shift to prevention whilst strengthening protection' (Department for Education and Skills 2004b: 3). The consultative Green Paper *Every Child Matters* (Chief Secretary to the Treasury 2003) had originally been launched as the government's response to a very high profile child abuse public inquiry into the death of Victoria Climbié (Laming 2003). Major organisational change followed the 2004 Children Act, including the replacement of local authority social service departments with departments of children's services which combined local authority education and children's social care responsibilities. However, the changes were much broader than simply being concerned with overcoming the problems related to cases of child abuse. The priority was to intervene at a much earlier stage in children's lives in order to prevent a range of problems both in childhood and in later life, including poor educational attainment, unemployment, crime and antisocial behaviour. The ambition was to improve the outcomes for all children and to narrow the gap in outcomes between those who did well and those who did not. The outcomes were defined in terms of: being healthy; staying safe; enjoying and achieving; making a positive contribution; and achieving economic well-being. Together, these five outcomes were seen as key to improving 'well-being in childhood and later life'. It was a very ambitious programme of change and was to include *all children*, as it was felt that any child, at some point in their life, could be seen as vulnerable to some form of risk and therefore might require help. The idea was to identify problems before they became chronic. Two figures included in the Green Paper (Figures 3.1 and 3.2) are particularly helpful in understanding how the reform of children's services was conceptualised.

All children in the population are included in the triangle in Figure 3.1 and categorised according to their level of vulnerability, while in Figure 3.2 services are organised according to whether they are specialist, targeted or universal. The idea was that problems were identified as quickly as possible to ensure they did not escalate and that services were integrated to ensure that this took place.

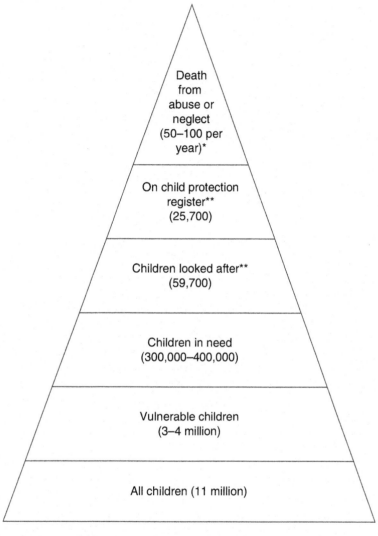

Figure 3.1 Every Child Matters: categorising children (subject to Crown copyright)
*These children may or may not be on the child protection register, nor looked after, nor vulnerable.
**These children are included in the 'children in need' figure, and not all children on the child protection register are children looked after.

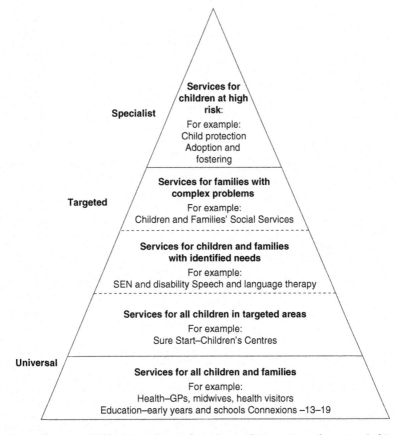

Figure 3.2 *Every Child Matters*: Targeted services within a universal context (subject to Crown copyright)

The model informing the changes was very much influenced by a public health approach to prevention and has been characterised as 'the paradigm of risk and protection-focused prevention' (France and Utting 2005) informed by risk factor analysis (RFA) (France, Freiberg and Homel 2010), whereby the knowledge of risk factors derived from prospective longitudinal research is drawn upon to design particular programmes and to reorientate mainstream services. The work of David Farrington in relation to youth crime prevention was particularly influential (Farrington 1996, 2000, 2007). What was attractive to policy makers was that a range of overlapping personal and environmental 'risk factors' were identified, not only in relation to future criminal behaviour, violence and drug abuse, but also for educational failure, unsafe sexual behaviour and poor mental health (Dryfoos 1990; Mrazek and Haggerty 1994; Goldblatt and Lewis 1998). The

Green Paper stated that: 'we have a good idea what factors shape children's life chances. Research tells us *that the risk of experiencing negative outcomes* is concentrated in children with certain characteristics' (Chief Secretary to the Treasury 2003: 17, emphasis added), and that these included:

- low income and parental unemployment;
- homelessness;
- poor parenting;
- postnatal depression amongst mothers;
- low birth weight;
- substance misuse;
- individual characteristics, such as intelligence;
- community factors, such as living in a disadvantaged community.

The more risk factors a child had, the more likely it was that they would experience 'negative outcomes', and it was 'poor parenting' that was seen to play the key role. Identifying the risk factors and intervening early provided the major strategy for overcoming the social exclusion of children and avoiding problems in later life.

However, the role of prevention was not only to combat the negatives involved but also to enhance the positive opportunities for child development via maximising protective factors and processes. The approach was informed by the work of Michael Rutter (1990) who conceived of risk and protection as processes rather than fixed states and saw protectors as the basis for opening up opportunities. The timing of interventions was crucial for, if they were to have the most impact, the 'early years' were key and success depended on recruiting parents – usually mothers – to the role of educators. The notion of protection was thus much wider than simply protection from harm or abuse. In trying to maximise childhood 'strengths' and 'resilience', the idea of risk was itself reframed in far more positive ways (Little, Axford and Morpeth 2004; Axford and Little 2006).

To achieve the outcomes, the ECM changes aimed to integrate health, social care, education and criminal justice agencies and thereby overcome traditional organisational and professional 'silos'. Such a development required agencies and professionals to share information so that risks could be identified early and opportunities maximised. To take this forward, a variety of new systems of information, communication and technology (ICT) were to be introduced – including the Common Assessment Framework (CAF), ContactPoint and the Integrated Children's System (ICS).

The *Common Assessment Framework* (CAF) provides an important insight into the way 'risk' to children was rethought in the context of ECM and the way practice was to be reconfigured as a result. The CAF was an electronic assessment form to be completed by any professional when they considered a child to have 'additional needs' that required the involvement of more than one service. It included a wide-ranging set of data covering most aspects of a child's

52 *Nigel Parton*

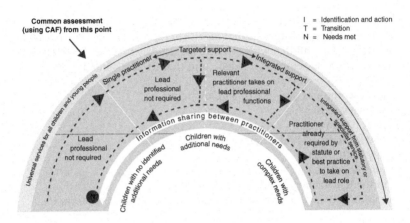

Figure 3.3 Processes and tools to support children and families (subject to Crown copyright)
Source: *Common Assessment Framework for Children and Young People: Practitioners' Guide* (CWDC 2009: 8).

health and development, including details about parents and siblings. The CAF was designed to identify those children who might not progress towards the five ECM outcomes without additional services and therefore operated at the level of secondary prevention (or targeted services). The diagram in Figure 3.3, taken from the CAF *Practitioners' Guide* (Children's Workforce Development Council 2009), provides a helpful picture of how the processes and tools designed to integrate children's services and support early intervention were conceived, particularly in the context of Figures 3.1 and 3.2 earlier.

The eCAF clearly demonstrated how the importance of early intervention and the growing use of ICT were seen as central for the transformation of children's services in England by New Labour. The focus of concern had broadened considerably from those children who might suffer child abuse or 'significant harm' to include all children, particularly those who were at risk of poor outcomes and therefore who might not fulfil their potential. In the process, the systems designed to screen and identify those in need of attention had grown in size and complexity and the challenges and responsibilities placed upon a wide range of agencies and practitioners increased considerably (Parton 2010). As a result, it seemed that important changes were taking place in the relationships between children, families and the state, which I characterised at the time as the emergence of the 'preventive-surveillance state' (Parton 2008a, 2010).

Baby Peter Connelly and the rediscovery of child protection

While the *ECM: Change for Children* programme (Department for Education and Skills 2004a) was presented by the New Labour government as its response to the Laming Report (Laming 2003) into the death of Victoria Climbié, a number of commentators argued that the reforms had the effect of marginalising child protection (Munro and Calder 2005; Smith 2008). This, however, was to change following the events of November 2008.

On 11 November 2008 two men were convicted of causing or allowing the death of 17-month-old Baby Peter Connelly, one of whom was his stepfather. The baby's mother had already pleaded guilty to the charge. During the trial the court heard that 'Baby P', as he was referred to at the time, was used as a 'punch bag'; and that his mother had deceived and manipulated professionals with lies and on one occasion had smeared him with chocolate to hide his bruises. There had been over 60 contacts with the family from a variety of health and social care professionals and he was pronounced dead just 48 hours after a hospital doctor failed to identify that he had a broken spine. He was the subject of a child protection plan with Haringey local authority in London – the local authority which had been at the centre of failures to protect Victoria Climbié back in 2000.

The media response was immediate and very critical of the services, particularly the local authority (Jones 2012; Warner 2013). The largest-selling daily tabloid newspaper, the *Sun*, ran a campaign aimed at getting the professionals involved in the case sacked from their jobs under the banner of 'Beautiful Baby P: Campaign for Justice' (*Sun*, 15 November 2008). Two weeks later the newspaper delivered a petition to the Prime Minister containing 1.5 million signatures, and claiming it was the largest and most successful campaign of its sort ever. In addition, a large number of Facebook groups, comprising over 1.6 million members, were set up in memory of Baby Peter and seeking justice for his killers. This weight of expressed opinion put major pressure on the then government minister, Ed Balls, to be seen to be acting authoritatively in order to take control of the situation. He responded by:

- ordering the Office for Standards in Education, Children's Services and Skills (Ofsted), the Healthcare Commission and the police inspectorate to carry out an urgent Joint Area Review (JAR) of safeguarding in Haringey;
- ordering the preparation of a new and independent serious case review following the publication of the original one on 12 November, which he deemed to be inadequate and insufficiently critical;
- appointing Lord Laming to carry out an urgent review of child protection in England;
- establishing a Social Work Task Force to identify any barriers that social workers faced in doing their jobs effectively; make recommendations for improvements and the long-term reform of social work; and to report in the autumn of 2009.

On receipt of the JAR on 1 December 2008, which he described as 'devastating', the minister announced he was using his powers under the

Education Act 1996 to direct Haringey to remove the Director of Children's Services, Sharon Shoesmith. Later that month she was sacked by the council without compensation and with immediate effect. In April 2009 Haringey Council also dismissed four other employees connected to the Baby Peter case – the Deputy Director of Children's Services, the Head of Children in Need and Safeguarding Services, the Team manager, and the Social Worker. In addition, the paediatrician who examined Baby Peter two days before his death but missed the most serious injuries was suspended from the medical register; and the family doctor who saw Baby Peter at least 15 times and was the first to raise the alarm about the baby's abuse was also suspended from the medical register.

Very quickly, reports surfaced that it was becoming very difficult to recruit and retain staff nationally to work in children's social care, particularly social workers, and that morale was at an all-time low (Local Government Association 2009). The case was clearly having wide-scale reverberations. A number of influential commentators, including the House of Commons Children, Schools and Families Parliamentary Committee (House of Commons 2009) began to argue that the threshold for admitting children into state care was too high. Not only should Baby Peter have been admitted to care some months before his death, but his situation was not seen as unusual. Similarly, the Children and Family Court Advisory and Support Service (CAFCASS 2009) produced figures which demonstrated that there were nearly 50 per cent more care applications to court in the second half of 2008–9 compared with the first half of the year; demand for care cases was 39 per cent higher in March 2009 compared with March 2008; and the demand for care continued to remain at an unprecedentedly high level for the first two quarters of 2009–10, with June 2009 having the highest demand for care ever recorded for a single month.

The death of Baby Peter and the intense and rancorous social and media reaction clearly engendered a sense of very high anxiety amongst government officials and children's services managers and practitioners (Garrett 2009). It was also notable that the report produced by Lord Laming in March 2009 was entitled *The Protection of Children in England* (Laming Report 2009) and that both this and the government's response (HM Government 2009) were framed in terms of 'child protection'. Whereas previously policy and practice had been framed in terms of 'safeguarding and promoting the welfare of the child', it now seemed that concerns about child protection had, again, moved centre stage.

At the same time as rediscovering child protection, central government also seemed to rediscover the importance of professional social work. It is, perhaps, a particular irony that the area where social work had been so heavily criticised for over 30 years, child protection, was the area of practice where it continued to be seen as having a key role to play, and the failures in the Baby Peter case seemed to reinforce this even further. The work of the Social Work Task Force, which reported in late 2009 (Social Work Task Force

2009), was clearly central in this regard, and the government made it clear that a major contribution to the improvement in child protection practice was crucially dependent on the rejuvenation of a well-trained, respected social work profession (HM Government 2010b).

Developments in the wake of the death of Baby Peter had the effect of reinforcing the importance of child protection at the centre of safeguarding policy and practice and reinforcing the central role that social work played in this. For while the period since the mid-1990s, particularly since the introduction of the ECM reforms, had emphasised a much broader and more positive approach to risk, the narrow forensic approach to child protection, which was so dominant in the early 1990s, had clearly been (re)confirmed as lying at the heart of current and future attempts to 'safeguard children' (HM Government 2010a). It seemed that government was determined to ensure that while there should be a continued emphasis upon early intervention, this should not deflect from ensuring that children were protected from significant harm. Child protection was very much seen to lie – in terms of Figures 3.1 and 3.2 reproduced above – at the sharp end, or apex, of any attempts to 'safeguard and promote children's welfare'. In many respects, the post-Baby Peter changes could be seen to consolidate one of the central aims of the ECM reforms of wanting to bring about 'a shift to prevention whilst strengthening protection' (Department for Education and Skills 2004b: 3).

It is notable that social work was to operate almost exclusively at this sharp end of child protection. Whilst there had been a considerable expansion in preventative and early intervention services from the mid-1990s, no longer were these seen as being in the province of mainstream social work (Frost and Parton 2009; Parton 2009). This had been made explicit in *Every Child Matters: Change for Children in Social Care* (Department for Education and Skills 2004c), published at the same time as *Every Child Matters: Change for Children* (Department for Education and Skills 2004a).

> Social workers and social care workers need to be at the heart of the ECM *Change for Children* programme. 'You play a central role in trying to improve outcomes for the most vulnerable through your work with children in need including those in need of protection, children who are looked after and disabled children' (Department for Education and Skills 2004c: 2).

It was social workers who were given the key and overriding responsibility for operating the child protection system, and this had changed very little from the situation in the early 1990s. Following the death of Baby Peter, social workers became more concerned than ever with forensically investigating, assessing and managing cases of child abuse in a context which was more high profile and procedurally driven than ever before. For example, the revised *Working Together* published in March 2010 (HM Government 2010a), produced primarily in response to recommendations in the Laming

Report, *The Protection of Children in England*, increased in length from 231 pages to 390 pages compared to the 2006 version (HM Government 2006). Thus, while the final 18 months of the New Labour government witnessed something of a revaluing of social work and a renewed recognition of the complexities involved, the actual focus and organisation of the work became even more prescribed and framed by its statutory and procedurally defined roles and responsibilities.

The period after November 2008 was also notable for an increased sense of anxiety and defensiveness in the way children's social care was operating, and there was clear evidence that it was having to cope with a large increase in referrals together with a growth in the number of children subject to a child protection plan, an increase in the numbers of children taken into care and a growth in Section 47 enquiries (Association of Directors of Children's Services 2010). Increasingly, it seems that early intervention was being interpreted as the need to formally intervene earlier with the increased possibility that children would be placed on a child protection plan, placed on a statutory order or taken into care (Hannon, Wood and Bazalgette 2010).

What also became evident by the end of the New Labour government in May 2010 was that there was a growing range of criticisms and concerns being expressed about the way policy and practice in this area had developed during the previous ten years. These criticisms were no longer focused only on the tragic deaths of young children and the failure of professionals to intervene, but on the fact that many of changes introduced may have had the unintended consequence of making the situation worse.

In particular, the introduction of the new electronic ICT systems, such as ContactPoint and the Integrated Children's System (ICS), came in for considerable criticism (Shaw et al. 2009; Shaw and Clayden 2009; Shaw, Morris and Edwards 2009; White et al. 2010). Not only did such systems seem to increase the range and depth of state surveillance of children, young people, parents and professionals (Parton 2006, 2008a; Anderson et al. 2009) and undermine individual and family privacy (Roche 2008), but they did not seem to work as intended. In particular, they seemed to have the effect of deflecting front-line practitioners from their core task of working directly with children, young people and parents (Hall et al. 2010); increasing the bureaucratic demands of the work (Parton 2008b; Broadhurst et al. 2010a, 2010b; White, Hall and Peckover 2009); and catching practitioners in an 'iron cage of performance management' (Wastell et al. 2010), unable to exercise their professional judgement in order to safeguard children and promote their welfare (Peckover, White and Hall 2008; White, Hall and Peckover 2009).

In addition, in broadening the focus of what was meant by risk there had been an elision or conflation (Munro 2009; Parton 2010) of concerns about children and young people who might be *at risk* from a whole variety of threats, including abuse, with other concerns about children and young people who might *pose a threat* to others, particularly by falling into crime or antisocial behaviour. The agendas around the care and control of children and young people and those who might be either victims or villains were in danger of becoming very blurred (Sharland 2006; James and James 2008). In attempting to widen and deepen attempts at early intervention in order to improve the outcomes for all children, while also trying to strengthen the systems of child protection, there was a real danger that there would be a growth in attempts at what Michael Power has called 'the risk management of everything' (Power 2004). Rather than overcoming the defensiveness, risk avoidance and blame culture so associated with the child protection system in the 1990s, it seemed that these characteristics were increasingly permeating the whole of the newly integrated and transformed children's services. Such concerns were heightened in the highly anxious context following the death of Baby Peter which seemed to prioritise an approach to practice based on 'strict safety' and a 'logic of precaution'. Increasingly, the language of risk was in danger of being stripped of its association with the calculation of probabilities and was being used in terms of not just preventing future harm but also avoiding the 'worst case' scenario (Ericson 2007; Hebenton and Seddon 2009).

The Coalition, child protection and the authoritarian neoliberal state

Soon after coming to power in May 2010, the Conservative/Liberal Democrat Coalition government announced it was introducing two changes to which the Conservative Party had committed themselves in their election manifesto (Conservative Party 2010) and for which they had been arguing ever since the furore over Baby Peter Connelly's death. ContactPoint was scrapped as from August 2010 and serious case reviews were in future to be published in full. However, and perhaps more significantly, the government also announced the establishment of an independent review of child protection in England to be chaired by Eileen Munro, a qualified and experienced social worker and Professor of Social Policy at the London School of Economics.

The Review was published in three parts (Munro 2010, 2011a, 2011b; Parton 2012) and clearly aimed to bring about a paradigm shift in child protection policy and practice:

> The final report sets out the proposals for reform which, taken together, are intended to create the conditions that enable professionals to make the best judgments about the help to give to children, young people and families. This involves moving from a system that has become over-bureaucratised and focused on compliance to one that values and develops professional expertise and is focused on the safety and welfare of children and young people. (Munro 2011b: 6)

It seemed that a major priority was to reverse a trend which had been evident for many years whereby the dominating response to tragedies in child protection had been to substitute *confidence in systems* for *trust in professionals*, particularly social workers (Smith 2001).

The overall aim of the final report (Munro 2011b) was to develop a child protection system which valued professional expertise; it recommended that the government revise *Working Together* to 'remove unnecessary or unhelpful prescription and focus on essential rules for effective multiagency working and on the principles that underpin good practice' (Munro 2011b: 7). Inspection was also seen as a key negative influence on front-line practice and needed reforming.

The Review was also clear, along with the other reviews established by the Coalition government (Field 2010; Allen 2011a, 2011b; Tickett 2011), that it wished to emphasise the importance of 'early help', for 'preventative services can do more to reduce abuse and neglect than reactive services', and it recommended that the government should place a duty on local authorities and their statutory partners to secure sufficient provision of 'local early help services for children, young people and families'. In addition the Review made a number of recommendations designed to improve accountability and emphasised the importance of the local authority acting as the lead agency while wanting to strengthen the role of Local Safeguarding Children Boards (LSCBs).

But perhaps the most significant recommendations related to the role and practice of social workers. For, if there was to be a reduced reliance upon procedures, central guidance and targets, the authority and practice of professionals needed to be improved, and it was social workers who were seen as the key professionals in the reformed child protection system. The Review therefore aimed to build on the report of the Social Work Task Force (2009) and the work of the Social Work Reform Board, which had been established to implement the recommendations of the Task Force. In particular, it recommended that each local authority should designate a Principal Child and Family Social Worker at senior management level to represent the views and experiences of front-line staff to all levels of management; a Chief Social Worker should be appointed to advise government and inform the Secretary of State's annual report to parliament on the workings of the Children Act 1989; local authorities should review and redesign the way that child and family social work was delivered; and a range of changes should be introduced by both local authorities and higher education to improve the training, capabilities and overall professional development of social workers.

The government appeared supportive of the Review's analysis and conclusions and accepted 9 of the 15 recommendations outright. The government clearly saw the Review as consistent with its overall approach to the reform of public services: 'The government is determined ... to work with all involved with safeguarding children to bring about lasting reform ... that means reducing central prescription and interference and placing greater trust in local leaders and skilled frontline professionals in accordance with the principles set out in the Government's Open Public Services White Paper' (Department for Education 2011: 5, para.2).

As I have argued elsewhere (Parton 2012, 2014), a major problem with the Review was that it never really addressed what it meant by child protection and, in particular, never addressed the fact that the problem of child maltreatment is generally agreed to be around ten times more prevalent than the number of cases that are ever referred to official agencies (Radford et al. 2011); if this was seriously addressed, child protection, health, welfare and criminal justice agencies would be completely submerged.

However, the above quotation and explicit reference to the *Open Public Services* White Paper demonstrated that the government felt that the Review was quite consistent with its overall agenda for the reform of public services. Unlike New Labour, which had placed children right at the centre of its reforms, the Coalition government made it very clear that it was the reduction of public finance debt which was its overriding and most urgent political priority. It also made it clear that it wished to decentralise power and reduce the role of the central state – to move from policies that emphasised 'Big Government' to those that emphasised 'the Big Society' (Ellison 2011). However, what became increasingly apparent was that the Coalition reform of public services was far more radical than anything seen previously, including the Conservative governments of Margaret Thatcher and John Major (1979–97). I have characterised the nature of the Coalition approach as the move to an authoritarian neoliberal state which has a number of key elements (Parton 2014) and for which the *Open Public Services* White Paper (HM Government 2011), the severe cuts to public service expenditure and the introduction of a number of more authoritarian and coercive interventions were key.

The *Open Public Services* White Paper made it clear that every public service at all levels of government should be opened up to delivery by a wide range of providers, primarily the private and, to a lesser extent, the voluntary, charitable and third sectors. This quickly started to happen across health, education, criminal justice and local authorities. While such policies had been evident under New Labour, the changes under the Coalition were much more wide-ranging, rapid and sweeping in nature.

From the outset the government introduced major plans for the reduction of public expenditure, including cuts of 28 per cent for local authorities over the course of the parliament. Not only were these to be 'front-end loaded' in the first year, but they were greatest in the poorest areas of the North, the Midlands and some London boroughs (Ramesh 2012). It was also clear that families with children were no longer considered a priority group in welfare spending in the way they had been under New Labour (Stewart 2011; Churchill 2012). The *Every Child Matters: Change for Children* programme was quietly but clearly dropped and there was a significant shift towards targeting the cuts to both children's benefits and services, including Sure Start Children's Centres (HM Treasury 2010). An analysis by the Institute of Fiscal Studies indicated that households with children would lose by more than those without children at all parts of the income distribution as a result of the government's changes to tax and benefits (Brewer 2010).

A survey by the Directors of Children's Services estimated that the cuts in local authority children's services for the financial year 2010/11 averaged 13 per cent, ranging from 6 to 25 per cent (Higgs 2011) and Children's Centres and early years services took a disproportionate cut in the overall reductions to education budgets (Chowdry and Sibieta 2011). Because of the speed and size of the budget reductions the voluntary sector, which relied on central and local government for much of its income, was particularly hard hit and it was estimated that children's charities experienced a greater proportion of public sector reductions (8.2 per cent) that year compared with the voluntary sector as a whole (7.7 per cent) (Children England 2011; Gill, La Ville and Brady 2011).

It became increasingly apparent that the *Munro Review*'s emphasis on the importance of 'early help' was being undermined. Research carried out for the NSPCC (Chartered Institute of Public Finance and Accountancy 2011) found that local authority children's social care budgets faced reductions of over 23 per cent and that it was cuts to early intervention and preventative services which were taking the brunt. This was likely to result in greater demand for child protection services and it was clear that these were already under considerable pressure. Similar findings were forthcoming in research carried out for the Family and Parenting Institute (Hopwood, Pharoah and Hannon 2012).

There was clear evidence of the growth in demand upon the statutory elements of children's social care such that the trends evident following the social reaction to the death of Baby Peter Connelly continued. Between 2009/10 and 2011/12:

- while the number of referrals to children's social care remained stable at just over 600,000 per annum (having been 538,500 in 2007/08), the number of initial assessments went up from 395,300 to 451,500 (319,900 in 2007/09);
- the number of registered child protection plans increased from 44,300 to 52,100 (34,000 in 2007/08);
- the number of children in care increased from 64,400 to 67,050 (59,360 in 2007/08). (Department for Education annual *Characteristics of Children in Need in England* and *Children Looked After in England*)

The number of applications for care to the courts increased even more dramatically, from 6,241 in 2007/08 to 8,832 in 2009/10 to 11,055 in 2012/13 (CAFCASS 2013).

We can see a clear shift to an emphasis upon statutory child protection work, what the Association of Directors of Children's Services called 'increases in safeguarding activity' (Brooks, Brocklehurst and Freeman 2012: 6).

It also became evident that the government was of the view that more children needed to be taken into care. This was confirmed in a significant speech by Michael Gove, the Secretary of State, in November 2012 (Gove 2012), when he also argued strongly that there had been a failure in leadership in relation to child protection over a number of years and that adults' interests had been overriding the needs of children.

In addition, and following a major campaign for reform by *The Times* newspaper, fronted by Martin Narey (Narey 2011), the retired Chief Executive of Barnardo's, the government launched a major initiative to 'speed up adoptions and give vulnerable children loving homes' (Department for Education 2012). The plan was to ensure that adoption became a mainstream option for children in care. Local authorities were required to reduce delays in all cases and would not be able to delay adoption in order to find a suitable ethnic match; it would be easier for children to be fostered by approved prospective adopters while the courts considered the case for adoption; and if suitable adopters could not be found within three months, the case would have to be referred to a new National Adoption Register.

Following a key recommendation of the *Munro Review*, and after a lengthy delay, the Coalition government published a revised version of *Working Together* in March 2013 (HM Government 2013). While it had the same title as the previous guidance (Department of Health et al. 1999; HM Government 2006, 2010a) and did not change the definition of many of the key concepts in the 2010 version (HM Government 2010a) – namely: safeguarding and promoting the welfare of children; child protection; abuse; physical abuse; emotional abuse; sexual abuse; neglect; and children – in other respects it had a number of important differences to the previous guidance. Significantly, the document had been reduced in size from 399 to 95 pages and the number of footnotes from 273 to 43. In addition the *Assessment Framework* no longer had the status of statutory guidance. This reflected the view of both the *Munro Review* and the government that the growing bureaucratisation of the work was a direct result of the growth in the central prescription and the length and complexity of *Working Together*. It was claimed that the revised guidance clarified the core legal requirements and made much clearer what individual professionals and organisations should do to keep children safe and promote their welfare.

While the focus of the guidance continued to be 'safeguarding and promoting the welfare of children', this was no longer set out in the context of the *ECM: Change for Children* programme and its emphasis on 'integration'. The 2013 guidance adopted 'a child-centred and coordinated approach to safeguarding' (para.8). 'Social workers, their managers and other professionals should always consider the plan from the child's perspective. *A desire to* think the best of adults and to hope they can overcome their difficulties should not trump the need to rescue children from chaotic, neglectful and abusive homes' (HM Government 2013: 22, emphasis added). The theme of 'rescuing children from chaotic, neglectful and abusive homes' ran through the guidance and very much reflected the emphasis in other elements of the Coalition government's policies of intervening early, admitting more children into care and investing in adoption.

Thus while the language of 'safeguarding and promoting the welfare of the child' was retained, we can see a significant shift in the guidance towards a much more explicit 'child protection orientation' (Parton 2014). It was not simply that any reference to the *ECM: Change for Children* programme had been dropped but that the idea of 'supporting families', which had been so important ever since the 'refocusing debate' in the mid/late 1990s, had all but disappeared. For example, Chapter 1 of the 1999 *Working Together* (Department of Health et al. 1999) was entitled 'Working together to support children and families' and emphasised that the guidance was based on 'partnership' and an 'integrated approach'. This emphasis was no longer present in the 2013 *Working Together* (HM Government 2013). No longer did it seem that the idea of 'partnership' with parents was given any major prominence.

Conclusion

I am therefore arguing that if we take these various developments together we can identify a significant shift in government policy concerned with child protection and safeguarding from that developed from the mid-1990s onwards, particularly compared to the changes introduced by the ambitious and wide-ranging ECM reforms. While changes were evident in the immediate fallout following the scandal related to Baby Peter Connelly, these have now been taken to a new level and increasingly it seems that intervention in families has become more coercive and authoritarian. The range of universal and secondary prevention benefits and services has been reduced and the role of the state in other areas has become more 'authoritarian' and much more willing to intervene in certain families with the full weight of statute behind it. At the same time the levels of poverty and deprivation have been growing and the private sector has been playing an increasingly major role in the organisation and delivery of services. Not only has the state been commercialised and residualised, it has become, for certain sections of the population, much more authoritarian. All are key elements in what I characterise as the emergence of an authoritarian neoliberal state in services for children and families (Parton 2014).

References

Allen, G. (2011a). *Early Intervention: The Next Steps – An Independent Report to Her Majesty's Government*. London: HM Government, Cabinet Office.

Allen, G. (2011b). *Early Intervention: Smart Investment Massive Savings – The Second Independent Report to Her Majesty's Government*. London: HM Government, Cabinet Office.
Anderson, R., Brown, I., Dowty, T., Inglesant, P., Heath, W. and Sasse, A. (2009). *Database State*. York: Joseph Rowntree Reform Trust.
Association of Directors of Children's Services. (2010). *Safeguarding Pressures Project: Results of Data Collection, April 2010*. Manchester: ADCS.
Audit Commission. (1994). *Seen But Not Heard: Coordinating Community Health and Social Services for Children in Need*. London: HMSO.
Axford, N. and Little, M. (2006). 'Refocusing Children's Services towards Prevention: Lessons from the Literature'. *Children & Society* 20(4): 299–312.
Brewer, M. (2010). 'The Spending Review and Children'. Presentation to the All Party Parliamentary Group for Children, 29 November. House of Commons.
Broadhurst, K., Wastell, D., White, S., Hall, C., Peckover, S., Thompson, A., Pithouse, A. and Davey, D. (2010a). 'Performing 'Initial Assessment': Identifying the Latent Conditions for Error at the Front-Door of Local Authority Children's Services'. *British Journal of Social Work* 40(2): 349–51.
Broadhurst, K., Hall, C., Wastell, D., White, S. and Pithouse, A. (2010b). 'Risk, Instrumentalism and the Humane Project in Social Work: Identifying the Informal Logics of Risk Management in Children's Statutory Services'. *British Journal of Social Work* 40(4): 1046–65.
Brooks, C., Brocklehurst, P. and Freeman, S. (2012). *Safeguarding Pressures: Phase 3*. Manchester: The Association of Directors of Children's Services.
Butler, I. and Drakeford, M. (2011). *Social Work on Trial: The Colwell Inquiry and the State of Welfare*. Bristol: Policy Press.
CAFCASS (Children and Family Court Advisory and Support Service). (2009). *CAFCASS Care Demand – Latest Quarterly Figures: 20 October 2009*. London: CAFCASS.
CAFCASS (Children and Family Court Advisory and Support Service). (2013). *Cafcass Care Application Annual figures: March 2013*.London: CAFCASS.
Chartered Institute of Public Finance and Accountancy (CIPFA). (2011). *Smart Cuts? Public Spending on Children's Social Care*. London: NSPCC.
Chief Secretary to the Treasury. (2003). *Every Child Matters* (Cm 5860). London: HMSO.
Children England. (2011). *Counting the Cuts: The Impact of Public Spending Cuts on Children's Charities*. London: Children England.
Children's Workforce Development Council. (2009). *Common Assessment Framework for Children and Young People: Practitioners' Guide. Integrated Working to Improve Outcomes for Children and Young People*. Leeds: CWDC.
Chowdry, H. and Sibieta, L. (2011). *Trends in Education and School Spending. IFS Briefing Note*. London: Institute for Fiscal Studies.
Churchill, H. (2012). 'Family Support and the Coalition: Retrenchment, Refocusing and Restructuring'. In M. Kilkey, G. Ramia and K. Farnsworth (eds), *Social Policy Review 24: Analysis and Debate in Social Policy 2012*. Bristol: Policy Press.
Conservative Party. (2010). *Invitation to Join the Government of Britain: The Conservative Manifesto 2010*. London: The Conservative Party.
Dale, P., Davies, M., Morrison, T. and Waters, J. (1986). *Dangerous Families: Assessment and Treatment of Child Abuse*. London: Tavistock.
Department for Education. (2011). *A Child-Centred System: The Government's Response to the Munro Review of Child Protection*. London: Department for Education.
Department for Education. (2012). *An Action Plan for Adoption: Tackling Delay*. London: Department for Education.

Department for Education and Skills. (2004a). *Every Child Matters: Change for Children*. London: DfES.
Department for Education and Skills. (2004b). *Every Child Matters: Next Steps*. London: DfES.
Department for Education and Skills. (2004c). *Every Child Matters: Change for Children in Social Care*. London: DfES.
Department of Health. (1988). *Protecting Children: A Guide for Social Workers Undertaking a Comprehensive Assessment*. London: HMSO.
Department of Health. (1995). *Child Protection: Messages from Research*. London: HMSO.
Department of Health. (2001). *Studies Informing the Framework for the Assessment of Children in Need and their Families*. London: HMSO.
Department of Health, Department of Education and Employment, Home Office. (2000). *Framework for the Assessment of Children in Need and their Families*. London: HMSO.
Department of Health, Home Office, and Department of Education and Employment. (1999). *Working Together to Safeguard Children: A Guide to Inter-agency Working to Safeguard and Promote the Welfare of Children*. London: HMSO.
Dryfoos, J. G. (1990). *Adolescents at Risk: Prevalence and Prevention*. Oxford: Oxford University Press.
Ellison, N. (2011). 'The Conservative Party and the "Big Society"'. In C. Holden, M. Kilkey and G. Ramia (eds), *Social Policy Review 23: Analysis and Debate in Social Policy, 2011*. Bristol: Policy Press.
Ericson, R. V. (2007). *Crime in an Insecure World*. Cambridge: Polity Press.
Farrington, D. (1996). *Understanding and Preventing Youth Crime*. York: Joseph Rowntree Foundation.
Farrington, D. (2000). 'Explaining and Preventing Crime: The Globalisation of Knowledge'. *Criminology* 38(1): 1–24.
Farrington, D. (2007). 'Childhood Risk Factors and Risk-Focused Prevention'. In M. Maguire, R. Morgan and R. Reiner (eds), *The Oxford Handbook of Criminology* (4th edn). Oxford: Oxford University Press.
Field, F. (2010). *The Foundation Years: Preventing Poor Children Becoming Poor Adults – Report of the Independent Review on Poverty and Life Chances*. London: HM Government, Cabinet Office.
France, A., Freiberg, K. and Homel, R. (2010). 'Beyond Risk Factors: Towards a Holistic Prevention Paradigm for Children and Young People'. *British Journal of Social Work* 40(4): 1192–210.
France, A. and Utting, D. (2005). 'The Paradigm of "Risk and Protection-Focussed Prevention" and Its Impact on Services for Children and Families'. *Children & Society* 19(2): 77–90.
Frost, N. and Parton, N. (2009). *Understanding Children's Social Care: Politics, Policy and Practice*. London: Sage.
Garrett, P. M. (2009). 'The Case of "Baby P": Opening up Spaces for Debate on the "Transformation of Children's Services?"'. *Critical Social Policy* 29(3): 533–47.
Gilbert, N. (ed.). (1997). *Combatting Child Abuse: International Perspectives and Trends*. New York: Oxford University Press.
Gill, C., La Ville, I. and Brady, M. L. (2011). *The Ripple Effect: The Nature and Impact of the Cuts on the Children and Young People's Voluntary Sector*. London: National Children's Bureau.
Goldblatt, P. and Lewis, C. (eds). (1998). *Reducing Offending*. Home Office Research Study No. 187. London: HMSO.

Gove, M. (2012). 'The Failure of Child Protection and the Need for a Fresh Start'. Speech at the Institute for Public Policy Research, 16 November. www.education. gov.uk/inthenews/speeches/900217075/gove-speech-on-child-protection (accessed 16 November 2012).

Hall, C., Parton, N., Peckover, S. and White, S. (2010). 'Child-centric Information and Communication technology (ICT) and the Fragmentation of Child Welfare Practice in England'. *Journal of Social Policy* 39(3): 393–413.

Hannon, C., Wood, C. and Bazalgette, L. (2010). *In Loco Parentis*. London: Demos.

Hebenton, B. and Seddon, T. (2009). 'From Dangerousness to Precaution: Managing Sexual and Violent Offenders in an Insecure and Uncertain Age'. *British Journal of Criminology* 49(3): 343–62.

Higgs, L. (2011). 'Exclusive Survey: Youth Services and Children's Services Worst Hit as Cuts Average 13 per cent'. *Children and Young People Now* (25 January): 6–7.

HM Government. (2006). *Working Together to Safeguard Children: A Guide to Inter-agency Working to Safeguard and Promote the Welfare of Children*. London: HMSO.

HM Government. (2009). *The Protection of Children in England: Action Plan; The Government Response to Lord Laming*, Cm 748. London: DCSF.

HM Government. (2010a). *Working Together to Safeguard Children: A Guide to Inter-agency Working to Safeguard and Promote the Welfare of Children*. London: DCSF.

HM Government. (2010b). *Building a Safe and Confident Future: Implementing the Recommendations of the Social Work Task Force*. London: DCSF, DH and BIS.

HM Government. (2011). *Open Public Services White Paper*. Cm8145. London: HMSO.

HM Government. (2013). *Working Together to Safeguard Children: A Guide to Inter-agency Working to Safeguard and Promote the Welfare of Children*. London: Department for Education.

HM Treasury. (2010). *Spending Review 2010*. London: HMSO.

Home Office, Department of Health, Department of Education and Science, and the Welsh Office. (1991). *Working Together Under the Children Act 1989: A Guide to Arrangements for Inter-Agency Cooperation for the Protection of Children from Abuse*. London: HMSO.

Hopwood, O., Pharoah, R. and Hannon, C. (2012). *Families on the Front Line? Local Spending on Children's Services in Austerity*. London: Family and Parenting Institute.

House of Commons Children, Schools and Families Committee. (2009). *Looked After Children*. http://www.publications.parliament.uk/pa/cm200809/cmselect/cmchilsh/111/11106.htm (accessed 6 August 2009).

James, A. and James, A. (2008). 'Changing Childhood in the UK: Reconstructing Discourses of "Risk" and "Protection"'. In A. James and A. James (eds), *European Childhoods: Cultures, Politics and Childhoods in Europe*. Basingstoke: Palgrave Macmillan.

Jones, R. (2012). 'Child Protection, Social Work and the Media: Doing as Well as Being Done To'. *Research, Policy and Planning* 29(2): 83–94.

Laming Report. (2003). *The Victoria Climbié Inquiry: Report of the Inquiry by Lord Laming* (Cm 5730). London: HMSO.

Laming Report. (2009). *The Protection of Children in England: A Progress Report*. London: HMSO.

Little, M., Axford, N. and Morpeth, C. (2004). 'Risk and Protection in the Context of Services for Children in Need'. *Child and Family Social Work* 9(1): 105–18.

Local Government Association. (2009). *Councils Struggling to Recruit Social Workers in Wake of Baby P*. London: LGA.

Lonne, B., Parton, N., Thomson, J. and Harries, M. (2009). *Reforming Child Protection*. London: Routledge.
Mrazek, P. J. and Haggerty, K. J. (eds). (1994). *Reducing Risks for Mental Disorders: Frontiers for Preventive Intervention Research*. Washington, DC: Institute of Medicine/National Academy Press.
Munro, E. (2009). 'Managing Societal and Institutional Risk in Child Protection'. *Risk Analysis* 29(7): 1015–23.
Munro, E. (2010). *The Munro Review of Child Protection, Part One: A System's Analysis*. London: Department for Education.
Munro, E. (2011a). *The Munro Review of Child Protection: Interim Report. The Child's Journey*. London: Department for Education.
Munro, E. (2011b). *The Munro Review of Child Protection: Final Report. A Child-Centred System*. Cm 8062. London: Department for Education.
Munro, E. and Calder, M. (2005). 'Where has Child Protection Gone?' *Political Quarterly* 76(3): 439–45.
Narey, M. (2011). *Narey Report on Adoption*. Special Supplement of *The Times*, 5 July.
Parton, C. and Parton, N. (1989). 'Child Protection, the Law and Dangerousness'. In O. Stevenson (ed.), *Child Abuse: Public Policy and Professional Practice*. Hemel Hempstead: Harvester Wheatsheaf.
Parton, N. (1985). *The Politics of Child Abuse*. Basingstoke: Palgrave Macmillan.
Parton, N. (1991). *Governing the Family: Child Care, Child Protection and the State*. Basingstoke: Palgrave Macmillan.
Parton, N. (1996). 'The New Politics of Child Protection'. In J. Pilcher and S. Wagg (eds), *Thatcher's Children? Politics, Childhood and Society in the 1980s and 1990s*. London: Falmer Press.
Parton, N. (ed.) (1997). *Child Protection and Family Support: Tensions, Contradictions and Possibilities*. London: Routledge.
Parton, N. (2006). *Safeguarding Childhood: Early Intervention and Surveillance in a Late Modern Society*. Basingstoke: Palgrave Macmillan.
Parton, N. (2008a). 'The Change for Children Programme in England: Towards the "Preventive-Surveillance State"'. *Journal of Law and Society* 35(1): 166–87.
Parton, N. (2008b). 'Changes in the Form of Knowledge in Social Work: From the "Social" to the "Informational"?'. *British Journal of Social Work* 38(2): 253–69.
Parton, N. (2009). 'From Seebohm to Think Family: Reflections on 40 Years of Policy Change in Statutory Children's Social Work in England'. *Child and Family Social Work* 14(1): 68–78.
Parton, N. (2010). 'From Dangerousness to Risk: The Growing Importance of Screening and Surveillance Systems for Safeguarding and Promoting the Well-being of Children in England'. *Health, Risk and Society* 12(1): 51–64.
Parton, N. (2011). 'Child Protection and Safeguarding in England: Changing and Competing Conceptions of Risk and Their Implications for Social Work'. *British Journal of Social Work* 41(5): 854–75.
Parton, N. (2012). 'The Munro Review of Child Protection: An Appraisal'. *Children & Society* 26(2): 150–62.
Parton, N. (2014). *The Politics of Child Protection: Contemporary Developments and Future Directions*. Basingstoke: Palgrave Macmillan.
Parton, N., Thorpe, D. and Wattam, C. (1997). *Child Protection: Risk and the Moral Order*. Basingstoke: Palgrave Macmillan.
Peckover, S., White, S. and Hall, C. (2008). 'Making and Managing Electronic Children: E-assessment in Child Welfare'. *Information, Communication and Society* 11(3): 375–94.

Pithers, D. (1989). 'A Guide through the Maze of Child Protection'. *Social Work Today* 20(18): 8–19.
Powell, M. (ed.). (2008). *Modernising the Welfare State: The Blair Legacy*. Bristol: Policy Press.
Power, M. (2004). *The Risk Management of Everything: Rethinking the Politics of Uncertainty*. London: Demos.
Radford, L., Corral, S., Bradley, C., Fisher, H., Bassett, C., Howat, N. and Collishaw, S. (2011). *Child Abuse and Neglect in the UK Today*. London: NSPCC.
Ramesh, R. (2012). 'Council Cuts Targeted Towards Deprived Areas'. *The Guardian*, 14 November: 9.
Roche, J. (2008). 'Children's Rights, Confidentiality and the Policing of Children'. *International Journal of Children's Rights* 16(4): 431–56.
Rutter, M. (1990). 'Psychosocial Resilience and Protective Mechanisms'. In J. Rolf, A. S. Masten, D. Cichetti, K. H. Nuechterlein and S. Weintraub (eds), *Risk and Protective Factors in the Development of Psychopathology*. Cambridge: Cambridge University Press.
Sharland, E. (2006). 'Young People, Risk Taking and Risk Making: Some Thoughts for Social Work'. *British Journal of Social Work* 36(2): 247–65.
Shaw, I. and Clayden, J. (2009). 'Technology, Evidence and Professional Practice: Reflections on the Integrated Children's System'. *Journal of Children's Services* 4(4): 15–27.
Shaw, I., Bell, M., Sinclair, I., Sloper, P., Mitchell, W., Dyson, P., Clayden, J. and Rafferty, J. (2009). 'An Exemplary Scheme? An Evaluation of the Integrated Children's System'. *British Journal of Social Work* 39(4): 613–26.
Shaw, I., Morris, K. and Edwards, A. (2009). 'Technology, Social Services and Organizational Innovation *or* How Great Expectations in London and Cardiff Are Dashed in Lowestoft and Cymtyrch'. *Journal of Social Work Practice* 23(4): 383–400.
Smith, C. (2001). 'Trust and Confidence: Possibilities for Social Work in High Modernity'. *British Journal of Social Work* 31(2): 287–305.
Smith, R. (2008). 'From Child Protection to Child Safety: Locating Risk Assessment in the Changing Landscape'. In M. C. Calder (ed.), *Contemporary Risk Assessment in Safeguarding Children*. Lyme Regis: Russell House.
Social Work Task Force. (2009). *Building a Safe, Confident Future: The Final Report of the Social Work Task Force*. Nottingham: Department of Children, Schools and Families.
Stewart, K. (2011). 'A Treble Blow? Child Poverty in 2010 and Beyond'. In C. Holden, M. Kilkey and G. Ramis (eds), *Social Policy Review 23: Analysis and Debate in Social Policy 2011*. Bristol: Policy Press.
Tickell, D. C. (2011). *The Early Years: Foundations for Life, Health and Learning – An Independent Report on the Early Years Foundation Stage to Her Majesty's Government*. London: Department for Education.
Waldfogel, J. (1998). *The Future of Child Protection: How to Break the Cycle of Abuse and Neglect*. Cambridge, MA: Harvard University Press.
Warner, J. (2013). '"Heads Must Roll"? Emotional Politics, the Press and the Death of Baby P. *British Journal of Social Work* (advance access, 4 March). DOI: 10.1093/bjsw. bct039.
Wastell, D., White, S., Broadhurst, K., Peckover, S. and Pithouse, A. (2010). 'Children's Services in the Iron Cage of Performance Management: Street-level Bureaucracy and the Spectre of Svejkism'. *International Journal of Social Welfare* (early access, 9 May), 19(3), 310–20.

White, S., Broadhurst, K., Wastell, D., Peckover, S., Hall, C. and Pithouse, A. (2009). 'Whither Practice – Near Research in the Modernization Programme? Policy Blunders in Children's Services'. *Journal of Social Work Practice* 23(4): 401–11.

White, S., Hall, C. and Peckover, S. (2009). 'The Descriptive Tyranny of the Common Assessment Framework: Technologies of Categorization and Professional Practice in Child Welfare'. *British Journal of Social Work* 39(7): 1–21.

White, S., Wastell, D., Broadhurst, K. and Hall, S. (2010). 'When Policy O'erleaps Itself: The "Tragic Tale" of the Integrated Children's System'. *Critical Social Policy* 30(3): 405–29.

4
Child Trafficking
Known Unknowns and Unknown Knowns

Julia O'Connell Davidson

Commenting on whether there was evidence that Saddam Hussein's regime was involved in supplying weapons of mass destruction to terrorist groups, Donald Rumsfeld, then US Secretary of Defense, famously told the press: 'There are known knowns. These are things we know that we know. There are known unknowns. That is to say, there are things that we know we don't know. But there are also unknown unknowns. There are things we don't know we don't know.' These 'unknown unknowns' were the threats from Saddam that could not even be imagined or suspected (Žižek 2004).

Rumsfeld's formulation resonates closely with dominant discourse on human trafficking in general, and child trafficking in particular. 'Trafficking' is understood to involve the forcible movement of people for purposes of exploitation, and individual cases in which either adults or children have been subject to very violent and also very particular forms of exploitation and abuse are presented as the things we know that we know about this phenomenon. The prevalence of such cases in any given sector, country or region appears as the 'known unknown'. Virtually every governmental, intergovernmental and non-governmental organisation (NGO) report and 'factsheet' on trafficking includes a statement to the effect that because trafficking is an illegal industry, it is difficult to ascertain exactly how many victims there are; it then follows this up with a sizeable and frightening estimate. For example, 'It is very difficult to assess the real size of human trafficking because the crime takes place underground, and is often not identified or misidentified. However, a conservative estimate of the crime puts the number of victims at any one time at 2.5 million' (UNODC 2013). There are also 'unknown unknowns'. The assumed links between trafficking and terrorism, organised crime, paedophile rings, corruption, and so on, are discussed as representing unknown threats to national security and the core values of liberal democratic societies.

Slavoj Žižek (2004) observes that in his 'amateur philosophizing' on the known and the unknown, Rumsfeld 'forgot to add the crucial fourth term: the "unknown knowns," the things we don't know that we know – which is precisely, the Freudian unconscious, the "knowledge which doesn't know itself"'. And where Rumsfeld was preoccupied by the threat of 'unknown unknowns', Žižek points out that if we focus on the treatment of Iraqi prisoners in Abu Ghraib (or indeed on the many thousands of civilians killed and maimed by cluster bombs in the Iraq conflict), danger seems to inhere as much, or more, in 'unknown knowns', that is, 'the disavowed beliefs, suppositions and obscene practices we pretend not to know about, even though they form the background of our public values' (2004).

This chapter asks whether similar 'unknown knowns' operate in relation to what is described as child trafficking. Are there things that are in fact knowable or known, but that politicians, policy makers, as well as many journalists, activists and members of the general public in liberal democratic societies would prefer not to know? What knowledge and which practices does dominant discourse on child trafficking camouflage, conceal and enable us to disavow? The chapter begins by tracing the way in which, over the past two decades, child trafficking has been constructed as a global social problem of immense proportions, then moves to consider the 'known unknowns' and the 'unknown knowns' that dominant discourse on child trafficking conjures with.

Child trafficking as a two-for-one crisis

Towards the end of the twentieth century, childhood – and then, slightly later, migration – became the focus of intense moral and political anxiety and debate in Western liberal democracies. The sense of crisis surrounding both topics has continued into the second decade of the twenty-first century, and is especially apparent and intense in discourse on 'child trafficking', a discourse that knits both sets of anxieties together to produce one particularly horrifying spectre.

So far as childhood is concerned, the threats began to be noted and discussed in academic and popular writings from the 1970s. Childhood was described as having been lost (Elkind 1981), or disappeared (Postman 1982), and children were increasingly represented as suffering as a consequence of being thrust prematurely into a stressful and corrupting adult world. By the turn of the century, the idea that childhood was in crisis and that children were at risk had come to be widely accepted (Kehily 2010). Popular anxiety about childhood and children has had many different focal points over the past 30-odd years (they grow up too soon, they remain dependent too long; they are too thin, too fat, too dim, too tested, too undisciplined, too pressured, too consumerist, and so on), but one of the enduring features of this childhood-in-crisis discourse is a preoccupation with sex.

From the 1970s on, academic, policy, professional and public interest in child abuse grew rapidly in the United States and Western Europe, and, as Joel Best (1993: 71) notes, what had earlier been discussed as incest and child molestation were brought under this umbrella and renamed as 'child sexual abuse'. Child sexual abuse quickly became big business for academics, publishers and mental health treatment and recovery service providers (Itzin 2000: 2). It also became big media business. The stories that were increasingly told and retold in newspapers, magazines and books, as well as on talk shows and in soap operas, through the 1980s and 1990s contributed to a discourse in which the problem of child sexual abuse was one of epic proportions. As James Kincaid (1998) has observed, these were stories about an epidemic of child molesting, a terror lurking in every nook and cranny, a horror that touched all of us, a problem that was ever-growing, inescapable and insoluble.

By the 1990s, alarm about the sexual abuse of children by paedophiles in positions of trust and authority was being further amplified by concerns about what was termed the 'commercial sexual exploitation of children' (CSEC). Tales of CSEC mirrored the more general story of child molesting as a huge and growing problem with almost unimaginably grave consequences (O'Connell Davidson 2005). Campaigners described commercially sexually exploited children as often 'so severely injured that it is not possible to rehabilitate them to a normal life. Most children who end up in the sex industry are also soon infected with HIV/Aids or other illnesses and die before they are adults' (Rädda Barnen 1996: 16). These themes were picked up and reworked by journalists in countless articles telling stories of children sold into prostitution by their parents, then 'rescued by good outsiders for a brief period of happiness before dying' (Montgomery 2001: 23). According to campaigners, the exponential growth of CSEC represented the dark underbelly of globalisation and recent technological advances, and added another layer of horror to the sexual abuse of children: the idea that there were people who profited from promoting and organising 'the most abhorrent of crimes – sexual molestation of children' (ECPAT 1996: 10).

The link between criminality and globalisation was being much more widely made in the 1990s. In the context of more porous borders in the post-Cold War era, transnational crime, especially immigration crime, was increasingly perceived as a threat to national sovereignty and security. Indeed, border crossing came to be regarded as a security issue, and 'human trafficking' first entered into public and policy consciousness through the lens of this concern. In the most general of terms, 'trafficking' is understood to involve the transportation of persons by means of coercion or deception into exploitative or slavery-like conditions. However, when it began to be identified as a significant problem in the mid-1990s, the focus was very much upon cases in which women and girls were forced into prostitution, especially women and girls forced into prostitution against the backcloth of the immense political, economic and social upheavals taking place in former Eastern Bloc countries.

For governments of affluent Western liberal democratic states, such cases were indicative of a much larger problem of 'transnational organised crime', which, especially post-9/11, was regarded as linked to terrorism and other security threats. A speech by George W. Bush to the United Nations General Assembly in 2003 illustrates how potent a cocktail of fear could be produced through the blending of anxieties about sex, childhood and border crossings:

> Each year, an estimated 800,000 to 900,000 human beings are bought, sold or forced across the world's borders. Among them are hundreds of thousands of teenage girls, and others as young as five, who fall victim to the sex trade. This commerce in human life generates billions of dollars each year – much of which is used to finance organised crime. There's a special evil in the abuse and exploitation of the most innocent and vulnerable. The victims of the sex trade see little of life before they see the very worst of life – an underground of brutality and lonely fear. (Cited in Lee 2011: 109)

Certainly, governments have been willing to spend billions of dollars on fighting this 'special evil', especially upon measures to 'secure' borders (in 2012, the US federal government spent US$18 billion on border enforcement; Gonzalez 2013). They have also been willing to fund certain forms of research and advocacy, as well as various intervention programmes designed to combat trafficking. The growing political and public interest in trafficking and associated opportunities for fund raising provided many human and child rights international organisations and NGOs with an incentive to re-badge some or all of their existing activities as 'anti-trafficking' work. Those campaigning against CSEC, for example, were quick to reposition it as a problem closely aligned with trafficking. As more and more governmental organisations, NGOs and researchers came to view trafficking as the topical and 'hot' human rights issue, the term experienced 'domain expansion' (Best 1993), and came to embrace a large and disparate collection of global social problems and rights violations. By the millennium, concerns about child labour, domestic servitude, enforced criminal activity, underage, servile or forced marriage, benefit fraud, inter-country adoption and fostering, and child soldiers, as well as child prostitution, were all included under the umbrella of 'child trafficking'.

Again, the fund raising, awareness raising and campaigning materials produced by child rights NGOs and agencies stress the immense scale of the problem ('Every year, worldwide, an estimated 1.2 million children are trafficked'; UNICEF 2009). And again, even though trafficked children are said to be present in many different settings, such materials typically emphasise the link between 'child trafficking' and sexual exploitation (O'Connell Davidson 2011). The focus on child prostitution works to emphasise the profoundly

Child Trafficking 73

damaging consequences of 'trafficking' and, once this is clearly established in the reader's mind, campaigners move to observe that all 'trafficked' children are destined for ruthless exploitation. Whether this takes place in the sex industry or another context, the consequences are equally horrifying: 'Once separated from their family [trafficked children] can become malnourished and neglected, and are subjected to violence and sexual abuse. They are also at risk of HIV infection. Trafficked children are driven by fear. Their traffickers control them with threats, rape, violence and drugs' (UNICEF 2007).

The global reach of this crime is also said to be phenomenal. As one campaigning journalist recently blogged, child trafficking 'is perhaps one of the most unimaginable practices in existence in today's world. However, it is real and it is happening even outside my very own doorstep in Minneapolis, Minnesota'. The same blog highlights the most recent twist to dominant discourse on child trafficking, which involves talk of what is termed 'internal' or 'domestic' child trafficking. This takes us back to the anxieties about child sexual abuse that grabbed the popular imagination in the 1980s and 1990s, and ensures that it is not just migrant children who are imagined as being at risk of trafficking. What was in the past described as 'grooming', or abuse by a group of paedophiles or child molesters, is now relabelled as 'trafficking' because the children concerned are not abused in their own homes but 'are moved away from their home town to other locations, for the purpose of sexual exploitation' (Barnardo's 2013), or even simply 'taken to private residences in the same area ... for sexual exploitation by other adult males' (CEOP 2009).

This move substantially increases the estimated number of children 'at risk' of trafficking in countries like the UK and the US. Some organisations claim that more than 200,000 American children are vulnerable to being 'sex trafficked' into strip clubs, street prostitution, escort services and brothels in the United States. In the UK, a much publicised case in 2012, in which five men in Rotherham had engaged in abusive relationships with minors and were found guilty of rape and/or sexual activity with a child, was widely described as illustrative of a significant 'internal trafficking' problem. Labour MP Denis MacShane commented that though 'an evil gang of internal traffickers' had been sent to prison, 'it is clear that the internal trafficking of barely pubescent girls is much more widespread' (BBC 2012).

As with narratives about sexual child abuse, we are presented with a paradox: child trafficking is monstrous and unthinkable and yet at the same time rampant; only the most depraved of perverts could wish to use child prostitutes and only the most vile of criminals could bring themselves to exploit a child, and yet there is a huge and growing market for children's bodies. As James Kincaid (1998: 10) remarks in relation to the more general narrative of child molesting:

> The story is ... cagily baited, mysterious, self-perpetuating, inescapable. It is a story of monsters and purity, sunshine and darkness, of being chased

by the beast and finding your feet in glue, of tunnels opening onto other tunnels, of exits leading to dead walls. Our story of child molesting is a story of nightmare, the literary territory of the Gothic. On the face of it, the Gothic is not a promising form for casting social problems. Instead of offering solutions, such tales tend to paralyse; they do not move forward but circle back to one more hopeless encounter with the demon. Why would we want that?

Why do we want to tell a story about a world in which millions of children are being torn from their homes, then raped, beaten, brutalised, sexualised and exploited by organised criminal gangs? Is it because we know that this story provides an accurate description of what is going on?

The threat of child trafficking: known and unknown unknowns

There are, sadly, many well-documented individual cases in which children have been subjected to extreme and violent forms of abuse and exploitation. We know about these cases and we know that we know about them. We do not, however, know the number of such cases or whether this number has increased, decreased or remained constant over any given time period. As Chris Jenks (1996: 92) has noted, 'child abuse is not an original event, there has never been a historical period nor a particular society in which children were not exploited, sexually molested and subjected to physical and psychological violence'. Though patterns of reporting of child sexual abuse may have been changing in the 1980s, there is no real evidence to suggest that the flurry of concern about abuse was a response to a sudden rise in its incidence. Nor is there anything new about the exploitation of children in the sex trade. Where prostitution has existed, so too has what would now be deemed 'child prostitution', and for as long as people have been taking erotic photographs of adults, they have also been producing 'child pornography'. As with child abuse more generally, it would be virtually impossible to produce empirical evidence either to support or refute the claim that more children are commercially sexually exploited today than ever before, or indeed to measure the extent of the phenomenon in the contemporary world (Ennew 1986). The same points hold good in relation to 'child trafficking'.

As with 'human trafficking' more generally, one reason why we do not know how widespread the problem is simply that clandestine phenomena are more difficult to measure than legally sanctioned and visible ones. This is the methodological difficulty that anti-trafficking campaigners emphasise when they present examples of particularly dramatic and harrowing individual cases, and claim that they are the tip of an iceberg of unknown dimensions. But the methodological problems presented by efforts to measure 'trafficking' run deeper than this. It is not simply that 'traffickers' have an interest in concealing their activities, in the same way that, say, people who smoke illegal drugs have an interest in concealing this practice. There are also definitional problems which mean that, unlike the question of whether or not someone has ever smoked marijuana, the question of whether or not someone has been 'trafficked' is a matter of judgement, not of fact.

In 2000, the UN Convention Against Transnational Organized Crime was adopted by the UN General Assembly along with two new protocols – one on smuggling of migrants and one on trafficking in persons, especially women and children. In these protocols, 'trafficking' is defined as a wholly non-consensual process involving the recruitment and transportation of persons by means of deception or coercion for purposes of exploitation, while 'smuggling' is said to be a mutually agreed arrangement between smuggler and smuggled person. This distinction between smuggling and trafficking was and remains important to state actors. Human rights activists often regard all migrants who end up in forced labour and slavery-like situations as 'victims of trafficking' (VoT) no matter how they arrived in these conditions. But those who wish to control and restrict immigration and/or limit governments' humanitarian obligations to migrants wish to distinguish between 'deserving' victims of trafficking (who are imagined as having exercised absolutely no choice or agency at any stage of the process) and 'undeserving' smuggled or 'illegal' migrants (who are deemed to have brought suffering upon themselves through their own actions and choices).

However, the UN Trafficking Protocol states that if children have been recruited and transported 'for purposes of exploitation', they have been 'trafficked' no matter if they consented to move. This may at first appear to allow us to sidestep questions about choice and agency where children are concerned, and so make it simple to draw a line between children who are VoTs and children who are not. Yet the Protocol does not offer a definition of 'exploitation', and as Moravcsik (1998: 173) points out in a discussion of slavery, 'exploitation', like 'force', is a slippery notion: 'What constitutes inappropriate economic exploitation depends partly on what alternatives were or could have been envisaged within a given situation ... [and similarly] what counts as force ... and what restrictions any society might have to invoke under certain circumstances are left to be determined in context.'

As defined in the UN Protocol and employed by governmental actors, NGOs and others, 'trafficking' intersects with a wide array of different markets, institutions and practices. Though some of these are almost universally condemned and criminalised, others are socially tolerated and may even be socially valued. In most countries, including those in the affluent world, it is legally and socially acceptable for a person below the age of 18 to enter many labour markets and to marry, and in some countries also to join the armed forces. Likewise, adoption and private fostering are not regarded as categorical wrongs in the way that child prostitution is, but rather as potentially positive and desirable for some children. We cannot therefore state that anyone who organises or facilitates a child's movement for adoption or fostering is, ipso facto, moving them 'for purposes of exploitation'. And as the key elements of what might be deemed to constitute exploitation range along a continuum rather than existing as either/or options, we are left with the tricky question of just how bad a child's experience needs to be in order for the people who facilitated her movement to be viewed as 'traffickers'. Even if arranged illegally and for a third party's financial gain, distinguishing between a child who has been 'trafficked' and a child who has been 'smuggled' into foster care is no simple matter given that expectations regarding the amount of unpaid labour that children will provide within households vary cross-nationally and within nations, as do social norms regarding the powers that adults can properly exercise over children. Children's independent labour migration presents similar difficulties. Just how exploitative does work have to be for a child migrant to be considered a 'VoT'?

What is described as 'trafficking' takes place in a range of very different contexts, and understanding of what constitutes 'exploitation' varies between these contexts. This significantly complicates questions about how the 'trafficked child' is to be distinguished from other children who have been moved, or whose movement has been facilitated, by third parties (O'Connell Davidson 2011). It follows that the number of 'VoTs' is unknown not simply because trafficking is a criminalised and clandestine activity, but also because 'VoTs' do not actually exist as some kind of prior, objective or legal category of persons that can be counted by researchers or form the object of policy interventions.

It might be objected that 'victim of trafficking' does exist as an administrative category in a number of states. As far as migrants are concerned, it is a status assigned to those who are considered deserving of protection and assistance on grounds that they have experienced the particular constellation of coercive and exploitative practices during the migratory process and at the point of destination that the relevant authorities understand as 'trafficking'. However, if anti-trafficking campaigners were to focus on those who were actually afforded this status, a very different picture of the scope and scale of the problem would emerge. Indeed, one of the most remarkable features of the figures that are bandied around about trafficking is the gap – or chasm – between the numbers of observed and estimated VoTs. In the United States, for example, the Bush administration spent more than $150 million on efforts to identify and assist an estimated 50,000 VoTs annually brought into the country, but just 1,362 people were certified by the US Department of Health and Human Services as victims of human trafficking between 2000 and 2007 (O'Connell Davidson 2006; Markon 2007; see also Weitzer 2007). Of them, only 131 were minors (US Department of Justice 2008).

Anderson (2013: 144) observes that in the United Kingdom there is a similar mismatch between the anti-trafficking rhetoric that speaks of hundreds or even thousands of victims brought across our borders, and the practice of victim identification. Between April and November 2009, 477 people were referred to the National Referral Mechanism (NRM) as potential VoTs – the NRM having been introduced as part of a strategy for improving procedures for the identification of trafficked persons. Of these, 371 were from non-EU states, 72 from EU states excluding the UK, and 34 were UK nationals. 'The "positive identification" rate of cases as a whole was 19 per cent, that of UK nationals was 76 per cent, EU nationals 29.2 per cent, and nationals of non-EU states 11.9 per cent ... So in practice, UK nationals are far *more* likely to be found to be victims of trafficking than are non-EU nationals' (Anderson 2013: 144).

The provenance and basis for the figures about trafficking routinely and forcefully given by governmental and non-governmental organisations is largely unknown (Feingold 2010). Where their basis has become visible, it has done little to inspire confidence in the figures. For instance, though widely cited and hugely influential on international policy, US government estimates of the numbers of trafficked persons have even been criticised by the US Government Accountability Office, which noted, among other things, the fact that these estimates were developed by one person who did not document all his work, and commented on the absence of an effective mechanism for estimating the number of victims of trafficking (Shah 2007; Morehouse 2009).

As noted at the outset of this chapter, when speaking of child trafficking, NGOs, politicians and policy makers generally make a point of stating that we do not know the size or scope of the problem. And yet the continual repetition of dramatic yet ephemeral estimates of the scale of child trafficking alongside graphic accounts of very distressing individual cases produces a strong conviction that we do know that this 'known unknown' is huge. There is equal certainty about the 'unknown unknowns' of trafficking in general and child trafficking in particular. For although 'trafficking' is described as a crime against the person, it is also presented as one that threatens the collective as well as the individuals affected. So, for example, Rizer and Glaser (2011) assert that though a single case of involuntary servitude or forced prostitution would not constitute a breakdown of national security, 'taken as a whole, in the context of human trafficking, these crimes indeed represent a breach of national security ... human trafficking rots the fabric of our society and, as a result, has a destructive effect on the United States' national security'.

In the remainder of this chapter, I want to consider what is masked by this confident vision of what we know about the unknown scale and harms of child trafficking.

Child trafficking and 'unknown knowns' about immigration regimes

The factors that underpin migration in the contemporary world are many and varied, but uneven economic development, international debt and the neoliberal policy measures with which it is associated form part of the background context against which many people – whether aged above or below 18 – make the decision to migrate. Governments in the developing world also often have a strong economic interest in emigration, not least because remittances from migrants can substitute for social welfare that they are unable to provide. Recorded remittances alone received by developing countries in 2010 far exceeded the volume of official aid flows and constituted 'more than 10 percent of Gross Domestic Product (GDP) in many developing countries' (World Bank 2011). But though many people have very good reasons for wishing to migrate, opportunities for legally authorised migration are limited. In the context of ever more restrictive immigration policies by governments of migrant-receiving countries, and the securitisation of borders mentioned above, the market for clandestine migration services has expanded and diversified (Kempadoo, Sanghera and Pattanaik 2005; Alpes 2011). Very often, adults and children fleeing war and persecution to seek asylum are also dependent on such clandestine migration services in order to make their escape.

Clandestine migration is not necessarily physically dangerous – journeys made with fake documents are often no more or less risky than those with genuine travel papers. However, death during transit is nonetheless the starkest risk to many irregular migrants. It is estimated that between 3,861 and 5,607 people – adults and children – died in the 15 years up to 2009 as a result of the US government's border security policies on the US–Mexico border, for example. Clearly, as with estimates about the scale of 'trafficking', estimates of deaths related to border controls need to be treated with caution. However, determining whether or not a person is dead does not require subjective judgement in the way that determining whether or not a person is a VoT does, and more children dying while border crossing was one of the significant trends revealed by a review of deaths of children who were Mexican or Central American residents and who died in Pima County, Arizona during the years 1995–2004 (Bowen and Marshall 2007). Meanwhile, between 1993 and 2011, the organisation UNITED for Intercultural Action documented 15,551 deaths of refugees and migrants attributable 'to border militarisation, asylum laws, detention policies, deportations and carrier sanctions' (UNITED 2011). Their data are not fully disaggregated by age, but nonetheless show that children are amongst the dead. Rape and sexual exploitation is another risk that children and women migrating by irregular channels are known to face.

Once in the country of destination, irregular migrant children continue to be at risk of physical and psychological harm, not only or always from the criminal gangs that feature in dominant discourse on 'child trafficking', but from state actors. Migrant children are held in detention centres, which are widely recognised as unsuitable for children; there have been reports of police brutality against migrants in detention, including attacks on children; of children locked in for 22 hours a day and denied access to education; of children dying as a result of lack of medical treatment, fires and suicide (Human Rights Watch 2002; Fekete 2007). Cases of families being separated in detention centres and of breastfeeding mothers being detained separately from their babies have also been reported (Refugee Council 2003).

Children with migrant parents whose immigration status is irregular may witness violence perpetrated against their parents, and may indeed be subject to it themselves, in the process of deportation proceedings. Even without actual violence, deportation is a terrifying experience that can suddenly uproot children and transport them to a land they do not know (Golash-Boza 2012), and that can also lead to children's separation from their parents. In the United States, undocumented migrants are increasingly at risk of being picked up by the immigration authorities, detained and deported under the Criminal Alien Program and the Secure Communities Program. During the first half of 2011, around 46,000 undocumented migrant parents are believed to have been separated from their US-born children as a result, and in the same year, 'in Los Angeles alone, it is estimated that one in sixteen children who are part of this city's child welfare system are the children of detained or deported undocumented Mexican immigrant parents' (Rosas 2012: 82). Furthermore, as Rosas (2012: 82) notes:

> Although federal laws require child welfare departments to reunify children with any parent able to provide for the safety of the child, in reality ... [f]orced removal from the United States makes it difficult for [migrants] to satisfy standards that would afford them parental rights under the law ... Moreover, rather than pursue family reunification at all costs, child welfare departments have resorted to terminating parental rights altogether.

This practice has resulted in the placement of over 5,000 children of deported immigrant parents in foster care. And where much research and policy attention has been devoted to the forced movement of children across borders through 'trafficking', very little has been paid to the forcible return of child migrants to their countries of origin by state actors. This happens to several different groups of child migrants: those who are deported with their families; those who are deported on their own; and those who have been identified as VoTs, but who are not deemed to be at risk of further rights violations upon return to their home country. Even when children who have been identified as VoTs are involved, such decisions are not always monitored, and data on what happens to children after they have been returned are not routinely gathered (Bloch and Schuster 2005). A report on the UK Border Agency (UKBA) in 2010 accused the agency of 'systematic disregard' for children, putting them on planes out of the country with no checks on their safety or welfare. A total of 334 unaccompanied children who claimed asylum in Britain between 2004 and 2010 were deported, most to their first European point of entry, and often left there destitute and homeless (Dugan 2010).

Undocumented migrants, both adult and child, are one of the groups facing the greatest risks of poverty and social exclusion in Europe today (PICUM 2007). Whether children are with their parents or not, 'illegality' represents a barrier to education, services, justice and social protection, and exposes them to additional harm from state actors (Bloch and Zetter 2009). The list could go on, but the central point is that children who migrate, especially if they move through irregular channels, can be exposed to many of the same risks and dangers that anti-child-trafficking campaigners identify as the harms of trafficking: violence; sexual abuse; HIV infection; forcible separation from their family; incarceration in appalling conditions. They too can be terrorised, driven by fear, face discrimination, suffer psychologically, and experience low self-esteem and suicidal feelings. Summing up the wrongness of trafficking, UNICEF (2007) states: 'Not only does trafficking violate every child's right to be protected and grow up in a family, it also deprives them of education and opportunity.' But immigration regimes can also do all of this to a child and more. In dominant discourse on child trafficking, this fact remains an unknown known.

Child trafficking and 'unknown knowns' about childhoods

The history and sociology of childhood(s) show that although there are observable physical, developmental and psychological differences between human beings over the course of life spans, and although babies and small children necessarily depend on older persons for their survival, there are no pre-given 'adults' and 'children' and there is no 'childhood' that can be abstracted from culture and society (Cunningham 1995). Indeed, in the same way that Judith Butler (1990) argues that gender is not 'the cultural inscription of meaning on a pregiven sex', but rather the 'very apparatus of production whereby the sexes themselves are established', so we might argue that the concept of childhood is the apparatus that produces 'adult' and 'child' as fixed, opposed categories.

From the nineteenth century on, in Western liberal societies, a romantic ideal of childhood as an innocent and enchanted period of life without the responsibilities and cares of adulthood has held a strong grip on popular and policy thinking, and has informed, and continues to inform, an insistence that children should be protected from exposure to what are imagined as 'adult' domains. As Cunningham (1995) notes, in the twentieth century, international organisations sought to export this Western vision of childhood. The International Labour Organization (ILO) had set itself the goal of abolishing child labour at its formation in 1919, and by 1973 'was envisaging a world where no child under the age of sixteen engaged in any form of productive work' (Cunningham 1995: 204). Likewise, the United Nations' 1989 Convention on the Rights of the Child (CRC), which is the most ratified instrument of international law, is explicitly premised on the assumption that 'children' constitute a clearly identifiable group distinct from adults (hence the need to establish and codify children's rights, rather than assuming that children are covered by existing human rights' declarations, charters and conventions). Because it gives rights to children 'only and in so far as they are children' (Archard 1993: 3), it also necessarily enshrines and universalises a particular understanding childhood.

Critics of the CRC argue that the ideal of childhood it encodes is peculiar to the Western, economically developed world (Montgomery 2001; Punch 2003). It universalises an ideal of childhood as a state of immanence, innocence, incompetence and dependence, and of children as lacking the capacities, attributes and obligations required for full and equal participation in economic, political and cultural life. Even the boundary of childhood enshrined in the United Nations Convention on the Rights of the Child and assumed in dominant discourse on child trafficking (0–18 years) reflects the experience of the minority of children who live in affluent economically developed societies, where a combination of government policies on housing, health care, education, employment and taxation typically serve to force children into dependence on adults until the age of 18, and even beyond. In economically developing nations (and even in poorer families in affluent countries), by contrast, it is not the norm for young people to remain in education or training or in a state of complete economic dependency until their eighteenth birthday. Cultural ideals regarding childhood also vary, and in some regions of the world children are understood to have responsibilities towards their families, as well as rights (Hashim and Thorsen 2011).

International organisations and NGOs campaigning against child trafficking frame trafficking as a violation of children's rights, and call on governments to recognise their obligations to ensure that children enjoy rights to protection from violence, economic exploitation, hazardous work, and sexual exploitation and abuse. At the same time, however, they stress that the children who are vulnerable to trafficking 'often come from poor families and lack economic and educational opportunities. Children who have been separated from their families, have minimal education, lack vocational skills or have few job opportunities are most at risk' (UNICEF 2010). These are pretty much identical to the factors that have more generally been identified as triggering children's independent migration (Whitehead and Hashim 2005), and migration even into what are, in absolute terms, poor and exploitative working conditions can improve rather than diminish some children's life chances. Labour migration can, for example, allow children to escape settings in which they are expected to undertake extensive and heavy labour without pay for their own families and enjoy few of the basic rights set out in the CRC, and afford them opportunities to develop relationships or skills, and to earn an income that allows them to save and buy the things necessary for their progression into adulthood (Grier 2004; Hashim and Thorsen 2011).

The most fundamental motive for independent labour migration is children's 'need or desire for income' (Whitehead and Hashim 2005: 28), but since opportunities for persons under the age of 18 to migrate independently (and legally in the case of cross-border migration) are extremely restricted, children frequently rely on intermediaries of one sort or another and/or enter into some form of indebtedness in order to realise their migratory projects. This does create a dependency that places them at risk of exploitation and abuse by those who arrange their migration. But not all intermediaries cheat or abuse the children they help to migrate, and even when children are abused or exploited by such intermediaries, they may still end up living and working in conditions that they regard as preferable to those they have left (see Anarfi et al. 2006; Hashim and Thorsen 2011; Howard 2012; Okyere 2013).

The need and desire to move for work on the part of people below the age of 18 is not visible in dominant discourse on child trafficking. As noted above, the UN Trafficking Protocol makes consent irrelevant in the case of persons below the age of 18 who are moved for purposes of exploitation, but fails to define 'exploitation'. In fact, it would be extremely difficult to come up with a neutral, standard and universal measure of 'exploitation', and judgements about when child labour becomes a worse form of child labour, as the ILO itself acknowledges, are not easily made. Yet in the absence of such a definition, and in the presence of a discourse about childhood as a period of carefree innocence and dependence, it is all too easy for anti-trafficking measures to simply become anti-child labour migration measures. As a number of studies have shown, this is indeed what is happening on the ground. In the name of protecting children from 'trafficking', barriers to all forms of independent child migration are being set in place, thereby making it harder for children to access the potentially positive effects of migration (Busza, Castle and Diarra 2004; Bastia 2005; Kapur 2005; Hashim and Thorsen 2011; Howard 2012).

Such measures are based on the assumption that children are always better off remaining at home with their families. This not only disregards the fact that not all families are in a position to support children economically until they reach the age of 18, but also the fact that families are not actually always the safest place for children. Indeed, the uncritically positive emphasis on the family in dominant discourse on child trafficking is curious, given that, statistically, families appear to pose a far greater risk to children than 'traffickers'. It was noted above that in the seven years between 2000 and 2007, the US Department of Health and Human Services certified just 131 foreign national minors as victims of human trafficking. Yet in 2007 alone, the US National Child Abuse and Neglect Data System reported an estimated 1,760 child fatalities as a result of abuse and neglect, and one or both parents were responsible for around 70 per cent of these deaths (Child Welfare Information Gateway 2008). Running away from home, which appears in discourse on child trafficking simply as an indicator that a child is 'at risk of trafficking', may be a way to escape neglect, abuse and violence for some children.

It is known that children are not always safe at home or with their families, just as it is known that the lived experience of the vast majority of persons under the age of 18 in the contemporary world is far from that described and celebrated in the Western romantic vision of 'childhood'. And yet somehow these knowns become unknown in dominant discourse on child trafficking.

Child trafficking and 'unknown knowns' about children

The categories 'adult' and 'child' are fundamental to people's moral identity in contemporary Western societies (Ribbens McCarthy, Edwards and Gillies 2000: 787), and the child/adult dualism and its associated binaries (innocence/experience, passivity/activity, powerless/powerful, object/subject) play a central in the psychic, social, economic and political lives of members of liberal democratic societies (O'Connell Davidson 2005). And yet these dualisms are 'all very wobbly', requiring 'massive bolstering' (Kincaid 1992: 7) precisely because, despite their centrality to the way we make sense of our society and private lives, they do not map neatly onto observable reality and are therefore easy to destabilise.

Just as the lives led by most children in most of the developing world do not match up to the Western romantic ideal of 'childhood', neither does the idea of children as entirely vacant, passive and object-like generally match up with adults' experience of real, live children. Often to the dismay of their parents and teachers, children do not actually lack will or agency, and older children and teenagers especially can and do evaluate the choices they face on the basis of knowledge and experience, albeit limited and partial. When they take a course of action that most would regard as undesirable, it is not necessarily because they have been coerced or manipulated by an adult, or because their immaturity leaves them unable to grasp the severity of the possible consequences. Sometimes it simply reflects the bleakness of the choices they face.

For example, not every child who is found in prostitution is selling sex because a 'trafficker' or 'pimp' is forcing them to do so. Dull economic compulsion operates on persons under, as well as above, the age of 18, and there is plenty of research to show that some teenagers enter prostitution because they need to support themselves and/or their own children or other dependants, and either cannot find other forms of paid work, or prefer prostitution to the other earning options open to them (Mayorga and Velasquez 1999; Montgomery 2001; Hubbard 2002; O'Connell Davidson 2005). And because children are social beings, ideas about honour, duty and/or social status can also inform their subjective evaluation of different possible courses of action. There is research to show that some children use prostitution as a means to escape a situation that they subjectively perceive as more painful, debasing and soul destroying than trading sex (for example, Montgomery 2001; O'Connell Davidson and Sánchez Taylor 2001; Soderlund 2005).

Children are 'active in the construction and determination of their own social lives' (Jenks 1996: 51), and this is true of children in prostitution, as well as children in general. It does not, of course, mean that they can control the conditions in which they live or that they should be viewed as authors of their own destinies. To the extent that they make their own social lives, they, like adults, do so in circumstances that are given to them by history. But to understand why many children end up selling sex, it is nonetheless important to think about children as agents, as existent rather than nascent social and emotional beings. A child who is neglected, or physically and verbally abused by its carers, or who is forced to conform to the grimly regimented, emotionally empty routine of life in a large state-run orphanage, or who is constantly made the object of homophobic bullying and denied opportunities to express his or her sexuality, can experience this as an extinguishing of her- or himself as a full person. To run away, even if that means using prostitution as a means of survival, can thus be experienced as an assertion of the self as subject, not as being transformed into an object.

My point is not that prostitution should be recognised as a legitimate form of work for persons under the age of 18, but rather, to paraphrase William Faulkner (1961), that, left with a choice between grief and nothing, some people will choose grief, and this is true of children as well as adults. If we want them to make different choices, it is necessary to address the nothingness of their alternatives. In reproducing a vision of children as non-agential, dominant discourse on child trafficking allows policy makers not to know this, and so to pursue policies that intensify both the grief that can attend on migration and the nothingness of remaining at home.

Conclusion

In dominant discourse on child sex trafficking, innocent, passive and trusting children are snatched from the safe and protective arms of their families and thrust, unwilling and unknowing, into a nightmare of relentless sexual and physical violence at the hands of brutal thugs and a vast but unseen army of depraved perverts who pay for sex with children. As with the master narrative of child molesting, the telling and retelling of this story provides a means through which to reassert a vision of 'children' as empty, vulnerable, dependent and biddable, as the opposite of sex, the opposite of us, and so also a vision of ourselves as good and worthy 'adults'. The Gothic story of child molesting works to protect socially cherished ideals of childhood, Kincaid (1998) argues, and it is these ideals, as opposed to actual, real children, in which we are most invested.

In addition to protecting our investment in a particular vision of childhood, popular and policy discourse on 'child trafficking' works to defend a set of beliefs about the goodness of the family and the liberal democratic state. The hyper-visibility of 'sex trafficking' renders invisible the 'obscene practices' to which migrant children are routinely subject at the hands of state actors, or as a result of their preventative and deterrent immigration policies (Enenajor 2009), and conceals the ways in which states are a source of risk for non-migrant children through their welfare policies.

Finally, dominant discourse on child trafficking perpetuates a discourse about children's rights to family and nationality that overlooks the vast material inequalities between families and between nations in terms of their capacity to guarantee children's well-being, and the fact that for this reason (as well as, sometimes, others), the right to leave the family and to independent existence may be more important than the right to remain in a family, and migrating may be in the child's best interests.

References

Alpes, J. (2011). 'Bushfalling: How Young Cameroonians Dare to Migrate'. PhD thesis, Universiteit van Amsterdam.
Anarfi, J. et al. (2005). *Voices of Child Migrants*. Sussex University, Development Research Centre on Migration, Globalisation and Poverty. www.migrationdrc.org (accessed 7 February 2014).
Anderson, B. (2013). *Us & Them: The Dangerous Politics of Immigration Control*. Oxford: Oxford University Press.
Archard, D. (1993). *Children: Rights and Childhood*. London: Routledge.
Barnardo's. (2013). 'Sexual Exploitation'. http://www.barnardos.org.uk/what_we_do/campaigns/sexual_exploitation_campaign.htm (accessed 14 January 2014).
Bastia, T. (2005). 'Child Trafficking or Teenage Migration? Bolivian Migrants in Argentina'. *International Migration* 43: 4.
BBC. (2012). 'Five Rotherham Men Jailed for Child Sex Offences'. http://www.bbc.co.uk/news/uk-england-south-yorkshire-11696508 (accessed 14 January 2014).
Best, J. (1993). *Threatened Children: Rhetoric and Concern about Child Victims*. Chicago: University of Chicago Press.
Bloch, A. and Schuster, L. (2005). 'At the Extremes of Exclusion: Deportation, Detention and Dispersal'. *Ethnic and Racial Studies* 28(3): 491–512.

Bloch, A. and Zetter, R. (2009). *No Right to Dream: The Social and Economic Lives of Young Undocumented Migrants in Britain*. London: Paul Hamlyn Foundation.
Bowen, K. and Marshall, W. (2007). 'Deaths of Mexican and Central American Children along the US Border: The Pima County Arizona Experience'. *Journal of Immigrant and Minority Health* 10(1): 17–21.
Busza, J., Castle, S. and Diarra, A. (2004). 'Trafficking and Health'. *British Medical Journal* 328: 1369–71.
Butler, J. (1990). *Gender Trouble: Feminism and the Subversion of Identity*. London: Routledge.
CEOP. (2009). *Strategic Threat Assessment: Child Trafficking in the UK*. Child Exploitation and Online Protection (CEOP) Centre. www.ceop.police.uk/Documents/child_trafficking_report0409.pdf (accessed 7 February 2014).
Child Welfare Information Gateway. (2008). Child Abuse and Neglect Fatalities: Statistics and Interventions. US Department of Health and Human Services. http://www.childwelfare.gov/pubs/factsheets/fatality.cfm.
Cunningham, H. (1995). *Children and Childhood in Western Society Since 1500*. Harlow: Pearson Education.
Dugan, E. (2010). 'Children deported from UK alone with no safety checks'. *Independent*, 11 April.
ECPAT. (1996). *ECPAT Newsletter*, No. 16. Bangkok: ECPAT.
Elkind, D. (1981). *The Hurried Child: Growing Up Too Fast Too Soon*. Reading, MA: Addison Wesley.
Enenajor, A. (2009). 'Rethinking Vulnerability: European Asylum Policy Harmonization and Unaccompanied Asylum Seeking Minors'. *Childhoods Today* 2(2): 1–24.
Ennew, J. (1986). *The Sexual Exploitation of Children*. Cambridge: Polity Press.
Feingold, D. (2010). 'Trafficking in Numbers: The Social Construction of Human Trafficking Data'. In P. Andreas and K. Greenhill (eds), *Sex, Drugs and Body Counts*. Ithaca, NY: Cornell University Press.
Faulkner, W. (1961). *The Wild Palms*. Harmondsworth: Penguin.
Fekete, L. (2007). 'Detained: Foreign Children in Europe'. *Race & Class* 49(1): 93–104.
Golash-Boza, T. (2012). *Due Process Denied: Detentions and Deportations in the United States*. London: Routledge.
Gonzalez, J. (2013). 'President Obama calls on Congress to act on immigration reform while patrolling the border has become big business for the government'. *New York Daily News*, 30 January. http://www.nydailynews.com/opinion/gonzalez-militarizing-border-new-version-war-drugs-article-1.1250959 (accessed 14 January 2014).
Grier, B. (2004). 'Child Labor and Africanist Scholarship: A Critical Overview'. *African Studies Review* 47(2): 1–25.
Hashim, I. and Thorsen, D. (2011). *Child Migration in Africa*. London: Zed.
Howard, N. (2012). 'Protecting "Children" in Southern Benin? Anti-Trafficking Policy in Need of Politics and Participation'. *Rights Work*. http://rightswork.org/2012/07/protecting-children-in-southern-benin-anti-trafficking-policy-in-need-of-politics-and-participation/ (accessed 14 January 2014).
Hubbard, D. (ed.). (2002). *'Whose Body Is It?' Commercial Sex Work and the Law in Namibia*. Windhoek: Legal Assistance Centre.
Human Rights Watch. (2002). 'Nowhere to Turn: State Abuses of Unaccompanied Migrant Children by Spain and Morocco'. Human Rights Watch. www.hrw.org.
Itzin, C. (2000). 'Child Sexual Abuse and the Radical Feminist Endeavour'. In C. Itzin (ed.), *Home Truths About Child Sexual Abuse*. London: Routledge.
Jenks, C. (1996). *Childhood*. London: Routledge.

Kapur, R. (2005). *Erotic Justice: Law and the New Politics of Postcolonialism*. London: Glasshouse.
Kehily, M. (2010). 'Childhood in Crisis? Tracing the Contours of "Crisis" and Its Impact upon Contemporary Parenting Practices'. *Media, Culture & Society* 32(2): 171–85.
Kempadoo, K., Sanghera, J. and Pattanaik, B. (eds). (2005). *Trafficking and Prostitution Reconsidered*. London: Paradigm.
Kincaid, J. (1998). *Erotic Innocence: The Culture of Child Molesting*. Durham, NC: Duke University Press.
Kincaid, J. (1992). *Child-Loving: The Erotic Child and Victorian Culture*. New York: Routledge.
Kofman, E., Phizacklea, A., Raghuram, P. and Sales, R. (2000). *Gender and International Migration in Europe*. London: Routledge.
Lee, M. (2011). *Trafficking and Global Crime Control*. London: Sage.
Markon, J. (2007). 'Human trafficking evokes outrage, little evidence'. *Washington Post*, 23 September.
Mayorga, L. and Velasquez, P. (1999). 'Bleak Pasts, Bleak Futures: Life Paths of Thirteen Young Prostitutes in Cartagena, Colombia'. In K. Kempadoo (ed.), *Sun, Sex and Gold: Tourism and Sex Work in the Caribbean*. New York: Rowman & Littlefield.
Montgomery, H. (2001). *Modern Babylon? Prostituting Children in Thailand*. Oxford: Berghahn.
Moravcsik, J. (1998). 'Slavery and the Ties That Do Not Bind'. In T. Lott (ed.), *Subjugation and Bondage*. Oxford: Rowman & Littlefield.
Morehouse, C. (2009). *Combating Human Trafficking*. Wiesbaden: VS Verlag fur Sozialwissenschaften.
O'Connell Davidson, J. (2005). *Children in the Global Sex Trade*. Cambridge: Polity Press.
O'Connell Davidson, J. (2006). 'Will the real sex slave please stand up?' *Feminist Review* 83: 4–22.
O'Connell Davidson, J. (2011). 'Moving Children: Child Trafficking, Child Migration and Child Rights'. *Critical Social Policy* 31(3): 454–77.
O'Connell Davidson, J. and Sánchez Taylor, J. (2001). *Children in the Sex Trade in the Caribbean*. Stockholm: Save the Children Sweden.
Okyere, S. (2013). 'Are Working Children's Rights and Child Labour Abolition Complementary or Opposing Realms?'. *International Social Work* 56(1): 80–91.
PICUM. (2007). 'PICUM's Comments on the Communication from the Commission on "Policy Priorities in the Fight against Illegal Immigration of Third-Country Nationals"'. Platform for International Cooperation on Undocumented Migrants, Brussels, 12 February.
Postman, N. (1982). *The Disappearance of Childhood*. New York: Vintage Books.
Punch, S. (2003). 'Childhoods in the Majority World: Miniature Adults or Tribal Children?' *Sociology* 37(2): 277–95.
Rädda Barnen. (1996). *Barnen Och Vi*. Special Feature Issue. Stockholm: Rädda Barnen.
Refugee Council. (2003). 'Refugee Charities Tell Government to Stop Detaining Children'. www.refugeecouncil.org.uk.
Ribbens McCarthy, J., Edwards, R. and Gillies, V. (2000). 'Moral Tales of the Child and the Adult: Narratives of Contemporary Family Lives under Changing Circumstances'. *Sociology* 34(4): 785–803.
Rizer, A. and Glaser, S. (2011). 'Breach: The National Security Implications of Human Trafficking'. *Widener Law Review* 17(69): 69–94.

Rosas, A. (2012). 'Some Children Left Behind: Families in the Age of Deportation'. *Boom: A Journal of California* 2(3): 79–85.

Shah, S. (2007). 'Undocumented Migrants and Trafficked Victims: Critiques and Contexts of U.S. Anti-Trafficking Policies'. *Georgetown Journal on Poverty Law and Policy* 9(1).

Soderlund, G. (2005). 'Running from the Rescuers: New U.S. Crusades against Sex Trafficking and the Rhetoric of Abolition'. *NWSA Journal* 17(3): 64–87.

UNICEF. (2007). Child Trafficking: More Precious than Gold. www.unicef.org.uk/campaigns/campaign_detail.asp?campaign=2&thesource=yt.

UNICEF. (2010). End Child Exploitation. http://www.unicef.org.uk/campaigns/campaign_sub_pages.asp?page=3.

UNITED. (2011). United for Intercultural Action: European Network against Nationalism, Racism and Fascism, and in Support of Migrants and Refugees. www.unitedagainstracism.org (accessed 14 January 2014).

UNODC. (2013). Human Trafficking FAQs. http://www.unodc.org/unodc/en/human-trafficking/faqs.html (accessed 14 January 2014).

US Department of Justice. (2008). 'Attorney General's Annual Report to Congress and Assessment of the US Government Activities to Combat Trafficking in Persons Fiscal Year 2007'. http://www.justice.gov/archive/ag/annualreports/tr2007/agreporthumantrafficking2007.pdf (accessed 7 February 2014).

Weitzer, R. (2007). 'The Social Construction of Sex Trafficking: Ideology and Institutionalization of a Moral Crusade'. *Politics & Society* 35: 447–74.

Whitehead, A. and Hashim, I. (2005). 'Children and Migration'. Background paper for DFID Migration Team. Unpublished.

World Bank. (2011). *Migration and Remittances Factbook 2011*. http://siteresources.worldbank.org/INTLAC/Resources/Factbook2011-Ebook.pdf.

Žižek, S. (2004). 'What Rumsfeld Doesn't Know That He Knows About Abu Ghraib'. http://www.lacan.com/zizekrumsfeld.htm.

5
'What have the Romans ever done for us?'
Child Poverty and the Legacy of 'New' Labour

Danny Dorling

My first child was born during Tony Blair's first term of office, my second during his second, and my third during his third (and final) term. Tony himself was born in the same year as Mrs Thatcher's twins. His generation, and (much later) mine, was the generation of Thatcher's children. His, and 'New' Labour's legacy, were Thatcher's grandchildren.

In 2010 'New' Labour won no fourth term in office, but neither did the Conservatives win outright power. Many people wanted an end to the Thatcherism that had come to characterise 'New' Labour (Dorling 2010a), but they had no serious alternative to turn to. What they got in 2010 with the coalition could be seen partly as a continuation of a trend set in place during 1979, and not much altered during the 13 years of New Labour rule from 1997. In 2010 it was claimed that when the electorate were:

> Invited to embrace five more years of a Labour government, and of Gordon Brown as Prime Minister, it [was] hard to feel enthusiasm. [And that] Labour's kneejerk critics can sometimes sound like the Monty Python's People's Front of Judea asking what the Romans have ever done for us. The salvation of the health service, major renovation of schools, the minimum wage, civil partnerships and the extension of protection for minority groups are heroic, not small, achievements. (*Guardian*, 30 April 2010)

But just how heroic had 'New' Labour really been, especially when it came to child poverty?When that editorial in the *Guardian* newspaper was published, during the onset of the British General Election in 2010, I suspected I might be one of these designated 'kneejerk critics'. I had kept quiet during that election campaign. Thatcher's election itself, in 1979, had been aided (some thought) by critics of 'Old' Labour back in the late 1970s (the 'pink professors'). But what I want to argue here is that the key and oft reiterated central undertaking made by the 1997–2010 'New' Labour administration that governed Britain in the early years of the twenty-first century was not honoured. This undertaking had been announced by Prime Minister Tony Blair in the annual Beveridge lecture of 1999: being poor, he said, 'should not be a life sentence': it was a '20 year mission – but I believe it can be done' (BBC News 1999).

Blair's pledge to end child poverty was reaffirmed by his successor Gordon Brown at the Labour Party conference of 2008:

> Brown acknowledged that economic times were 'tough' but said the government was 'in it for the long haul', set to achieve the complete elimination of child poverty by 2020. He also promised to continue record investment in Sure Start (the government's pre-school programme, begun in 1998) and introduce free nursery education for two-year-olds in up to 60 areas. He said: 'For me, the fairer future starts with putting children first – with the biggest investment in children this country has ever seen. It means delivering the best possible starts in life with services tailored to the needs of every single precious child .... (Ahmed 2008)

Once the 'New' Labour government had departed the political stage, it was possible to make a more sober appraisal of the 'Blair years' in relation to state of the nation's children. Here I concentrate on statistics that cover the period 1997 to 2005. During those years the proportion of children living in a family that could not afford to take a holiday away from home had risen; so had the number (and proportion) of children whose parents could not afford to let them have friends round for tea; likewise the number of children who were too poor to pursue a hobby and the number of children living in single-parent families without access to a car. All these statistics first came to light in preliminary work on child poverty undertaken in national surveys and revealed in 2010 (Dorling 2010b). Today that work is largely complete, as part of the massive recent ESRC-funded project 'Poverty and Social Exclusion', and the results can be viewed in detail at: www.poverty.ac.uk/.

This chapter offers an alternative assessment of 'New' Labour's record on child poverty to that story of relative success which some on the centre-left like to believe. It argues that 'New' Labour travelled in the very direction it had specifically promised not to travel. In his Beveridge lecture, Blair had said: 'In Beveridge's time the welfare state was associated with progress and advancement. Today it is often associated with dependency, fraud, abuse, laziness. I want to make it once again a force for progress' (BBC, 1999). It is important to remember that it was Tony Blair, not David Cameron, who said those words.

In office, 'New' Labour pursued a populist and punitive approach, happy to label benefit claimants as feckless and to regard taxation as the Victorians had done – as similar to giving to charity, something one did for the poor. One life-long Labour supporter explained in 2013 that there had been doubts all along: 'Blair had not been leader long when I was told by a distinguished and dedicated Labour MP: "The trouble with Tony is that he's a Tory"' (Flintoff 2013). That Labour MP thought that those who were not Tories in the party would be able to control Tony and his group. They were wrong.

The real militant tendency had come into Labour from the right, not the left, and on poverty 'New' Labour peddled myths that the poor were lazier than the rich; they introduced 'no fifth option', and rhetoric of being 'tough on the causes', of teaching 'money management', having 'fraud crackdowns', and 'benefit squeezes', especially for those 'feckless' adults without children. And in doing all this they propagated five myths:

Myth 1: 'They' are lazy and just don't want to work.
Myth 2: 'They' are addicted to drink and drugs.
Myth 3: 'They' are not really poor – they just don't manage their money properly.
Myth 4: 'They' are on the fiddle.
Myth 5: 'They' have an easy life on benefits.

The Coalition government that came to power in 2010 took this language on gladly, and added a myth of this own (The Churches 2013):

Myth 6: 'They' caused the deficit.

The Coalition claimed that the poor in Britain, children as well as adults, and especially families that contained 'more children than they could afford', did not deserve what they had. The Coalition government of 2010 began almost immediately upon taking office to single out this group of the poor, and to suggest that partly through 'New' Labour's support for them, and partly through their own indolence, it was these people who had brought down the nation's economy. 'New' Labour had created the environment that made such arguments believable.

By extending 'New' Labour's rhetoric the Coalition government began, quite successfully, to increase hatred for the poor. They did this to try to justify cutting benefits, moving poorer families out of London and other places where the rich wanted more of the housing. Because they talked of still caring, in the way (and using the language) that 'New' Labour had talked of caring, and in the way a charity worker might talk of caring, much of the electorate did not notice the ground shifting. That shift had begun with Thatcher. It was not continuous, but more often than not, even under Labour, it continued to move the centre-ground towards the right long after she had left office.

The 'New' Labour Government had made some significant achievements for children. It greatly reduced the numbers living in the very worst of poverty. It both improved education chances and narrowed education divides and it governed over a period when young people's chances of gaining a job improved greatly, especially in the poorest areas, and national youth suicide rates fell quickly (in contrast to the previous Conservative administration, and subsequent period). However, when it came to assessing their legacy as regards inequality overall and the access to income and wealth enjoyed by different groups of children in the UK, 'New' Labour's record was poor. As the exhaustive Economic and Social Research Council (ESRC) survey recently found, by 2012, 'More children lead impoverished and restricted lives today than in 1999' (Gordon et al. 2013).

'New' Labour also paved the way, on so many fronts, for some of the worst policy decisions of the next government. 'New' Labour introduced student tuition fees, which the next government could increase to £9,000 a year (making them the most expensive in Europe). 'New' Labour began the privatisation of the National Health Service, which the next government could then expand upon. And they allowed life-chances between young adults to diverge rapidly, which is why the young parents of today are bringing their children up in such widely differing circumstances. Above all else, it is that increase in inequality which makes it easier now for people in Britain *not* to see others' children as like theirs.

An heroic Labour government from 1997 to 2010 would have achieved so much more. It would have been heroic to have reduced income and wealth inequalities. By doing so, 'New' Labour could have reduced both the rates of real poverty, and the waste, pollution and excesses of the rich. It would have been heroic to have refused to take part in America's wars, as Labour refused to do when in power from 1964 to 1970. It is possible to look back at every progressive government elected to power in Britain before 1979 and find evidence of heroism. In contrast, 'New' Labour excelled only at fighting and 'losing small wars' (Ledwidge 2011). It may have been 'New' Labour's military escapades that most diverted the attention of those in that party who could have salvaged its progressive credentials when it was in office. Had so many eyes not been turned towards Iraq during 'New' Labour's second term in office, more people in that party might have spotted the war on poverty faltering at home. The cost of the war in Iraq also reduced the resources that could have been spent within the UK.

But it was not just in fighting expensive and harmful overseas wars that the last Labour government squandered its chance to leave office with most ordinary people better off than when it had gained power. It would have been heroic to have reined in the bankers before the crash. In comparison with contemporary governments in other countries, and with progressive politics in Britain's past, and with the 1997 dream that 'things can only get better', 'New' Labour fell far short.

Here is what Julian Baggini had to say on Labour's record in office in that same issue of the *Guardian* that the comment on Romans was made:

I think this has been an under-appreciated government. The last 13 years have been immeasurably better than the previous 18, and the return to Conservatism, in its current shape at least, appals me. But the game is up, both for a system which protects two parties which most people do not support, and a government that just cannot now hope to be re-elected with a majority. (Baggini 2010)

What do we find when, instead of announcing 'immeasurably better', we actually measure? Below, I'll list a few attempts to measure this allegedly immeasurable betterment. These attempts were from those first surveys which became available in 2010, and I include them here to show that it was even possible during the last year of Labour's period in power to tell that the wrong trajectory was being taken. What has happened since, under the Coalition, has accelerated the growing gaps between rich and poor. The rot began earlier, ultimately with Thatcherism, but continued under New Labour.

Among British adults during the 1997–2005 Blair years, the proportion unable to make regular savings rose from 25 per cent to 27 per cent; the number unable to afford an annual holiday away from home rose from 18 per cent to 24 per cent; and the national proportion who could not afford to insure the contents of their home climbed a percentage point, from 8 per cent to 9 per cent. However, these national proportions conceal the way in which the rising exclusion has hit particular groups especially hard, not least a group that the Blair government had said it would help above all others: children living in poverty. The sources for all these facts are all detailed in Dorling (2010b). Brown's years as Prime Minister were a little less damning, but too short and turbulent a time to easily dovetail with the statistics.

The findings of that major ESRC research project on poverty through to 2010/2011, which was released during 2013, reveal more on trends in poverty during all the combined Blair and Brown years. What that survey also revealed is a growing hardness in attitudes that accompanied New Labour's period in office and was then cemented in place by the first two years of Coalition government:

Harsh economic times have resulted in reduced minimum expectations of a social life for both adults and children. In 1999, nearly two thirds of the population believed that being able to have friends or family for a meal or a drink once a month was a necessity but this had dropped to under a half by 2012. Similarly, for children, being able to have their friends to visit for tea or a snack once a fortnight was seen as a necessity by the majority in 1999 but it now just falls short of the 50% approval mark. (Gordon et al. 2013: 7)

The comparison of poverty surveys taken towards the start and end of Tony Blair's time in office showed that, of all children, the proportion living in a family that could not afford to take a holiday away from home (or just to visit relatives) rose between 1999 and 2005, from 25 per cent to 32 per cent. This occurred even as the real incomes of most of the poorest rose; they just rose more for the affluent, making holidays more expensive for all and subtly changing what it meant to go on holiday.

The more recent statistics now show how living conditions for the poor fell from 1999, with most of the harm occurring in the 'New' Labour years, but a little being added since then. In 1999 only 3 per cent of households could not afford to keep their home warm. By 2012 that proportion was 10 per cent (Gordon at al. 2013: 12). Energy bills had risen, but the governments had allowed them to rise. Partly as a result of that, by 2012 one in ten households had damp in their home, a higher proportion than at any time since the 1970s. Perhaps because of these revelations, in his September 2013 party conference speech the (not so 'New' anymore) Labour leader Ed Miliband pledged to prevent energy companies increasing fuel bills in the future. He was labelled a socialist, as if that were an insult.

During the 'New' Labour (essentially Thatcherite) years, the rich became richer and housing became more expensive and more unequally distributed. The number of school-age children who had to share their bedroom with an adult or sibling over the age of ten and of the opposite sex rose from 8 per cent to 15 per cent nationally by 2005. Encouraging buy-to-let landlords in a new wave of privatisation did not help reduce overcrowding.

It was in London that such overcrowding became most acute and where sharing rooms rose most quickly. Keeping up appearances for the poor in London was much harder than in Britain as a whole, not simply because London had less space, but because within London other children were so often very wealthy, and quickly becoming so much wealthier under 'New' Labour. However, their rising wealth did not correlate with an increase in the medium income of families with children rising by much. In general, as the richest 1 per cent got much richer, and the 9 per cent below them became a little richer, the bottom 90 per cent got relatively poorer (Dorling 2013).

Greatly reducing the numbers of children living in households below 60 per cent of medium incomes still leaves many children in those households, or only just over that threshold. On average it became harder for a child to live a life according to the norms of society in 2005 as compared to 1999 because overall inequalities increased as mean incomes rose faster than mediums. Even among children at the same school, the incomes of their parents had diverged and, consequently, standards of living and expectations of the norm did too. Between 1999 and 2012 an extra half a million households in Britain found themselves to be overcrowded and not adequately housed when the same criteria were used to assess at both dates;

an extra 2 per cent could not afford fresh fruit daily as compared to 1999; 3 per cent more could not afford 'meat, fish or a vegetarian equivalent'; 2 per cent more than before 'New' Labour gained power could not afford two meals a day (Gordon et al. 2013, p. 12). That was Thatcherism continued, and that might be why Labour in 2013 began to promise to stand up for ordinary people more.

Nationally, the proportion of children who said their parent(s) could not afford to let them have friends round for tea doubled, from 4 per cent to 8 per cent by 2005. The proportion who could not afford to pursue a hobby or other leisure activity also rose, from 5 per cent to 7 per cent, and the proportion who could not afford to go on a school trip at least once a term doubled, from 3 per cent to 6 per cent. For children aged below five, the proportion whose parents could not afford to take them to playgroup each week also doubled under the Blair government, from 3 per cent to 6 per cent.

By 2012, 3 per cent of families could not afford properly fitting shoes for their children, twice as many as in 1999, and all other measures of clothing difficulty rose for the worst of groups. Some four million households could not afford an item seen as vital in 2012 as compared to 1999, like a telephone or washing machine. By 2012, 26 per cent of all children in Britain were living in families who could not afford a holiday other than staying with friends and family for even just one week in the year. In 1999 that proportion had been 22 per cent (Gordon et al. 2013: 14). This all became worse once the Coalition government gained power, but it was getting worse before that time too.

Concealing poverty becomes ever more difficult in an age of high and increasingly unequal consumption, and it becomes easier for us to imagine why someone might be tempted to go further into debt in order to pay for a playgroup rather than spend another day at home with a toddler or to pay for a school trip rather than pretend to be ill that day. Debt rose greatly amongst families with children under 'New' Labour. The worst off resorted to the increasing number of dodgy lending and saving schemes set up by loan sharks, or Christmas clubs such as Farepak, which went bust in 2006 and where the savers were not aided by 'New' Labour.

One Farepak victim made it clear what growing inequality meant:

> I have got four children, all at various ages. Like I say, you can't tell the little two, Father Christmas can call next door, but he can't call here you know. And with my husband being on sick as well, having to pay the mortgage and feed four kids and whatever, and £37 a week is not a lot. (Spalek and King 2007)

In April 2010, it was reported that 'Customers who paid for hampers from Farepak are expected to receive less than £50 each, even as accountants and lawyers handling the liquidation rack up millions in fees' (*The Times*, 27 April 2010). By 2013, the families first robbed by Farepak were still awaiting proper compensation and were still paying off the new debts that they had taken out to pay for the Christmas that Farepak never covered. But it is everyday expenses now, not saving for Christmas, that pose a greater problem.

The second most expensive of all consumption items are housing costs – rents or mortgages – and these have also diverged as income inequalities have increased. Having to move to a poorer area, or being unable to move out of one, is the geographical reality of social exclusion. People get into further debt trying to avoid this.

The most expensive consumer item is a car. The combination of the expense and necessity of car ownership is the reason why not having a car is, for many, a contemporary mark of social failure. It is also closely connected to why so many car firms were badly hit so early on in the financial crash of 2008, as they were selling debt as much as selling cars. By 2008/9, two out of three children in Britain living in a household without a car were living with only one parent.

The chattels and behaviour that signal what it means to be poor change over time and in accordance with what most others have. By 2009, not having a car (outside of London) was, for a family – like not being able to go on the cheapest of summer holidays – a sign of stigma. The continued Thatcherism spanning 1979 to 2013 has pulled people further and further apart socially. Some now have more holidays than anyone ever had in 1979, and many have fewer. Some lack the space to park all of their cars, and others whose parents had one car now have none.

Growing poverty of experience – fewer being able to partake in the norms of society – was the outcome of having a government that was seriously relaxed about the rich becoming richer, 'as long as they paid their taxes' – as stated by 'New' Labour architect and government minister Peter Mandelson in a speech to California computer executives in 1998. (But 'New' Labour cut Her Majesty's Review staff, thereby reducing tax inspectors' abilities to chase the rich for their payments.)

The gaps between all families grew: between 'celebrity' and 'entrepreneur', between the 'affluent' and the merely 'hard working', and between those below them painted as being 'a bit slovenly', and those a little more 'down-in-the-mouth'. As the very rich got richer still, even those people 'earning' just a few thousand a week in income less than them began to feel a little worse off. And all the time the language kept on becoming harsher as the gaps between us grew.

Council housing became social housing, with the word 'social's' implications of charity rather than rights. All this set the scene for what the Coalition then did. The moral argument against allowing inequality to grow had not been won by 'New' Labour because it was not believed by enough at the top of 'New' Labour. Not in practice.

Taxation became viewed by some in 'New' Labour as a form of charity: something one 'did' for the poor, not something you did for yourself too. Jobseeker's Allowance of £9 a day was fine (as long as 'one' never imagined having to live off it oneself). But charity, or child tax credits, or Sure Start centres, are simply not enough if the income gaps between people are allowed to turn into chasms. Whether our gaps can be considered cracks or chasms can be established by looking at other similarly affluent societies.

International comparisons of the quintile range of income inequality are some of the most telling comparisons that can be made between countries. By 2005, after eight years of 'New' Labour government, the richest fifth received 7.2 times more income on average than the poorest fifth each year – up from 6.9 times in 1997. According to the United Nations Development Programme's Annual Report (the most widely used source), this ratio has been 6.1 to 1 in Ireland; 5.6 to 1 in France; 4.0 to 1 in Sweden; and 3.4 to 1 in Japan. By contrast, in the United States that same ratio of inequality was 8.5 to 1. Between 1997 and 2005 the UK moved 0.3 points towards US levels of inequality, or almost one quarter of the way along the path to becoming as socially unequal as people are in the United States.

The great and the good of 'New' Labour mostly cared. But caring was not enough given thinking that had been rewired by too many years of living under growing inequality. The people who make up what is left of the party that governed until 6 May 2010 mostly know that it made huge mistakes, that what it did was not enough compared with what most other politicians in most other affluent countries in the world achieve today; not enough compared with what the 1906 or 1910 or 1945 or 1964, or even the 1974 governments achieved, all with less time and much less money.

This chapter was originally intended as a piece to be published by the Child Poverty Action Group in 2012. At the last minute they declined to publish it. The reason they gave was this:

Dear Danny,

Many thanks for your piece on inequality during the Labour years. It's particularly interesting to think about how widening inequalities have affected our view of the norm in recent years, as well as how they potentially explain surging debt levels over the 2000s.

When we looked at all the pieces together for the progress report, however, we realised that this piece did not fit the overall narrative well i.e. that the strides made on child poverty, while falling short of the interim target, were significant and meaningful, and hence should not be dismissed as many in government and elsewhere are currently doing.

Given that the purpose of the progress report is to head off a negative interpretation of HBAI [the Households Below Average Income report issued by the Department of Work and Pensions] *when it is released, we have struggled a bit to work out how to slot your piece into the project. I hope you do* not mind too much but we decided after some discussion not to run a chapter on inequality. ...

They were right. What I say above did not fit their overall narrative of that time well. The overall narrative, by 2012, was for there still to be broad agreement between the two parties of coalition and the (now not so 'New') Labour Party. All these products of the Thatcher consensus largely agreed on what was best for Thatcher's grandchildren. They differed a little over how much pain they thought it was acceptable for the poor to bear. They all agreed that it would be nice not to have too many very poor children, too many living on below 60 per cent of median incomes, and to limit the numbers of extremely poor pensioners that could be seen, but other than that there was little – for them – to be done.

On 14 June 2012 the HBAI figures referred to in the quote above were released. A day later, in the analysis of them it was reported: 'Average private incomes fall over 7% in the three years to 2010–11.' This was the leading sentence of the Institute for Fiscal Studies' press release (IFS 2012). The IFS did report that despite 'New' Labour missing its final child poverty target between 1998–9 and 2010–11, it was still the case that: 'Annual entitlements to net state support – that is, benefits and tax credits minus direct taxes – rose by an average of £4,000 per year for the poorest half of households with children.' 'New' Labour had reduced the worst effects of child poverty for many children not quite at the bottom by increasing cash or tax-break handouts. But this was a policy measure that was easy to partly dismantle after 2011.

For adults without children, including those just about to become new parents, by the end of the 'New' Labour years:

> relative poverty among working age adults without children remains close to its highest level since at least 1961. ... [and] Even more striking is the fact that absolute poverty (based on a poverty line fixed at 60% of the 1996–97 median income, adjusted for inflation) among working aged adults without children was no lower in 2010–11 than in the 1970s on an after-housing-costs basis (and only a little lower on a before-housing costs basis). (IFS 2012)

Conclusions

Between the 1970s and 2010 something changed which ensured that those at the bottom of society in the UK saw their economic position stagnating despite the growing wealth and income of most in society. When 'New' Labour took power in 1997, and consequently took responsibility for Thatcher's grandchildren, they increased state welfare payments to poorer families considerably and also introduced a minimum wage for those in work. However, none of this was enough to achieve their poverty targets, nor to cement real change, the more progressive parts of which could not have so easily been undone by the incoming Coalition government.

If many people continue to believe that 'New' Labour did reduce child poverty considerably then there is little hope in the immediate future of real reductions under any of the three main political parties. This is because being in poverty means not being able to take part in the normal life of society. At the extremes, it means going hungry and, for a child, going to school with no underwear on. Your classmates realise this when you change for PE, or when they discover that you lied about your summer holiday, or when you can't go on the school trip, or to a friend's birthday party.

Thatcherism and its 'New' Labour appendage leave the children and grandchildren of the rich in a worse, more ignorant place as well as leaving their contemporaries among the poor worse off as well (BBC 2004; Holden 2008; Revoir, Thomas and Grant 2009). It is not hard to show how poverty has become more felt, more acute, as inequalities have grown. It is far harder to understand how putting the affluent on a pedestal – supposedly there because of their achievements – will so often lead to the ridicule, embarrassment and failure of many of the rich. Lottery winners are the most obvious group who so frequently find all is not rosy upon winning their millions, but many former chief executive officers of banks and other multi-million salaried former tycoons have fallen from a great height to ignominy in recent years. As Ed Miliband put it in that 2013 leader's speech, a rising tide lifts a few yachts, but not all boats. When inequality rises it demeans both rich and poor. Dignity is a feature of more equal societies – for everyone.

Notes

Danny Dorling was Professor of Human Geography at the University of Sheffield when this article was written. He is currently the Halford Mackinder Professor of Geography at the University of Oxford. For a longer and better referenced (although a little dated) version of this argument and accounting, see *Injustice: Why Social Inequality Persists* (Policy Press, 2009). An early long version of the chapter first appeared as an article in *Poverty*, the journal of the Child Poverty Action Group, in 2010; here the argument has been made a little firmer.

References

Ahmed, M. (2008). 'Gordon Brown Vows to Enshrine Child Poverty Pledge in Law'. *Community Care*, 24 September. http://www.communitycare.co.uk/articles/24/09/2008/109514/gordon-brown-labour-will-legislate-to-end-child-poverty-by-2020.htm.

Baggini, J. (2010). Quoted in part in the *Guardian*, 1 May 2010, p. 37 and in full at www.guardian.co.uk/commentisfree/2010/apr/30/lib-dems-tories-election.

BBC News. (1999). 'UK Politics Pledge to Eliminate Child Poverty'. 18 March. http://news.bbc.co.uk/1/hi/uk_politics/298745.stm.

BBC News. (2004). Profile: Mark Thatcher. 26 August. http://news.bbc.co.uk/1/hi/uk_politics/3597196.stm.
Dorling, D. (2010a). 'New Labour and Inequality: Thatcherism Continued?' *Local Economy*, 25(5–6) (August–September): 406–23. www.dannydorling.org/?page_id=1286.
Dorling, D. (2010b). *Injustice: Why Social Inequality Persists*. Bristol: Policy Press, pp. 117–43.
Dorling, D. (2013). 'Fairness and the Changing Fortunes of People in Britain'. *Journal of the Royal Statistical Society A* 176(1): 97–128. www.dannydorling.org/?page_id=3597.
Flintoff, I. (2013). 'Tony Blair's legacy for Labour and the world'. *The Guardian*, 28 February. www.guardian.co.uk/politics/2013/feb/28/tony-blair-legacy-labour-world.
Gordon, D., Mack, J., Lansley, S. and at least 12 others. (2013). *The Impoverishment of the UK*. ESRC Report. Bristol: PSE UK Reports. www.poverty.ac.uk/pse-research/pseuk-reports.
Holden, W. (2008). 'Sink or swim with the Iron Mother'. *Daily Mail*, 15 September. http://www.dailymail.co.uk/home/books/article-1055239/Sink-swim-Iron-Mother-A-SWIM-ON-PART-IN-THE-GOLDFISH-BOWL-Carol-Thatcher.htm.
IFS. (2012). 'Average private incomes fall over 7% in the three years to 2010–11'. Press Release, 15 June. www.ifs.org.uk/pr/pr2_hbai2012.pdf.
Ledwidge, F. (2011). *Losing Small Wars: British Military Failure in Iraq and Afghanistan*. London: Yale University Press.
Revoir, P., Thomas, L. and Grant, C. (2009). 'Chiles reveals EXACTLY what Carol Thatcher said in "golliwog" chat as she insists she did say sorry before she was fired'. *Daily Mail*, 7 February. http://www.dailymail.co.uk/news/article-1136005/Chiles-reveals-truth-Carol-Thatchers-golliwog-gaffe.html.
Spalek, B. and King, S. (2007). 'Farepak victims speak out: an exploration of the harms caused by the collapse of Farepak, 2007'. For the full report, see www.crimeandjustice.org.uk/farepakvictims.html.
The Churches. (2013). *The Lies We Tell Ourselves: Ending Comfortable Myths about Poverty*. Report from the Baptist Union of Great Britain, the Methodist Church, the Church of Scotland and the United Reformed Church, March. www.ekklesia.co.uk/files/truth_and_lies_report_final.pdf.
The Guardian. (2010). 'General election 2010: The liberal moment has come'. 30 April. www.guardian.co.uk/commentisfree/2010/apr/30/the-liberal-moment-has-come.
The Times. (2010). 'Report on Farepak – now behind Rupert Murdoch's firewall'. See paper copy of the paper on 27 April, or pay for access via: http://business.timesonline.co.uk/tol/business/industry_sectors/consumer_goods/article7108918.ece.

6
'When I give food to the poor ...'
Some Thoughts on Charity, Childhood and the Media

Stephen Wagg

In the now widely repeated words of Dom Helder Camara (1909–99), Roman Catholic Archbishop of Olinda and Recife in Brazil, 'When I give food to the poor, they call me a saint. When I ask why so many people are poor, they call me a communist' (see, for example, O'Shaughnessy 2009). Giving aid to the poor, especially when they are children, is, in mainstream public and media discourse, a matter simply for congratulating the donors, great and small, and not for arguing over the whys and wherefores. So the central assertion of this chapter is that contemporary media campaigns such as Children in Need and Comic Relief inevitably depoliticise child poverty by treating it simply as a regrettable fact and paying little attention to its causes. Equally, since they exclude any political analysis of the causes of child poverty, other political assumptions are being affirmed through the transaction of these projects. The chapter offers a brief discussion of some of the prevailing contemporary discourses on child poverty, noting points of continuity with ways of framing poverty in the past, while at the same time contending that they have a particularity, borne of globalised and neoliberal times. Arguably, one of the points of continuity has been the feature of celebrities in the definition and address of poverty. There has, similarly, been regular recourse to already-familiar arguments about child poverty in the UK – notably, that it is a myth, or, alternatively, that it is regrettable and the fault of self-serving politicians or of derelict and/or conniving parents. But new media discourses are also at work, which reflect the break-up of the postwar welfare consensus. These new discourses often reveal a willingness on the part of commentators or other crucial actors to criticise anti-child poverty campaigns as mere posturing on the part of the campaigners. Alternatively, they may imply that child poverty and the combating of this poverty should be matters for individual action alone.

Child poverty, political celebrity and the British: a brief history

The debate about, and address of, child poverty in Britain seems, in modern times, always to have been bound up with celebrity – usually political or quasi-political celebrity. The nineteenth century had Dr Thomas Barnardo (1845–1905) and the (seventh) Earl of Shaftesbury (1801–85); the late twentieth and early twenty-first century has the Irish singers Bono and Sir Bob Geldof along with a cadre of show business celebrities sporting false red noses, historic signifiers of the clown.

Barnardo was a protégé of Shaftesbury and was part of the Ragged Schools Movement of the mid-nineteenth century, which was dominated by Shaftesbury, a Tory landowner and philanthropist. Barnardo's work with children was, like much of its contemporary equivalent, dependent on private benefaction and donation and he is described by one of his biographers as 'a first class publicist' (Wymer 1954: 144). Barnardo's homes taught religion and useful toil (see, in particular, Williams 1943) but, because at the time the state assumed minimal responsibilities for children – they belonged to the private realm of the family – child rescuers such as Barnardo often saw themselves as defying the law, the state taking the view that children in difficulties were the responsibility of their families. He was subject also to public scepticism: 'My facts were scouted,' he once said, 'my inferences derided' (Wymer 1954: 64). There were, of course, other notables in the child rescue movement – Thomas Bowman Stephenson (1839–1912), Edward de Mountjoie Rudolf (1852–1933), Benjamin Waugh (1839–1908) and Selina Sutherland (1839–1909) have all been celebrated by historians in this regard (see Swain and Hillel 2010). Stephenson founded the National Children's Home and Waugh the National Society for the Prevention of Cruelty to Children; both were ministers, the former a Methodist and the latter a Congregationalist. Rudolf, who began the Waifs and Strays Society in south London, worked under the auspices of the Church of England. Similarly, Sutherland, feted as a child rescuer in nineteenth-century Australia, operated via the Presbyterian Church (see Swain 2013). The work of these campaigners is important to note here for two reasons: first, because the history of child poverty is to a significant degree the history of prominent personalities operating outside the state; and, second, because the paradigm within which they dealt with the impoverished children was organised around religion and/or work.

Between the late 1880s and the 1940s the British state gradually brought child welfare under public jurisdiction and, although the family remained central to the official ethos of child welfare, the work of volunteer organisations such as Barnardo's receded as the post-1945 political consensus took root.

From the 1970s onward, however, there were perceptible challenges to, and ruptures in, this consensus: the right to national assistance was no longer taken for granted in some quarters and the term 'scrounger' entered public discourse. In this baleful development the role of the media was crucial: in their book *Images of Welfare* (Golding and Middleton 1982), sociologists Peter Golding and Sue Middleton wrote of the reawakening and orchestration of residual attitudes to the poor, ones which stressed the need for efficiency (in the face of overweening government bureaucracy) and morality (the decency inherent in hard work and good housekeeping) and dealt in pathology (so that poverty was explicable only in individualistic terms). In effect acknowledging the rise of neoliberalism, they wrote: 'A society so firmly anchored in an ethic of competition and reward will only with difficulty dispose of scarce resources to those conspicuously unsuccessful in a system ostensibly offering equal opportunity to all. For success to glisten seductively to the winners, the failure of poverty must display its burden of guilt and shame' (Golding and Middleton 1982: 244). Other media sociologists noted renewed talk of poverty in British mass media and politics in the late 1980s and early 1990s (see, for instance, Meinhof and Richardson 1994). The television documentary *Breadline Britain in the 1990s* (a TV series made by London Weekend Television and shown in the spring of 1991) proved an especial lightning rod for media/political debate.[1] The dominant mood of the popular press, according to one writer, became one of apparent vigilance in exposing the supposed artifice behind anti-poverty campaigning. For example, an anti-poverty advertising campaign launched by the trade union the National Association of Local Government Officers (NALGO) in 1992 drew claims by the *Daily Mail*, the *Daily Express* and the *Evening Standard* that children depicted as suffering serious social problems (compounded by health difficulties such as Down's syndrome or premature birth) were actually living in comfort. Parents of the children were said to have been either paid or deceived. There was denunciation of 'NALGO lies', with the implication that child poverty was a myth and/or that anti-child poverty campaigners deceitful (see Street 1994: 54–6). A further, equally important, media assumption flowed from these insinuations: since there wasn't any significant poverty in contemporary Britain, and people who claimed otherwise were lying, this purported lack of poverty could form part of the basis for constructing a persuasive British identity, set against the ('genuinely' impoverished) '"Third World" and its afflictions: drought, cyclones, earthquakes, dictators, tribal wars ...' (Street 1994: 63–4). This not-in-the-UK perspective almost certainly remains the most widely accepted view of child poverty. When, in 2011, UK Prime Minister David Cameron was confronted on ITV's *This Morning* programme with the prospect that 100,000 children would pass below the poverty line as a consequence of recent government measures, he retorted: 'I think there is a real problem with the way we measure child poverty in this country. Because it's done on relative poverty, if you increase the pension, that means more children are in poverty. I think that's illogical' (see Curtis 2011).

Child poverty, media and contemporary opinion – *Poor Kids*: a case study

Poor Kids was a documentary shown by various BBC television channels between June and August 2011.[2] Its declared and principal aim was to give a voice to, and thus illuminate the experiences of, children in poverty. The Orange website invited viewers' responses;[3] the various responses to *Poor Kids*, which are given a rough categorisation here, offer some guide to current public thinking about child poverty in the UK. The themes were, in the main, familiar: poverty was ascribed, as in Victorian times, to individual failings or to the abstract derelictions of 'politicians; there was sympathy and praise for the fortitude of the children involved'; there were assertions that charity should begin at home (in the UK); and there was also a glimpse of a new, identifiably neoliberal discourse. The selected responses below are reproduced verbatim.

1. *Child poverty is down to bad management/parenting*:
having watched this programme i can only fell sorry for the kids and the way there parents are letting them down. before people get on there high horses im a single parent and survuved on benifits. my house was always clean and tidy and there was always food in the cupboard and clothes could be brought cheaply from asdatescoetc food was more supermarket labels than not but we were well fed. by the way i also smoke and enjoyed the odd drink. what do the parents do with there money?
... wrote one respondent.

    IF YOU CANT FEED THEM – DON'T BREED THEM!. When ever I hear about so called 'POVERTY' its ALWAYS the same class of people that are involved, so, I will say to these mothers (fathers if any) why not sort your own lives out before knocking out kids for the rest of us 'TAX PAYERS' to keep. If a child is put into 'POVERTY' because of the loss of he/she parents then yes, feel sorry and help if we can but, the majority of these 'POVERTY CHILDREN' are due to ignorant people whom should have had the SNIP & TUCK
... said another.

2. *Society; social class; the system; corrupt/lazy politicians are to blame*
How can this still be in Britain 2011 it is shamefull every government agency should feel ashamed.I won't mention childrens charities they just fill their own coffers,year after year smiling faces of TV personalities urging people to give, isnt it time we saw where the money went to I mean published audited accounts on the internet for us all to see where every penny as gone, not some community care worker telling

us how they now have 2 plastic swings and a slide.Who can be trusted to help these poor children, the MP that buys a floating duck island, or the ones that have two homes on expenses, or the social workers that get money for old rope????

3. *Altruism*
This really touched me. It made of grateful for everything I have. I particularly thought of Sam and his sister. Their dad adores them and is doing his best to get a job. As a child who had her head stuck in her books because I knew education was the key to the future, I felt particularly sad for Kayleigh. I hope all these kids do well. I would love to send something to sam and Kayleigh. Can someone please email me how to in about doing this. Thanks.

4. *Put British kids first; charity begins at home*
I didn't see the documentary, but I can imagine how terrible the circumstances would be for these poor children.until we stop sending billions to the EU, and curb immigration, so that only those who honestly have nowhere else to go are admitted, this problem will sadly just worsen. I feel ashamed to be British at times.

5. *Praise for the children as individuals*
Those children are the future ... and they came across as beautiful souls who are more intellegent than the people running the country!education, self respect and love every child deserves this and adults are the ones who should teach and show it. people have no respect for each other so children do as they see unless guided. a moving programe to make us think if we all did a little ...

One particular perspective, however, ventured outside of this consensus and was voiced by Brendan O'Neill. O'Neill runs a website called *spiked*, which emerged from the ashes of the magazine *Living Marxism*, along with the libertarian 'Institute of Ideas'. He blogs for the right-wing *Telegraph* website. O'Neill challenged the concept of 'child poverty', but bedded his critique in populist rhetoric:

> *Poor Kids*, the much-lauded, late-night BBC documentary in which the children of struggling adults speak directly to camera about their lives, sums up everything that is wrong with today's salacious and Dickensian focus on so-called 'child poverty'. In circumventing the adult world, elbowing aside problematic parents and guardians in favour of letting the kids 'have a voice', the documentary exposes the extent to which the problem of poverty has been infantilised. Poverty is no longer treated as a social problem involving unemployed adults with insufficient incomes, but

rather as a moral problem involving grubby-mouthed, empty-stomached urchins whom the chattering classes must tweet and blog their bleeding-heart concern for. It is like something straight out of the Victorian era, though dolled up in PC lingo. (O'Neill 2011)

If this apparent plea by a *Telegraph* writer for more consideration to be given to material factors in assessing child poverty startled readers, O'Neill seemed to wish to discuss the matter no further, scorning the 'outpourings of commentariat concern for less well-off children, a kind of mass advertising of one's moral sensitivity and goodness, in place of any genuine ideas for how to lift adults (and their dependants) out of poverty. Well, who needs a serious political debate about adult poverty and its causes when we can gawp at modern-day Oliver Twists and tell the world how sad they make us feel?' (O'Neill 2011).

This is a deceptive, and decidedly contemporary, discourse. O'Neill appears to be calling for a 'grown-up' debate about poverty and why the adults in the lives of impoverished children have no jobs. But his real concern is to question the motives of those who campaign against child poverty through the media. Some of the tools that O'Neill employs for this dismissal are of their time: with a postmodern sleight-of-hand, he reduces child poverty to a media text and to the supposedly self-serving motives of the people producing and consuming that text. To reduce anti-poverty initiatives to a series of poses would have been unthinkable before 1980, but this formulation has become an accepted part of the political vocabulary of the twenty-first century. In his recent memoir, Tony Blair (British Prime Minister 1997–2007) expressed a 'dislike' for some aid NGOs (non-governmental organisations), remarking that they had 'learned to play the media game perfectly' (Blair 2010: 559).

Meanwhile, child poverty – and poverty generally – has been rendered increasingly as a matter for individual husbandry and/or intervention. British television channels, for example, carry regular adverts for Wonga. com, a company founded in 2006 and backed by some of the world's leading venture capitalist firms.[4] Wonga are ostensibly dedicated to helping people who are short of money to manage their finances. The company rapidly acquired a reputation as a 'loan shark company' acting as 'payday lenders' preying on poor families and charging as much as 4,200 per cent interest to borrowers. Their sponsorship of the Premier League football club Newcastle United in October of 2012 drew strong protests on Tyneside,[5] suggesting that these new assumptions about poverty – that the poor must learn to manage their finances and are fair game for apparently predatory loan companies – are not uncontested. Also in 2006, the *Secret Millionaire* format (since taken up in the United States, Australia and the Irish Republic) was adopted by the UK's Channel 4; here a millionaire spends several days moving incognito in an impoverished community before revealing their true identity and donating money to individuals designated as deserving.[6]

The politics of 'feed the world' initiatives: child poverty and the media since *Live Aid*

Poor Kids, though recent, was not typical of contemporary media commentary on child poverty; most modern political and media discourse about poor children now concentrates on those living in poorer countries. The Conservative/Liberal Democrat coalition that took office in 2010 soon affirmed its commitment to overseas aid and politicians doubtless speak for many in implying that 'underdeveloped' countries remain the locus of 'real' child poverty. In the autumn of 2011 Secretary of State for Overseas Development Andrew Mitchell gave the UK government's support to the campaign to stamp out malaria, while emphasising the gulf between Britain and other countries in this regard:

> These children die from diseases which no child in Britain dies from. If three children in my [Sutton Coldfield] constituency died of malaria, it would be a front-page story for weeks in Britain. We are dealing with a scale of deprivation and poverty out of all proportion to anything we see in Britain. It is part of being British. We are determined not to balance the books on the backs of the poorest people in the world. [It] is the right thing to do, but it is also very much in our national interest. (Grice 2011)

This view has certainly been strengthened in the public mind by an ongoing series of celebrity-led charity media events in the wake of the best-selling record 'Do They Know It's Christmas?' in 1984, the proceeds of which went to famine relief in Ethiopia, and the Live Aid event of the following year. Comic Relief, which mobilised comedians to engage, and engage their public, in charitable activities was inaugurated that same year; the first 'Red Nose Day' was held in 1988. Sport Relief, drawing in prominent sportspeople to support similar causes, was added in 2002. Among a number of media initiatives to promote children's charities, only the BBC's annual Children in Need telethon supports UK charities, urging donors to help the children 'on your doorstep'. Poverty and deprivation are part of their remit, but much funding goes to 'organisations in the UK working with children who have mental, physical or sensory disabilities [or] behavioural or psychological disorders'.[7] Comic Relief, by contrast, has an avowedly global focus and parallel events are now held in countries beyond the UK.[8]

Since celebrities have long since become 'walking news items',[9] they and their fund-raising events have become in all probability the chief source of public information about the matter of addressing child poverty. Much publicity, for example, attended comedy actor David Walliams' swimming of the English Channel in July 2006[10] and the charity triathlon undertaken by comedian John Bishop in March 2012 (see Anisiobi and Dadds 2012); both feats were the subject of TV documentaries and were in aid of Sport Relief.

On 23 March 2012 Walliams acted as guest editor of *The Independent* daily newspaper, all proceeds from the edition passing once again to Sport Relief. These campaigns are, at the same time, *narratives*. They are implied accounts of why the world is as it is – popular pedagogies (ways of learning through popular culture), to adopt the apt phrase concocted by Kellner and Kim.[11] As such, they become more explicit when challenged. In this regard one of the most telling challenges has come from within the (now huge) contingent of comedians invariably enlisted in the propagation of the Red Nose charity. Mark Steel, a stand-up comic and newspaper columnist, wrote in 2004:

> My first experience of [raising money for charity] was as a scout during bob-a-job week, when you'd walk the streets offering to spend all day grafting for a shilling that would be taken straight back off you, a charming tradition recently adopted throughout half of Asia by Nike and Gap. One day perhaps, we'll live in a world in which the starving are fed, and if world leaders want to finance a war they have to hope for a Christmas number one. (Steel 2004)

This pithy observation, like Dom Camara's original (and equally pithy) remark, draws attention to the *creation* of world poverty[12] and to the political priorities of the major powers. Aside from the commercial objectives of the trans- or multinational corporations (like Nike), these might include control of the world's oil supplies, maintenance of massive 'Third World' debt and domination of global financial institutions such as the International Monetary Fund and the World Bank. There is, moreover, some significance in the fact that Steel is a comedian, one of the few interested in bridging private troubles and public issues,[13] comedy now being a chief source of viewpoints outside of an increasingly narrow political consensus.

The point of these charitable initiatives, then, to paraphrase Camara and Steel and to reverse Marx's famous dictum,[14] is *not* to change the world. In 2008 the writer Sarfraz Manzoor compared Live Aid unfavourably with the earlier liberal campaign Rock Against Racism (RAR):

> Where RAR [was] about raising awareness, Live Aid was about raising funds. While there are some parallels – rock stars performing in a large outdoor venue for a good cause – the Live Aid and later Live 8 concerts [of 2005] were very different in their ambitions to Rock Against Racism. Three months after the 1978 concert in Victoria Park, Bob Geldof, then lead singer of The Boomtown Rats, told *Sounds* magazine he did not believe in political rallies, adding 'I think all revolutions are meaningless'. The Live Aid and Live 8 concerts were huge spectacles designed for a mass television audience; the audience members were witnesses, not activists. Live 8 did advertise itself as being about 'justice, not charity' but the level

of participation demanded was modest: a text message to register concern, a click on an on-line petition. Rock against Racism was a grassroots movement which encouraged members to campaign and challenge those in power .... (Manzoor 2008)

Moreover, critics were keen to point out the contradictions in the immanently anti-revolutionary politics in which the celebrity charity initiatives were rooted. For example, in 2009 a coalition of Irish aid groups accused the rock band U2, whose leader 'Bono' is a leading campaigner against world poverty, of hypocrisy in moving their business to the Netherlands for tax purposes. The band's manager, Paul McGuinness, stated that 'like any other business, U2 operates in a tax-efficient manner' (Michaels 2009).[15]

Another important aspect of post-Live Aid celebrity charity culture is that it has become a theatre for the assertion of the Great Men Theory of History,[16] wherein things happen because powerful males make them happen, more structural interpretations having been ruled inadmissible. After all, if all revolutions are meaningless, how is history made (and poverty, therefore eradicated)? 'Like it or not,' said Sir Bob Geldof[17] rebuking anti-G8 protestors in 2010,

> the agents of change in our world are the politicians. Otherwise you're always outside the tent pissing in. They stay inside their tent pissing back out at you. This is futile. My solution is to get inside the tent and piss in there. The G8 has become a pointless ritual where the marchers and the wankers dressed as clowns (wow! Radical) get to throw stones at cops miles from the decision makers, who can't even hear them, and the cops get to crack some heads. I can do rock n roll, they can do marching. (Lewis 2010)

(The 'politicians' cited in this discourse seldom come from Africa, although Geldof himself has not been blind to some of the historical ironies in promoting aid to Africa, a continent now widely acknowledged to have been depleted by European conquest. In a book of 2006, based on his tour of the continent, Geldof quotes with approval an African joke – Question: 'What did they use in the Congo before they had candles?' Answer: 'Electricity' – see Geldof 2006: 120.)

Bono, the other leading celebrity *animateur* of these anti-child poverty campaigns, made similar remarks six years earlier when he addressed the British Labour Party Conference in Brighton: 'I love them both: John Lennon ... and Paul McCartney. I'm also fond of Tony Blair and Gordon Brown. They are kind of the John and Paul of the global development stage, in my opinion. But the point is, Lennon and McCartney changed my interior world – Blair and Brown can change the Real World.'[18]

The political assumptions here seem clear enough: protest and street agitation for social change is futile; history is made by powerful men – political celebrities and access to them, usually by other celebrities, is the only way to influence events; child poverty is the province of the social and political elite; the public will be co-opted as consumer-donors. These elites have communed around two key assumptions: first, that aid must concentrate on children because, as argued in the Brandt Report of 1980 (Brandt Commission 1980), poorer countries crucially lack the infrastructure to give them the 'start in life' taken for granted in 'the West'; and, second, the trigger for this aid must come from the titans of Western popular culture. 'There are 20 million children in school now because of what went on that week and they [The Pink Floyd] were emblematic,' said Geldof in 2011, reflecting on the band's reunion for Live 8.[19] The politicians, for their part, welcomed the opportunity to deal on a celebrity-to-celebrity basis. Geldof and Bono, wrote Tony Blair later, were 'both genuinely committed [and] properly knowledgeable', the latter possessing 'an absolutely natural gift for politicking' (Blair 2010: 554–5). Blair made it clear that he preferred to negotiate with them than with aid organisations (NGOs), who rejected 'free trade' and 'basically took the position that "globalisation is a rich-country conspiracy"'(Blair 2010: 559–60).

For the mainstream media, then, celebrity intervention with the world's leading political figures (the President of the United States, the Pope etc.) and a co-opted (usually young) public in their charity T-shirts and red noses, offers the best (sometimes the only perceptible) defence against a world, in which, to adopt Zygmunt Bauman's bleak dictum, 'everything may happen, but nothing can be done' (Bauman 2002: 18).

Come slumming: celebrity charity, child poverty and mitigation

This final section offers some thoughts on the politics inherent in the growing practice of placing celebrities temporarily in the situation of the children they are raising money for. It draws on another case study – *Famous, Rich and in the Slums*, a two-part documentary film made by the BBC for the Red Nose Day of 2011. For this film, four celebrities (two actors, an actor-comedian and a veteran TV presenter) visited Kibera, a huge slum adjoining the Kenyan capital Nairobi, and spent time with some of its young inhabitants. 'Stripped of all possessions,' read the publicity material,

> they're left alone for a week to live, work and survive in one of the most impoverished places on earth – the slums of Kibera, Kenya. It's estimated that up to **1 million people** live in an area measuring just 1.5 square miles. People in Kibera do back-breaking labour in unsanitary conditions for as little as **50p per day**. Open sewers run through streets and pit-latrine toilets are often shared by up to **1,000 people**. **20% of children** in Kibera don't live to the age of five. **Donate and Make a Difference.** Your

cash could help us to improve living conditions in slums across Africa and make a massive difference to countless people's lives.
   Small Amounts, Big Difference £8. In Kenya, £8 is all it takes to feed a child, who's lost both their parents to AIDS, for two weeks.[20]

I suggest that initiatives of this specific nature involve a series of interlinked *mitigations*. Mitigation is especially important to the conduct of celebrity, because contemporary celebrity itself is very ambiguous – morally, socially and politically. Celebrities are symbols of an (albeit mythical) open society. Their status derives from popular acclaim but, since we are all assumed to have had the same chances in life, their success automatically indicts the majority of us who have failed to climb the ladder to success, who therefore enjoy neither wealth nor fame and relate to celebrities either as fans or as 'ordinary members of the public'. There is, thus, a tension in our typical attitude towards celebrities. Admiration mixes with resentment. As the writer Zadie Smith once remarked: 'Groupies hate musicians. Moviegoers hate movie stars. Autograph men hate celebrities. We love our gods. But we do not love our subjection.'[21] This ambiguity is, of course, routinely exploited by the popular media and lies at the heart of the 'build-them-up/knock-them-down' strategy on which the tabloid press now subsists. So celebrity, enjoyed by the most conspicuously wealthy members of an increasingly unequal society, has to be mitigated. Equally, and on the other hand, in an increasingly secular, hedonistic and acquisitive society the notion of giving requires a new paradigm – it, too, has to be mitigated, for fear of 'compassion fatigue', a term of comparatively recent vintage.

In relation to child poverty charity, this mitigation works in several ways. First, as with Red Nose discourse generally, a paradigm of *play* is established (as opposed to Barnardo's culture of religion and work). Four friendly celebrity visitors, sporting and dispensing red plastic noses, may briefly lift the spirits of impoverished African children, but this also salves the process of *giving* in a postmodern society based increasingly on consumption, pleasure and self-advancement: 'consume-laugh-give' is the exhortation. After all, it's important to remember that the bulk of the charity donation in these campaigns comes from the public. As Steel said in 2010, instead of appealing for '£3,000 ... to feed this village', the (very wealthy) Bono should simply '*give it to them*'.[22]

Second, such spectacles (increasingly a 'reality television' staple in the wider media world) mitigate the wealth and soft life of the celebrities – and particularly of comedy, an inherently hedonistic medium. These celebrities, is the clear implication, can tough it out with the best of them. Besides, they care. (Such mitigations may similarly drive the growing phenomenon of 'slum tourism', for which Kibera is a popular destination – see Obombo 2010.[23])

112 Stephen Wagg

Third, this latter consideration moves the discourse onto the plane of the *im*material. There is a massive and acknowledged (note the title of the film – *Famous, Rich and in the Slums*) wealth difference between the locals and their visitors, but an implied democracy of the emotions: the celebrities and the poor children laugh and cry together – the comedian and actor Lenny Henry, for example, is seen weeping and being consoled by a local man.[24] This becomes part of a spiritual journey undertaken by the celebrity. Drawing again on Bono's speech to the Labour Party Conference in 2004, the singer informed his audience:

> Another very tall, grizzled rock star, my friend Sir Bob Geldof, issued a challenge to 'feed the world'.
> It was a great moment, it changed my life. That summer, my wife Ali and I went to Ethiopia, on the quiet, to see for ourselves what was going on. We lived there for a month, working at an orphanage. The locals knew me as 'Dr. Good Morning'. The children called me 'The Girl with the Beard'. Don't ask. But let me say this – Africa is a magical place. And anybody who ever gave anything there got a lot more back. A shining, shining continent, with beautiful royal faces ... Ethiopia not just blew my mind, it opened my mind.[25]

Fourth, Comic Relief interventions help to mitigate contemporary television itself – to sanction its current practices. The twenty-first century has seen the rise in many countries of 'reality television', which the media sociologist Nick Couldry has described as a 'theatre of cruelty' expressing the harsh 'truths' of neoliberal philosophy (Couldry 2008: 3). These programmes include *Big Brother* (shown in the UK on Channel 4, 2000–10; Channel 5, 2011–), which films a group of individuals in close confinement and invites viewers to vote to evict one of them from this closed environment; *Dragon's Den* (BBC2, 2005–), which shows aspiring entrepreneurs whose business ideas are often ridiculed by a resident panel of tycoons; *The Apprentice* (BBC 2, 2005–7; BBC1, 2007–), wherein young people invariably lose their dignity in competing to work for the self-consciously boorish multi-millionaire Sir Alan Sugar; and *The Weakest Link* (BBC1, 2000–12, but franchised in over 50 countries), in which an aggressive host puts general knowledge questions to contestants and invites open conflict between them – unsuccessful players exit along a 'Walk of Shame'. Plainly these are lessons in the bleak realities of life in a market society and all have softened their harsh message with a Red Nose special – *Big Brother* in 2001; *The Weakest Link* in 2001 and 2003; *The Apprentice* in 2007 and 2009; and *Dragon's Den* in 2009. In the Red Nose *Celebrity Big Brother* of 2001, viewers were told that participant Vanessa Feltz, who had recently been divorced and had the contract for her TV talk show cancelled, would soon 'show signs of strain'. 'You've probably seen how passionate the whole thing was, how emotional,' said commentator Davina McCall, 'but it's all for Comic Relief.'[26]

Fifth, and finally, a good deal of discussion has, not surprisingly, concerned the motivation of the celebrities who, once a year, call on the public to donate money to combat world child poverty: surely, the criticism runs, they're doing it for publicity – an advantageous presentation of their professional selves. Lenny Henry, a veteran of 25 years of Comic Relief, recently said of the inception of the whole post-1985 fund-raising project: 'We'd had some of the richest people in the world singing about "Feed the world". Of course, there was going to be some criticism [that they were trying to] big themselves up, but, actually, over the years, I've not seen that ...'[27] Similarly, in 2013 scriptwriter Richard Curtis, regarded as the creator of Comic Relief, dismissed the suggestion that the event was 'a smug pratfest' or 'a vehicle for washed-up celebrities trying to revive flagging careers': 'My experience tells me it's nonsense. One Direction, who have done the Comic Relief single this year, are the biggest boy band in the world; they don't need more publicity' (Vallely 2013). It might be suggested that Curtis is here simply dismissing a straw-man argument; in any event, questioning the sincerity of the celebrity participants is of marginal importance. But it should nevertheless be remembered that celebrities, Geldof's and Bono's assertions notwithstanding, do not make history in circumstances of their own choosing. Celebrity, as Rojek points out, is socially constructed – it is a 'cultural fabrication', concocted and nurtured by press, PR, fashion and other impression management professionals (Rojek 2001: 10). And not only is it constructed, it is zealously *policed* – something that no observer of the public controversy over the hacking of celebrities' telephones by tabloid journalists,[28] or of proceedings of the subsequent Leveson Inquiry of 2011–12, could reasonably doubt.[29] There can be little doubt, either, that celebrities and their advisers are aware of the fine line they tread between media approval and media vilification. After Live Aid, its organiser Bob Geldof was offered a fortnight's free holiday in Mauritius by the island's government. 'I got out my atlas,' Geldof wrote later. 'Mauritius was dangerously close to Africa in my limited conception of geography. I could envisage the headline: "Geldof Suns on Beach as Nearby Millions Starve". With regret I turned it down and opted to visit a friend who had a farmhouse in a quiet part of Ibiza' (Geldof, with Vallely, 1986: 391).

Conclusion

As in Victorian times, poverty-stricken children depend heavily for relief on the campaigning of prominent public figures. Without questioning the benevolent intent of the people involved, it is important to say that the contemporary culture of media campaigns to mitigate child poverty have the parallel function of mitigating the cult of celebrity. They do so by turning an *objective* phenomenon – celebrities as conspicuous tokens of an unequal distribution of wealth – into a *subjective* one: people who care about the world's poor. At other times, as we have seen, a reverse discourse may be deployed in which the *objective* – real poverty, be it suffered by children or adults – is reduced to the *subjective* – that is, to the 'bleeding heart' liberalism or the media game-playing of the people who publicise it. Two further things are vitally important about this process. First, not only does the pattern of economic power relations that produces and sustains world poverty go unchallenged, but the money raised by celebrity campaigns comes chiefly not from government, global corporations or wealthy celebrities, but from the temporarily red-nosed public – office workers, schoolchildren, television viewers and the like. Second, in the neoliberal political culture of the twenty-first century, childhood – and the poverty that attaches to it – is the only life course fully viable for these projects. As I observed earlier, the contemporary political lexicon of aspiration and free trade compels adults to seek their own salvation; all they can reasonably expect, in the moral vocabulary of neoliberalism, is a 'start in life'. Sallying forth in red noses to assist beleaguered adults wouldn't command the same level of support. In this regard neoliberalism shuns history and social context: 'Yes, we needed increased aid,' reflected Tony Blair, 'but the purpose was to help get Africa on its own feet, with no rubbish about not being able to govern because of the wicked colonial past' (Blair 2010: 555).

Acknowledgement

Thanks to Peter Bramham, Peter Golding and Jane Pilcher for reading a draft of this essay and making helpful suggestions as to how it might be improved.

Notes

1. 'The *Breadline Britain in the 1990s* survey was funded by London Weekend Television (LWT) with additional funding from the Joseph Rowntree Foundation and was carried out by Marketing and Opinion Research International (MORI). It was conceived and designed by Joanna Mack and Stewart Lansley for Domino Films, with the help of Brian Gosschalk of MORI.' See Jonathan Bradshaw et al., *Perceptions of Poverty and Social Exclusion 1998: A Preparatory Report* (Bristol: Townsend Centre for International Poverty Research, 1998). Available at: www.bris.ac.uk/poverty/pse/99-Pilot/99-Pilot_Intro.doc (accessed 12 February 2013).
2. See www.bbc.co.uk/programmes/b011vnls (accessed 12 February 2013).
3. See http://blogs.orange.co.uk/tv/2011/06/poor-kids-bbc-children-poverty-line-courtney-paige-sam.html (accessed 27 September 2011). This blog has been taken down since the research was completed. However, readers may like to read a TV Blog by the *Poor Kids*' director Jezza Neumann: '*Poor Kids*: A Child's View of

Growing Up in Poverty'. Posted Tuesday 7 June 2011: www.bbc.co.uk/blogs/tv/posts/poor-kids (accessed 24th January 2014).
4. Errol Damelin, founder and CEO of Wonga.com received a number of 'Entrepreneur of the Year' awards in 2010. See www.guardian.co.uk/megas/errol-damelin (accessed 28 February 2013).
5. See, for example, www.dailymail.co.uk/sport/football/article-2215020/We-wont-step-inside-Wonga-Arena-Newcastle-fans-hit-24m-sponsorship-deal.html (accessed 28 February 2013).
6. For details, see Channel 4 website: www.channel4.com/programmes/the-secret-millionaire (accessed 28 February 2013).
7. See BBC Children in Need website: www.bbc.co.uk/programmes/b008dk4b (accessed 12 February 2013).
8. See Comic Relief website: www.comicrelief.com/about-us (accessed 12 February 2013).
9. This telling phrase may have originated with the Cultural Studies academic and writer Dick Hebdige. See Hebdige (1974: 5).
10. See http://news.bbc.co.uk/sport2/hi/tv_and_radio/sport_relief/5143966.stm (accessed 12 February 2013).
11. See Kellner and Kim (2010). I'm grateful to Michael Silk and Jessica Francombe for drawing my attention to this concept.
12. A phrase now generally associated with the writing of Teresa Hayter. Her *The Creation of World Poverty* was first published in London by Pluto Press in 1981 and republished in Oxford by Third World First in 1990 – see Hayter (1981) and Hayter (1990). Hayter's book was a response to the so-called Brandt Report of 1980, *North–South: A Programme for Survival*, published by the UN. It called, among other things, for rich Northern countries to aid poorer Southern ones – an exhortation roughly in keeping with the Live Aid/Comic Relief ethos – see Brandt Commission (1980).
13. Older readers will recognise this phrase of C. Wright Mills. See Mills (1970: 9–17).
14. 'The philosophers hitherto have only interpreted the world in various ways; the thing, however, is to change it.' Karl Marx, 'Theses on Feuerbach', in *Collected Works*, vol. V, p. 8 (Moscow: Progress Publishers, 1976). Quoted in Heilbroner (1991: 152).
15. For an acute political analysis of Bono's relationship to charity and world politics, along with further references to writing on 'celebrity humanitarianism', see Browne (2013).
16. This is now, largely, a 'common-sense' notion, but originated in the work of nineteenth-century philosophers such as Thomas Carlyle. In his *On Heroes, Hero-Worship and the Heroic in History*, based on lectures first given in 1840, Carlyle wrote: 'For, as I take it, Universal History, the history of what man has accomplished in this world, is at bottom the History of the Great Men who have worked here'. See Carlyle (1841: 1).
17. Geldof, born in the Republic of Ireland in 1951, was given an honorary knighthood in 1986, the year after Live Aid.
18. 29 September 2004. Transcript available at the @U2 website: http://www.atu2.com/news/transcript-of-bonos-speech-at-labour-party-conference.html (accessed 13 February 2013).
19. *The Pink Floyd Story: Which One's Pink?* BBC4, 20 September 2011.
20. From: http://www.rednoseday.com/whats-on/tv-listings/famous-rich-and-in-the-slums (accessed 5 October 2011).

21. The observation by Zadie Smith appeared in the Review section of the *Guardian* on 3 September 2005, p. 19. I've made this argument in previous writing, notably Wagg (2007) and Wagg (2011).
22. On the BBC TV programme *Room 101*, February 2010. Available at: www.youtube.com/watch?v=f-TmxuhZCn8 (accessed 13 February 2013).
23. For a wider discussion of slum tourism, see Frenzel et al. (2012).
24. This can be seen at: www.bbc.co.uk/news/uk-21333472 (accessed 13 February 2013).
25. 29 September 2004. Transcript available at the *@U2* website: http://www.atu2.com/news/transcript-of-bonos-speech-at-labour-party-conference.html (accessed 13 February 2013).
26. *Celebrity Big Brother* for Comic Relief 2001 was broadcast on Channel 4 between 9 and 16 March, with updates every ten minutes on BBC1.
27. See www.bbc.co.uk/news/uk-21333472 (accessed 13 February 2013).
28. The controversy began in 2005. See www.bbc.co.uk/news/uk-14124020 (accessed 13 February 2013).
29. See www.levesoninquiry.org.uk/ (accessed 13 February 2013).

References

Anisiobi, J. J. and Dadds, K. (2012). 'That's just blown me away': Comedian John Bishop finally ends Week of Hell charity triathlon, raising £1.6m for Sport Relief.' *Mail Online*, 2 March. www.dailymail.co.uk/tvshowbiz/article-2109290/John-Bishop-Sport-Relief-challenge-Comedian-ends-Week-Hell-charity-triathlon.html (accessed 23 October 2013).
Bauman, Z. (2002). *Society Under Siege*. Cambridge: Polity Press.
Blair, T. (2010). *A Journey*. London: Hutchinson.
Brandt Commission. (1980). *North–South: A Programme for Survival*. London: Pan Books.
Browne, H. (2013). *The Frontman: Bono (In the Name of Power)*. London: Verso.
Carlyle, T. (1841). *On Heroes, Hero-Worship and the Heroic in History*. Available online: www.gutenberg.org/files/1091/1091.txt (accessed 23 October 2013).
Couldry, N. (2008). 'Reality TV, or the Secret Theatre of Neoliberalism'. *Review of Education, Pedagogy and Cultural Studies* 30: 3–13.
Curtis, P. (2011). 'Is David Cameron right to dispute the poverty figures?' *Guardian Politics Blog*, 1 December. www.guardian.co.uk/politics/reality-check-with-pollycurtis/2011/dec/01/child-benefit-poverty (accessed 12 February 2013).
Frenzel, F. with Koens, K. and Steinbrink, M. (eds). (2012). *Slum Tourism: Poverty, Power and Ethics*. London: Routledge.
Geldof, B., with Vallely, P. (1986). *Is That It?* Harmondsworth: Penguin.
Geldof, B. (2006). *Geldof in Africa*. London: Arrow Books.
Golding, P. and Middleton, S. (1982). *Images of Welfare: Press and Public Attitudes to Poverty*. London: Martin Robertson.
Grice, A. (2011). 'It is our moral duty to help the world's poor'. *The Independent*, 1 October. www.independent.co.uk/news/uk/politics/it-is-our-moral-duty-to-help-the-worlds-poor-mitchell-tells-tories-2364069.html (accessed 12 February 2013).
Hayter, T. (1981). *The Creation of World Poverty*. London: Pluto Press.
Hayter, T. (1990). *The Creation of World Poverty* (2nd edn). Oxford: Third World First.
Hebdige, D. (1974). 'The Kray Twins: A Study of a System of Closure'. Stencilled Occasional Paper. Birmingham: University of Birmingham Centre for Contemporary Cultural Studies.

Heilbroner, R. (1991). *The Worldly Philosophers*. Harmondsworth: Penguin.
Kellner, D. and Kim, G. (2010). 'YouTube, Critical Pedagogy and Media Activism'. *Review of Education, Pedagogy and Cultural Studies* 31(5): 3–36.
Lewis, P. (2010). 'Geldof condemns lame and ineffective anti-poverty campaigners'. *The Independent*, 2 April. Available at: www.guardian.co.uk/music/2010/apr/02/bob-geldof-anti-poverty-campaigners-starsuckers (accessed 13 February 2013).
Manzoor, S. (2008). 'The year rock found the power to unite'. *The Observer*, 20 April. Available at: www.guardian.co.uk/music/2008/apr/20/popandrock.race (accessed 13 February 2013).
Meinhof, U. and Richardson, K. (eds). (1994). *Text, Discourse and Context: Representations of Poverty in the British Mass Media*. Harlow: Longman.
Michaels, S. (2009). 'U2 accused of robbing the world's poor'. *The Guardian*, 27 February. Available at: www.guardian.co.uk/music/2009/feb/27/u2-irish-aid-group-coalition (accessed 13 February 2013).
Mills, C. W. (1970). *The Sociological Imagination*. Harmondsworth: Pelican.
Obombo, K. M. (2010). *Slum Tourism in Kibera, Nairobi, Kenya: Philanthropic Travel or Organised Exploitation of Poverty?* Saarbrucken: Lambert Academic Publishing.
O'Neill, B. (2011). 'Poverty is a serious social problem – but "child poverty" is often an excuse for sentimental PC rhetoric'. 13 June. http://blogs.telegraph.co.uk/news/brendanoneill2/100091936/poverty-is-a-serious-social-problem-%E2%80%93-but-child-poverty-is-often-an-excuse-for-sentimental-pc-rhetoric/ (accessed 4 October 2011).
O'Shaughnessy, H. (2009). 'Helder Camara – Brazil's archbishop of the poor'. *The Guardian*, 13 October. Available at: www.theguardian.com/commentisfree/belief/2009/oct/13/brazil-helder-camara (accessed 23rd October 2013).
Rojek, C. (2001). *Celebrity*. London: Reaktion Books.
Steel, M. (2004). 'The depressing truth about Live Aid'. *The Independent*, 18 November. Available at: www.independent.co.uk/voices/commentators/mark-steel/the-depressing-truth-about-live-aid-533624.html (accessed 13 February 2013).
Street, B. (1994). 'The International Dimension'. In U. Meinhof and K. Richardson (eds), *Text, Discourse and Context: Representations of Poverty in the British Mass Media*. Harlow: Longman, pp. 47–66.
Swain, S. (2013). 'Child Rescue'. http://www.emelbourne.net.au/biogs/EM00333b.htm (accessed 21 March 2013).
Swain, S. and Hillel, M. (2010). *Child, Nation, Race and Empire: Child Rescue Discourse, England, Canada and Australia, 1850–1915*. Manchester: Manchester University Press.
Vallely, P. (2013). 'Twenty-five years of laughing in the face of tragedy'. *The Independent on Sunday*, 3 February.
Wagg, S. (2007). 'Angels of Us All? Football Management, Globalisation and the Politics of Celebrity'. *Soccer and Society* 8(4): 440–58.
Wagg, S. (2011). '"Her Dainty Strength": Suzanne Lenglen, Wimbledon and the Coming of Female Sport Celebrity'. In S. Wagg (ed.), *Myths and Milestones in the History of Sport*. Basingstoke: Palgrave Macmillan, pp. 122–40.
Williams, A. E. (1943). *Barnardo of Stepney: The Father of Nobody's Children*. London: George Allen & Unwin.
Wymer, N. (1954). *Father of Nobody's Children: A Portrait of Dr Barnardo*. London: Hutchinson.

7
A Coming or Going of Age?
Children's Literature at the Turn of the Twenty-First Century

David Rudd

Children's literature, as a discrete entity, is commonly traced back to the eighteenth century in England, to a time when the new middle classes began to carve out a protected space for their progeny. Distinct commodities were developed, including games, furniture and clothing – and, of course, books, seen as perfect vehicles to instruct and entertain the future citizenry. The Romantics rounded out and mythologised this new being, the child, as innocent, pure and, therefore, unsullied by adult society. By the end of the Victorian period, the 'cult of the child', as it became known, was at its height, with the desirability of remaining a child, a Peter Pan, in the cultural ascendant. However, a century on from the *fin de siècle*, at the *fin de millennium*, this image had been severely questioned. The 'century of the child', as Ellen Kay (1900/1909) then termed it, had ended, and with it, a growing number of voices proclaimed a new century that foresaw the child's disappearance, or death, even (Winn 1984; Postman 1994; Buckingham 2000). This chapter explores how this crisis over the child manifests itself in the era of Thatcher's grandchildren. On the one hand, there are writers who celebrate a new freedom to discuss issues more candidly with children – whether about war, the Holocaust, homelessness, the family, racism, abuse, drugs, ecology, or sex and sexuality – whereas others fear that this very openness is destroying childhood, formerly defined in terms of protection, of relative innocence.

Such debates, though, all too easily lose direction because of a tendency to reduce the child to a symbol, juxtaposed with that equally amorphous being, 'the adult'. Instead of demographically representative childhoods, then, we, as a society, have usually defaulted to a privileged, white, middle-class being, readily evoked in discourses about moral decline, whether to expose the dangers of fairy tales, chapbooks, penny dreadfuls, comics, films, television, video or the Internet (e.g., Winn 1984; Postman 1994; cf. Pearson 1983; Springhall 1998). Actual children who, say, were once forced to work down the mines or up chimneys, and for whom *any* entertainment would have been an uplifting luxury, are lost to view. Certainly, this historical example is provocative, but from what we know about child abuse today, about children as carers and workers, about their status as refugees and as homeless (Göncü 1999; Goddard et al. 2004; Lancey 2008), we might suggest that children's books could still do with being more varied in their representations of childhood, in order to avoid that twee, angelic stereotype. However, as childhood is such a sensitive issue, its representation is always going to be subject to criticism, and barometric shifts are frequent. Thus, there is currently an outcry over what has been termed 'sick-lit' for the young (Pauli 2013), with the *Daily Mail* criticising, among other works, Anne Fine's *The Road of Bones* (2006), an allegorical tale about a young person caught up in the icy, deathly totalitarianism of Soviet Russia. Naturally, Fine would defend her portrayal, and yet, in 2009, she too was critical of some other works for children, suggesting that 'realism has gone too far' (Fine 2009).

My general argument in this chapter is that this was a period of contradictory tensions. Sociologically, it was typified as a time when there was a shift away from individual identity being shaped by traditional institutions (the Church, the school, the workplace); instead, there was an emphasis on one's identity being a more personal construct, facilitated by the various images that the media paraded before us. This notion of 'identity politics' continued a trend begun in the 1980s. One of the key proponents of this shift was the influential sociologist Anthony Giddens, who not only put forward his model of the 'third way' (1998), itself suggesting a more individual, ethical capitalism shaping the future, but was himself actively courted by Tony Blair, with Giddens' ideas informing the PM's agenda.

While Giddens was generally optimistic, though, there were wider, global issues that underlined continued threats to the world order, against which an individual nation could do little. These were summed up in Ulrich Beck's term, the 'risk society' (1992), which pointed out how modernisation had exposed us to threats beyond natural 'acts of God'. The Chernobyl disaster (1986) was a key example, but there were others, particularly linked to terrorist attacks, which were themselves often seen to be the result of a polarising, Muslim–Christian divide. Moreover, even disasters formerly seen as natural, it was realised, could have been caused by human action (as with global warming), and an anti-globalisation movement became increasingly vocal. Finally, the 1990s also saw some horrific ethnic conflicts (e.g., in Africa, the Balkans, the Caucasus) that also had their effects on the UK, as refugees sought asylum here, many of whose young would have experienced very different childhoods from most in the West.

While these shifts undoubtedly had an impact on some of the fiction for children at this time, with the decline in the influence of traditional organisations (the Church, schooling and the workplace) making itself felt, Giddens' arguments did not really take account of the effects such shifts would have on what was formerly a clearer distinction between child and adult. Thus we find various linguistic attempts to capture this problematic semantic space: 'adultification', 'infantalisation', 'adultescence', 'kidulthood', 'tweenager', and 'rejuvenile' (cf. Postman 1994; Giroux 2000; Cross 2008). It was also at this time that the word 'crossover' was coined, making overt (and more acceptable) a phenomenon that had always existed: of adults and children reading the same books (Knoepflmacher and Myers 1997; Beckett 1999; Falconer 2009). Undoubtedly, bestsellers like the 'Harry Potter' series made the most of this in their marketing campaigns, but they neither initiated nor sustained the phenomenon. The crisis over childhood (whether *it* was 'adultised' or *adulthood* was 'infantilised') had deeper roots, though the millennium certainly exacerbated concerns in the way that it marked the end of one era and the beginning of another, suggesting, simultaneously, a sense of nostalgia and apocalypse.

Though concerns about the young were widespread in the West, in the UK it was the murder, in 1993, of the toddler James Bulger by two other children (both 10-year-olds) that gave the discourse about the 'death of childhood' a dark, ironic twist. Innocence itself was seen to have perished, albeit James's death was not without precedent, either in reality (Paul 2003; Loach 2009) or in fictionalised form (e.g., Golding 1954; March 1954). Moreover, in the public imagination, the actions of Bulger's young killers became conflated with those of the American children who took firearms to school to gun down their peers, a subject that, again, would later take fictional form (Strasser 2000; Shriver 2003). Other disturbing issues concerning children were also regularly aired over this period: high youth unemployment; loutish behaviour, both amongst the more mature ('men behaving badly') and the younger (dealt with through ASBOs and curfew orders); the use of the Internet by paedophiles, cyber-bullies and pornography peddlers; a concern that children were becoming precociously sexual, and, in general terms, were simply out of control (Palmer 2006). As ever, a spate of television programmes attested to this, where children's bad behaviour was exhibited to experts who, over the course of the show, returned 'brats' to 'proper' childhood (e.g., *Supernanny, The House of Tiny Tearaways, Brat Camp*). And yet, while terms like 'pester power' were bandied about, less attention seemed to be paid to the way that children were being increasingly targeted as a market for a plethora of desirable goods (Seiter 1993; Cross 1997; Steinberg and Kincheloe 1997; Kenway and Bullen 2001). Moreover, though accused of growing up too quickly (Elkind 1981), the pressures of schooling seemed to emphasise 'hot-housing'; and, if children were termed antisocial, it was equally the case that they were being deterred from playing in public spaces, a more solitary, bedroom culture being preferred.

In general, then, as the above neologisms suggest, notions of 'coming of age' had ceased to hold their former significance, notions compounded by the demise of many working communities (e.g., in the mining and steel industries), the loss of permanent employment and increased debt, such that many thirty-somethings found themselves still dependent within the family home (making popular another acronym, Kippers: Kids In Parents' Pockets Eroding Retirement Savings, and further TV programmes, like *Young, Dumb and Living Off Mum*). While these dispiriting factors need taking into account, and certainly coloured some of the more dystopian children's fiction of this period, it is also the case that there was a general feeling of optimism in the air, as the decade climbed out of the recession of the early 1990s and Tony Blair, mentioned earlier, appeared like a saviour figure for the Labour Party.

Harry Potter and the new millennium

It seems more than coincidental that Blair's years as Prime Minister chime exactly with the Harry Potter publishing phenomenon (1997–2007), the former sweeping through Whitehall like a new broom, just as Harry Potter, at Hogwarts, actually rode one. Youth was in the air (literally, in the latter's case), and, at 43, Blair was the youngest British PM for almost two centuries, standing in stark contrast to what was seen as the more staid Thatcher and Major years, the latter famously evoking a cosy 'country of long shadows on cricket grounds, warm beer, invincible green suburbs, dog lovers and pools fillers and ... Shakespeare ... in school' (Seldon and Baston 1997: 370).[1] Blair had once played in a rock band, making Downing Street part of 'Cool Britannia', courting trendy Britpop stars. Youth, then, was valorised, and particularly so as a result of the recent convergence of new technologies, like the Internet and mobile phone, which seemed to be understood, almost intuitively, if not magically, by the new generation.

It was this technological revolution, I think, that was partly responsible for the resurgence in fantasy, which J. K. Rowling's Harry Potter seemed to spearhead: the idea of a digital equivalent of our everyday world existing alongside our own, which those in the know could access and manipulate (Hutchby and Moran-Ellis 2001; Weber and Dixon 2007; Rosen 2008). Prior to this, a more realistic style of children's writing had prevailed, which extended through Labour's darker days of the strike-filled 1970s and into the leaner Thatcher and Major years.

But fantasy now seemed less remote, associated less with separate worlds (like Tolkien's Middle-earth) than realms that coexisted, which is how Rowling depicts the relationship between her Wizard and Muggle realms, of course, albeit both are committed to capitalism (in line with Giddens' third way). The wizarding world thus offers us little that is innovative in social, political or spiritual terms (unlike what we find in C. S. Lewis's or Ursula Le Guin's fantasy fiction). Instead, we have an all-too-familiar consumerism, in which Muggles and Wizards indulge equally, with (for the latter) Diagon Alley doing an excellent trade in the latest models of broomstick (Harry's victory in his first Quidditch tournament is partly ensured thanks to the superior 'spec' of the Nimbus 2000 racing broom; Rowling 1997). And, of course, with life imitating art, a huge consumer industry quickly sprang up attendant on the books, then the films, with a glut of academic works appearing in their wake (the majority published only partway through the actual series; e.g., Zipes 2000; Nel 2001; Blake 2002; Eccleshare 2002; Whited 2002; Anatol 2003; Heilman 2003).

Like Blyton, Rowling uses traditional storytelling techniques, with feisty children overcoming malignant adults. But even though Rowling also opted to set her series in a boarding school, it maintained a contemporary feel. This was partly a result of Blair's pronouncement that his 'three main priorities for government' were 'Education, education, education', which had turned the youthful National Curriculum – thanks to league tables – into something requiring far more commitment, resulting in schools running breakfast, lunchtime and post-school clubs, let alone homework circles in the evenings, and even 'booster' classes at the weekends. Like traditional boarding school children, then, it was very hard for the young to escape the school regime.

Rowling also touched on other contemporary concerns, many encapsulated in Harry's overweight, overindulged and bullying cousin, Dudley Dursley, who seemed to be a product of bad parenting and a slothful lifestyle; in fact, the one in need of a brat camp. In contrast, Harry and his chums were seen to represent proper childhood. Harry was the traditional Cinderella orphan from 'below stairs', brought up by step-parents and abused accordingly. But, like Cinderella, his background was also one of privilege, as was Blair's (unlike Major's) in attending the 'Eton of the North', Fettes College; indeed, half Blair's initial cabinet were public school products, with another quarter coming from traditional grammar schools.

A number of critics have drawn attention to this question of privilege in Harry Potter, too; for, while Dumbledore might play down the 'purity of blood', arguing that 'it matters not what someone is born, but what they grow to be' (Rowling 2000: 614–15), the Muggles are continually represented as second-class citizens who, like children themselves, find much of what goes on in the world concealed from them. There is therefore the continual question of why the wizarding world does not intervene more. For instance, we hear that Dumbledore had Gellert Grindelwald imprisoned in Nurmengard in 1945, after the latter's despicable deeds in 'mainland Europe', and, of course, as Daragh Downes (2010: 167) points out, 'we think of a certain other Teutonic dark wizard. We hear pure-blood philosophy; we think of Aryan supremacy. We hear Nurmengard; we think of Nuremberg'. These historical coordinates can only point to one event, and yet Rowling steers around it. So, while we hear 'truly inspirational stories of wizards and witches risking their own safety to protect Muggle friends and neighbours' (quoted in Downes 2010: 167), still we want to ask: 'what can possibly have stopped wizards and witches from intervening when Jewish, Gypsy,

Communist and Homosexual Muggles were falling victim to an earlier, and immeasurably more lethal, pure-blood ideology?' (ibid.: 167–8). Whereas, in more distinct worlds, such as Tolkien depicts, the possible parallels between Nazgul and Nazi become less problematic.

Even if Rowling's two realms chose not to interact, though, the parallels between reality and fantasy are arresting. Thus both Blair and Potter would fight a War on Terror (which the hardening of fundamentalist faiths, crystallised in the events of 9/11, exhibited), and each ends his respective journey demonstrating his faith, the messianic Potter shown to be 'the instrument of ... deep good laws of magic', displaying Christian love (Gupta 2009: 173), and Blair converting to Catholicism and establishing his Faith Foundation.

It certainly seemed an irony that Rowling's series, in many ways quite orthodox in its expressions of faith, should have been so extensively attacked by Christian fundamentalists, whereas Philip Pullman's trilogy, *His Dark Materials* (1995–2000), emerged relatively unscathed. The latter was far more provocatively critical of organised religion – and, many thought, of Catholicism in particular. Certainly, Pullman's work celebrates the coming of a Republic of Heaven, where the emphasis is on individual choice (in the fashioning of identity), rather than something imposed by political and religious institutions, and is thus reminiscent of the shift towards personal responsibility that Giddens outlined.

But it is still perplexing that, in the twenty-first century, there should be such an interest in alternative realms, with angels, vampires and werewolves everywhere – perhaps most famously, and successful commercially, in Stephenie Meyer's 'Twilight' series (2012) – which had sold an extraordinary 85 million copies by 2010 (Carpenter 2010; although Rowling's Potter books were estimated to have topped 450 million by 2011). I have already suggested that the popularity and accessibility of computerised virtual worlds had something to do with this shift towards fantasy, producing a strange fusion of the materialistic and the ineffable. There was also, in the West at least, a postmodern sensibility that questioned all overarching 'grand narratives', religious or secular, while maintaining a soft spot for the quirky and unorthodox (cf. Žižek 1991), whether involving aliens, angels or other mythological figures (we find a similar reaction in the nineteenth century, when, in the face of more secular explanations of the world, orthodox religion suffered a severe blow and more marginal beliefs thrived, in spiritualism, fairies and pagan deities, such as Pan, who appears in countless works at this time, returning a spiritual meaningfulness to nature; Dingley 1992). Lastly, as also mentioned above, two of the world's main religions were becoming increasingly polarised, giving many of the apocalyptic fantasies of this period a more credible basis.

The figure of the child, however, though its innocence had been queried, remained a redemptive being in many children's books of the noughties, as witnessed in the work of Rowling and Pullman. Moreover, each of these writers seemed keen to preserve the generic sanctity of children's fiction; thus, although Harry Potter ages across the series, he experiences few of the sexual stirrings of adolescence we find elsewhere (see below); Lyra, too, hero of Pullman's trilogy, though she comes of age, is forced to accept that what has become the leaky vessel of her world must be resealed, such that she ends up more confined at the trilogy's conclusion.

Elsewhere in his crossover novel Pullman had seemed to challenge the adult–child binary (something that his winning of what had formerly been the 'adult' Whitbread Book of the Year award, seemed to consolidate[2]). However, his lauding of the power of children's books over adult ones then seemed to polarise this very binary: 'children's books have dealt with ultimate questions, where do we come from, what's the nature of being a human being, what must we do to be good', issues he found absent from 'books that adults read', which have often, 'in recent years ... dealt with the trivial things, such as does my bum look big in this or will my favourite football team win the cup ...' (quoted in Blake 2002: 83–4). This was fairly partisan rhetoric, for, as ever, there were equally frivolous children's works (e.g., *The Day My Bum Went Psycho* by Andy Griffiths, 2001; or Alan Durant's 2001 'Bad Boyz' series about 'football-mad kids'), just as many 'adult' works of the time probed deeper, ontological issues (e.g., Peter Carey, Stevie Davies, Jonathan Franzen, David Mitchell, V. S. Naipaul and Ali Smith also published in 2001).

Nevertheless, Pullman certainly stimulated a debate that was already in the air, with, on the one hand, writers like A. S. Byatt (2003) expressing concern about culture's infantilisation with the 'childish adult' reading Rowling, whereas, on the other, champions of children's literature articulated the opposite concern, about adultification; as Julia Eccleshare (2004: 213) put it, '"crossover" books run the risk of riding roughshod over the absolute essence of the children's book [such that we] end up with no children's books that are aimed solely at children'. However, I'd argue that these entrenched notions of the 'essence' of either child or adult persisted precisely because these categories were no longer so secure: there was a slippage, as suggested earlier.

In particular, adolescence spread, both up and down the chronological scale, making it seem more a lifestyle choice than a stage of development. This is a theme that Frank Cottrell Boyce wittily explored in *Cosmic*, whose narrator, Liam, is six feet tall at age 13, and can pass as an adult; as he says, 'everyone lies about their age. Adults pretend to be younger. Teenagers pretend to be older. Children wish they were grown up. Grown-ups wish they were children' (Boyce 2008: 3). Even medical bodies seemed to accept the spread of youth in this era, with the Society for Adolescent Medicine shifting its definition of the end of adolescence from 26 years old (in 1995) to 34 in 2002 (Danesi 2003: 162). In postmodern terms, then, the idea of us as 'human becomings' rather than 'human beings' held more attraction, with diet, drugs and cosmetic surgery all aiding the realisation of this state (as others have noted, the teddy boy, the original British subcultural hero, was by this time an established pensioner, as were 'sixties' rock rebels like The Rolling Stones and The Who).

The preoccupation with adolescence and the idea of an eternal, youthful beauty are certainly part of the attraction of Meyer's incredibly successful 'Twilight' books (2005–8), which might otherwise appear rather dated, reactionary texts (with their stress on virginity, aligned with the 'True Love Waits' movement). But the youthful appeal of the central, elderly vampire family, the Cullens, is irresistible, as is their old-fashioned, considerate behaviour, and especially Edward's unselfish attentiveness towards his girlfriend, Bella. Moreover, by including a considerable number of more traditional vampires (and, indeed, werewolves), the books also held onto that darker side of adolescence outlined earlier, in which teenagers are depicted as a strange and dangerous species living amongst us (the title of Danesi's 2003 book exploring adolescence – *My Son Is an Alien* – is indicative).

Scott Westerfeld's *Uglies* (2005) is the first volume in a similar series that captures this ambivalence around teenagers. At age 16, they are surgically rendered 'pretty', playing up to stereotypes of adolescent narcissism and conformity. However, there is also the underlying idea that youth would otherwise be ugly, or 'revolting'. Thus the operation, unbeknown to those operated on, also alters their minds, making them docile, 'pretty-minded' (and petty-minded, too). Needless to say, there's a rebel cell working against such state control, which Westerfeld explores across the series. Pullman's alternative-world trilogy, discussed earlier, makes a similar point, with the church experimenting on children, subjecting them to a form of castration ('intercision') which circumvents the complications of puberty, rendering youth zombie-like and compliant. As noted earlier, with the prescriptive National Curriculum increasing its hold, and the young finding themselves under greater surveillance elsewhere (via, for example, ASBOs, curfews and league tables), the control of young minds was something of particular concern at this time.

Crossover fiction

From this perspective, a particularly interesting work is Mark Haddon's *The Curious Incident of the Dog in the Night-Time* (2003), the first UK book to be officially published in 'crossover' format (i.e., with two different covers, one for adults and one for children, albeit the text within was identical). Though not stated in the novel itself, the dust jacket informs us that the 15-year-old protagonist, Christopher Boone, 'has Asperger's' – a condition that had only been officially recognised in 1994.[3] And, as we read the novel, we come to realise why Christopher's psychological condition is downplayed, for strange as some of his ways appear (he hates the colours yellow and brown, does not like being touched, and comprehends neither metaphor nor facial expression), in others he is no different from teenagers across the Western world with their fads and aversions. Thus, like many other young people, Christopher is simply struggling to come to terms with the way the world operates, seeking to discover its underlying rules and ways of being, and, in the process, uncovering the fact that humans are not as logical or consistent as they might think. As he points out, 'the Bible ... says *Thou shalt not kill* but there were the Crusades and two World Wars and the Gulf War and there were Christians killing people in all of them' (Haddon 2003: 38).

But for all his belief in logic, Christopher is delightfully capricious in some of his own behaviour. Hence the chapters in his first-person narrative are given prime numbers simply because, as he informs us, 'I like prime numbers' (14), although he is content to let his footnotes amble ordinally. The main attraction of prime numbers, Christopher tells us, slipping dangerously close to metaphor before asserting that he speaks in simile only, is that they are 'what is left when you have taken all the patterns away', hence they are 'like life. They are very logical but you could never work out the rules' (15). For many readers, this might sound a contradiction: life is anything but logical. Moreover, Christopher's claim that he 'solved the mystery of Who Killed Wellington?' (268) – the dog of the title – also proves untrue: rather than deducing this answer, or even appreciating the emotional state that led to his father committing 'canicide', his father simply confesses his crime to Chris. Thus, the numbers that stand between Christopher's primes are the places where ordinary, ordinal life, in all its obdurate detail, gets in the way for our protagonist. The 'curious incident', then, is something of a 'dead dog', whereas 'the elephant in the room' (to use a more voguish metaphor) escapes Christopher completely.

He thus wanders through society in the manner of a *flâneur*, observing life without letting it contaminate him. In fact, he likes to imagine himself alone 'in a spherical metal submersible' several miles down in the sea (10). His idea of being a private eye therefore puts far more emphasis on his personal space, as a 'private I'.[4] In many respects, then, Christopher is not far removed from Holden Caulfield, central character in J. D. Salinger's *Catcher in the Rye*, 50 years his predecessor (Salinger 1951). Both are confused teenagers, but are nonetheless effective interrogators of our society's values. They lay adolescence bare in the manner suggested by Julia Kristeva, who famously suggested that adolescence comprised 'less an age category than an open psychic structure' (1990: 8), which suggests anything but it being a life choice; rather, it becomes a time when choices and meanings are interrogated, when one discovers one doesn't fit in; in short, as Kristeva (1991) puts it in another context, we find that we are strangers to ourselves. Hence adolescent gaucheness can be triggered at any time by anyone who feels 'out of synch' with the world, questioning its prohibitions, its rules, orderings and the range of identities it has to offer – small wonder that this book had crossover appeal at the time.

In fact, as Haddon's novel avoided any easy polarisation between rational, mature and caring adults on the one hand, and children, as their antithesis, on the other, in many ways it makes a stronger claim to crossover status. It raises more questions than it offers solutions. Thus, for example, we might be distinctly uncomfortable that the kind of dystopic society depicted by Westerfeld or Pullman is something that would likely appeal to Christopher. Indeed, in what sounds very much like an extended metaphor, Christopher wistfully dreams that 'nearly everyone on the earth is dead, because they have caught a virus', to which only those who don't comprehend metaphor or facial expression are resistant, 'special people [... who] like being on their own' (Haddon 2003: 243).

Our sense of normality is thereby questioned, and the hypocrisies of our society uncovered as we consider the messy lives of the adults in the book, and start to realise how adolescents can become the scapegoats of a society where adults are often the ones 'out of control', not only attacking fellow Christians, but innocent dogs, too. The media might panic about school shootings, then, but set alongside adult atrocities, they are not only singularly rare (Males 1996, 1998; Baxter 2008) but also need putting in context, occurring predominantly in societies where adults have approved the right to bear arms.

Some of David Almond's protagonists form a useful contrast with Haddon's Christopher, though there are similarities, too, perhaps especially evident in *Skellig* (1998), where the eponymous figure describes himself in hybrid terms as '[s]omething like you, something like a beast, something like a bird, something like an angel' (Almond 1998: 158). Like Christopher, Skellig causes us to reconsider our knowledge of the world, and our place within it, but whereas Christopher would be dismissive of angels (as he is of fairies), Michael, *Skellig*'s protagonist, is more open. This goes to the heart of debates about the shift from modernity, which Christopher seems to epitomise – its attempt 'to *dis-enchant [...in its] declaration of reason's independence*' – to a more postmodern 're-enchantment' (Bauman 2001: x; cf. Bennett 2001), as exhibited by Michael.

As with Pullman's work, Almond's novels are fascinated by the latter, with both authors invoking William Blake, who declared, 'May God us keep / From Single vision & Newton's sleep!' (Blake 1972: 818). So, although the monetarist vision of Thatcherism had left some regions of the UK particularly bleak, especially after basic industries, like mining, had collapsed, Almond's Tyneside stories retain a feel for the numinous, which is most lyrically expressed in his volume of short stories, *Counting Stars* (2000), with its revelations about everyday existence. Thus, again in the face of an increasingly virulent, globalised capitalism (a grand narrative that was certainly not ending), and a hardening of the divide between a stark materialism and a fundamentalist commitment to faith, Almond manages to carve out a more spiritual, optimistic space – one, again, that draws on uncanny angels and monsters (Almond 2005, 2008).

Finally, Almond's books should be mentioned for the way that they question traditional notions of masculinity, which were certainly in crisis at this time, partly as a consequence of Thatcher's dismantling of some traditionally 'male' industries. Alternative masculinities began to be explored, as in films like *The Full Monty* (1997), following the demise of the steel industry, but also in more child-oriented works, like Lee Hall's *Billy Elliot* (2000; Burgess 2001a). Here, in 1984–5, the confrontation between the Thatcher government and the miners was at its most bitter. To his beleaguered family (his widowed father and older brother), the 11-year-old Billy seems to betray all that they stand for: the solid camaraderie of North-East mining manhood confronted by a would-be ballet-dancer (a soft Southern 'poof', in their terms). Almond's work also shows us both sides of this crisis, as we witness older versions of masculinity struggle in an age in which the very term 'working class' became increasingly empty of meaning – just as the notion of a 'Labour' party also became problematic, with Blair very much defining himself as both the 'new man' and New Labour, and with his wife, Cherie, maintaining her prestigious career as a barrister. (In fact, Blair reduced his workload in 2000 when his son Leo was born, with his government introducing paid paternity leave three years later.) Almond's *Clay* (2005) and *The Savage* (2008) each feature an atavistic, male bully (Mouldy and Hopper), whom the heroes, Blue Baker and Davie respectively, have to confront. Not only do the protagonists discover inner resources, but they also uncover some rather darker, brutal aspects of themselves, which are brought to the surface during their respective struggles. In *Skellig*, by contrast, we have the more sensitive Michael, who starts to experience an uneasiness in the company of his old mates, Coot and Leakey, finding himself happier with the more intuitive and mindful Mina.

Louis Sachar's *Holes* (1998, filmed by Andrew Davis, 2003), though an American book, also proved very popular in the UK, and explores similar ideas (like Almond's books, it too has a magical realist feel to it, with its coincidence-heavy plot). The overweight protagonist, Stanley Yelnats, is sent to an arid correction camp for a crime he has not committed. The Camp itself is a testosterone-charged place, and Stanley certainly finds himself becoming a leaner and fitter male. However, traditional masculinity is by no means secure here: it is interrogated and undermined, with the patronymic character, 'Mister Mister', overdetermined in his masculinity, suffering at the hands of the far more powerful, female Warden. Stanley and his friend Zero, though both outsiders, manage to right the wrongs of Camp Green Lake through their tender regard for one another, to the extent that this arid landscape turns lush and verdant again; indeed, it becomes a Girl Scout Camp. The novel ends with Zero's mother, a woman silenced by history and circumstance, not simply speaking, but singing (using the more semiotic, sensory aspects of language – Kristeva 1984). *Holes* deals with a number of issues that tend to fall between the cracks of mainstream discourse (the title itself is indicative, and the reader is advised, towards the end, 'to fill in the holes yourself' – Sachar 1998: 231). Gender and fatness are two such issues, but race and class are also present, with both main characters coming from poor immigrant backgrounds, one white, one black.

Over this period in the UK, though, the most well-known children's book about race was Malorie Blackman's clever reversal of the social coding of black and white in *Noughts & Crosses* (2001), which makes black people Crosses, or top dogs, while the Noughts are, much like Zero in *Holes*, given 'zero' status, as nothings, noughts. The historical outcome of this coding, like the game 'Noughts and Crosses' (a meaning somewhat lost in the American equivalent, 'Tic Tac Toe'), is thereby made to seem more of a lottery, although the consequences prove anything but a game. Unfortunately, this binary coding does tend to oversimplify things, precisely reducing it to black and white, rather than opening up the far greater richness of ethnic diversity that was so characteristic of this period, especially given the arrival in Britain of so many asylum seekers from Eastern Europe and Africa, as dealt with in a number of other sensitive works, like *Christophe's Story* (Cornwell 2006), about a Rwandan refugee, or Benjamin Zephaniah's *Refugee Boy* (2001), about an Ethiopian lad, whereas others are more general (e.g., Ben Morley's *The Silence Seeker*, 2009 – the title based on a mishearing of the word 'asylum'). However, as is often the case with narratives concerned with individual representatives of a country, there's a tendency to default to masculine protagonists.

Dealing with the contemporary horrors of ethnic cleansing probably also allowed people to take a more open look at the events of the Holocaust (Russell 1997; Kertzer 1999), realising that, with similar events occurring elsewhere (as in Rwanda, mentioned above), children could not, and should not be sheltered from this dark history. Thus picture books, like Jo Hoestlandt's *Star of Fear, Star of Hope* (2000) and Tony Johnston's *The Harmonica* (2004), opened up this topic; and for older readers, there was the extremely popular *The Boy in the Striped Pyjamas* by John Boyne (2006), though many found it compromised by the hero's naivety (an example of the overplayed, Romantic child figure). Morris Gleitzman's popular trilogy, starting with *Then* (2009), is certainly more hard-hitting, but Markus Zusak's *The Book Thief* (2006) remains the most rewarding, if demanding read, featuring a feisty young heroine, whom even Death, the narrator, takes to heart. From this mordant perspective, the book could deal with Nazi atrocities in a more sardonic and, therefore, far less didactic manner.

Millennial matters

This raises the perennial problem for writers of children's works: how to address thorny issues without turning books into moralising tracts that lack credible and fallible characters. Having discussed several of the powerful voices of this period, then, I'd now like, more briefly, to mention some of the other key concerns of the era – although a number of these have already been touched on in works mentioned earlier (Harry Potter, for instance, also addresses notions of prejudice, racial purity and bullying).

First, let me discuss what I shall term 'body issues', including birth, gender, sex, and sexual abuse. Over this period, such matters hit the headlines in various forms. Generally there seemed to be more awareness and openness about bodies, with writers like Babette Cole (1995, 2001) leading the way; not only did such books inform youngsters about gender, puberty and the 'facts of life', but managed to do so in a humorous and, therefore, less embarrassing way. A more scatological perspective also emerged, perhaps inspired by Roald Dahl's work, as shown in Holzwarth and Erlbruch's classic picture book, *The Story of the Little Mole Who Knew It Was None of His Business* (2001) and works for slightly older children, like Dav Pilkey's 'Captain Underpants' (1997–) and Claire Freeman's *Aliens Love Underpants* (2007–) series. There also seemed more of an attempt, possibly in the wake of the Spice Girls (most active, professionally, between 1994 and 2000) and 'girl power', to present gendered behaviour in less stereotypical ways, without simply reversing the polarity, as earlier works had done. *Billy Elliot* certainly achieves this, as do several of Jacqueline Wilson's works (most famously, her Tracy Beaker books, 1991–),[5] and, more recently, Jeff Kinney's *Diary of a Wimpy Kid* (2007–) series.

Books that explored alternative sexualities also became more in evidence, though, once again, there seem to be more of these available for gay boys; for example, Alex Sánchez's popular 'Rainbow Boys' trilogy (2001–5) and David Levithan's *Boy Meets Boy* (2003), with, for the more literary-minded, Jamie O'Neill's exceptionally beautiful *At Swim, Two Boys* (2001). It may be that girl relationships never suffered quite the same stigma as boys', but some memorable, overt portrayals of lesbianism did appear at this time; for example, M. E. Kerr's *Deliver Us From Evie* (1994) and Julie Burchill's *Sugar Rush* (2004), which was also televised. Otherwise, girls had to turn to 'adult' classics, like those by Jeanette Winterson (1985) and Sarah Waters (1998, 2002), at least until well into the noughties. Moreover, works addressing the two latter initials of 'LGBT' (Bi- and Trans-sexual) remained far less in evidence. Certainly, this was a fraught period for young adults of alternative sexuality, with the law initially discriminating against them, until it was challenged by a 17-year-old boy in 1997. Furthermore, the revised Sexual Offences Act (2003), which, though it mostly sought to address issues around paedophilia, the bugbear of this period, did also manage, bizarrely, to criminalise all sexual touching between teenagers (Carvel 2003).

Each of the areas alluded to above requires comment, both the inappropriate touching (and worse) of children (by adults or, indeed, other children), and the more natural – if illegal! – erotic explorations of teenagers. Certainly, this era produced some sensitive works that attempted the very difficult task of protecting innocence while making it more savvy. They also avoided scapegoating that bogeyman, the paedophile, recognising that most abuse occurs within the family (e.g., Hessell 1987; Kleven 1997). This aspect was also brilliantly explored in Bryan Talbot's *The Tale of One Bad Rat* (1995), a work for older readers which was told in a format becoming increasingly popular over this period: the graphic novel. As his title suggests, Talbot draws on Beatrix Potter's work in order to tell a dark story of parental abuse, also touching sensitively on issues around drugs, teenage prostitution and homelessness.

Despite figures attesting to the growth in young teenagers' sexual activities, Young Adult (YA) fiction remained reticent, with many still looking back to Judy Blume's *Forever* (1975). Authors like Melvin Burgess in the UK and Lauren Myracle in the US did, however, challenge what they saw as a rather outdated reticence about the topic. Burgess's most controversial titles, *Lady: My Life as a Bitch* (2001b), giving a teenage girl's perspective on the 'joy of sex' – but only after she has been transformed into canine form – and *Doing It* (2003), providing the views of three, horny, teenage boys, were much criticised, with Children's Laureate Anne Fine (2003) declaring that the latter would have girls 'begging their parents to send them to single sex schools'. In contrast, Myracle's books were aimed distinctly at girls, bearing titles like *ttyl* (2005) and *ttfn* (2007), notably using text-speak throughout.

There are several points to make here. First we must note that children's (or YA) fiction is still very much subject to generic conventions, which not only prove hard to break, but, when they are broken, cause an outcry (as, more recently, has 'sick-lit'). But secondly, we must observe that this restriction on children's reading is *merely* generic, given that the National Curriculum for Key Stage 4 (i.e., 14- to 16-year-olds) includes 'English literary heritage' authors like James Joyce and D. H. Lawrence, both of whom had had their work prosecuted for obscenity. This is where labelling makes all the difference, as other 'adult' works popular in their time with literate teenagers attest; for example, Philip Roth's *Portnoy's Complaint* (1969), Erica Jong's *Fear of Flying* (1973) Martin Amis's *The Rachel Papers* (1973), Ian McEwan's *First Love, Last Rites* (1975), Julian Barnes's *Metroland* (1980), Will Self's *Cock & Bull* (1992), or Helen Fielding's *Bridget Jones's Diary* (1996). It is also worth noting that all the above works appeared after 'Sexual intercourse began in 1963', as Philip Larkin jokingly expressed it, referring, once again, to Lawrence (*Lady Chatterley's Lover*). For it was also the case that explicit sexual acts were absent from most adult books before this date: sex was not particularly the yawning divide that it would later become. Lastly, although there is no 'Bad Sex Award' for children's books (the award was established by the *Literary Review* in 1993), it is the case that many of these YA attempts are equally awkward (ironically, Rowling was mooted to be a contender for the award, albeit for her adult novel, *The Casual Vacancy*, but her writing was considered 'not nearly bad enough'; Kennedy 2012). The tension, then, between works like *Doing It* and *Twilight* (which might almost have been subtitled 'Not Doing It'), is reflected in this period's sobriquet – the naughties or the noughties – with very few YA books achieving anything like a more rounded, sensitive treatment of sex, though exceptions like William Nicholson's *Rich and Mad* (2009) deserve mention.

Abuse, both sexual and otherwise, would also feature in many books for children, as it had in earlier periods, but the new media had also introduced new forms, such as cyber-bullying. Moreover, the pressure on teenagers to conform had resulted in far greater attention being paid to body image, with a frightening growth in eating disorders, in drug and alcohol abuse, and other forms of behaviour that could present a threat to the body, from 'mild' self-harming (e.g., cutting) to suicidal behaviour (e.g., Kaysen 2000). Once again, many worthy books were published that addressed these problems, but helpful as many such titles clearly are, it always seems that the more successful works are those that manage to treat these issues in more everyday terms, and without resolving them too summarily. Thus Jacqueline Wilson's *Girls Under Pressure* (1998) is certainly a page-turning story, with the 13-year-old protagonist developing an eating disorder after being called 'fat'. But then, after visiting an older girl from school, hospitalised as a result of anorexia, she quickly overcomes her problem. It is not quite the 'QED' of Christopher, but some readers might prefer grittier works, like Ibi Kaslik's *Skinny* (2004), Judith Fathallah's *Monkey Taming* (2006) or Natasha Friend's *Perfect* (2004); or, on cutting, Joanna Kenrick's cleverly titled *Red Tears* (2007); or, for more suicidal behaviour, linked to cyber-bullying, Julie Anne Peters' *By the Time You Read This, I'll Be Dead* (2010). On the other hand, a book such as Meg Rosoff's *How I Live Now* (2004) manages to incorporate many of these issues – around eating disorders and self-harming (and, come to that, incest as well, with a first-cousin love affair) – without making them overly intrusive or too tidily resolved.

A final issue of body image that became increasingly significant in these years was cosmetic surgery. Again, notions of uniformity are a common theme in YA literature, and when linked with 'mainstream' looks, are even more powerful, making An Na's *The Fold* (2008) a sensitive exploration of the dilemma a Korean girl faces in having a blepharoplasty, as it is known, to make her eyelids more 'Western'. Many science fiction works over this period looked at the darker implications of such surgery, like Westerfeld's *Uglies*, discussed earlier, or, moving more into the territory of post-human engineering, Rodman Philbrick's *The Last Book in the Universe* (2000), where – as in Huxley's *Brave New World* – the class system has been genetically underpinned, with your average 'normals' living in the Urbs (concrete jungles) whilst the superior 'proovs' (i.e., improved ones) live in a sunny Eden. The book's narrator, Spaz, is not even a 'normal', as his name might intimate: he is a 'Deef', or 'defective' (an epileptic).

Philbrick's work introduces yet another issue that became more in evidence, thanks to a vocal disability rights lobby. Again, while there are worthy stories that concentrate on particular problems, these do have a tendency to have the condition define the character, rather than seeing it simply as an aspect of their person (Saunders 2004). Philip Ridley's *Scribbleboy* (1997) is a good example of a work that avoids this trap, despite featuring main characters who are, respectively, a wheelchair user and a boy with a bad stammer. Likewise, Jamila Gavin's *Coram Boy* (2000) not only features a character with learning difficulties (a 'simpleton'), but also deals with teenage pregnancy (in the eighteenth century), bullying, slavery and the general ill-treatment of children. Haddon's *Curious Incident* also deserves mention again, where the Asperger's label doesn't appear overtly in the text at all.

I'll finish this section by mentioning what was perhaps the most sustained concern to have featured among the many complex issues in children's fiction over this period: the environment. A huge number of books addressed ecological issues, often within a dystopic context – and many of these, simultaneously, dealt with related issues, such as post-humanism, poverty and warfare. Once again, the best were those that created wholly credible worlds populated with believable characters. M. T. Anderson's *Feed* (2002) is all too plausible, with the title referring to a future form of the Internet, which is routinely implanted at birth, allowing consumer profiling to reach into our very capillaries, raising questions about agency and identity (and questioning the viability of Giddens' faith in personal empowerment, too), situating the whole story in a very polluted and depleted world. Anderson's novel falls into the relatively new subgenre of 'cyberpunk', whereas Philip Reeve's *Mortal Engines* (2001), the first of a quartet, is more 'steampunk' (like Pullman's trilogy). The premise of this subgenre is that the nineteenth century's key form of power continued to develop and shape the future. In Reeve's world, it is shown in the huge, mechanical, mobile cities that consume each other in a bid to secure scarce resources, in what is termed 'Municipal Darwinism'.

Conclusion

The notion of steampunk epitomises what had been a central concern of this period with its Janus-faced straddling of the millennium. On the one hand, it looked back nostalgically to what was seen as a more carefree period of childhood, and, on the other, it looked forward, sometimes positively, but often with apprehension. Much of the former mood – positive, liberating and technologically enabled – came with the ebullience of new millennial thinking. We have seen it in Rowling's work ('You're a wizard, Harry!'), in Pullman's *His Dark Materials*, and in an explosion of other, imaginatively conceived fantasies. But optimism also colours more realistic works, too, which address issues both of personal concern (around identity and the body) and of wider social and historical import, including darker topics like the Holocaust, ethnic cleansing, racism and sexual abuse. Not only can we point to the increasing visibility of children's books across this period, both in terms of market success and cultural recognition, but also to the emergence of crossover fiction, with adults openly engaging with texts seen to be for the young (albeit, often packaged differently).

However, this phenomenon was part of a larger debate about society becoming more infantilised or adultised, depending on one's perspective. I have suggested, though, that each of these terms is inadequate in trying to retain what is a false binary – which is something that books like Haddon's *Curious Incident* query, several of the 'adult' characters therein also experiencing adolescent angst, finding themselves as ongoing 'human becomings'. Once again, this shift is partly driven by developments in IT, such that no one can rest on their existing knowledge, but it is also informed by a general sense of social instability – around globalisation, deregulation, terrorism, political and social realignments, and threats of ecological disaster. Though Britain had its local social climate, it was also more than previously affected by global shifts in this 'risk society'.

The result, then, is not a happy, crossover melting pot. We end up not liberated from stereotypes of age, any more than we have been liberated from the inequalities of class, gender or ethnicity. We have all, in fact, been made more dependent through stricter forms of government control and surveillance (contra Giddens), as we find ourselves entered into the various 'league tables' of modern life, and to which we are thereafter indebted. As Heinz Hengst (2005: 23) puts it, 'children [... are] "new arrivals" in societies and cultures in which adults are not really at home either'.

Some of the books, above, have discussed this in allegorical ways, whereas others are more direct and cynical, earning them the current label, 'sick-lit'. However, such works have not appeared in a vacuum, for they reflect the concerns and moods of the time. Suzanne Collins' immensely successful trilogy, beginning with *The Hunger Games* (2008), is a case in point, tapping into many of these issues. It centres on a future society, 'Panem', which references 'Pan-am', meaning all-American, but also the Latin phrase *panem et circenses*, 'bread and games', referring to the Roman way of appeasing people and diverting them from real issues of power and inequality. In Panem, there is an annual Games in which young representatives (12- to 18-year-olds) are arbitrarily selected to represent their area, and fight to the death in a televised spectacle. Youth is central and, typically, the young and attractive are championed, but it is also seen as fearful and deadly (the 'cult' of the child has here morphed into its 'cull'). The personas constructed around the chosen 'tributes', the makeovers they endure, plus the need for sponsorship, make this televised spectacle simultaneously distasteful and compelling, and we, so used to reality TV – to *Big Brother* and *Supernanny* – recognise our complicity in the process (and read on avidly). The Games thus capture many elements of the risk society, and, beyond that, show how the invisible hand of government, through the media, orchestrates and controls the rebellion that eventually occurs. The success of these books, though, together with a growing number of critical non-fiction works that take issue with our overly regulated, mediatised and controlled society – especially towards its young (Levine 2002; Gill 2007; Piper and Stronach 2008; Louv 2010) – suggests that what has been termed 'sick-lit' might still be homeopathic in its effects, perhaps to the benefit of Thatcher's future great-grandchildren.

Notes

1. Ironically, Major's background and education was relatively humble compared to Blair's. In this famous 1993 Mansion House speech, Major also quotes another Blair – Eric, better known as George Orwell.
2. The rules had been changed in 2000, when it was expected that Rowling might win – though she was ultimately beaten by Seamus Heaney with his translation of *Beowulf*.
3. See Greenwall (2004) for more detail, and for consideration of the growing number of books on this syndrome. Haddon's publication was itself preceded by one written by 13-year-old Luke Jackson, *Freaks, Geeks and Asperger Syndrome: A User Guide to Adolescence* – certainly about his own condition, but also about adolescence per se.
4. The term 'Private I' actually precedes 'Private eye', the 'I' originally standing for 'Investigator.
5. Despite 'Harry Potter', Wilson's books were actually the most popular library books in the UK over the 2000–10 decade. news.bbc.co.uk/1/hi/entertainment/arts_and_culture/8512613.stm.

References

Almond, D. (1998). *Skellig*. London: Hodder.
Almond, D. (2000). *Counting Stars*. London: Hodder.
Almond, D. (2005). *Clay*. London: Hodder.
Almond, D. (2008). *The Savage*, illustrated by D. McKean. London: Candlewick Press.
Amis, M. (1973). *The Rachel Papers*. London: Jonathan Cape.
Anatol, G. L. (ed.). (2003). *The Harry Potter Phenomenon: Critical Essays*. Westport, CT: Praeger.
Anderson, M. T. (2002). *Feed*. Somerville, MA: Candlewick Press.
Bauman, Z. (2001). *Intimations of Postmodernity*. London: Routledge.
Baxter, K. (2008). *The Modern Age: Turn-of-the-Century American Culture and the Invention of Adolescence*. Tuscaloosa, AL: University of Alabama Press.
Beck, U. (1992). *Risk Society: Towards a New Modernity*. London: Sage.
Beckett, S. L. (ed.). (1999). *Transcending Boundaries: Writing for a Dual Audience of Children and Adults*. New York and London: Garland.
Bennett, J. (2001). *The Enchantment of Modern Life: Attachments, Crossings, and Ethics*. Princeton, NJ: Princeton University Press.
Billy Elliot. (2000). Dir. Stephen Daldry. London: BBC Films/Tiger Aspect Pictures/StudioCanal/WT[2] Productions.

Blackman, M. (2001). *Noughts & Crosses*. London: Random House.
Blake, A. (2002). *The Irresistible Rise of Harry Potter: Kid-Lit in a Globalised World*. London: Verso.
Blake, W. (1972). *Complete Writings ...*, ed. G. Keynes. Oxford: Oxford University Press.
Blume, J. (1975). *Forever*. New York: Bradbury Press.
Boyce, F. C. (2008). *Cosmic*. Basingstoke: Palgrave Macmillan.
Boyne, J. (2006). *The Boy in the Striped Pyjamas*. London: David Fickling.
Buckingham, D. (2000). *After the Death of Childhood: Growing Up in the Age of Electronic Media*. Cambridge: Polity Press.
Burchill, J. (2004). *Sugar Rush*. London: Pan Macmillan.
Burgess, M. (2001a). *Billy Elliot*. Frome: Chicken House.
Burgess, M. (2001b). *Lady: My Life as a Bitch*. London: Andersen Press.
Burgess, M. (2003). *Doing It*. London: Andersen Press.
Byatt, A. S. (2003). 'Harry Potter and the childish adult'. *The New York Times*, 7 July. www.nytimes.com/2003/07/07/opinion/harry-potter-and-the-childish-adult.html.
Carpenter, S. (2010). 'Young adult lit comes of age'. *Los Angeles Times*, 8 March. http://articles.latimes.com/2010/mar/08/entertainment/la-et-young-adult8-2010mar08.
Carvel, J. (2003). 'New bill will make teenage kisses illegal'. *The Guardian*, 11 July. www.guardian.co.uk/uk/2003/jul/11/ukcrime.childprotection.
Cole, B. (1995). *Mummy Laid an Egg!* London: Red Fox.
Cole, B. (2001). *Hair in Funny Places*. London: Red Fox.
Collins, S. (2008). *The Hunger Games*. London: Scholastic.
Cornwell, N. (2006). *Christophe's Story*, illus. K. Littlewood. London: Frances Lincoln.
Cross, G. (1997). *Kids' Stuff: Toys and the Changing World of American Childhood*. Cambridge, MA: Harvard University Press.
Cross, G. (2008). *Men to Boys: The Making of Modern Immaturity*. New York: Columbia University Press.
Danesi, M. (2003). *My Son Is an Alien: A Cultural Portrait of Today's Youth*. Lanham, MD and Oxford: Rowman & Littlefield .
Dingley, R. (1992). 'Meaning Everything: the Image of Pan at the Turn of the Century'. In K. Filmer (ed.), *Twentieth Century Fantasists: Essays on Culture, Society and Belief in Twentieth-Century Mythopoeic Literature*. London: Macmillan, pp. 47–59.
Downes, D. (2010). 'Harry Potter and the Deathly Hollowness: A Narratological and Ideological Critique of J. K. Rowling's Magical System'. *International Research in Children's Literature* 3(2): 162–75.
Durant, A. (2001). *Kicking Off*. London: Walker.
Eccleshare, J. (2002). *A Guide to the Harry Potter Novels*. London: Continuum.
Eccleshare, J. (2004). 'The Differences between Adult and Child Fiction'. In P. Pinsent (ed.), *Books and Boundaries: Writers and Their Audiences*. Lichfield: Pied Piper, pp. 213–15.
Elkind, D. (1981). *The Hurried Child: Growing Up Too Fast Too Soon*. Reading, MA: Addison-Wesley.
Falconer, R. (2009). *The Crossover Novel: Contemporary Children's Literature and Its Adult Readership*. New York: Routledge.
Fathallah, J. (2006). *Monkey Taming*. London: Random House.
Fine, A. (2003). 'Filth, which ever way you look at it'. *The Guardian*, 29 March. www.guardian.co.uk/books/2003/mar/29/featuresreviews.guardianreview24.
Fine, A. (2006). *The Road of Bones*. London and New York: Doubleday.
Fine, A. (2009). 'Children's books are too bleak'. *The Telegraph*, 25 August. www.telegraph.co.uk/culture/books/booknews/6085928/Childrens-books-are-too-bleak-says-Anne-Fine.html.

Freeman, C. (2007). *Aliens Love Underpants*, illus Ben Court. New York and London: Simon & Schuster.
Friend, N. (2004). *Perfect*. Minneapolis, MN: Milkweed.
Full Monty, The. (1997). Dir. P. Cattaneo. London: Channel 4 Films.
Gavin, J. (2000). *Coram Boy*. London: Egmont.
Giddens, A. (1998). *The Third Way: The Renewal of Social Democracy*. Cambridge: Polity Press.
Gill, T. (2007). *No Fear: Growing Up in a Risk Averse Society*. London: Calouste Gulbenkian.
Giroux, H. A. (2000). *Stealing Innocence: Youth, Corporate Power and the Politics of Culture*. Basingstoke: Palgrave Macmillan.
Gleitzman, M. (2009). *Then*. London: Penguin.
Goddard, J., McNamee, S., James, A. L. and James, A. (eds). (2004). *Politics of Childhood: International Perspectives, Contemporary Developments*. Basingstoke: Palgrave Macmillan.
Golding, W. (1954). *The Lord of the Flies*. London: Faber & Faber.
Göncü, A. (ed.). (1999). *Children's Engagement in the World: Sociocultural Perspectives*. Cambridge: Cambridge University Press.
Greenwall, B. (2004). 'The Curious Incidence of Novels about Asperger's Syndrome'. *Children's Literature in Education* 35(3): 271–84.
Griffiths, A. (2001). *The Day My Bum Went Psycho*. London: Pan.
Gupta, S. (2003). *Re-Reading Harry Potter*. Basingstoke: Palgrave Macmillan.
Gupta, S. (2009). *Re-Reading Harry Potter* (2nd edn). Basingstoke: Palgrave Macmillan.
Haddon, M. (2003). *The Curious Incident of the Dog in the Night-Time*. London: Jonathan Cape.
Heilman, E. E. (ed.). (2003). *Harry Potter's World: Multidisciplinary Critical Perspectives*. New York and London: RoutledgeFalmer.
Hengst, H. (2005). 'Complex Interconnections: The Global and the Local in Children's Minds and Everyday Worlds'. In J. Qvortrup (ed.), *Studies in Modern Childhood: Society, Agency, Culture*. Basingstoke: Palgrave Macmillan, pp. 21–38.
Hessell, J. (1987). *What's Wrong with Bottoms?* illus. M. Nelson. London: Hutchinson.
Hoestlandt, J. (2000). *Star of Fear, Star of Hope*, illus. J. Kang. London: Walker.
Holes. (2003). Dir. A. Davis. Burbank, CA: Walt Disney Pictures.
Holzwarth, W. and Erlbruch, W. (2001). *The Story of the Little Mole Who Knew It Was None of His Business*. London: Chrysalis.
Hutchby, I. and Moran-Ellis, J. (2001). *Children, Technology and Culture: The Impacts of Technologies in Children's Everyday Lives*. London: Routledge.
Jackson, L. (2002). *Freaks, Geeks and Asperger Syndrome: A User Guide to Adolescence*. London: Jessica Kingsley.
Johnston, T. (2004). *The Harmonica*, illus. R. Mazellan. Watertown, MA: Charlesbridge.
Kaslik, I. (2004). *Skinny*. London: HarperCollins.
Kay, E. (1900/1909). *The Century of the Child*. New York: Putnam's.
Kaysen, S. (2000). *Girl, Interrupted*. London: Virago.
Kennedy, M. (2012). 'Bad sex awards 2012 shortlist …'. *The Guardian*, 20 November. www.guardian.co.uk/books/2012/nov/20/bad-sex-award-2012-shortlist.
Kenrick, J. (2007). *Red Tears*. London: Faber & Faber.
Kenway, J. and Bullen, E. (2001). *Consuming Children: Education – Entertainment – Advertising*. Buckingham and Philadelphia: Open University Press.
Kerr, M. E. (1994). *Deliver Us from Evie*. New York: Harper.
Kertzer, A. (1999). '"Do You Know What 'Auschwitz' Means?" Children's Literature and the Holocaust'. *The Lion and the Unicorn* 23(2): 238–56.

Kinney, J. (2007). *Diary of a Wimpy Kid*. New York: Abrams.
Kleven, S. (1997). *The Right Touch: A Read-Aloud Story to Help Prevent Child Sexual Abuse*, illus. J. Bergsma. Bellevue, WA: Illumination Arts.
Knoepflmacher, U. C. and Myers, M. (eds). (1997). '"Cross-Writing" and the Reconceptualizing of Children's Literature Studies'. *Children's Literature* 25 (Special Issue).
Kristeva, J. (1984). *Revolution in Poetic Language*, trans. M. Waller. New York: Columbia University Press.
Kristeva, J. (1990). 'The Adolescent Novel'. In J. Fletcher and A. Benjamin (eds), *Abjection, Melancholia, and Love*. London: Routledge, pp. 8–23.
Kristeva, J. (1991). *Strangers to Ourselves*, trans. L. S. Roudiez. New York: Columbia University Press.
Lancey, D. (2008). *The Anthropology of Childhood: Cherubs, Chattels, Changelings*. Cambridge: Cambridge University Press.
Levine, J. (2002). *Harmful to Minors: The Perils of Protecting Children from Sex*. Minneapolis: University of Minnesota Press.
Levithan, D. (2003). *Boy Meets Boy*. New York: Knopf.
Loach, L. (2009). *The Devil's Children: A History of Childhood and Murder*. London: Icon.
Louv, R. (2010). *Last Child in the Woods: Saving our Children from Nature-Deficit Disorder*. London: Atlantic Books.
Males, M. (1996). *The Scapegoat Generation: America's War on Adolescents*. Monroe, ME: Common Courage Press.
Males, M. (1998). *Framing Youth: 10 Myths about the Next Generation*. Monroe, ME: Common Courage Press.
March, W. (1954). *The Bad Seed*. New York: Rinehart.
Meyer, S. (2012). *The Twilight Saga*. London: Little, Brown.
Morley, B. (2009). *The Silence Seeker*, illus. C. Pearce. London: Tamarind.
Myracle, L. (2005). *ttyl*. New York: Abrams.
Myracle, L. (2007). *ttfn*. New York: Abrams.
Na, A. (2008). *The Fold*. New York: Putnam's.
Nel, P. (2001). *J. K. Rowling's Harry Potter Novels*. London: Continuum.
Nicholson, W. (2009). *Rich and Mad*. London: Egmont.
O'Neill, J. (2001). *At Swim, Two Boys*. New York: Scribner.
Palmer, S. (2006). *Toxic Childhood: How the Modern World Is Damaging Our Children and What We Can Do About it*. London: Orion.
Paul, J. (2003). *When Kids Kill: Unthinkable Crimes of Lost Innocence*. London: Virgin.
Pauli, M. (2013). '"Sick-lit"? Evidently young adult fiction is too complex for the Daily Mail'. *The Guardian*, 4 January. www.guardian.co.uk/books/2013/jan/04/sick-lit-young-adult-fiction-mail.
Pearson, G. (1983). *Hooligan: A History of Respectable Fears*. Basingstoke: Palgrave Macmillan.
Peters, J. A. (2010). *By the Time You Read This, I'll Be Dead*. New York: Hyperion.
Philbrick, R. (2000). *The Last Book in the Universe*. New York: Scholastic.
Pilkey, D. (1997). *The Adventures of Captain Underpants*. New York and London: Scholastic.
Piper, H. and Stronach, I. (2008). *Don't Touch! The Educational Story of a Panic*. London: Routledge.
Postman, N. (1994). *The Disappearance of Childhood*. New York: Random House.
Pullman, P. (2007). *His Dark Materials*. New York and London: Random House.
Reeve, P. (2001). *Mortal Engines*. London: Scholastic.

Ridley, P. (1997). *Scribbleboy*. Harmondsworth: Penguin.
Rosen, L. D. (2008). *Me, Myspace and I: Parenting the Net Generation*. London: Palgrave Macmillan.
Rosoff, M. (2004). *How I Live Now*. London: Penguin.
Rowling, J. K. (1997). *Harry Potter and the Philosopher's Stone*. London: Bloomsbury.
Rowling, J. K. (2000). *Harry Potter and the Goblet of Fire*. London: Bloomsbury.
Russell, D. L. (1997). 'Reading the Shards and Fragments: Holocaust Literature for Young Readers'. *The Lion and the Unicorn* 21: 267–80.
Sachar, L. (1998). *Holes*. London: Bloomsbury.
Salinger, J. D. (1951). *The Catcher in the Rye*. New York: Little, Brown.
Sánchez, A. (2001). *Rainbow Boys*. New York: Simon & Schuster.
Saunders, K. (2004). 'What Disability Studies Can Do for Children's Literature'. Disability Studies Quarterly 24(1). http://dsq-sds.org/article/view/849/1024.
Seiter, E. (1993). *Sold Separately: Children and Parents in Consumer Culture*. New Brunswick: Rutgers University Press.
Seldon, A. and Baston, L. (1997). *Major: A Political Life*. London: Weidenfeld & Nicolson.
Shriver, L. (2003). *We Need to Talk About Kevin*. Berkeley, CA: Counterpoint.
Springhall, J. (1998). *Youth, Popular Culture and Moral Panics: Penny Gaffs to Gangsta-Rap, 1830–1996*. Basingstoke: Palgrave Macmillan.
Steinberg, S. R. and Kincheloe, J. L. (eds) (1997). *Kinder-Culture: The Corporate Construction of Childhood*. Boulder, CO: Westview Press.
Strasser, T. (2000). *Give a Boy a Gun*. New York: Simon & Schuster.
Talbot, B. (1995). *The Tale of One Bad Rat*. Milwaukie, OR: Dark Horse.
Waters, S. (1998). *Tipping the Velvet*. London: Virago.
Waters, S. (2002). *Fingersmith*. London: Virago.
Weber, S. and Dixon, S. (eds). (2007). *Growing Up Online: Young People and Digital Technologies*. Basingstoke: Palgrave Macmillan.
Westerfeld, S. (2005). *Uglies*. New York: Simon and Schuster.
Whited, L. A. (ed.). (2002). *The Ivory Tower and Harry Potter: Perspectives on a Literary Phenomenon*. Columbia and London: University of Missouri Press.
Wilson, J. (1991). *The Story of Tracy Beaker*. London: Doubleday.
Wilson, J. (1998). *Girls Under Pressure*. London: Corgi.
Winn, M. (1984). *Children without Childhood: Growing Up Too Fast in the World of Sex and Drugs*. Harmondsworth: Penguin.
Winterson, J. (1985). *Oranges Are Not the Only Fruit*. London: Pandora.
Zephaniah, B. (2001). *Refugee Boy*. London: Bloomsbury.
Zipes, J. (2000). *Sticks and Stones: The Troublesome Success of Children's Literature from Slovenly Peter to Harry Potter*. London and New York: Routledge.
Žižek, S. (1991). *Looking Awry: An Introduction to Jacques Lacan through Popular Culture*. Cambridge, MA: MIT Press.
Zusak, M. (2006). *The Book Thief*. London: Pan Macmillan.

8
Punishment, Populism and Performance Management
'New' Labour, Youth, Crime and Justice

Tim Newburn

Introduction

My chapter in *Thatcher's Children?*, the volume preceding this, charted the re-emergence of 'authoritarian populism' during the Major administration of the early 1990s. Despite their tough crime rhetoric, the Home Office during the preceding Thatcher administrations, principally under the stewardship of Douglas Hurd, had continued much of the penal-welfarist tradition of earlier periods, seeking to control the prison population and to place considerable emphasis on identifying sources of 'treatment' that would reduce or prevent crime. A sea change occurred from around 1993 when, challenged continuously and ferociously by his parliamentary shadow Tony Blair, the then Home Secretary Michael Howard took youth justice policy (indeed criminal justice policy generally) in a highly punitive direction. In this chapter I want to look at developments in youth justice since that period and, in particular, to examine the spectacular changes wrought by the 'New' Labour governments from 1997 onward. Although youth justice was one of 'New' Labour's more carefully thought-through policy domains, a decade and a half later it remains territory that is complex to characterise, and one in which an overall pattern is far from easy to discern. Through the establishment of the Youth Justice Board and the introduction of a raft of other reforms, 'New' Labour's 'new' youth justice became increasingly centralised and performance-managed.

Successive Labour home secretaries also continued with broadly populist and increasingly punitive stances in relation to much youthful criminality. From the abolition of *doli incapax*, through the substantial increase in the numbers of children incarcerated, to the net-widening consequences of the 'antisocial behaviour agenda', it is possible to see aspects of a new culture of control emerging in the decade from the mid-1990s. Yet, simultaneously, the largest experiment with restorative justice was also set in train by 'New' Labour, and recent years appear to have seen both a reduction in the number of 'first time entrants' to the youth justice system and declining numbers of juveniles in prison.

Populist punitiveness and the rise of managerialism

The early 1990s saw something of a sea change in the politics of juvenile justice. Well-publicised urban disturbances in 1991 (Campbell 1993) and an emergent moral panic about so-called 'persistent young offenders' (Hagell and Newburn 1994) played an important role, but the 'tipping point' was the murder of two-year-old James Bulger, following his abduction from a shopping centre in Bootle, Liverpool, and the subsequent arrest, prosecution and imprisonment of the two ten-year-old boys responsible. The tone of most of the press coverage – despite the age of the offenders – was unforgiving in its punitiveness (Franklin and Petley 1996) and ushered in a new political era of populism and punitiveness in relation to young offenders. At the forefront of this punitive turn was then Home Secretary, Michael Howard, who sought to capture the public mood with his promotion of the idea that 'prison works'. Whereas in previous eras such unabashed penal populism might have been expected to provoke some opposition, within parliament the quickly 'modernising' Labour Party was itself adopting a fairly radical 'tough on crime' stance. The predictable consequence was a series of government reforms, little resisted by the Opposition, leading inexorably to a swift and substantial rise in the use of youth custody.

The other major influence on mid-1990s youth justice was the Audit Commission. Initially established to promote economy, efficiency and effectiveness in public services, the Audit Commission's first target in the criminal justice field was policing. By the middle of the decade, however, it had turned its attention to the youth justice system and, in an enormously influential report published in 1996 (Audit Commission 1996), it described the youth justice system as uneconomic, inefficient and ineffective. It was critical of the cautioning system, especially 'repeat cautioning', and expressed dismay at what it saw as the absence of coordinated working within the youth justice system. Indeed, in its most damning indictment it suggested that 'overall, less is done now than a decade ago to address offending by young people. Fewer young people are now convicted by the courts, even allowing for the fall in the number of people aged 10–17 years, and an increasing proportion of those who are found guilty are discharged' (ibid.: para.69). The system, the Commission argued, needed to be streamlined, speeded up and greater attention given to early preventive work.

'New' Labour's 'new youth justice'

The Commission's analysis formed the basis for the Labour Party's core Home Affairs policy proposals as it planned for office in the lead-up to the 1997 General Election (Newburn 1998). Post-election, its flagship legislation in this field, the Crime and Disorder Act 1998, took a firmly managerialist approach to youth justice, emphasising inter-agency cooperation, the necessity of overall strategic planning, the creation of key performance indicators and active monitoring of aggregate information about the system and its functioning by the newly created Youth Justice Board (YJB). In addition to building on the managerialist initiatives introduced under the last Conservative administration, the new Labour government also initiated a series of reforms which introduced new penalties and earlier intervention and extended the reach of the state.

Within its restructured system of penalties, 'New' Labour promised increased, and earlier, interventions in the lives of young offenders and those 'at risk' of becoming young offenders. The Crime and Disorder Act scrapped the existing cautioning system, replacing it with a reprimand (for less serious offences) and a final warning – effectively a 'two strikes' system with less discretion and reduced opportunities for diverting young offenders from court. A further raft of changes increased the reach of the criminal justice system, and indeed that of the state more generally. One of the more controversial elements of the 1998 Act was the repeal of *doli incapax*, the rebuttable[1] common law presumption that young children (aged 10–13) are insufficiently mature to fully understand the consequences of their conduct and therefore should not be dealt with via the criminal justice system. The provision was removed on the grounds, as Home Secretary Jack Straw argued at the time, that the idea 'that children aged 10 to 13 do not know the difference between serious wrongdoing and simple naughtiness flies in the face of common-sense'. Thus, 30 years after the Children and Young Persons Act 1969 had provided for the minimum age of criminal responsibility to be raised to 14, 'New' Labour moved the system in the opposite direction.

In addition, 'New' Labour also began to develop a controversial menu of antisocial behaviour (ASB) initiatives which, initially in many parts of the country at least, sat outside the multi-agency YOT (Youth Offending Team) structures. In Opposition they had been much influenced by the Wilson and Kelling (1982) 'Broken Windows' thesis[2] and once in office began to introduce a range of measures where there was no necessity for there to be the commission of a criminal offence, thus enabling local agencies to tackle 'low-level disorder'. Most controversial was the antisocial behaviour order (ASBO), designed to combat behaviour 'likely to cause harassment, alarm or distress to one or more persons not of the same household'. ASBOs were civil orders lasting a minimum of two years, breach of which was a criminal offence carrying a maximum sentence, in the Crown Court, of five years. Although there was initial reluctance to use the orders, in 2003 the whole policy was given high-profile political impetus through the establishment of a unit within the Home Office (ASBU, later renamed the 'Respect' Unit) which encouraged use of the new powers, including those enabling courts to impose ASBOs post-conviction for a criminal offence (known colloquially as CRASBOs). The number of ASBOs imposed, including those on children, increased dramatically despite significant international and domestic criticism (European Commissioner for Human Rights 2005: paras 109–11; and see Millie et al. 2005; Simester and Von Hirsch 2006). The most serious concerns being expressed concerned the suggestion that the minimum order was often so long and the number of prohibitions imposed usually so excessive, that breach was made likely. Consequently, following breach, ASBOs were dragging into custody some young people who would not previously have got there or, possibly more commonly, were providing an evidential short cut for the police to fast track persistent young offenders into custody (Home Affairs Committee 2005).

Finally in this regard, 'New' Labour also extended the custodial plans set in train by their Conservative predecessors. The building programme for Secure Training Centres continued and a new, generic custodial sentence, the Detention and Training Order (DTO), was introduced. Lasting from 6 to 24 months, half the sentence being served in custody and half in the community, the DTO replaced the Secure Training Order (STO) (for 12–14 year olds) and detention in a Young Offender Institution (YOI) (for 15–17 year olds). After the Criminal Justice Act 2003 young offenders also became liable for indeterminate sentences for public protection (IPPs) and by the end of 2007, 51 boys under 18 were serving such sentences (HMI Prisons/HMI Probation 2008: para.6.3). The DTO represented an increase in the powers of the youth court to impose custodial sentences. The maximum period of detention in a YOI for 15- to 17-year-olds had been six months for a single offence: the DTO has a maximum of two years. Further, though the STO for 12- to 14-year-olds already provided for a two-year maximum, 'New' Labour replaced the strict criteria for offenders under 15 relating to 'persistence' with the provision that the sentence be available where the court 'is of the *opinion* that he is a persistent offender' (emphasis added). The courts, including the Court of Appeal, interpreted this power rather broadly.

Two key planks of 'New' Labour's 'new youth justice', therefore, were managerialism, on the one hand, and a broadly populist retributivism, on the other. This is not the whole picture, however, for they also sought to expand – very significantly – the scope for reparative and restorative justice. Following the Youth Justice and Criminal Evidence Act 1999, a new primary sentencing disposal was introduced in England and Wales – the referral order. It is a mandatory sentence, of between 3 and 12 months, for 10- to 17-year-olds pleading guilty and convicted for the first time by the youth court; unless the crime is serious enough to warrant custody or the court orders an absolute discharge, the disposal involves referring the young offender to a youth offender panel (YOP). Drawing on the Scottish hearings system, family group conferencing and victim offender mediation, panels are to comprise local community volunteers as well as a professional youth justice worker, and are attended by the parents of the offender as well as, in principle, the victim and their supporters. The intention is that the panel will provide a forum away from the formality of the court. The aim is that the panel devise a 'contract' and, where the victim chooses to attend, for them to meet and talk about the offence with the offender. It is intended that negotiations between the panel and the offender about the content of the contract should be led by the community panel members. The contract should always include reparation to the victim or wider community and a programme of activity designed primarily to prevent further offending.

Trends in youth crime and youth justice

Trends in youth crime are difficult to assess. Neither of our two major crime measures – police-recorded crime statistics and the Crime Survey for England and Wales – is especially helpful in identifying the age of the perpetrator. Both sources, however, suggest that crime overall has been in decline since the mid-1990s. The nature and extent of this fall remains contested but on the surface it seems likely that there has been some diminution overall in youth crime in recent years. Although influenced by many factors, some support for this conclusion is found in the declining number of 'proven offences' (offences resulting in a reprimand, final warning or conviction) by young people – which declined by almost half between 2001/2 and 2011/12 (see Figure 8.1). The most significant falls were in relation to the less serious offences – motoring offences and criminal damage – with much smaller falls in relation to the more serious offences such as those involving drugs and violence, and robbery the only major category increasing.

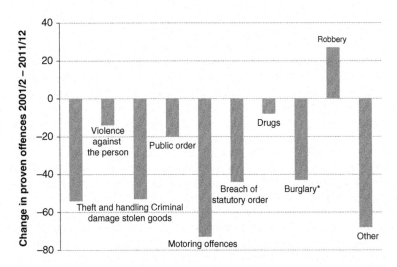

Figure 8.1 Reduction in proven offences by young people, 2001/2 to 2011/12 (subject to Crown copyright)
Source: Ministry of Justice (2013b) (supplementary tables).

'New' Labour, Youth, Crime and Justice   145

Notwithstanding what appear to be declining youth crime levels, there are good reasons for believing that in the last decade and a half (and likely longer) the number of young people dealt with by the youth justice system has actually had more to do with political and managerial initiatives affecting how the system reacts to children and young people than it has crime trends. Figure 8.2 shows the number of first-time entrants – those not previously in receipt of a reprimand or final warning, nor convicted in court – into the youth justice system over the past decade.

Leaving aside those subject to reprimand or warning, in terms of formal court-based sentencing the big change since the turn of the century, as Table 8.1 illustrates, has been the significant decline in the use of discharges and fines and their displacement by the referral order, potentially the jewel in the crown of 'New' Labour's youth justice reforms.

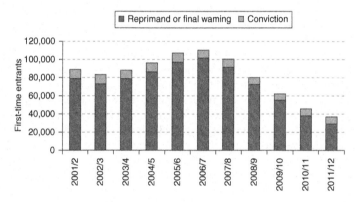

Figure 8.2 First-time entrants into the youth justice system, 2001/2 to 2011/12 (subject to Crown copyright)
Source: Ministry of Justice (2013b).

Table 8.1 Young people sentenced for all offences, by type of sentence, 2001/2 to 2010/11 (%)

	2001/2	2002/3	2003/4	2004/5	2005/6	2006/7	2007/8	2008/9	2009/10	2010/11
Discharge	18	15	15	13	13	13	13	12	12	13
Fine	23	16	15	16	15	12	11	10	10	8
Referral order	2	20	27	27	31	32	33	33	35	34
Community sentence	43	37	32	32	32	33	35	35	34	31
Custody	8	8	7	6	6	6	6	6	6	6
Other	6	4	4	5	3	3	3	3	3	4
TOTAL SENTENCED	94,870	93,436	94,533	94,623	96,539	94,583	95,328	86,818	78,561	72,039

Source: Ministry of Justice (2013b) (supplementary tables).

However, the referral order has to date not fulfilled its restorative justice potential. As early assessments and later YJB monitoring data attest, a very small proportion of referral orders result in the active participation of victims and there are big variations in the proportion who do from one YOT to another (Crawford and Newburn 2003; Morgan and Newburn 2007). There is now a case for many offenders being dealt with not post-prosecution and conviction by YOPs, but by out-of-court panels, along the lines of Scottish hearings or restorative justice conferences similar to those in use in Northern Ireland. This case rests on the grounds that there is overwhelming evidence that restorative justice conferences in which victims participate result in greater victim satisfaction and that frequency of reoffending is reduced (Shapland et al. 2008). The most controversial sanction available for children, however, is of course custody. Although the use of youth custody had fallen both proportionately and absolutely by the end of 'New' Labour's third administration (Figure 8.3), it was nevertheless substantially higher in 2010 than had been the case in the early 1990s and it also remained the highest in Western Europe.

Declining youth custody rates in recent years have occurred despite the continuing rise in the adult prison population and the continuing use of the language of 'punishment' and 'enforcement' rather than 'welfare' (Graham 2010). Behind the scenes a number of fairly successful initiatives aiming at penal restriction have been taken, with penal and children's pressure groups publishing highly critical reports on the high use of custody for very young children who have not committed grave crimes (Glover and Hibbert 2009); for children on remand (Gibbs and Hickson 2009); who have learning difficulties (Talbot 2010); or have multiple disadvantages (Jacobson et al. 2010).

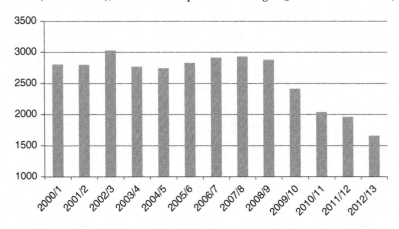

Figure 8.3 Average custodial population (under 18), 2000/1 to 2012/13 (subject to Crown copyright)
Source: Ministry of Justice (2013b) (supplementary tables).

These followed reports on the high reliance on physical restraint within custodial institutions (Carlile Report 2006) and the repeated deaths of children in custody (Goldson and Coles 2005). The welter of criticism and the overall shrinkage in the number of children being drawn into the youth justice system generally (see Allen 2011), have led to a dramatic fall in custody rates in some localities, and have also contributed to the significant fall nationally.

How are we to understand the spike in criminal sanctioning around 2006/7, and the general decline since that point? What has been happening? In part, and this claim has certainly been made by the Youth Justice Board (YJB), the increased expenditure and effort put into early interventions would appear to be having some impact on youthful offending (though reoffending rates continue to be stubbornly high; Ministry of Justice 2013a). The YJB pointed to the impact of Youth Inclusion Programmes and others (YISPS, parenting programmes and SSPs) and suggested collectively they had prevented over 20,000 young people entering the criminal justice system in a single year alone (2008/9, as claimed in the YJB Press Statement of 26 November 2009). There is every indication that this is likely a considerable exaggeration and, at best, the conclusion would be that it remains unclear to what degree the drop in the number of first-time entrants is a consequence of targeted early interventions with children at risk delivered through YOTs (cf. Mackie et al. 2008).

Notwithstanding the potential impact of such interventions, in fact, what these statistical trends really reveal is an interesting story about out-of-court penalties and the impact of target setting on the behaviour of public bodies. In short, the expansion in the sanctioning of young people in the early 2000s, followed by the steep decline in recent years, is almost wholly the result of the government setting national targets for what it referred to as 'offences brought to justice' (OBTJs). Labour administrations became increasingly preoccupied with what they saw as a growing 'attrition rate' in the criminal justice system whereby a decreasing proportion of crimes committed ended with formal sanctioning. The OBTJ targets were designed to reverse this process by requiring criminal justice agencies, and the police in particular, successfully to increase the number of offenders being sanctioned each year. The key to so doing was the newly introduced out-of-court penalties that were available from 2004 onward.

In effect, perverse incentives were introduced which led to considerably increased action in relation to relatively minor offences, primarily via the imposition of ASBOs, penalty notices for disorder (PNDs) and reprimands and final warnings. The spike in overall numbers sanctioned from 2004 to 2007 was attributable almost entirely to the introduction in 2003 of such penalty notices (in effect, on-the-spot fines) for 16- to 17-year-olds combined with increased use of the traditional out-of-court sanctions – reprimands, final warnings and conditional cautions – over the past decade.

Similarly, the decline that has occurred in the formal sanctioning of children and young people since 2007/8 is partly a result of the drop-off in the use of ASBOs, but is more particularly a consequence of the declining use of reprimands and final warnings, and also the falling use of PNDs.

Of all the 'New' Labour initiatives in the justice field, probably the best known – at least for a period – was the ASBO. When first introduced there was considerable reluctance in most parts of the country to seek ASBOs. But the Prime Minister, Tony Blair, and successive home secretaries, were not to be deflected and repeatedly kick-started the ASB initiative with major speeches, and in 2003, a unit (the ASBU) was created within the Home Office to promote local activism. Further legislation (the Criminal Justice and Court Services Act 2000, the Criminal Justice and Police Act 2001,the Police Reform Act 2002 and, in particular, the Anti-Social Behaviour Act 2003) added a raft of additional powers which the courts, police and local authorities were encouraged vigorously to use. To a degree, all this promotional activity was successful, for the number of ASBOs rose markedly and the term 'ASBO' became part of the everyday lexicon. Nevertheless, from 2005/6 the use of the order started to decline quite dramatically (Figure 8.4).

Indeed, around this time it became increasingly clear that the ASBO was by no means uniformly popular with Labour ministers: in 2007, for example, Secretary of State for Children, Schools and Families Ed Balls observed that, "It's a failure every time a young person gets an ASBO. It's necessary – but it's not right ... I want to live in the kind of society that puts ASBOs behind us."[3] It was the arrival of the Coalition government in 2010 that appeared to signal the beginning of the end for the ASBO.

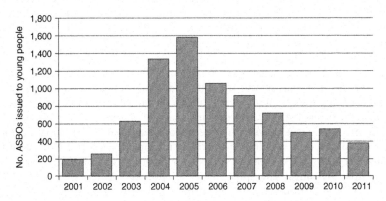

Figure 8.4 Trends in the use of ASBOs for young people, 2001–11 (subject to Crown copyright)
Source: Ministry of Justice (2013b).

Theresa May, the Home Secretary in the new government, outlined a change of direction:

> Labour introduced a ludicrous list of powers for tackling anti-social behaviour – the ISO, the ASBI, the ASBO and the CRASBO. Crack house closure orders; dog control orders; graffiti removal orders, litter and noise abatement orders, housing injunctions and parenting orders. (And that's not even all of them!) These sanctions were too complex and bureaucratic – there were too many of them, they were too time consuming and expensive and they too often criminalised young people unnecessarily, acting as a conveyor belt to serious crime and prison ... [The latest] ASBO statistics have shown that breach rates have yet again increased – more than half are breached at least once, 40% are breached more than once and their use has fallen yet again, to the lowest ever level. It's time to move beyond the ASBO.

The decline of the ASBO is only part of the picture of a marked shift away from the use of out-of-court sanctions. A similar trend can be found in relation to the use of reprimands, final warnings and conditional cautions (the latter were introduced in 2009), which have decreased by 18 per cent since 2010/11 and by 69 per cent since 2006/7 (see Figure 8.5) and PNDs (Figure 8.6).

The heavy use of out-of-court sanctions by the police to meet their OBTJ targets was both acknowledged and criticised by Sir Ronnie Flanagan, the then Chief Inspector of Policing, in his major review of policing in 2008. The OBTJ target, he said, had 'the unintended effect of officers spending

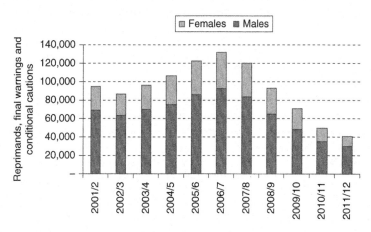

Figure 8.5 Trends in reprimands, final warnings and conditional cautions (subject to Crown copyright)
Source: Ministry of Justice (2013b).

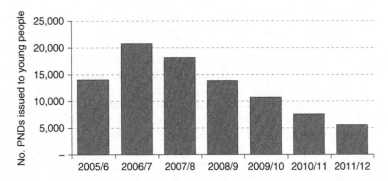

Figure 8.6 Trends in penalty notices for disorder (PNDs) for young people, 2005/6 to 2011/12 (subject to Crown copyright)
Source: Ministry of Justice (2013b).

time investigating crimes with a view to obtaining a detection, even when that is clearly not in the public interest. An example of such would be a low level playground common assault' (Flanagan Report 2008: 10). What Flanagan identified was that government targets pushed the police in particular towards minor offences committed by children and young persons – the so-called 'low hanging fruit'. Use of PNDs, reprimands and final warnings had risen most steeply in relation to juveniles, particularly children under 14 years, and when in 2007 the OBTJ target was modified so as to focus now on 'serious, violent, sexual and acquisitive offences', and was finally abandoned altogether in 2010 by the incoming Coalition government, the fall was steepest for juveniles (see Farrington-Douglas and Durante 2009: 12–14): the police no longer got Brownie points for recording minor youth offences and criminalising youth. Given that the best research evidence suggests that, all other things being equal, criminalising children is criminogenic – that is, the likelihood of reoffending is increased rather than diminished (see McAra and McVie 2007) – it seems probable that 'New' Labour's managerialist, target-driven policing policies in the first decade of the twenty-first century exacerbated the problem of youth crime and has left a legacy of adult, career criminality which could have been avoided (Morgan and Newburn 2012).

The positive element of this story, therefore, is that after many years in which the number of young people being sanctioned – by courts or through other means – increased, the last few years have seen a significant change of direction. The numbers entering the system are declining and, at its apex, the numbers in custody are also falling. Further, there seems to have been something of a rethink in relation to out-of-court disposals. The vast increase in PNDs and the like has also been stemmed, and the unintended consequences of the privileging of the OBTJ targets have now also been largely mitigated. And, yet, there remain very good reasons to avoid complacency in this field. It remains the case, for example, that the number of children and young people sentenced to custody is still significantly higher than it was in the mid-1990s when overall crime levels peaked. Furthermore, custodial sentences given to young offenders also tend to be longer than was the case 20 years ago. Finally, rates of imprisonment remain considerably higher than is the case in neighbouring European countries such Germany and France. 'New' Labour's 'new' youth justice was in part, therefore, the child of post-Thatcher Conservatism (as practised by Michael Howard). 'New' Labour never threw off the populist punitivism it constructed for itself whilst in opposition between 1993 and 1997, Howard's time as Home Secretary. For all the talk of 'tough on crime, tough on the causes of crime',[4] the second part of the mantra never came to rival in emphasis the prominence of the first.

Young people and policing

In 2010 an independent commission on youth crime and justice published the results of a two-year inquiry into youth justice, under the title *Time for a Fresh Start* (Independent Commission 2010). The Commission was particularly critical of what it saw as the 'continuing and deep rooted failings' (ibid.: 17) of the youth justice system. More particularly, it accused politicians of ignoring the evidence (on the balance of probabilities) that offending had declined in both frequency and seriousness in the previous decade, and suggested that the current approach lacked coherence, largely as a result of what it described as 'an inflated political arms race' in policy making (ibid.: 5). Moreover, and rightly, it went on to observe that: 'The youth justice system tends to target and recycle "the usual suspects" again and again, especially young people from deprived neighbourhoods and certain black and minority ethnic groups ... children and young people from black and mixed heritage backgrounds are disproportionately stopped and searched, arrested, prosecuted and sentenced to custody' (ibid.: 25; and see Feilzer and Hood 2005).

Given this emphasis, it was somewhat surprising therefore to find that the Commission appeared to have paid relatively little attention to the policing of young people, and the implications of such interactions for the operation of the criminal justice system. We know that contact with the police is a far from unusual occurrence for certain categories of young people (McAra and McVie 2005). Indeed, research suggests that young working-class males, especially from ethnic minorities, who have an active 'street life' – or who exhibit what in some contexts has simply been termed 'availability' (MVA and Miller 2000) – are particularly likely to experience 'adversarial' contact with the police (Aye Maung 1995; Flood-Page et al. 2000). Confirming the Independent Commission's observation above, McAra and McVie's

(2005) Edinburgh-based research offers concrete evidence that the police disproportionately target the 'usual suspects'. Whilst they are in the first instance 'suspects' because of their behaviour (including often the volume and seriousness of their alleged offending), 'once identified as a troublemaker, this *status* appears to suck young people into a spiral of amplified contact, *regardless* of whether they continue to be involved in serious levels of offending' (2005: 9). Their conclusion from the analysis of police–youth interaction suggests that although the police in some respects adhere to the aim of avoiding the criminalisation of young people, an unintended outcome of police discretion is the creation of a stigmatised 'permanent suspect population' (2005: 27) of young people. Similar patterns can be seen in relation to the contested territory of 'stop and search' – an area of police activity which has substantially expanded in the quarter-century since the passage of the Police and Criminal Evidence Act 1984 (PACE).

So, what does the future hold? Can we expect the use of out-of-court disposals to continue to decline? It is possible, but there are significant challenges. The Coalition government is piloting the new 'community trigger' – where local agencies will be compelled to take action if several people in the same neighbourhood have complained and no action has been taken; or the behaviour in question has been reported to the authorities by an individual three times and no action has been taken (Home Office 2011). On the one hand, this might be viewed as a welcome democratic shift but, on the other, it might also be seen as a reform which carries the potential for ever-greater intervention in the lives of young people. The results from the initial pilots are at best inconclusive (Home Office 2013).

The broader context is one, of course, of financial austerity and public service cuts, including to policing. How this will play out will undoubtedly be affected by the very significant changes to police governance included in the Police Reform and Social Responsibility Act 2011. The introduction of directly elected Police and Crime Commissioners (PCCs) to replace police authorities changes the policing landscape markedly, and has the potential (though this is only *potential* at the moment) to stimulate further, localised 'penal populism'. The entry of PCCs into the politics of local policing could easily lead to increased pressure on the police to make greater rather than reduced use of their powers to criminalise youth. These pressures may be particularly acute in urban areas where youth gang-related offences are most troubling and which attract substantial mass media attention. This is speculative, of course. However, on the assumption that the emergence of these new political contests has at least the potential to lead to calls for greater use of formal police powers in respect of youth crime and antisocial behaviour, it reinforces the need to think carefully now about the principles upon which we would wish police activity in this area to be governed and, if necessary, restricted.

The police are the gatekeepers to the criminal justice system and, as such, play a significant role – as illustrated above – in determining which, and how many, young people end up before the courts or being otherwise dealt with. But there is another element to the story of young people and policing – one that lies outside of formal sanctioning – that also needs to be borne in mind. It is one perhaps best illustrated by aspects of the England riots of 2011. Played out over four days and nights, the disturbances, which were particularly evident in London, Birmingham, Manchester, Salford and Liverpool, illustrated the depth of the hostility and distrust that continues to exist between a section of our young people and the police. Sparked by the shooting of a young black man – Mark Duggan – by the police in north London, the initial disturbances occurred in the north London district of Tottenham but in the following days spread across the capital city and beyond. Lives were lost, tens of millions of pounds of destruction caused, and thousands eventually prosecuted and punished.

What brought thousands of young people onto the streets in August 2011? Perhaps predictably, the answer is complex. Despite the usual descriptions of 'mindless' activity, and 'copycat' or opportunistic behaviour stripped of political meaning, many young people talked about a pervasive sense of 'injustice'. This was both economic – the lack of jobs, money, opportunity – and social – how they felt they were treated. In the *Guardian*/LSE *Reading the Riots* study (*Guardian*/LSE 2011), we described the rioters as 'a group that felt dislocated from the opportunities they saw available to others'. Alongside this, it was impossible to watch the scenes from parts of London and other English cities in August 2011 and not be struck by the opportunistic greed on display. 'Shopping for free', or 'like a normal shopping day ... but with no staff in the shop', as one 18-year-old put it, was an exciting possibility raised for many when the rule of law appeared briefly to have been suspended. Some of the rioters talked about getting their 'just rewards', seeing the goods they looted as payback to a consumerist world from which they were excluded. Indeed, in many respects it was the scale and centrality of the looting that occurred in August 2011 that distinguished those riots most obviously from the disorders that had occurred in previous decades. As such, the riots arguably also illustrated another uncomfortable fact about contemporary England: that individualistic greed was now a more prominent part of its culture than it had ever previously been.

What emerged most strongly from the initial phase of *Reading the Riots*, in which large numbers of rioters were interviewed, however, was a longstanding frustration – indeed anger – with the police. Of all those interviewed, well over four-fifths said policing was an 'important' or 'very important' factor in the riots. Across the cities in which the research was conducted, rioters talked about their antagonistic relations with the police. Their accounts varied in intensity – from descriptions of poor relations and negative experiences on the one hand to a violent, almost visceral hatred of the police on the other. In some ways it should come as little surprise that the police were the focus of such negative emotions. In part they were no doubt the straightforward product of the role the police had to play in responding to the riots. In addition, the simple fact that the police are the most visible manifestation of the state leads to them becoming a 'condensation symbol' (Edelman 1977) for broader grievances and concerns and makes them a predictable and easy target. And, yet, it was also clear that the emotions and attitudes expressed by the rioters went beyond this.

Some respondents' problems with the police were longstanding. For others, the experiences were more recent and often stemmed from personal experience of alleged poor treatment. Some rioters' accounts concerned overt police violence but, more regularly, the complaints focused on perceived disrespect, impoliteness and the unfair or illegitimate use of police power. In the latter regard, the use of the power to stop and search was very much the symbolic heart of the complaints. There is considerable evidence that police use of stop and search, under PACE 1984 and other legislation, has been on the increase in the last decade or more (see Figure 8.7).

So far as the rioters were concerned, there were three main issues raised in relation to stop and search: that it was conducted unreasonably, unfairly or with prejudice; that it occurred so frequently as to amount to harassment; and that the conduct of individual stops involved rudeness, aggression and occasionally violence. Academic discussions of stop and search focus primarily on issues of disproportionality (Miller 2010), and in interview black respondents brought up stop and search far more often than their white counterparts. In particular, they described feeling stereotyped by the police and many attributed their regular experiences of stop and search to their ethnicity. Indeed, the implication that prejudice was deeply inscribed in police practice was articulated even by those who had had little direct experience of stop and search. Both the excessive use of the power to stop and search, and an arrogance or aggression which was described as often accompanying such encounters, led to a significant level of disenchantment.

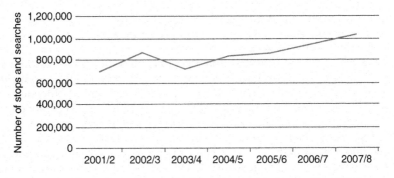

Figure 8.7 Stops and searches under PACE 1984 and other legislation, 2001–8
Source: Equality and Human Rights Commission (2010).

At best, many of the young people that were involved in the riots saw the police as an organisation that simply interfered in their lives and regularly antagonised them. At worst, such was the level of hostility that the police became the focus of a deeply visceral anger. There is now a considerable body of literature illustrating that the degree to which the police exercise their power in ways that are viewed as impartial, fair and respectful has significant implications for their legitimacy (Jackson et al. 2012). What the riots at least potentially illustrate is that for a significant section of our urban youth, their everyday experiences and treatment at the hands of the police serve to reinforce their already existing sense of alienation and marginalisation – feelings arising from the fragile socioeconomic position they occupy in contemporary Britain. Whilst the operation of the youth justice system, and the numbers of young people being criminalised and sanctioned, are important considerations therefore, they are only part of the picture that should concern us. Beyond that, the deeply problematic relationships that many young people – black and white – have with the police is something which should be of considerable concern and ongoing scrutiny.

A final comment

Clearly, youth justice in the last two decades has been subject to very considerable change – and reform that has come from a number of different directions. 'New' Labour's initial foray, primarily via the 1998 Crime and Disorder Act, cemented its promise to be 'tough on crime'. It was also deeply managerialist in approach, rapidly expanding central state oversight and control of local youth justice activity. Additionally, 'New' Labour's interpretation of its 'tough on the causes of crime' part of the brief centred on significantly enhanced early intervention in the lives of young offenders, and those 'at risk', and also saw the emergence of a range of orders focused not just on offenders, but also on their parents; and, most radically of all, it also increasingly focused attention on relatively low-level, sub-criminal activities – generally referred to as antisocial behaviour (ASB). It also subsequently, via other legislation, sought to add a major experiment in restorative justice to the many reforms underway.

One consequence of Labour's obsession with ASB, and with performance measurement, was a very considerable spike in the numbers of young people being drawn into the criminal justice system and, subsequently, sanctioned. Recent years have seen something of a reverse, with fewer first-time entrants to the youth justice system, all the way through to declining numbers incarcerated. Indeed, there's even been something of a shift away from ASBOs and PNDs. While these recent changes are to be welcomed, they must be put in context and set against the very considerable net widening and mesh thinning that the whole ASB movement helped to foster. The numbers entering the system, and entering prison, may be in decline, but they remain higher than was the case a decade or so ago.

Then there is the issue of the more general treatment and position of young people. Many of those involved in the 2011 riots targeted their anger and violence towards the police, and some at least argued that this was 'payback' for the mistreatment they felt they had regularly received. The riots also illustrated the perilous position many young people now occupy in modern Britain. In the immediate aftermath, the then Justice Secretary Ken Clarke said that what most disturbed him about the riots 'was the sense that the hardcore of rioters came from a *feral underclass*' (Clarke 2011, emphasis added). By combining Charles Murray's 'underclass' terminology' (Murray 1984) with the imagery of wild animals on the loose, Clarke's implication was that we have among us a class of people who are subject to far too little control, who assume that it is their right to be idle and not work, and who are generally nasty and brutish. This, the phrase implied, was all we needed to know or to understand.

Yet within a short period of time, government data were painting a rather different – or at least more nuanced – picture. Ministry of Justice research, which combined court data with information from the Department for Work and Pensions and the Department for Education, revealed a pattern of considerable social deprivation. More than one in three adults that were prosecuted (35 per cent) were claiming out-of-work benefits compared with fewer than one in eight of the working-age population in general. Forty-two per cent of young people were in receipt of free school meals compared with 16 per cent of all pupils in maintained secondary schools. Finally, young people appearing before the courts were significantly more likely to come from areas of high deprivation – with almost two thirds coming from one of the 20 per cent most deprived areas. Most significantly perhaps, two thirds of the juveniles were found to be classified as having some form of special educational need compared with one fifth of secondary school pupils more generally, and the educational achievement levels at Key Stage 2 (the end of primary education) of those arrested in the riots was very significantly below that of the population generally. Indeed, only approximately half of the young people appearing in court had reached the expected level in English or Maths compared with over three quarters of the population generally.

Understood in the context of social deprivation, or what in recent years might have been referred to as social exclusion, these data don't look all that extraordinary. There is now considerable social research, including government research, which shows how truancy and exclusion from school, and low educational attainment, are both strongly identified as 'risk factors' in relation to involvement in crime (see, for example, Department for Education 2012). Add into that mix living in a socially deprived neighbourhood, and the young people who feature in the statistical releases on riot-related arrests and prosecutions look rather like we might expect them to – a group, as Ken Clarke put it, 'cut off from the mainstream'. The last 20 years have seen political interest in tackling social exclusion grow and subsequently very substantially ebb. So far as the riots were concerned, by and large our political leaders were unwilling to enter into any full-scale discussion of such matters and preferred to retreat into well-worn political rhetoric about individual personal responsibility and moral inadequacy. Yes, many young people did set out to steal, inflict damage or engage in dreadful acts of violence during the riots. They did so often with the feeling, in their own words, that they had 'nothing to lose'. For all the social reforms since the early 1990s, including those to youth justice, too many of our young people feel that they have an insufficient stake in the future, and precious few legitimate opportunities to play a full part in the society they see all around them. To that extent they are very much the children (or possibly grandchildren) of the new right philosophies that have held sway since the 1980s.

Notes

1. Legally, a rebuttable assumption is one made by a court that is taken to be true unless someone successfully contests it.
2. The thesis is that maintaining and monitoring urban environments in good order may stop further disorder and prevent the escalation of criminality.
3. Quoted in www.guardian.co.uk/politics/2007/jul/28/ukcrime.immigrationpolicy (accessed 17 June 2013).
4. A widely invoked phrase taken from a radio broadcast by then shadow Home Secretary, Tony Blair, in 1993. According to Blair's biographer, the phrase was actually Gordon Brown's (Rentoul 1995).

References

Allen, R. (2011). *Last Resort: Exploring the Reduction in Child Imprisonment 2008–2011*. London: Prison Reform Trust.

Audit Commission. (1996). *Misspent Youth: Young People and Crime*. London: Audit Commission.

Aye Maung, N. (1995). *Young People, Victimisation and the Police: British Crime Survey Findings on the Experiences and Attitudes of 12–15 Year Olds*. London: Home Office.

Campbell, B. (1993). *Goliath: Britain's Dangerous Places*. London: Methuen.

Carlile, Lord, of Berriew QC (2006). *An Independent Inquiry into the Use of Physical Restraint, Solitary Confinement and Forcible Strip Searching of Children in Prisons, Secure Training Centres and Local Authority Secure Children's Homes*. London: Howard League for Penal Reform.

Clarke, K. (2011). 'Punish the feral rioters but address our social deficit too'. *The Guardian*, 5 September.

Crawford, A. and Newburn, T. (2003). *Youth Offending and Restorative Justice: Implementing Reform in Youth Justice*. Cullompton: Willan.

Department for Education. (2012). *A Profile of Pupil Exclusions in England*. London: Department for Education.

Edelman, M. (1977). *Political Language*. New York: Academic Press.

Equality and Human Rights Commission. (2010). *Stop and Think: A Review of Stop and Search Powers in England and Wales*. London: EHRC.

European Commissioner for Human Rights. (2005). *Report by Mr Alvaro Gil-Robles, Commissioner for Human Rights, on His Visit to the United Kingdom 4–12 November (2004*. Strasbourg: Council of Europe.

Farrington-Douglas, J. and Durante, L. (2009). *Towards a Popular Preventative Youth Justice System*. London: IPPR.

Feilzer, M. and Hood, R. (2005). *Differences or Discrimination: Minority Ethnic Young People in the Youth Justice System*. London: Youth Justice Board.

Flanagan Report. (2008). *The Review of Policing by Sir Ronnie Flanagan: Final Report*. London: HMIC.

Flood-Page, C., Campbell, S., Harrington, V. and Miller, J. (2000). Youth Crime: Findings from the 11998/99 Youth Lifestyles Survey. London: Home Office.

Franklin, B. and Petley, J. (1996). 'Killing the Age of Innocence: Newspaper Reporting of the Death of James Bulger'. In J. Pilcher and S. Wagg (eds), *Thatcher's Children? Politics, Childhood and Society in the 1980s and 1990s*. London: Falmer Press.

Gibbs, P. and Hickson, S. (2009). *Children: Innocent until Proven Guilty. A Report on the Overuse of Remand for Children in England and Wales and How It Can Be Addressed*. London: Prison Reform Trust.

Glover, J. and Hibbert, P. (2009). *Locking Up or Giving Up? Why Custody Thresholds for Teenagers Aged 12, 13 and 14 Needs to be Raised*. London: Barnardo's.

Goldson, B. and Coles, D. (2005). *In the Care of the State? Child Deaths in Penal Custody in England and Wales*. London: Inquest.

Graham, J. (2010). 'Responding to Youth Crime'. In D. J. Smith (ed.), *A New Response to Youth Crime*, Cullompton: Willan.

Guardian/LSE. (2011). *Reading the Riots: Investigating England's Summer of Disorder*. London: *Guardian*/LSE.

Hagell, A. and Newburn, T. (1994). *Persistent Young Offenders*. London: Policy Studies Institute.

HMI Prisons/HMI Probation. (2008). *The Indeterminate Sentence for Public Protection: A Thematic Review*: London: HMI Prisons/HMI Probation.

Home Affairs Committee. (2005). *Anti-Social Behaviour*. Fifth Report. London: HMSO.

Home Office (2011). *More Effective Responses to Anti-Social Behaviour*. London: Home Office.

Home Office. (2013). *Empowering Communities, Protecting Victims: Summary Report on the Community Trigger Trials*. London: Home Office.

Independent Commission. (2010). *Time for a Fresh Start: The Report of the Independent Commission on Youth Crime and Antisocial Behaviour*. London: Police Foundation/ Nuffield Foundation.

Jackson, J., Bradford, B., Stanko, E. A. and Hohl, K. (2012). *Just Authority? Trust in the Police in England and Wales*. Oxford: Routledge.

Jacobson, J., Bhardwa, B., Gyateng, T., Hunter, G. and Hough, M. (2010). Punishing Disadvantage: A Profile of Children in Custody. London: Prison Reform Trust.

Mackie, A., Hubbard, R. and Burrows, J. (2008). *Evaluation of the Youth Inclusion Programme*. London: Morgan Harris Burrows/YJB.

McAra, L. and McVie, S. (2005). 'The Usual Suspects? Street-life, Young People and the Police'. *Criminology and Criminal Justice* 5(1): 5–36.

McAra, L. and McVie, S. (2007). 'Youth Justice? The Impact of System Contact on Patterns of Desistance from Offending'. *European Journal of Criminology* 4(3): 315–45.

Miller, J. (2010). 'Stop and Search in England: A Reformed Tactic or Business as Usual?' *British Journal of Criminology* 50(5): 954–74.

Millie, A., Jacobson, J., McDonald, E., and Hough, M. (2005). *Anti-social Behaviour Strategies: Finding a Balance*. Bristol: Policy Press and Joseph Rowntree Foundation.

Ministry of Justice. (2013a). *Proven Reoffending Statistics Quarterly Bulletin*. London: Ministry of Justice.

Ministry of Justice. (2013b). *Youth Justice Statistics* (and supplementary tables). London: Ministry of Justice.

Morgan, R. and Newburn, T. (2007). 'Youth Justice'. In M. Maguire, R. Morgan and R. Reiner (eds), *The Oxford Handbook of Criminology*. Oxford: Oxford University Press.

Morgan, R. and Newburn, T. (2012). 'Youth Crime and Justice: Rediscovering Devolution, Discretion, and Diversion?' In M. Maguire, R. Morgan and R. Reiner (eds), *Oxford Handbook of Criminology* (5th edn). Oxford: Oxford University Press.

Murray, C. (1984). *Losing Ground: American Social Policy 1950–1980*. New York: Basic Books.

MVA and Miller, J. (2000). *Profiling Populations Available for Stops and Searches*. Home Office Policing and Reducing Crime Unit, Police Research Series Papers No 131. London: Home Office.

Newburn, T. (1998). 'Tackling Youth Crime and Reforming Youth Justice: The Origins and Nature of New Labour Policy'. *Policy Studies* 19(3–4): 199–212.

Rentoul, J. (1995). *Tony Blair*. London: Little, Brown.

Shapland, J., Atkinson, A., Atkinson, H., Dignan, J., Edwards, L., Hibbert, J., Howes, J., Johnstone, J., Robinson, G. and Sorsby, A. (2008). *Does Restorative Justice Affect Reconviction? The Fourth Report from the Evaluation of Three Schemes*. London: Ministry of Justice.

Simester, A. P. and Von Hirsch, A. (2006). 'Regulating Offensive Conduct through Two-Step Prohibitions'. In A. Von Hirsch and A. P. Simester (eds), *Incivilities: Regulating Offensive Behaviour*. Oxford: Hart Publishing.

Talbot, J. (2010). *Seen and Heard: Supporting Vulnerable Children in the Youth Justice System*. London: Prison Reform Trust.

Wilson, J. Q. and Kelling, G. (1982). 'Broken Windows'. *Atlantic Monthly* (March): 29–38.

9
Children's Rights Since Margaret Thatcher

Marc Cornock and Heather Montgomery

Introduction

The year 1979 – the year Margaret Thatcher became Prime Minister – was declared by the United Nations as the International Year of the Child. It was also the year when there was a major, international push to codify children's rights and to begin the drafting process of the United Nations Convention on the Rights of the Child – the first international, legally enforceable treaty to focus specifically on children. A year after Mrs Thatcher left office, in 1991, the UK ratified the UNCRC, enshrining its ideals in UK law and agreeing to be accountable to the United Nations for ensuring that children's rights were implemented in the UK. Thatcher's grandchildren, therefore, are those who came to adulthood under a new era of children's rights and, more than any other generation, are those on whom the impact of these social changes is most apparent and who are the ones most likely to be able to claim and benefit from these rights. Yet the legacy from the Thatcher years is a complex one. British children, we are told, are now the unhappiest in Europe (as well as the fattest and most academically underachieving). UNICEF, as well as the Committee on the Rights of the Child, continually upbraids the British government for failing to fulfil its duties under the UNCRC, and there are repeated claims in the media that British childhood is in crisis and that British children are the unhappiest in Europe, as well as the most stressed and over-sexualised. (These claims will be discussed later in the chapter, but for a full analysis of them see Kehily 2010. They are also discussed in this book: see the chapter by Jane Pilcher.)

This chapter will begin with a brief examination of how the UNCRC came to be ratified by the UK and how it interacts with and complements English and Welsh legislation. The UNCRC may be the most high profile and holistic piece of children's rights legislation but it does not stand alone and is part of a complex web of international and national laws which take as their basis the rights of children to participate, and be protected and provided for. This chapter will examine some of the main legislative changes that occurred in the period 1979–91 and will examine their legacy. It will end with suggestions of possible future dilemmas and challenges that implementing rights for all children will entail.

International children's rights legislation and the UK

Attempts to codify international standards for children's welfare have a long history, albeit one marked by good intentions and high aspirations rather than legislative impact. The UK has often been quick to sign such declarations and conventions but slower to implement and adapt their provisions into workable law. One of the first attempts to set out universal standards was the 1924 Geneva Declaration, which recognised adults' obligations to feed, care for, relieve and protect children wherever they lived. This document was adopted by the League of Nations in 1924 and approved again in 1934 but it had limited impact, except for its legacy as the first international human rights document that focused specifically on children. Signatories promised to incorporate its principles into their national laws, but they were not legally bound to do so, and few did. The 1924 Declaration was expanded into the Declaration of the Rights of the Child, which was adopted by the General Assembly of the United Nations in 1959. Like the Declaration, this stated in the Preamble that 'mankind owes to the child the best it has to give', but laid down no suggestions, or infrastructure, to ensure that rights were respected or that special protective measures were put in place (Van Bueren 1995).

Despite this, the 1959 Declaration provided the impetus for longer-term thinking about what children's rights meant and how they could be legally enforced. Several non-governmental organisations (NGOs), along with national governments, most notably Poland, began to lobby for a legally enforceable convention which would ensure that individual states were prepared to guarantee children's rights (Van Bueren 1995).[1] The year 1979 was designated the International Year of the Child by the UN and, a year before, in 1978, the Polish delegation to the 34th session of the UN Commission on Human Rights formally asked for the adoption of a UN Convention on the Rights of the Child. The UN agreed and set a deadline of ten years for the Convention to be drafted and opened for signature (Office of the United Nations High Commissioner for Human Rights 2007). The Convention was made up of 54 legally binding articles covering (among other things) children's right to health care, education, nationality and legal representation, but the fundamental principle behind the Convention was stated in Article 3: 'All actions concerning the child shall take full account of his or her best interests.' The rights set out in the UNCRC are often grouped into three categories known as the '3 Ps' of children's rights: their right to *provision* (i.e., their rights to food, housing or education); their right to *protection* (against exploitation and abuse); and most controversially, their right to *participation* (the right of children to take part in decisions made on their behalf, discussed later in this chapter).[2] Unlike previous international children's rights conventions, the UNCRC put in place an infrastructure for ensuring state compliance with its articles.[3] The UNCRC was ratified by the United Nations on 20 November 1989 and came into force on 2 September 1990. The UK signed the Convention on 19 April 1990, ratified it on 16 December 1991 and it came into force on 15 January 1992. It has since been ratified by every country in the world, except the USA and Somalia, and is the most ratified convention in the history of the United Nations.[4] It introduced, according to one commentator, a new ideology of childhood based on respect for children's dignity, which shifted the emphasis when intervening in children's lives 'from protection to autonomy, from nurturance to self-determination, from welfare to justice' (Freeman 1992: 3).

Despite this near universal enthusiasm for the UNCRC, implementing its articles has proved difficult and there have been, and still remain, some significant differences in how children's rights are envisaged in the UNCRC and how they are seen by national governments, including the UK. At a fundamental level there remain contesting ideologies of childhood and there is little agreement on what childhood is (or what should it be) or on how children should best be nurtured and protected. The UNCRC has been criticised for promoting a particular form of childhood, based on Westernised ideals of autonomy and individuality rather than on family harmony or mutual obligations between parents and children (Goodman 1996; Boyden 1997; Twan-Danso 2009). Others have seen it as a form of neocolonialism, imposing the standards of the West on other countries and holding them to account when they fail to fulfil them (Pupavac 2001).

On another level, there is disagreement about who is a child. Setting a chronological boundary of 18 may be a useful and necessary bureaucratic exercise but it ignores the realities of life for many children outside the West who work, marry and have their own children and fulfil adult social obligations at an age when they are themselves still designated as children (Montgomery 2009). At the beginning of childhood, the question of who is a child is even more problematic. The Convention refers to anyone under 18 but says nothing about when childhood starts (Cornock and Montgomery 2010). The Preamble says that 'the child, by reason of his physical and mental immaturity, needs special safeguards and care, including appropriate legal protection, *before* as well as after birth' (emphasis added) but does not discuss this further. Only four countries who ratified the Convention have clarified how they define childhood in this regard. China and the United Kingdom stated that they interpreted the Convention as applicable only following a live birth, while Argentina and Guatemala declared that Article 1 'must be interpreted to the effect that a child means every human being from the moment of conception up to the age of eighteen'. No other countries clarified their definition of childhood although the Holy See stated that it hoped the UNCRC 'will safeguard the rights of the child before as well as after birth'. This may have been a necessary compromise in drafting the UNCRC, in order to avoid being dragged into debates on abortion, but it leaves important questions unanswered and even unasked.

There have also been longstanding anxieties about granting children rights which would undermine other aspects of government policy and, even at the drafting stage, the UK expressed its concerns over those articles which concerned immigration (Office of the United Nations High Commissioner for Human Rights 2007). Once ratified, the UK lodged several reservations. In order to get the maximum possible numbers of signatures, states were allowed to ratify the UNCRC while lodging reservations about certain articles, meaning that there are some provisions of the Convention that states did not agree to incorporate into national law. When the UK first ratified the Convention, it lodged reservations about Article 37, which concerned the detention of young people alongside adults, and also to Article 22, which dealt with family reunification and asylum and immigration, thereby specifically excluding asylum-seeking children from the provisions of the UNCRC.[5]

Since the UK ratified the Convention there have been concerted attempts throughout the UK (both in Westminster and particularly in the devolved assemblies in Scotland and Wales) to create laws, administrative procedures and policy initiatives which support and implement children's rights, including the Children Acts of 1989 and 2004, the 2003 Every Child Matters agenda, and the 2007 Children's Plan.[6] Nevertheless bringing the provisions of the UNCRC into domestic law has proved problematic and controversial, for a number of reasons. First, the UK does not, in general, incorporate international treaties directly into domestic law but instead introduces specific legislation which enables it to comply with a particular treaty. Second, while the UNCRC sets out the rights that need to be ensured in practice, it is not prescriptive about how this is done and recognises that implementation need not be done by law alone but through a combination of legislative, administrative and other measures, and it is up to state parties who have ratified the Convention to decide how best to implement them.[7] Third, Article 4 recognises that resources are limited and governments have to make choices about what to fund and that such decisions are relevant when deciding what measures should be taken to implement the Convention. Finally, it is important to remember that some of the most important and far-reaching judgments in English law concerning children's rights have come about, not as a result of the UNCRC, but through previous Acts of Parliament and legislation such as the Children and Young Persons Act 1933 or the Protection of Children Act 1978 or through legal rulings such as the Gillick ruling, which will be discussed below. Children's rights were not invented by the UNCRC, and it is not the only legislation necessary to support children's rights. That said, Wales became the first of the UK nations to bring the provisions of the UNCRC into domestic law with the passing of the Rights of Children and Young Persons (Wales) Measure 2011 by the Welsh Assembly.[8]

Children's rights in the UK before and after the UNCRC

One of the fundamental changes concerning children's rights in the UK, in relation to their own bodies, came with the judgment in the 1986 Gillick case. It is impossible to overemphasise the importance of this case for child rights. Before Margaret Thatcher came to office, the legal position regarding children's right to self-determination over their bodies was unclear. During Mrs Thatcher's time in office the Gillick case challenged many of the preconceptions that were held regarding children's rights and the judgment helped to clarify the legal position in the years before the UNCRC was ratified.

The laws relating to children and their rights, seen from the perspective of the twenty-first century, were both archaic and confusing when Mrs Thatcher first became Prime Minister. Parental rights were generally taken to have precedence over the rights of the child such that a parent was in a position to restrict the place and way in which a child spent their time. Whilst this was seen as essential for the well-being and safety of a young child, the effect was to include all children up to the age of 18 years old. Over the years, various cases had been heard in the courts on this issue and had concluded that parental rights extended to this degree and also that parents could expect unquestioning obedience.[9] In the decade prior to Mrs Thatcher coming to office the legal position had softened somewhat; views of parental rights as all-encompassing and requiring unquestioning obedience were seen as being reflective of 'the attitude of a Victorian parent towards his children'.[10]

The Family Law Reform Act 1969 was one of the first pieces of legislation which reflected this relaxation in attitudes and tentatively supported a child's right to self-determination. Section 8 of the Act is particularly significant because it stated that:

(1) The consent of a minor who has attained the age of sixteen years to any surgical, medical or dental treatment which, in the absence of consent, would constitute a trespass to his person, shall be as effective as it would be if he were of full age; and where a minor has by virtue of this section given an effective consent to any treatment it shall not be necessary to obtain any consent for it from his parent or guardian.

(2) In this section 'surgical, medical or dental treatment' includes any procedure undertaken for the purposes of diagnosis, and this section applies to any procedure (including, in particular, the administration of an anaesthetic) which is ancillary to any treatment as it applies to that treatment.

This meant that a child who had reached the age of 16 was legally entitled to provide their own consent for medical treatment, without the need for their parents to do so, and even if their parents refused to consent. However, there was still uncertainty about the legal position of a child's self-determination since there was no mention of a child's right to withhold consent; also, the legal basis for providing medical treatment to a child under 16 without their parent's consent was still unclear. This latter uncertainty was to be resolved as a result of the Gillick case.

The Gillick case arose as a result of a circular issued by the then Department of Health and Social Security (DHSS) regarding family planning within which it was stated that, in certain cases which were described as 'exceptional', a doctor could lawfully advise and prescribe contraception for a girl under 16 without her parents' consent.[11] Mrs Gillick, a mother of five girls under the age of 16, wrote to the local area health authority seeking an assurance that none of her children would receive such advice or treatment whilst they were under 16 without her knowledge or consent. The local area health authority refused to provide this assurance. Mrs Gillick then challenged the lawfulness of the circular in the courts.

Mrs Gillick initially lost her case as the court found that the guidance in the circular was not unlawful. Mrs Gillick then went to the Court of Appeal who granted her a declaration that the circular was unlawful on the grounds that a child under 16 was not able to provide a valid consent to the advice and treatment. The DHSS then appealed to the House of Lords where the case was finally settled. The House of Lords judgment in the Gillick case provided that it was lawful to provide advice and contraception to a girl under the age of 16 without her parents' knowledge or consent. However, this was subject to certain guidelines laid down in the House of Lords judgment by Lord Fraser.[12]

As the law progressed during Mrs Thatcher's period of office, and subsequent cases came to be heard on the issue of a child's right to decide for themselves about medical treatment, it became apparent that there were in fact two outcomes from the Gillick case, and two terms emerged for these outcomes. One is that it became lawful to provide contraceptive advice and treatment to girls under the age of 16, subject to certain guidelines (Fraser guidelines). The other was that in certain circumstances a child under the age of 16 could now give consent in their own right ('Gillick competence') (Cornock 2007a: 142). However, it is further noted that:

> confusion has arisen regarding the two terms as a result of a fallacy that Mrs Gillick objected to the use of the term 'Gillick competence' and that the Fraser guidelines were introduced in its place. However, there is no evidence that Mrs Gillick objected to the use of the term. Fraser guidelines refer to a specific set of guidelines that Lord Fraser proposed in the

Gillick case ... [Whilst] Gillick competence, on the other hand, refers to the fact that some children under the age of 16 are able to give consent. (Cornock 2007a: 142)

Gillick competence is now a firmly established principle of the law relating to children and health care, such that it is referred to in most, if not all, cases that involve children and consent to treatment. It forms the basis for those children under 16 to be able to consent to medical treatment.

As a result of the judgment in the Gillick case, once a child has sufficient emotional and intellectual maturity to be able to fully understand the nature and effect of any proposed medical treatment that is offered, they are said to be 'Gillick competent' and treated as if they have the competence to provide a valid legal consent to that treatment. This means that if a Gillick competent child provides consent to a medical treatment, there is no legal duty to obtain consent from someone with parental responsibility over that child; the child's consent is sufficient and the person with parental responsibility has no right to override the child's consent. As Lord Scarman stated: 'I would hold that as a matter of law the parental right to determine whether or not their minor child below the age of sixteen will have medical treatment terminates if and when the chid achieves a sufficient understanding and intelligence to enable him or her to understand fully what is proposed' (Gillick at pages 188–9). Unfortunately, as we shall see later, the situation where a Gillick competent child refuses a medical treatment is not as enlightened.

In a subsequent case Lord Donaldson likened consent to a key that is capable of unlocking a door to medical treatment.[13] He noted that, like many locks, there is more than one key capable of opening it, and provided a person has one key, the use of other keys does not matter. In his analogy, both the Gillick competent child and their parents have keys to the lock. Provided that the child uses their key to unlock the door, what happens to the parents' key is irrelevant.

As a result of the Gillick case, parental rights, from a legal perspective, are now seen as dwindling as the child gains maturity rather than as an absolute right that suddenly ceases when the child reaches 18. Parental rights are, as far as the law recognises them, only valid so long as they promote the welfare and well-being of the child, until the child is able to make their own decisions.

As noted above, it is impossible to overstate the importance that the judgment in the Gillick case has had in the matter of a child's right of self-determination. Although she ultimately lost her case, Mrs Gillick provided an opportunity for children's rights to be debated in the highest court of the land and for its senior judges to clarify the position between the rights of a parent and those of a child in relation to self-determination. That debate and clarification has had a lasting legacy for children and child rights. Indeed, as Fortin states:

> well-informed parents can learn a great deal from the House of Lords decision in Gillick v West Norfolk and Wisbech Area Health Authority. It shows that, by the mid-1980s, a far more enlightened approach to the parental role was emerging, compared with that of earlier generations. Indeed the Gillick decision established new legal boundaries for parents' relationships with their adolescent children. It reflected the view that the law should encourage parents to stand back and permit their adolescents to reach important decisions with as little interference as possible. (Fortin 2003: 80–1)

White, Carr and Lowe (2002) are of the opinion that the Gillick judgment was influential on the subsequent Children Act 1989 which came into force on 14 October 1991. They assert that the Act (Children Act 1989) recognises the importance of ascertaining and taking into account the child's own wishes to an extent commensurate with his age and understanding. The question of whether the preferences of a mature child should not only be taken into account but be determinative of the matter in question provoked considerable debate during the passage of the Bill (2002: 3).

The Gillick case was heard before the UNCRC was ratified by the UK. Therefore it is not known how the UNCRC would have affected the Gillick judgment. However, in 2006, a case was brought before the courts that had similar issues to the Gillick case and both allows the judgment of the Gillick case to be read in light of the ratification of the UNCRC by the UK and also allows a more recent perspective to be taken on the issues of the Gillick case. The case in question was the Axon case.[14]

In this case, Mrs Sue Axon sought a declaration from the court that a doctor was not obliged to keep advice and treatment provided to a girl under 16 in respect to contraception, sexually transmitted infections or abortion confidential. Mrs Axon lost her case and did not receive the declarations she sought. In his judgment, the judge in the case, Justice Silber, paid particular attention to articles 5, 12, 16 and 18 of the UNCRC, stating that:

> The ratification by the United Kingdom of the United Nations Convention on the Rights of the Child in November 1989 was significant as showing a desire to give children greater rights (at paragraph 64) [and that the UNCRC] provisions provide further support for the general movement towards now giving young people greater rights concerning their own future while reducing the supervisory rights of their parents (at paragraph 115).

Justice Silber further stated that:

> the right of young people to make decisions about their own lives by themselves at the expense of the views of their parents has now become an increasingly important and accepted feature of family life ... in the light of this change in the landscape of family matters, in which rights of children are becoming increasingly important, it would be ironic and indeed not acceptable now to retreat from the approach adopted in Gillick (at paragraphs 79–80).

Therefore, the Axon case judgment has provided an opportunity for the Gillick judgment to be brought up to date, extended and reinforced in the light of the twenty-first century. Some 20 or so years after Mrs Thatcher left office, the principles of the Gillick case are still as relevant and valid as when they were decided.[15] As Lord Fraser held: '[the] parental rights to control a child do not exist for the benefit of the parent. They exist for the benefit of the child and they are justified only in so far as they enable the parent to perform his duties towards the child, and towards other children in the family' (Gillick at page 170).

It is with this in mind that children's rights can be discussed from a twenty-first-century perspective.

Children's rights in the early twenty-first century

Without doubt the years 1979–91 were crucial in the battle for children's rights and laid the basis for important changes concerning the role and status of children in the UK at a legislative, administrative and policy level. More difficult to judge, however, is whether these changes have improved children's lives, led to better childhoods, or closer and more supportive adult–child relationships. Here the evidence is less encouraging and, some 20 years after Mrs Thatcher left office, much of the optimism of the 1990s seems to have died away and the ideology of children as active citizens, empowered and equal to adults, does not appear to have filtered down into general discourse. Furthermore, it has been argued that there has been a general shift away from support for rights of individual autonomy and a greater suspicion of all human rights discourses. As the Children's Rights Alliance of England has argued: 'There is no doubt that now is an uncertain time for human rights, with conflicting messages from politicians about the future of the Human Rights Act and the viability of economic, social and cultural rights' (CRAE 2012: 2). Since 2000, the deaths of Victoria Climbié and Peter Connelly ('Baby P') have shown how there are still large gaps in provision and that even children's most basic rights to protection are still not always enforced.[16] There has been some progress in implementing participation rights and, in various fields, such as children's mental health services or in the provision for disabled children and young people, much emphasis has been placed on listening to what children themselves want, not simply imposing what is understood as medically best for them. In other areas too, we have seen the creation of Children's Ombudsmen in all four nations of the UK, a UK Youth Parliament, youth councils in Scotland, and in schools the concept of 'student voice' and pupil representation on school councils is now part of many schools' mission statement (for an evaluation of many such projects see the contributors to Percy-Smith and Thomas 2010). However, there are still some areas where children's rights to have a voice or opinion on matters which affect them are still not properly respected and children remain entirely dependent on adults to interpret and defend their best interests.

Despite the Gillick and Axon cases, the English legal system has consistently constrained a child's right to some autonomy over their body. Several notable court cases in the 1990s demonstrated the restrictions that the law has placed upon a child's ability to withhold their consent for medical procedures. In two cases in 1992, it was determined that even where a child was 'Gillick competent', their refusal to consent to treatment that was deemed to be in their best interests could be overruled by someone with parental responsibility or the court;[17] and, in 1999, a 15-year-old girl's refusal to have a heart transplant was overridden by the court on the basis that the girl's refusal of consent carried 'considerable weight' but was not decisive.[18] More recently, in 2003, a boy aged 16 and 10 months had his refusal to a blood transfusion, because of his religious beliefs, overruled by the court in his best interests.[19] The English courts have thus demonstrated a willingness to use the authority of their *parens patriae*[20] power to protect those who they believe are not acting in their own best interests, despite their competence.

Some academics have argued that children's rights have not transformed relationships between adults and children in the ways that had been anticipated and that far from being a time of autonomy, self-determination and justice, childhood is now often said to be a time of separation and even alienation from adulthood. A survey carried out by Barnardo's in 2008 found that 49 per cent of adults felt that children were a danger to themselves and others and 43 per cent thought that adults needed to be protected from children; 45 per cent agreed with the description of children as feral and 35 per cent agreed with the statement that 'it feels like the streets are infested with children' (Barnardo's 2008). Based on an analysis of media coverage and several non-governmental reports on the state of childhood, Mary Jane Kehily has argued that childhood is now seen and discussed in terms of crisis – children are perceived as being at risk as never before, with the institutions of the state, as well as their own parents, failing them. At the same time, they are seen as out of control, unhappy and a risk to themselves and others (Kehily 2010). To give one example, the 2009 Good Childhood Inquiry, based on the conclusions of 12 independent experts commissioned by The Children's Society to look at the state of British childhood, claimed that rates of depression and aggression among 15- and 16-year-olds had risen since the 1980s, that one in five children has a mental health problem, that one in twelve children intentionally self-harms on a regular basis and that children no longer play outside because of their parents' fears (Layard and Dunn 2009). Books such as Sue Palmer's 2006 *Toxic Childhood* made an influential contribution to the 'childhood in crisis' thesis by arguing that modern childhoods have become over-commercialised, too competitive, too reliant on technology and have left children stressed and unable to play. Such findings led the UK Children's Commissioner to comment in 2007, 'There is a crisis at the heart of our society', and this crisis is focused on childhood (Aynsley Green 2007: 12). Perhaps the most influential report of all was UNICEF's *Child Poverty in Perspective: An Overview of Child Well-being in Rich Countries* (UNICEF 2007). This report looked at six different aspects of children's lives – material well-being, health and safety, educational well-being, family and peer relationships, behaviours and risks and subjective well-being – and, using a variety of indicators and statistics, compared the experiences of being a child across Europe. The term 'well-being' was developed to explore children's quality of life, moving from a focus on basic needs and what children lacked to a more positive emphasis on the strengths of their present lives. Most importantly, it was designed so that children's own perceptions of their life were taken into account alongside a calculation of their material standards of living.[21] Therefore the indicators used by the UNICEF report ranged from rates of child poverty to less tangible issues such as family and peer relationships. However, the results, which were widely disseminated throughout the media, made for grim reading and seemed to show that the UK's children were at the bottom of the league table of rich nations in relation to emotional well-being. In contrast, the Scandinavian societies scored highly on nearly every measure, making childhood a seemingly happier and easier period of life in northern Europe than in the UK.[22]

Ever since the publication of this report it has become a truism that British children are among the poorest, most educationally under-achieving, unhappiest, most stressed and most emotionally deprived children in Europe, and that whatever legal rights British children have, it has not made their lives any better. Yet a closer reading of the report and an examination of the relationships between rights and well-being suggests the need for a more nuanced assessment of the state of British childhood. First, it must be remembered that children's rights and children's well-being are two very different prospects and that the UNCRC, national legislation, or indeed any human rights treaty, does not promise children the right to happiness or the right to loving parents or supportive peers. There is an important difference between rights and ideals and it is essential to differentiate between the desire for children's well-being and the legal responsibility to enforce this. It is possible to say, for example, that a child has a right to the best possible standard of living given the circumstances they live in, but it is not meaningful to say a child has a right to a happy childhood, no matter how desirable this might be. As Jack Donnelly has argued:

> We do not have human rights to all things that are good, or even all *important* good things. For example, we are not entitled – do not have (human) rights – to love, charity or compassion. Parents who abuse the trust of children wreak havoc with millions of lives every day. We do not, however, have a human right to loving, supportive parents. In fact, to recognize such a right would transform family relations in ways that many people would find unappealing or even destructive. (Donnelly 2003: 10–11)

When drafting the UNCRC, its authors were very careful not to set up legally meaningless rights. The Preamble states an ideal and recognises that in a perfect world all children would grow up in 'an atmosphere of happiness, love and understanding', but this is not, and never can be, a legally enforceable standard as no government or organisation can ensure that people are happy, loved or understood.

The UNICEF report itself has also been criticised for the indicators it used and how it interpreted them (see Morrow and Mayall 2009 for the most extensive critique of this work). While the authors of the report were cautious in their findings and recognised many of the problems with their work, the report was taken up in the media in an often sensationalistic way which twisted what was actually claimed. Virginia Morrow and Berry Mayall (2009: 224) give as an example the percentage of 11-, 13- and 15-year-olds who claimed to find their peers 'kind and helpful', an indicator on which British children scored very low and which contributed to the UK's low placement in the table. The 'finding' was rephrased by news media as a clear fact that children in the UK do not have good friendships. However, the question was part of a series about life at school, and related not to 'peers' nor to 'friends', but to 'classmates'. It is not surprising that children (in a competitive school regime) do not all regard all classmates as friends. However, the media seized on this finding: 'The report presents a sad picture of relationships with friends, which are so important to children. Not much more than 40% of the UK's 11, 13 and 15-year-olds find their peers "kind and helpful", which is the worst score of all the developed countries' (*Guardian*, 14 February 2007).

While Morrow and Mayall point out there is much to admire and discuss in the UNICEF report, and agree with its suggestion that children in the UK are not given the priority in social policy that they are in other countries in Europe, they also criticise it for relying on a deficit model of children's lives and looking at the negatives rather than the positives. This is not to say that a different focus would suggest that all was well with British childhood but it might show that things are not as problematic as is sometimes reported.

Other aspects of children's lives which have also been taken to indicate that childhood is in crisis, such as the fears over early sexualisation, the rise in obesity or the over-commercialisation of childhood, have also been challenged by those who argue that these are more complex phenomena than simply being symptoms of a crisis and part of the deteriorating experiences of childhood. Sara Bragg (2012), for example, has shown that despite the fear and multiple government reports over sexualisation, children themselves interpret the sexual images they see in the media in very different, multifaceted ways to adults and do not necessarily feel that their childhood is eroded because of them. Jantina de Vries (2007) has argued that modern concerns about obesity in childhood use ideas of medical risk and children's ill-health as a means of stigmatising the poor and marginalised as being out of control, feckless and gluttonous. She argues that childhood obesity is used by the state and its agencies as a way of marking out social divisions and reinforcing the differences between those children with slim, disciplined bodies and those children, who are usually poorer or members of ethnic minorities, who are seen as lacking in self-control and the cause of their own problems. Other studies of consumption and advertising and its impacts on children and how they understand and relate to it (see, for example, Buckingham 2011 and in this book) also point to the complexities of understanding contemporary childhood and challenge the idea that childhood today is necessarily worse than in the past just because it is different. Most importantly, such critical voices suggest that children themselves perceive childhood very differently to some adult commentators and do not see their own childhoods as being in crisis.

Looking forward

It is always dangerous to predict the future but it is also interesting to raise questions about what will happen to Thatcher's great-grandchildren, what social concerns and issues they will face and what impact the children's rights agenda of the late twentieth century will have on them. If sociologists and historians are to be believed, then it is a fair guess that their childhoods too will be seen as immensely problematic, challenging and even threatening to the adult world. Nostalgia is an essential part of much thinking on childhood and the temptation to see the current generation as worse off and unhappier than the one before is constant. Moral panics around childhood also have a long history and, while it is impossible to predict what these fears will coalesce round in the future, it is safe to assume that children will be at the heart of them.

Children's rights, and in particular the relationship between state, parents and child, will continue to be contested in the courts. Issues of immigration and provision for child asylum seekers and refugees are also likely to pit government policy against children's rights. An interesting area of development may be the application of the UNCRC to young persons in addition to children. Recognising that the UNCRC was created for the benefit of children (defined as under 18), in October 2012 the Welsh Assembly issued a consultation document on whether the protection afforded to children should apply to young persons (defined as those who have attained the age of 18 but are under 25) to allow them to reach their full potential.[23] It is also worth noting that the Rights of Children and Young Persons (Wales) Measure 2011 imposes a duty on Welsh Ministers to consider how far the UNCRC may be relevant and applied to young persons. Whether this will enhance or detract from the rights and protection of children under the UNCRC remains to be seen.

Some of the most intractable children's rights issues, however, are likely to arise over issues of cultural identity. Other European countries suggest some possible sources of conflict. In France, debates around the wearing of a veil as a symbol of religious expression have exposed the difficulties inherent in ensuring a child's right to an education in a secular state while also ensuring their rights to freedom of expression and religion (Scott 2010). These debates have also played out in Germany and Sweden where government attempts to curb parental rights to circumcise their infant sons in accordance with their religion are increasingly seen as being in conflict with children's rights to bodily integrity and protection from harm. In July 2012, this issue briefly became the subject of a court case in Germany when a doctor went on trial in Cologne after a 4-year-old boy developed complications after he was circumcised (Evans 2012). As a result, the German Medical Association advised doctors not to carry out non-medical circumcisions in the future in case they were prosecuted, although this directive was later overturned when politicians stepped in. While this particular case was based on issues of medical risk, it raised much more complex issues over children's right to protection versus those of their right to a cultural identity. In Sweden this debate focused even more clearly on the issue of competing rights and in 2001 the Swedish government enacted a highly controversial law that allowed only those certified by the National Board of Health to perform circumcision, effectively removing control of the procedure from religious practitioners.[24] The law on the circumcision of boys was reviewed in Sweden in 2005 and again in 2007 when some of the loudest voices behind the campaign to ban infant circumcision were those of children's rights organisations, most notably the Swedish Ombudsman for Children and Save the Children Sweden, the latter going so far as to call for Jews and Muslims to 'change their religion' (Schiratzki 2011: 39) in order to protect children's rights.[25]

The UNCRC has been criticised for its assumption of a universal child and in the future this will increasingly be an issue not only between countries but also within them. Children's rights continue to be contested because they raise difficult and sometimes intractable questions about the desirable relationships between adults and children and between the state and the family. They raise uncomfortable issues of who is a citizen and what citizenship should look like and whether it is parents, the state or children themselves who are best able to articulate and defend children's best interests. These are issues that have been debated since 1979 and are likely to be contested for some time to come. It may not be easy to predict what cases will come to court or spark media attention, but children's rights, with all their attendant dilemmas, problems and ideological complexities, will lie at the heart of social change because they are so fundamental to adult imaginings of future societies.

Notes

1. Why Poland was so central is a matter for debate. It might be argued that being seen as a pioneer of children's rights, at a time when Poland was part of the Soviet bloc and had a less than enviable reputation for political freedom, was a way of seizing the moral high ground. Others, perhaps less cynically, have attributed the Poles' particular interest in children's rights to the life and death of Janusz Korczak, a pioneer of children's welfare who died with the orphaned children he refused to leave behind in the Warsaw Ghetto in 1942 (Ennew 2000).
2. Although the UNCRC does not define participation explicitly, Article 12 states: 'The child has the right to express his or her opinion freely and to have that opinion taken into account in any matter or procedure affecting the child.' Other articles also affirm a young person's right to freedom of expression (Article 13), to freedom of association (Article 15), and to access appropriate information (Article 17).
3. Built into the UNCRC is a system of measuring and monitoring progress towards implementation and every five years all governments are expected to report their progress to the UN Committee on the Rights of the Child, which also takes statements from NGOs and other interested parties.
4. Until this time, Somalia has not had a functioning government able to sign or ratify an international treaty such as the UNCRC. The USA, on the other hand, signed the Convention in 1995 but has refused to ratify it because it claims that children's rights are best protected within families and by parents rather than the state. Furthermore, the US government argues that the Convention violates principles of national sovereignty and the rights of individual states.
5. The UK was heavily criticised in successive reports to the UN Committee on the Rights of the Child for these reservations and withdrew them in 2008.
6. The Children Act of 1989 established the right for children to be consulted (considered in the light of his or her age and understanding). Children would be invited by the courts and the welfare system to voice their opinions in matters such as where they would prefer to live after a parental divorce, or whether they wished to remain at home or go into care when there were concerns about child protection issues. The Children Act also upheld the right of children to apply for court orders in their own right. The next Children Act (2004) expanded children's rights to participation, built on the provisions of the previous Children Act, and provided the legislative framework to implement Every Child Matters (2003) and

the Children's Plan (2007). It also set out the reforms in health and education and established the office of the Children's Commissioner in England (Wales had established this post in 2001, as had Scotland and Northern Ireland in 2003).
7. In 2012 the Children's Rights Alliance for England (CRAE) launched a campaign for full incorporation of the UNCRC into domestic law. The Alliance argued that:
> The approach taken by successive UK governments to put children's rights into practice can be described as 'sectoral', the gradual examination of legislation in different areas in order to ensure compliance with the UN Convention on the Rights of the Child. However, this means that there is too often a focus on certain rights, certain settings and certain children to the exclusion of others, resulting in some rights being neglected and the obligation to consider children's views only being recognised in some contexts. Incorporation would provide something far more rigorous and routine than currently happens across the UK as a whole. (Children's Rights Alliance for England 2012: 2)
8. The legislation was passed by the Welsh Assembly on 18 January 2011 and subsequently approved by the Queen on 16 March 2011. The legalisation places a duty on Welsh Ministers to have due regard for the rights of a child, as laid down in the UNCRC, when exercising any of their functions.
9. Cases such as *R* v. *Howes* (1860) 3 E & E 332, where it was decided that a father is entitled to custody of his child until it attains the age of 21, and *Re Agar-Ellis, Agar-Ellis* v. *Lascelles* (1883) 24 Ch D 317, where a father lawfully restricted his 17-year-old daughter's communication.
10. Lord Denning in *Hewer* v. *Bryant* [1969] 3 ALL ER 578 at page 582.
11. *Gillick* v. *West Norfolk and Wisbech Area Health Authority* [1986] AC 112.
12. These guidelines are that the doctor:
> is satisfied on the following matters: (1) that the girl (although under 16 years of age) will understand his advice; (2) that he cannot persuade her to inform her parents or to allow him to inform the parents that she is seeking contraceptive advice; (3) that she is very likely to begin or to continue having sexual intercourse with or without contraceptive treatment; (4) that unless she receives contraceptive advice or treatment her physical or mental health or both are likely to suffer; (5) that her best interests require him to give her contraceptive advice, treatment or both without the parental consent. (Per Lord Fraser in Gillick at page 174)
13. *Re R (A Minor)(Wardship: consent to treatment)* [1992] Fam 11 CA.
14. *R (on the application of Axon)* v. *Secretary of State for Health* [2006] EWHC 37 (Admin).
15. This section has considered the position of children in England and Wales regarding their legal right to self-determination in relation to medical treatment. In Northern Ireland, the law adopts the same position to that of England and Wales. However, in Scotland there is a different approach. The Age of Legal Capacity (Scotland) Act 1991 effectively puts the common law provision of the Gillick case into statutory effect in Scotland. Section 2(4) states that 'A person under the age of 16 years shall have legal capacity to consent on his own behalf to any surgical, medical or dental procedure or treatment where, in the opinion of a qualified medical practitioner attending him, he is capable of understanding the nature and possible consequences of the procedure or treatment.'
16. Eight-year-old Victoria Climbié died in Haringey, London in 2000 from neglect and abuse by her guardians, who were her great-aunt and her great-aunt's partner. The abuse had been ignored and misdiagnosed by the local child protection and welfare agencies. A report into her death by Lord Laming called for improved safeguards and more integrated services but, despite this, the case of

Peter Connelly, 'Baby P', who, aged 17 months and living in the same borough as Victoria, was abused and killed by his mother, her partner and his brother in 2007, revealed further shortcomings in the care and protection provided to children (Laming 2009).
17. *Re R (A Minor) (Wardship: consent to treatment)* [1992] Fam 11 CA and *Re W (A Minor) (Medical treatment)* [1992] 4 All ER 627.
18. *Re M (Child: refusal of medical treatment)* 52 BMLR 124.
19. *Re P (A minor)* [2003] EWHC 2327 (Fam).
20. *Parens patriae* (or parent of the country) refers to the common law power of the monarch and courts to act as legal protector for those who are unable to protect themselves.
21. *Well-being* is a term that is now used regularly by policy makers, practitioners and academics but, not surprisingly, it has been controversial. For some it is problematic since it describes both a state of being and an outcome of intervention, while others see it as too conceptually vague (for an overview of the arguments for and against its use, see Punch 2013).
22. Many reasons can be put forward for the Scandinavians' high ranking in the table: better state-subsidised childcare, delayed entry to primary school, greater emphasis on pupils' social development and happiness than on academic or school achievement, fewer league tables, flexible working for parents and low crime rates. One of the most contentious is that these societies are more socially equal, with higher taxation and a more equitable distribution of wealth. Consequently, unlike in the UK, there is less of a gap between the richest and the poorest in society, which some have argued is a major cause of social stress and unhappiness (Wilkinson and Pickett 2010).
23. The consultation, entitled 'Should the Welsh Government apply the "Articles" in the United Nations Convention on the Rights of the Child (UNCRC) to young people aged 18–24yrs?', was issued on 8 October 2012. It is available at: http://wales.gov.uk/docs/phhs/consultation/121008consultationen.pdf.
24. This law led to protests across the world. A spokesman for the World Jewish Council claimed it was 'the first legal restriction placed on a Jewish rite in Europe since the Nazi era. This new legislation is totally unacceptable to the Swedish Jewish community' (quoted in Schiratzki 2011: 1).
25. Despite the interest in the German case, there have been no similar cases as yet in the UK. The current legal position in the UK is that 'it is lawful to perform a nontherapeutic procedure upon a child who is too young to be able to give their own consent, although it has to be demonstrated that the procedure is in the child's best interests. This can include religious factors and the need for the child to follow a specific religion' (Cornock 2007b: 349).

References

Aynsley Green, A. (2007). *Forward from the Children's Rights Commissioner for England. Five Year Plan.* London: 11 Million.

Barnardo's. (2008). *The Shame of Britain's Intolerance of Children.* www.barnardos.org.uk/news_and_events/media_centre/press_releases.htm?ref=42088 (accessed 27 September 2012).

Boyden, J. (1997). 'Childhood and Policy Makers: A Comparative Perspective on the Globalization of Childhood'. In A. James and A. Prout (eds), *Constructing and Reconstructing Childhood* (2nd edn). London: Falmer Press.

Bragg, S. (2012). 'Dockside Tarts and Modesty Boards: A Review of Recent Policy on Sexualisation'. *Children and Society* 26(5): 406–14.

Buckingham, D. (2011). *The Material Child. Growing up in Consumer Culture.* Cambridge: Polity Press.

Children's Rights Alliance for England. (2012). *Why Incorporate? Making Rights a Reality for Every Child.* London: CRAE.

Cornock, M. (2007a). 'Fraser Guidelines or Gillick Competence?' *Journal of Children's and Young People's Nursing* 1(3): 142.

Cornock, M. (2007b). 'Circumcision in Young Boys: A Legal Commentary'. *Journal of Children's and Young People's Nursing* 1(7): 348–9.

Cornock, M. and Montgomery, H. (2010). 'Children's Rights In and Out of the Womb'. *International Journal of Children's Rights* 19(1): 3–19.

de Vries, J. (2007). 'The Obesity Epidemic: Medical and Ethical Considerations'. *Science & Engineering Ethics* 13(1): 55–67.

Donnelly, J. (2003). *Universal Human Rights in Theory and Practice* (2nd edn). Ithaca, NY: Cornell University Press.

Ennew, J. (2000). 'The History of Children's Rights: Whose Story?' *Cultural Survival Quarterly* 24(2): 44–8.

Evans, S. (2012). 'German circumcision ban: is it a parent's right to choose?' http://m.bbc.co.uk/news/magazine-18793842 (accessed 20 August 2012).

Fortin, J. (2003). *Children's Rights and the Developing Law* (2nd edn). London: LexisNexis.

Freeman, M. (1992). 'Introduction: Rights, Ideology and Children'. In M. Freeman and P. Veerman (eds), *The Ideologies of Children's Rights*. Leiden: Martinus Nijhoff.

Goodman, R. (1996). 'On Introducing the UN Convention on the Rights of the Child into Japan'. In R. Goodman, T. and I. Neary (eds), *Case Studies on Human Rights in Japan*. Richmond: Curzon Press.

Kehily, M.-J. (2010). 'Childhood in Crisis? Tracing the Contours of "Crisis" and Its Impact upon Contemporary Parenting Practices'. *Media, Culture and Society* 32(2): 171–85.

Laming, W. H. (2009). *The Protection of Children in England: A Progress Report.* London: HMSO.

Layard, R. and Dunn, J. (2009). *A Good Childhood: Searching for Values in a Competitive Age.* London: Penguin.

Montgomery, H. (2009). *An Introduction to Childhood: Anthropological Perspectives on Children's Lives.* Oxford: Wiley-Blackwell.

Morrow, V. and Mayall, B. (2009). 'What Is Wrong with Children's Well-being in the UK? Questions of Meaning and Measurement'. *Journal of Social Welfare and Family Law* 31(3): 213–25.

Office of the United Nations High Commissioner for Human Rights. (2007). *Legislative History of the Convention on the Rights of the Child.* Vol. I. New York and Geneva: United Nations.

Palmer, S. (2006). *Toxic Childhood: How the Modern World Is Damaging Our Children and What We Can Do about It.* London: Orion.

Percy-Smith, B. and Thomas, N. (eds). (2010). *A Handbook of Children and Young People's Participation. Perspectives from Theory and Practice.* London: Routledge.

Punch, S. (2013). 'Resilience and Well-being'. In H. Montgomery (ed.), *Global Childhoods: Local Issues.* Bristol: Policy Press.

Pupavac, V. (2001). 'Misanthropy without Borders: the International Children's Rights Regime'. *Disasters* 2(2): 95–112.

Schiratzki, J. (2011). 'Banning God's Law in the Name of the Holy Family'. *The Family in Law Review* 5(35): 35–53.

Scott, J. W. (2010). *The Politics of the Veil*. Princeton: Princeton University Press.
Twan-Danso, A. (2009). 'International Children's Rights'. In H. Montgomery and M. Kellett (eds), *Children and Young People's World: Developing Frameworks for Integrated Practice*. Bristol: Policy Press.
UNICEF. (2007). *Child Poverty in Perspective: An Overview of Child Well-being in Rich Countries*. Florence: UNICEF Innocenti Research Centre.
Van Bueren, G. (1995). *The International Law on the Rights of the Child*. Dordrecht: Martinus Nijhoff.
Welsh Government. (2012). *Should the Welsh Government apply the 'Articles' in the United Nations Convention on the Rights of the Child (UNCRC) to young people aged 18–24yrs?* Consultation Document WG16064. wales.gov.uk/docs/phhs/consultation/121008consultationen.pdf (accessed 21 January 2014).
White, R., Carr, P. and Lowe, N. (2002). *The Children Act in Practice* (3rd edn). London: Butterworths LexisNexis.
Wilkinson, R. and Pickett, K. (2010). *The Spirit Level. Why Equality Is Better for Everyone*. London: Penguin.

Legislation

Age of Legal Capacity (Scotland) Act 1991
Children Act 1989
Children Act 2004
Children and Young Persons Act 1933
Family Law Reform Act 1969
Protection of Children Act 1978
Rights of Children and Young Persons (Wales) Measure 2011

Cases

Gillick v. West Norfolk and Wisbech Area Health Authority [1986] AC 112
Hewer v. Bryant [1969] 3 ALL ER 578
R v. Howes (1860) 3 E & E 332
Re Agar-Ellis, Agar-Ellis v. Lascelles (1883) 24 Ch D 317
Re M (Child: refusal of medical treatment) 52 BMLR 124
Re P (A minor) [2003] EWHC 2327 (Fam)
Re R (A Minor) (Wardship: consent to treatment) [1992] Fam 11 CA
Re W (A Minor) (Medical treatment) [1992] 4 All ER 627
R (on the application of Axon) v. Secretary of State for Health [2006] EWHC 37 (Admin)

10
Whiteboard Jungle
Schooling, Culture War and the Market at the Turn of the Twenty-First Century

Stephen Wagg

The Cambridge academic Stefan Collini wrote recently: 'One of the most fascinating yet elusive aspects of cultural change is the way certain ideals and arguments acquire an almost self-evident power at particular times ...' (Collini 2011). In relation to political discourse on British schooling at the turn of the twenty-first century, 'standards' fits this description. By then it had acquired the status of a political myth – that's to say, 'depoliticised speech', as in the work of Roland Barthes (Barthes 1973: 142). For much of the first decade of the twenty-first century, the notion that 'standards' – held, largely, to reside in the results of written tests – were falling and that the actions of successive governments would raise them went virtually unchallenged in the political mainstream.

The word 'choice' acquired a similar force. Despite the growing and widespread promotion of children's rights, the views of schoolchildren were seldom heard amid the hue and cry over 'standards'. Instead, their interests, like those of their parents, were invoked largely in their absence. In the process, some of the fundaments of British liberal educational thought were largely abandoned, at least at government and parliamentary level. There was decreasing sympathy, for example, for the thought, eloquently expressed as long ago as 1874 by the biologist Thomas Henry Huxley, that students, submitted to an excessive programme of examinations, 'work to pass, not to know' (Huxley 1874). But perhaps the most significant departure from the postwar educational consensus was the disinclination of key policy makers any longer to see a child's educational performance as being influenced by social factors. Alastair Campbell, Director of Communications and Strategy for Prime Minister Tony Blair (1997–2003), recalled a conversation with Blair in his diary, 30 August 2000, as follows: 'he said the problem with schools was uniformity of teaching. I said the problem was the background of poorer kids and he just rolled his eyes at me' (Campbell and Hagerty 2011b: 385). There can have been few moments in the transaction of British educational politics at the turn of the twenty-first century more symbolic than this one.

Amid these often dramatic changes in discourse a range of reforms of English schools has been introduced, many by the 'New' Labour governments in office between 1997 and 2010, and they have been associated in the public mind principally with Tony Blair, the party's leader and chief rhetorician between 1994 and 2007. It was Blair, of course, who, at the Labour Party conference of the autumn of 1996, declared that the party's three priorities, if elected the following year, would be 'Education, education and education'. In another noted oration, this time at his Sedgefield constituency in November of 2005, Blair asserted: 'Education is the spark that can light a love of learning – horizons broaden, imaginations are fired, confidence and ambition take root.' These seemingly admirable, if unspecific, statements gave little clue as to Labour's intentions for schools. In fact, as several writers have since argued, the administrations of Tony Blair (1997–2007) and Gordon Brown (2007–10) continued reforms that were already in progress. These reforms – essentially market in character – involved severing the link between state schools and local education authorities, introducing schools specialising in particular skills and curricula, and permitting private bodies, such as churches[1] and commercial companies to run schools. Greater selection has been sanctioned via the rhetoric of parental choice and the publication of league tables compelled by the Education Act of 1988. The process of what is, in effect, the privatisation of schooling has been accelerated with the coming to power of a Conservative–Liberal Democrat coalition in 2010: under the stewardship of Michael Gove the Department of Education has begun the promotion of 'free schools', purportedly on a model previously established in Sweden.

This chapter, a sequel to the one written for *Thatcher's Children?*, will provide a political analysis of the changes enacted over this period. It will argue that the changes (a) conform to a pattern of privatisation that has characterised Western politics since around 1980 and therefore transcend the purported philosophies or strategies of individual politicians or, for that matter, political parties; (b) at an electoral level they play to the aspirations (and fears) of a particular demographic – the upwardly mobile and/or lower-/middle-class voter; (c) meet the demands of international corporations now prominent in funding British political parties and seeking new markets; and (d) affirm the notion that schooling should serve the needs of business and individual self-advancement. It will dispute the idea widely propagated by government that the reforms enfranchise 'pupils and parents'.

'Permanent Maoist revolution': contemporary schooling – rhetoric and reform

Reforms to British schooling, and the transformation thereby of the lives of most British schoolchildren, have been, as previously indicated, part of a widespread trend in the industrialised world. The rhetoric that has accompanied these changes, however, has combined old-established notions and perspectives with newly minted terminology. Indeed, what amounts to a contemporary culture war[2] over schooling in Britain has generated an improbable melange of previously disparate political ideas. This culture war has been an asymmetrical conflict, with the education ministry, the main political parties, the schools inspectorate, leading businesses (including the influential global management consultants McKinsey[3]), religious bodies and large sections of the national press on one side and the teacher unions and various educationally progressive pressure groups on the other. The war has purportedly been about the (relentlessly invoked) 'standards' of educational achievement and related matters – classroom discipline, the competence of teachers and so on. But, for many observers, this simply provided the government of the day with a pretext for putting the schools into private hands – hands which alone, it was asserted, were capable of 'raising standards'.

Leading social theorists such as Bob Jessop have suggested that societies such as Britain have lately moved from their status as 'Keynesian welfare national states', established in the 1940s and 1950s, and become reconstituted as 'competition states', wherein 'workfare' takes priority over welfare – that is to say, economic policy predominates over, and shapes, social policy. The task of this state is 'to secure economic growth ... and ... competitive advantages for capitals based in its borders' (Jessop 2002: 96). This analysis is, generally speaking, a given in the work of the most acute academic observers of contemporary education. Sally Tomlinson, for example, writes of 'education in a post-welfare society' (Tomlinson 2005) and Stephen J. Ball, another leading chronicler, acknowledges Jessop's arguments in his book *Education plc*, the consequence for schooling being that the state is 'increasingly re-positioned as the guarantor, not necessarily the provider, nor the financier, of opportunity goods like education' (Ball 2007: 13; see also Ball 2008: 84). (The description of education as an 'opportunity good' marks the power of a new, market-based discourse in relation to what had been, until relatively recently, a 'public good'.)

The likelihood must be that the actual political progress towards the wholesale reorientation of British schooling was the result of complex behind-the-scenes lobbying and deliberation, which will have involved civil servants from the Department of Education,[4] lobbyists and representatives of major international companies and pressure groups/think tanks. The Education Act of 1988, for example, is known to have been strongly influenced by right-wing bodies such as the Hillgate Group, the Centre for Policy Studies and the Institute of Economic Affairs (Chitty 2001: 63). To this list must be added the growing influence of international bodies such as the Organisation for Economic Cooperation and Development (OECD) and, in particular, of its Programme for International Student Assessment (PISA), inaugurated in 1997 to evaluate national education systems and, specifically, the competence of 15-year-old pupils in reading, science and mathematics: governments across four continents (there are no African members of OECD) have understandably been anxious that their countries show up well in these international indices. The history of school reform, however, is invariably attributed to the inspiration of individual politicians. Inevitably, the role of these individuals in bringing about these reforms is (often greatly) exaggerated, but their importance in advocating them publicly invariably is not.

In this regard, an important step on the road towards the reshaping of British state schooling was taken by Labour Prime Minister James Callaghan in a speech at Ruskin College, Oxford, in October 1976 (Wagg 1996: 16–18), in which he spoke of 'the need to improve relations between industry and education'.[5] Since 1988, Ball notes, there has been a '"ratchet effect" of changing practical and discursive possibilities' (Ball 2007: 19) – an upheaval, both in the way that education was organised and in the vocabulary used to describe it. Evidence of this 'ratchet effect' can, of course, be found in the Education Reform ('Baker') Act of that year, which instituted a national curriculum, regular testing of pupils from the age of seven and the publication of league tables purporting to show the respective merits of schools based on test results. Schools were permitted to opt out of the control of local education authorities and a new kind of school – the City Technology College – was created to cater for pupils with special aptitudes (say, for science, sport or music). These latter would be, similarly, outside of local authority jurisdiction. Overall, the measures were centralising, taking schooling outside of the scope of local democracy and placing both the curricular direction and the funding of schools with the ministry. Teachers and local administrators would have decreasing influence over what was taught in British state schools.

The Conservative government of John Major (1990–7) worked within the logic of this new dispensation. In his memoirs, Major recalls reading reports that 'revealed a rash of low expectations and children performing below their natural abilities. Against that background, the creation of an Office of Standards in Education (OFSTED) was vital. From the outset I wished to set up a regular and fully independent inspection of schools' (Major 2000: 397). Established in 1993, this was, in effect, the privatised school inspectorate; its title showed the central place now accorded to the word 'standards' in the British politics of education and its role was plainly to police schools according the emergent, post-Baker priorities. (It is unlikely that OFSTED was Major's creation. It was, after all, wholly in keeping with the state's new role as 'guarantor-but-not-necessarily-provider', in the context of which Major had in 1991 announced a 'Citizens Charter', under which public services would be held to account.)

Of the new watchdog's work, Major judged: 'Under its chief inspectors, Professor Stewart Sutherland [a philosopher of religion] and Chris Woodhead [a former English teacher and deputy chief education officer]

OFSTED was quite fearless in condemning low standards and opening up information long hidden from parents' (Major 2000: 397). The notion of condemnation and the implication that information had previously been deliberately withheld from parents prefigured the sort destabilisation of public services identified by Ball as a common feature of the transition to a competition state, whereby these services and the people who perform them ultimately become objects of derision (Ball 2007: 20). Woodhead's time at OFSTED (1993–2000) was described by the liberal educationist Professor Tim Brighouse as 'a reign of terror' (Bangs, MacBeath and Galton 2011: 5), and Woodhead himself later conceded: '"Prickly, arrogant, confrontational, incapable of working with anyone". Yes, that is me. But it is what the Chief Inspector has to be if OFSTED is to maintain any semblance of independence' (Woodhead 2002: 108). Despite, or more probably because of, his fractious relationship with schoolteachers, Woodhead was confirmed in post by the incoming Labour administration in 1997, under which the destabilisation of state schools as a more-or-less taken-for-granted public service became more concerted.

The ten years of educational politics transacted between 1997 and 2007 are closely associated with the Prime Minister of the time, Tony Blair – an association certainly not discouraged in his autobiography. The Labour Party had been rebranded as 'New Labour' in 1996 with the issuing of the pamphlet *New Labour, New Life For Britain*. Rendered in political discourse as a 'move to the right' or 'embracing the centre ground', the document, in effect, accepted the emerging competition state. Thus, as Tomlinson observes, the Conservative and Labour manifestos at the General election of 1997 were 'remarkably similar' on education (Tomlinson 2005: 88). Indeed, John Major, his predecessor as premier, later accused Blair of stealing Conservative policies (on education and other matters), calling him a 'middle-of-the-road Tory' and a 'political kleptomaniac' (Major 2000: 592–3). But Blair's role was primarily ideological; he proselytised a view of schooling designed to dignify a set of radical changes already in train. Blair's ideological pitch was a radical reconfiguration of arguments that had been around in the politics and sociology of education (in Britain and elsewhere) since the 1950s. The Blair era also marks a time in the field of schooling when, to adopt Andrew Gamble's conceptualisation, the politics of power (state activity) and the politics of support (the ongoing struggle for the approval of the electorate) effectively merge (see Gamble 1974: 3–11). Back in 1995, Conservative education minister Gillian Shephard had privately noted the power of the words 'standards, discipline and chaos' to erode the public perception that state schools were short of money (Wagg 1996: 24), and stories making extravagant use of such words had long since become a staple in right-wing, mid-market newspapers such as the *Daily Mail* and the *Daily Express* (School Without Walls 1978). This was largely because, in a nominally open and 'aspirational' society, schooling is widely claimed to be the key to success in the job market. Therefore schooling is important to most people, particularly if they have children. Besides, the changes being made were likely to meet with strong resistance in some quarters and this would have to be countered ideologically. Indeed, by the early years of the twenty-first century a kind of culture war was, as I have suggested, being waged over Britain's state schools – something which leading protagonists seemed to acknowledge in their published thoughts on the subject: books by Woodhead (Woodhead 2002) and Melissa Benn, a leading campaigner against marketisation (Benn 2011), both had the word 'war' in their titles.

As Ball drily observes: 'Whatever else you could say about Labour's education policies, there is certainly no shortage of them' (Ball 2008: 86). Tomlinson enumerates around 50 separate initiatives in the field of education taken by the Blair government between May of 1997 and September 2000 (Tomlinson 2005: 92–3). Chief among these were: the establishment of a Standards and Effectiveness Unit in the Department for Education and Skills (1997); the publication of a White Paper called *Excellence in Schools*, containing a promise to 'raise standards in education', followed by a School Standards and Framework Bill (1997, made law the following year); a campaign to improve literacy (including instituting a 'literacy hour' in all state primary schools) (1997); the setting up of 25 'Education Action Zones'; the inauguration of the Sure Start programme for children aged 0–3 in deprived areas; receiving a report on *Education for Citizenship and the Teaching of Democracy in School* (1998); the expansion of 'specialist and beacon schools' (1999); tests for 12-year-olds (2000); and the creation of centrally funded 'city academies', modelled on 'charter schools' in the United States (2000). (In December 1998, David Blunkett, Labour's new Secretary of State for Education and Employment, expressed to Blair the fear that, such was the hectic nature of policy making, they appeared to be 'moving into a phase of "permanent Maoist revolution"' (Blunkett 2006: 101).

These moves, and numerous others, had enormous ramifications for the (already crumbling) postwar political consensus on schooling in British society. Britain's schools were still largely comprehensive in some form, although some grammar schools remained, along with city technology colleges – arguably a form of grammar school – and the option for schools to withdraw from local authority control had begun to undermine the comprehensive system. The Labour Party had a history of opposition to the selection (via the Eleven Plus examination) that had underpinned the post-1944 'tripartite' secondary school arrangement in state secondary schools, on the grounds that it disadvantaged the working-class child. A Labour government had called on local authorities to draw up plans for comprehensive schools in the mid-1960s and they had the support of the Labour movement in doing so. Moreover, the Labour Party had had a broad sympathy with the work of generations of sociologists of education who had written of the obstacles faced by working-class children in the education process (Wagg 1996: 10–12). The National Union of Teachers, founded in 1870, had supported the comprehensive ideal since the early 1940s and had become affiliated to the Trade Union Congress in 1969. The increased talk in government circles after 1997 of 'standards' and 'low expectations' ran contrary to all of that. In the judgement of Sally Tomlinson: 'Policy convergence between Conservative and Labour governments was most observable over one of the cruellest and most pointless policies developed in the wake of the Education Act 1993 [which, among other things, provided for schools to be placed under 'special measures'] – that of attacking so-called "failing schools".' These allegedly faltering institutions, she pointed out, were often former secondary modern schools, which were now comprehensives 'serving working class areas' (Tomlinson 2005: 79; see also 58–61). This argument cut no ice with 'New' Labour.

The rhetoric of Tony Blair on the schools issue has attracted special attention – Stephen Ball, for example, devotes six pages to it in his analysis of business involvement in British schooling (Ball 2007: 32–7). In Blair's many speeches and published ruminations a number of important themes emerge; in all of these instances, school reforms are presented not as the continuation of a marketising project emanating from the education ministry but as the fruits of Blair's personal vision. In the summer of 1995 Blair flew to Australia to speak at a conference held on Hayman Island by News Corporation, the multinational media conglomerate run by Rupert Murdoch. On his return he wrote an article in *The Times* (owned by News Corporation), reassuring readers that Labour Party policy on education was 'not devised to please the National Union of Teachers. It was devised to meet the concerns of parents' (Blair 2010: 98–9). Once in office, Labour launched immediate initiatives on literacy and numeracy. At the same time, Blair heightened the political talk of past and present failure. 'There's nothing wrong with old principles,' he told the Labour Party Conference of 2002, 'but, if the old ways worked, they'd have worked by now' (quoted in Ball 2007: 32). Blair, by contrast, would be reaching for the sky:

> It wasn't hard to persuade people to do something with failing schools, by which I mean schools that were to all intents and purposes basket cases – 10 per cent, 15 per cent, 20 per cent of pupils getting five GCSEs – but that was nowhere near the ambition I wanted. I take an essentially middle class view of public services, and you can't understand anything I tried to do to reform them without understanding that. I sent my own children to state schools; they were good state schools – but I wanted them to be even better. And they were, at least then, reasonably rare. It wasn't simply the schools getting ten per cent, 15 per cent or 20 per cent of their kids to the right level that concerned me, but the schools getting only 50 or 60 per cent. (Blair 2010: 272)

A number of vital consequences flowed from this stance. First, the inauguration of the Sure Start pre-school programme and the setting up of 'Education Action Zones' notwithstanding,[6] Blair and the education ministry showed little sympathy for the notion of mitigating circumstance. Hitherto, an influential body of opinion (led by sociologists, educationists and spokespeople from the left of the political spectrum) had held that the educational achievements of children and their schools could not be judged without regard to social context. Poverty, lack of parental support, minimal access to reading matter or other stimulation, 'restricted codes' of language, the fatalistic expectation of manual labour on the part of working-class lads ... these and other similar factors had all, at one time or another, been adduced to account for the comparative lack of progress made by the working-class pupil. Correspondingly, a host of social advantages would explain the continued success of those middle- and upper-middle-class children who prospered – especially those who passed, often generation after generation, from Britain's private schools, via the elite universities of Oxford and Cambridge, into well-paid, high-status jobs. In the emergent paradigm propagated by 'New' Labour, these arguments virtually disappeared and were replaced by a coarser explanation, in which the only significant variables lay in the school itself: teachers and head teachers. Now 'good' schools got good results simply because they were 'good', not because they had the most gifted, well-resourced or dedicated pupils. 'Equity,' wrote Blair later, 'could not and should never be at the expense of excellence' (Blair 2010: 578). This, in practice, had meant a tacit endorsement of Britain's public (i.e., private) and grammar schools and a rejection of the comprehensive school. In January 1995, while still in opposition, Blair had rejected the idea of taxing private schools, which, to the consternation of many educationists, were (and remain) registered as charities (Blair 2010: 87). 'The truth is,' insisted Blair in his memoirs, 'that both types of school [grammar and private] are good for other reasons too [i.e., aside from their middle-class intake and superior facilities]. They are independent. They have an acute sense of ethos and identity. They have strong leadership and are allowed to lead. They are more flexible. They innovate because no one tells them they can't. They pursue excellence.' Moreover, 'the way comprehensives were introduced and grammar schools abandoned was pretty close to academic vandalism' (Blair 2010: 579). And towards those parents and children without current access to private or grammar school education, Blair was sympathetic but resolute:

> In the end it often came down to this: if you introduced a really good school in an area of really average ones, lo and behold the parents all clamoured to get their children into the really good one. And, yes, of course that caused consternation among the parents that failed to get their children in, and the local councillors, teachers and so on. But, as

I used to argue: that simply cannot be a reason not to have the really good school; that must be a reason for analysing why the others are average or worse and changing them. (Blair 2010: 579–80)

Analysing them often entailed little more than an accentuation of the idea of 'low expectation' invoked by John Major: some schools, in Blair's judgement, simply 'accepted failure' (Blair 2010: 580). This was an unmistakeable shot across the bows of the teaching force: Dr Mary Bousted, general secretary of the Association of Teachers and Lecturers, recalled hearing Blunkett use a 'phrase which I'll never forget, "kids in Inner City Schools fail because the teachers have no expectation". I thought that was a shameful thing for a Labour minister to say' (quoted in Bangs, MacBeath and Galton 2011: 108–9). Changing these 'failing' institutions took the form of encouraging the creation of 'foundation schools' or academies, many of which would be sponsored by businesses or individual entrepreneurs. The key to these schools would be that they lay outside of state control – 'some remote bureaucracy', as Blair styled it – and that sponsors were 'determined and successful individuals' who 'brought that determination and drive for success into the school. And most of all, freed from the extraordinarily debilitating and often, in the worst sense, politically correct interference from the state or municipality, the academies just had one thing in mind, something shaped not by political prejudice, but by common sense: what will make the school excellent' (Blair 2010: 576–7).

None of this was incompatible with inclusive or emollient rhetoric and Blair and his speechwriters and communications advisers provided much of this. 'We should be proud of our education system, our teachers and staff,' Blair told an audience at Abraham Moss High School in Manchester in March of 2002, for example. 'There is, however, a lot more to do. We want to be the best. And we can be. The challenge is to educate not just the top twenty or thirty per cent well, but all our children' (quoted in Campbell and Hagerty 2012: 194). Later that year, this time at a school in East London, Blair said: 'Our goal is a Britain in which nobody is left behind, in which people can go as far as they have the talent to go' (quoted in Campbell and Hagerty 2012: 303).

Blair's speeches frequently married this rhetorical inclusiveness – what Ball calls 'peoplism' (Ball 2007: 35) – to an emphasis upon the importance of 'modernisation' (see, in particular, Finlayson, 1998) and 'globalisation' in relation to schooling. In 2005 he famously told the Labour Party conference: 'Some day, some party will make this country at ease with globalisation. Let it be this one. Some day we will forge a new consensus on our public services.'[7] The following year the rhetoric soared still higher when the party's spring conference in Blackpool was stirred in affirmation of Blair's resolve in 'preparing Britain for the competitive force of globalisation; we have to be the ones taking the hard decisions, meeting the challenges, explaining why change is the only way to make the nation, stronger, better, fairer'. 'So', he continued,

> what is the agenda that we are carrying through? It is to modernise our country, so that, in the face of future challenges, intense and profound for us and like nations, we are able to provide opportunity and security for all; not for an elite; not for the privileged few; but for all our people, whatever their class, colour or creed. (*Guardian*, 10 February 2006)

Along with 'modernisation' and 'globalisation', there were frequent invocations, in the speeches of Blair and other 'New' Labour spokespeople, of 'the knowledge economy' – a phenomenon Alex Nunn has called 'the "Knowledge Economy" cacophony' (Nunn 2002) – and 'the learning society', the latter a notion of lifelong learning first employed by educationists in the 1970s (see Hutchins 1970; Schon 1973; Husen 1974) and adopted by the OECD in the mid-1990s (Commission of the European Communities 1995).[8]

This breathless lexicon of a world in apparent flux, full of words that were by turns exciting, business-like and vague in their meaning – invariably bulwarked by invocations of the (equally indistinct) 'third way'[9] of governing – seemed to license 'New' Labour to take radical action on schools. In parliamentary and government circles, however, and in the purported pursuit of higher standards, objectives other than those hymned in Blairite rhetoric soon became evident.

'An inspector calls': contemporary schooling – resistance, critique and culture war

David Blunkett became the Blair government's first education secretary in 1997. His main difficulties in negotiating Labour's radical programme came initially from his own natural allies: his party, education academics and the myriad supporters of the concept of comprehensive schooling. Privately doubtful of some of the prevailing rhetoric of 'choice', 'efficiency gains' and 'productivity' in schooling (see Blunkett 2006: 48 and 87), he fretted over the reception the reforms would have among the previously taken-for-granted friends of Labour. Early in his stewardship, Blunkett appointed both Chris Woodhead and Tim Brighouse (a leading critic of Woodhead) to a task force on school standards. He told the National Association of Head Teachers conference in Scarborough, which had just voted unanimously for Woodhead's dismissal, that the pair had agreed to work together 'to benefit the country's children',[10] but Blunkett later admitted that he'd appointed Woodhead for 'rigour' and Brighouse to appease the 'liberal press' (Blunkett 2006: 19–20).

Veteran Labour politician Roy Hattersley, once perceived as on the right of the party but now an apparent spokesperson for its (shrinking) left, denounced the notion of 'failing schools'; Blunkett saw this – as many such criticisms were to be rendered – as 'not defending the children' (Blunkett 2006: 15–16). Later, when it became clear that these 'failing schools' and others would likely be turned over to private firms or become (largely independent) academies, it occurred to many critics that such schools would very likely now choose to select their intake. Blunkett had been mindful of the historic importance to the British Labour movement of doing away with the selective Eleven Plus examination (mostly achieved in the 1960s and 1970s) and, in the General Election campaign of 1997, had vowed 'no selection' under a Labour government. Once in office, however, Blunkett suggested that this had been a 'compromise ... in order not to be distracted from the agenda of standards and improvement for all children'; what he'd meant, he now claimed, was 'no *further* selection' (Blunkett 2006: 173, emphasis added). Blunkett now effectively severed Labour's longstanding dialogue with the liberal educationalists. Despite its increasing and inevitable diversity, the sociology of education remained (and is still) concerned with issues of class (see, for example, Tomlinson 2005; Ball 2006; Apple, Ball and Gaudin 2010). But the premise from which Blair and Blunkett now worked did not recognise sociological arguments so, understandably, Blunkett received a hostile reception when he visited the (previously influential) Institute of Education at London University in January of 1999. He accused them of talking 'middle class claptrap' and resolved to look elsewhere for advice (Blunkett 2006: 108–9).

In the place of social factors as the chief determinant of a school's overall performance, the Blair government and the inspectorate propounded the simple notion of the charismatic individual – the man or woman who provided 'good teaching', for instance, or the 'super head' that 'turned around' a troubled place of learning. The National College of School Leadership was established in Nottingham in 2000 and the notion of the 'super head' received growing affirmation in the media. The latter idea was flagged up in 1996:

> A new breed of super headteacher, paid over the odds and running more than one school, would be created by a Labour government. Under plans to be announced in a speech today by Tony Blair, the Labour leader, successful heads would be paid to take over nearby failing schools. They might run another secondary school as well as their own, or one or more feeder primary schools. (Judd 1996)

The idea soon found its way into popular media culture: the comedian and actor Lenny Henry played the role of a 'super head' in *Hope and Glory*, a BBC television drama that ran for two series between 1999 and 2000. Blair and his communications adviser Alastair Campbell discussed knighthoods and other honours for individual teachers (Campbell and Hagerty

2011a: 104, 235, 247). By the time 'New' Labour had left office, a journalist on the *London Evening Standard* was informing readers: 'They take on our worst performing schools in deprived areas with some of the toughest pupils in the capital and turn these so-called "unteachable" kids into stars. Superheads they call them, and although they're handsomely rewarded with salaries typically in excess of £120,000, they put in ferociously long hours and punch well above their weight when it comes to ramping up results' (Cohen 2011)

These myths (again, in Barthes' sense) had politically important corollaries, which Inspector Woodhead was among the first to recognise. Woodhead came to embody simultaneously the politics of support and the politics of power in relation to schooling. Apparently an acute reader of the political wind, he had begun as early as the mid-1990s to see that the growing emphasis on good teachers logically implied the existence of bad ones: in 1995, a few months into his appointment to OFSTED, he had claimed that 15,000 teachers were incompetent and should be dismissed. To many observers – for the government and the right-wing press – schools, good teaching and 'standards' now seemed to be whatever Woodhead said they were. The clear logic of the current narrative of 'failing schools', 'bad teachers' and 'super-heads' was to privatise schools, enabling heads to lay off unwanted teachers and strike local pay deals, thus breaking the negotiating power of teacher unions such as the NUT. (Campbell noted in his diary in June of 1995 that the NUT, doubtless concerned by the new political vocabulary of 'low expectation', had hired the prestigious public relations company Lowe Bell to advise them on their 'image'; Campbell 2010: 221–2.) Woodhead began to lobby for performance-related pay for teachers and for poor performers to be sacked; Blunkett perceived that Woodhead was seeking a lucrative contract to write for a right-wing newspaper, as well as pressing behind the political scenes (along with right-wing columnist Melanie Phillips) for more privatisation. Woodhead, wrote Blunkett, 'denounces everything around him' (Blunkett 2006: 194, 212). Woodhead resigned in 2000 and began to write for the right-wing *Daily Telegraph*; he also established a private education company.

By the end of the twentieth century there was, according to Tomlinson's calculation, a hierarchy of 13 different kinds of school in Britain (Tomlinson 2005: 103). At the time of Woodhead's resignation, *The Economist* calculated that: 'Since Labour came to power, no fewer than 604 schools have been put on, and come out of, "special measures". More than 100 failing schools have been closed altogether.'[11] By 2010, many were run or likely to be run by private firms[12] and private sponsors and private capital was extensively contracted to provide a range of educational services (Ball 2007). By and large, being freed from Blair's 'remote bureaucracy' (code for the local education authorities, finally marginalised in 2005), they were not subject to the National Curriculum, regarded as a vital prescription for schoolchildren only a dozen years earlier. According to Tony Blair, 'standards' were now appreciably higher: 'In 1997 there were nearly a hundred London schools with fewer than a quarter of pupils getting five GCSEs. By 2007, it was down to two' (Blair 2010: 650).

For the left, however – albeit now scarcely represented in the political mainstream – the crisis of 'standards' and 'failing schools' had always been confected. 'If you believed the papers and the politicians,' wrote Colin Sparks in 1997, 'everything is wrong in the schools and it is all the fault of teachers, aided by irresponsible single parents. Child centred learning and comprehensive education were mad ideas dreamed up by red teachers back in the 1960s. They have totally failed the nation. Schools churn out uneducated and unemployable young people with no values and no sense of discipline.' In Sparks's view, the evidence of exam passes – the conventional index of 'standards' – actually showed a steady improvement, especially since the introduction of GCSEs in 1986 (Sparks 1997: 3). For a number of distinguished and longstanding observers, the recent reforms, in Britain and elsewhere, were likely to reverse social and educational progress made since the 1960s, not advance it. The social class divide in state schooling, mitigated to a degree by comprehensivisation, was now being restored: by 1992, Sally Tomlinson argued, 'the creation of a market in education, driven by the self interest of knowledgeable parents and the competitive strategies of schools which had been forced, with varying degrees of reluctance, to market their schools to attract desirable customers, was ensuring a first and second division in state schooling' (Tomlinson 2005: 78). (The *Daily Mail* reported in October 2008 that parents were now hiring lawyers before applying for their children to go to popular state schools – see Clark 2008.) In the United States the educator and activist Jonathan Kozol argued that charter schools – begun in 1991 and, like many British schools now, independent but receiving public money – were reproducing 'apartheid' (i.e., a racial divide) in the American school system (Kozol 2005).

Similarly, the guiding assumption of the 'New' Labour years that schools must now produce 'human capital' to meet the requirements of 'globalisation' was called into question. In a thoroughgoing critique of the education consensus of the late twentieth century, veteran educationist Frank Coffield argued that human capital theory ignored other kinds of capital and had 'nothing to say about the sharpening polarisation in income and wealth both internationally and within the UK' (Coffield 1999: 483). It was also pointed out that the widely invoked transnational corporations, which were invariably placed at the centre of the globalisation thesis, usually trawled the globe looking for labour that was low-paid and flexible, rather than 'upskilled' (see, for example, Ball 2006: 68).

Such critiques were widespread, but, as this chapter has argued, they were either ignored or rejected by policy makers. So, aside from lecture halls, conferences and academic journals, the principal setting for opposition to changes visited on British schooling has been a burgeoning network of blogs, websites and pressure groups. These include the Campaign for State Education, the Local Schools Network, Comprehensive Future, the Socialist Educational Association (which is close to the Labour Party, although not, of course, its leadership), the Anti-Academies Alliance (which has strong trade union support, including that of the TUC and several teacher and other unions) and Changing Schools, which has the support of academics and cites research which calls the improving properties of academy schools into question.[13] These groups often have overlapping membership made up of MPs, school governors, teachers, students, parents and activists and their policies include what they see as fair admissions and broad curricula. They try to influence school policy at national and at local level but have often found themselves prisoners of the economic vocabulary in which schools are now routinely discussed: for example, as a result of progressive campaigns to salvage the notion of educational disadvantage, school league tables since 2003 have contained information on 'value added' to the pupil by his/her school. Opponents of the new orthodoxy have also found themselves, as I have argued, drawn into a culture war, struggling not only to salvage comprehensive schooling but to counter what Melissa Benn has called the 'apocalyptic picture of state education' (Benn 2011: 13) conjured by right-wing culture warriors. The careers of Chris Woodhead and Melanie Phillips suggested, if nothing else, that the same narrative of the degeneration of British state schooling, to which the tabloid newspapers returned so often, could also support substantial book sales and a prominent public profile. Woodhead produced two books on falling standards and the folly of much recent educational orthodoxy (Woodhead 2002, 2009); he wrote columns for the right-wing *Daily Telegraph* and *The Sunday Times*, became a professor at the (private) University of Buckingham and received a knighthood in 2011. In 1996 Phillips published a book called *All Must Have Prizes* (the title is taken from *Alice in Wonderland*), which accused teachers, among other things, of moral relativism and claimed that:

> British education is in a state of 'meltdown'. Throughout the system, from nursery classes to degree courses, the relationship between teacher and pupil has been undermined, and the idea that children should be taught a body of rules at all, whether in maths or grammar, is now taboo in many schools. Systematic instruction has given way to approximations and guesswork, resulting in a rising tide of illiteracy.[14]

She began writing (in a similar vein) for the *Daily Mail* in 2001. In 2013 she launched herself as a right-wing celebrity, with branded merchandise, in the United States (Cooper 2013). This media admixture of show business and right-wing educational politics threw up another celebrity in Katharine Birbalsingh, a New Zealand teacher and blogger of Caribbean heritage, who condemned the 'left wing straitjacket' in which British state schools were allegedly held at the Conservative Party conference of 2010 (Odone 2011). She has since published a book rendering her experiences as a teacher in a state school from the same perspective (Birbalsingh 2011) and set up a free school in the London borough of Brent. Toby Young, a Conservative journalist and experienced self-publicist (his memoir *How to Lose Friends and Alienate People* was turned into a film in 2008), was another successful blogger-on-education (for the *Telegraph*) and, availing himself of government reforms, the founder of the West London Free School in 2011.

It was probably inevitable, therefore, that when the Conservative Michael Gove was made Education Secretary in the Conservative–Liberal Democrat Coalition government of 2010, he would beat the same ideological drum. Gove soon became one of the most media-prominent members of the cabinet and his ministry was notable for two things in particular: the urgency with which schools were now pressed to become academies or free schools – bringing widespread accusations of bullying (see, for example, Garner 2013a) – and a series of populist-traditionalist announcements about contemporary schooling. For instance, he combined three classic signifiers in a speech at Brighton College in May of 2013: mining the now well-worn seam of 'low expectations', he suggested that 'most parents would want their children to read George Eliot's *Middlemarch*[15] rather than watch the teen vampire TV series *Twilight*' and attacked the teaching of history, 'reasserting his enthusiasm that pupils should grow up "knowing the story of our islands"' and claiming that the *Mr Men* children's books were being used as illustrative material in history classes (Warrell 2013). Here the themes of (a) failing teachers, (b) the dangers to children's minds of contemporary popular culture versus the uplifting properties of timeless 'great works of high culture' and (c) the (unpatriotic) neglect of the nation's triumphal history[16] were skilfully melded together. Earlier Gove's recently announced proposals for another National Curriculum were criticised as stunting children's ability to think by one hundred leading education academics in a letter to the national broadsheets (Bassey et al. 2013). This being a culture war, however – effectively, the politics of support writ large – the criticisms were, for the most part, not addressed directly. The critics were deemed simply to be outside the scope of legitimate debate, the boundaries of which were now, in neoliberal times, very tightly drawn. 'Many of the 100 academics,' the *MailOnline* website reassured its readers, 'are Left-wingers linked to Labour or the unions' (Levy and Chapman 2013). Gove himself used the same site to place his accusers in the political-cultural universe, rather than to deal with their arguments. He denounced the critics thus: 'the new Enemies Of Promise are a set of politically motivated individuals who have been actively trying to prevent millions of our poorest children getting the education they need'. He added that 'One of the letter's principal signatories claims to write "from a classical Marxist perspective"'; the article included a picture of the philosopher in question, with the caption 'The academics who criticised the coalition's plans for education wrote with reference to Karl Marx (pictured).'[17]

Conclusion: who will listen to the student voice?

As I observed at the beginning of this chapter, the views of children and the consequences for their childhood were largely absent from 20 or more years of often vehement and highly contentious political assertion and enactment on schooling. Much of what was said and done was said and done in the name of (equally absent) parents and global institutions. The socialist academic Terry Wrigley, however, wrote in 2006:

> In England and the US, the heartlands of neo-liberal reaction, childhood itself is being consumed. Children are tested to destruction, and learners stuffed with fragments of dead knowledge like turkeys for Christmas. Despite the government's rhetoric of 'raising standards', learning is being trivialised. Literacy is treated as a mere exercise, disconnected from pleasure and purpose, and knowledge is 'delivered' in the straitjacket of government-approved lesson plans. (Wrigley 2006: 8–9)

Moreover, in the febrile educational-political climate that has prevailed since the late 1980s, wherein the views of educationalists and teachers' bodies were summarily discounted, there has been scant opportunity for children to express theirs. Kay Tisdall has been one of a number of writers to argue that British schools have a poor record in recognising children's rights to participate in the running of their schools and that citizenship, introduced as a subject in the National Curriculum in 2002, might better be taught in schools via this participation, rather than by learning legal rights and duties (Tisdall 2010: 318–20). And it goes, virtually, without saying, that the ideological sound and fury dispensed by right-wing commentators brooks little encouragement for this kind of participation. On the web page of Amazon.com which advertises Melanie Phillips' *All Must Have Prizes*, a sympathetic reader's review states:

> I have been a secondary school teacher for 20 years an [sic] I have seen the moral chaos at first hand in some schools, in others, key members of senior management have decided to stop the rot and been successful in doing so. In my classes, I have always adopted a didactic and disciplinarian approach – if you decide to follow this course then you have to kiss your career good bye; if you want to be senior management, then a PC [politically correct] approach is the key, with lots of child-centered [sic] BS[18] in your CV to help your application along. Student voice is one

example of the madness, where children interview prospective teachers, I refuse to allow this.[19]

But Maggie Atkinson, the Children's Commissioner (appointed under the Children Act 2004) did not subscribe to the 'BS' perspective. She told the *Guardian* in 2011:

> We know from research that young people want to be more involved in the running of their schools. They particularly want to help select their teachers and give feedback on lessons. Where schools involve pupils well, it leads to better relationships, improved behaviour and higher attainment. For example, at one school we visited, the school council runs training sessions for teachers – giving feedback on their lessons. Teachers say this helps them improve, and they really value the feedback – even if they did find it a bit daunting at first. (Birkett 2011)

In any event, 2010 saw the most concerted and radical political action by schoolchildren in recent times – an event which was handled with some severity by the state and its apologists in the press. On taking office, the Coalition government announced a steep rise in university tuition fees (something that the Liberal Democrat Party, now part of the Coalition, had pledged in the General Election not to do) and tens of thousands of school pupils, having exploited their extra-school freedom to organise themselves via Facebook and Twitter (Foot 2011), took to the streets in protest. The *Telegraph* treated the matter not as one of political dissent, but as one simply of truancy and disorder. It posted the following message on its website: 'Did your local school allow pupils time off to demonstrate? Leave your comments below or email, in confidence, studentriots@telegraph.co.uk' (Bloxham et al. 2010). In London, 1,500 police were mobilised and young protesters 'kettled' (maintained in a confined space) for eight hours. Three schoolchildren (two boys of 16 and a girl of 14) challenged the legality of this in the High Court, claiming a breach both of their human rights and of the Children Act 2004 (BBC News 2011). They lost. One of the boys said: 'We were punished for protesting and everyone was left demoralised' (Radnedge 2011).

'Demoralised' had, over more than 20 years, become a word widely used to describe the mood of teachers in public employ. In the second decade of the twenty-first century, invocations of great literature and high culture notwithstanding, government and government-sponsored renditions of life in British schools had taken on a cartoon quality. The culture war over schools showed no signs of abating. In this war, prosecuted on behalf of the new competition state, denigration of teachers appeared to be a taken-for-granted part of the job description for an OFSTED inspector. Complaints of stress and government bullying were tantamount to cowardice. 'Let me tell you what stress is,' the new chief of OFSTED, former academy 'superhead' Sir Michael Wishaw, told an audience in May of 2012, 'Stress is what many of the unemployed young people today feel – unable to get a job because they've had a poor experience of school and lack the skills to find employment'; this was reported with evident approval in the right-wing press, the relevant article in the *Sun* being prefaced by the words: 'The schools watchdog yesterday told whingeing teachers: You don't know what stress is' (Schofield 2012). A year on, Wilshaw had introduced a shorter-notice inspection for schools and abolished OFSTED's 'satisfactory' grade; head teachers, meanwhile, began to plan their own school inspection service (Garner 2013b). In the spring of 2013 the Association of Teachers and Lecturers, the NUT (for the first time in its long history) and the National Association of Headteachers all passed overwhelming votes of no confidence in the serving education secretary (Gove).

In a purportedly open and 'aspirational' society, only 7 per cent of whose children were educated privately, it might have been thought an affront for a Coalition cabinet, less than half of whom had been schooled in the state sector,[20] to be disposing of public sector schools in this way. But the 'New' Labour rhetoric of the previous dozen years had given them licence. Private schools now were no longer privileged, simply 'good'. Thus, Prime Minister David Cameron, educated at the nation's most prestigious private school (Eton) and from a wealthy and long-established banking family, could tell the Conservative Party conference of 2012: 'And to all those people who say: he wants children to have the kind of education he had at his posh school ... I say: yes – you're absolutely right. I went to a great school and I want every child to have a great education. I'm not here to defend privilege, I'm here to spread it.'[21]

However, by the time this book was going to press late in 2013, even this further rupturing of the postwar political consensus on schooling was beginning to seem outdated. The rhetoric of schools policy was already moving in an even more radical, right-wing direction. This came principally from Dominic Cummings. A former Director of Strategy for the Conservative Party, Cummings had become special adviser to Michael Gove in 2011 and was widely held to be aggressive in pressing the government's reforms (see, for example, Cusick 2013). In the autumn of 2013, Cummings issued what appeared to be a personal manifesto (Cummings 2013). Cummings' (extended) argument makes great play with science, using the lack of acquaintance with it to condemn most of the world's education systems: 'The education of the majority even in rich countries is between awful and mediocre. In England, few are well-trained in the basics of extended writing or mathematical and scientific modelling and problem-solving.' He calls for Britain to become 'the leading country for education and science' (Cummings 2013: 1 and 2). It is speckled with graphs, tables, theorems and pictures of the cosmos, but as the liberal *Observer* (Helm 2013) and the right-wing *Daily Mail* (Edwards 2013) were equally swift to spot, Cummings used his vision of a science-based educational future to revive the long-discredited concept of Intelligence Quotient (IQ). This pushed the argument further away from social factors; children had, until only recently, been blank slates upon which dynamic new free schools could achieve hitherto undreamt-of high standards. Now, in Cummings' formulation, they became, in prospect, little brighter than their own biology. Cummings told of how he had invited Professor Robert Plomin of King's College London to lecture education ministry civil servants on the importance of genetics in the development of intelligence. Plomin had already been given a sympathetic hearing in the *Spectator* – effectively the house journal of the British Conservative Party – a few months previously, in which he tells his breathless interviewer (in an educational parallel to Val Gillies' arguments in this book) that 'Newborns may well have their DNA sequenced as a matter of course' (Wakefield 2013). The idea that intelligence was genetic had played little part in the British argument over schooling in over 50 years, although a coterie of academics – mostly in the United States and funded in many cases by far-right eugenicist bodies such as the Pioneer Fund – has continued its search for a biological base to human differences. In December of 1994 Plomin had been signatory to a letter to the *Wall Street Journal* in support of Herrnstein and Murray's book *The Bell Curve* (Herrnstein and Murray 1994) (which argued that intelligence in the United States determined class – including, of course, a largely African American working class) and of the possibility culture-free intelligence testing.[22]

In the short term, the rehabilitation of these long since marginalised researchers and their arguments provided important political rationales: they dignified the closing of Sure Start centres (something the Conservative Party had undertaken not to do in 2009[23]) and made more complex any argument a parent might in future have about 'value added' to their child by a commercially run school. In the longer term, it levered open a political Pandora's box labelled 'eugenics' which, in relation to British schooling, had been firmly closed since the middle of the previous century.

Acknowledgement

Thanks to Jane Pilcher, Peter Bramham and Terry Wrigley for helpful comments on an earlier draft of this chapter.

Notes

1. Churches have, of course, been involved in British schooling for centuries but church schools were effectively nationalised under the Education Act of 1870. Until recently, churches, generally speaking, ran schools under the aegis of,

and financed by, the state. These schools may now, with state funding, become independent 'academies', setting their own pay, conditions and curricula. Similarly, many religious bodies have been encouraged to establish 'faith schools' on the same basis.
2. The term 'culture war' has been popularised in contemporary debate chiefly by the American sociologist James Davison Hunter (Hunter 1991), who used it to analyse wrangles over American values during the 1980s. In adopting the concept I have also had in mind the (in)famous remark of the American right-wing ideologue Patrick Buchanan who, in September 1993, told an audience of Conservative Christians that 'culture is the Ho Chi Minh Trail of power': http://articles.sun-sentinel.com/1993-09-12/news/9309120179_1_buchanan-s-speech-new-party-culture-war (accessed 6 June 2013).
3. McKinsey are widely quoted in the publicity material of schools and companies operating in the new educational market. The fact that they are management consultancy and not a specifically educational body is, of course, highly illustrative of the direction that official thinking about schools has taken in recent times.
4. I adopted this vague term because of the rapid changes of title that the ministry itself underwent over an approximately 20-year period, as government planners searched for a suitably utilitarian branding. The British education ministry was known successively as the Department of Education and Science (1964–92), the Department of Education (1994–5), the Department for Education and Employment (1995–2001), the Department for Education and Skills (2002–7) and the Department for Children, Schools and Families (2007–10), before reverting to the Department for Education in 2010. During the period of its apparently more pastoral title (2007–10) there were separate ministries called respectively the Department of Business, Innovation and Regulatory Reform and Innovation, Universities and Skills.
5. The full text of the speech is available at: http://education.guardian.co.uk/thegreatdebate/story/0,9860,574645,00.html.
6. This pre-school programme reflected 'New' Labour's vestigial commitment to tackling poverty as an obstacle to educational achievement and was based on the same principles as Project Head Start, inaugurated by the Johnson administration in the United States in 1965. Significantly, Head Start came under the auspices of the Office of Economic Opportunity's Community Action Program and was regarded in the academic world as a flagship for 'compensatory education', a policy widely advocated by progressive educationists at the time. It presupposes, among other things, that children gain all the cultural capital they need in the first five years of life. Sure Start was wound down by the Conservative–Liberal Democrat coalition soon after it took office in 2010, but, in April 2013, Elizabeth Truss, Parliamentary Under Secretary for Education and Childcare, announced a 15-hours-a-week early learning programme for two-year-old children who were eligible for fee school meals.
7. See http://www.biogs.com/blair/speech27Sept2005.html (accessed 20 May 2013).
8. For an outline of the debate on 'the learning society' go to: http://www.infed.org/lifelonglearning/b-lrnsoc.htm (accessed 21 May 2013). For a fuller range of arguments see Ranson (1998).
9. This notion is most often associated with the sociologist and political consultant Anthony Giddens (Giddens 1998). The most powerful critique of Giddens' position was provided by Alex Callinicos (Callinicos 2001).
10. See http://www.bbc.co.uk/news/special/politics97/news/05/0530/blunkett.shtml (accessed 22 May 2013).

11. 9 November 2000. Available at www.economist.com/node/417977 (accessed 22 May 2013).
12. The BBC reported in August 2010 that a number of large companies, including Gems, Pearson, Serco, Tribal and Nord Anglia, doubtless attracted by the possibility of lucrative contracts, were looking to move into this emergent market and run 'free schools'. Zenna Atkins, Chair of OFSTED, became chief executive of Gems in 2010 (Richardson 2010).
13. The latter group's website can be found at: www.changingschools.org.uk/ (accessed 22 January 2014).
14. From Phillips' own website http://melaniephillips.com/all-must-have-prizes (accessed 23 May 2013).
15. First published in 1874. Its author, George Eliot, was one of four 'great English novelists' nominated by Cambridge lecturer F. R. Leavis in his book *The Great Tradition* (Leavis 1948). Remarks such as Gove's are rooted in the notions of inherently 'good' literature propagated by Leavis.
16. A pressure group called Defend School History formed in reaction to Gove's various pronouncements on history teaching. It was launched by history teacher Andy Stone: andystone2002@yahoo.com. In June of 2013 over one hundred lecturers and teachers took the remarkable step of writing to the press to claim that Gove's plans for school history, with its Anglocentric and triumphal emphases, might be illegal under the Education Acts of 1996 and 2002, which had called for a balanced and broad-based curriculum and forbad the promotion of partisan political views (see www.independent.co.uk/voices/letters/letters-13th-june-2013-full-list-of-signatories-8656150.html [accessed 15 June 2013]).
17. See www.dailymail.co.uk/debate/article-2298146/I-refuse-surrender-Marxist-teachers-hell-bent-destroying-schools-Education-Secretary-berates-new-enemies-promise-opposing-plans.html (posted 23 March 2013; accessed 13 June 2013). For a close analysis of Michael Gove's tenure as Secretary of State for Education (at the time of writing still unbroken), see Grant (2013). See also Benn (2011: 3–34).
18. A coy abbreviation, it seems, for 'bullshit'.
19. See http://www.amazon.co.uk/product-reviews/0751522740/ref=dp_top_cm_cr_acr_txt?ie=UTF8&showViewpoints=1 (posted 26 April 2009; accessed 24 May 2013).
20. See http://liberalconspiracy.org/2010/05/13/an-illustration-of-private-school-intake-of-the-new-cabinet/ (accessed 6 June 2013).
21. See www.newstatesman.com/blogs/politics/2012/10/david-camerons-speech-conservative-conference-full-text (accessed 6 June 2013).
22. See http://en.wikipedia.org/wiki/Mainstream_Science_on_Intelligence (accessed 18 November 2013).
23. In 2009, David Cameron said: 'Sure Start will stay, and we'll improve it. We will keep flexible working, and extend it.' Between the Coalition government taking power in 2010 and November 2013, 400 Sure Start centres had closed (see Wright 2013).

References

Apple, M. W., Ball, S. J. and Gaudin, L. A. (eds). (2010). *The Routledge International Handbook of the Sociology of Education.* Abingdon: Routledge.
Ball, S. J. (2006). *Education Policy and Social Class.* Abingdon: Routledge.
Ball, S. J. (2007). *Education plc: Understanding Private Sector Participation in Public Sector Education.* Abingdon: Routledge.

Ball, S. J. (2008). *The Education Debate*. Bristol: Policy Press.
Bangs, J., MacBeath, J. and Galton, M. (2011). *Reinventing Schools, Reforming Teaching*. Abingdon Routledge.
Barthes, R. (1973). *Mythologies*. St Albans: Paladin.
Bassey, M. and 99 others. (2013). 'Gove will bury pupils in facts and rules'. Letter to the *Independent*, 20 March, p. 20.
BBC News. (2011). 'Kettling of children at tuition fees protest challenged'. 7 June. www.bbc.co.uk/news/uk-england-london-13679665 (accessed 24 May 2013).
Benn, M. (2011). *School Wars: The Battle for Britain's Education*. London: Verso.
Birbalsingh, K. (2011). *To Miss With Love*. London: Penguin.
Birkett, D. (2011). 'The school I'd like: here is what you wanted'. *The Guardian*, 3 May www.guardian.co.uk/education/2011/may/03/school-i-would-like (accessed 24 May 2013).
Blair, T. (2010). *A Journey*. London: Hutchinson.
Bloxham, A., Hutchison, P., Edwards, R. and Roberts, L. (2010). 'Student tuition fees protest: schoolchildren bring chaos back to the streets'. *The Telegraph*, 25 November. www.telegraph.co.uk/education/educationnews/8158733/Student-tuition-fees-protest-schoolchildren-bring-chaos-back-to-streets.html (accessed 28 March 2013).
Blunkett, D. (2006). *The Blunkett Tapes: My Life in the Bear Pit*. London: Bloomsbury.
Callinicos, A. (2001). *Against the Third Way: An Anti-Capitalist Manifesto*. Cambridge: Polity Press.
Campbell, A. and Hagerty, B. (eds). (2010). *The Alastair Campbell Diaries*: Volume 1: *Prelude to Power 1994–1997*. London: Hutchinson.
Campbell, A. and Hagerty, B. (eds). (2011a). *The Alastair Campbell Diaries*: Volume 2: *Power and the People 1997–1999*. London: Hutchinson.
Campbell, A. and Hagerty, B. (eds) (2011b). *The Alastair Campbell Diaries*: Volume 3: *Power and Responsibility 1999–2001*. London: Hutchinson.
Campbell, A. and Hagerty, B. (eds) (2012). *The Alastair Campbell Diaries*: Volume 4: *The Burden of Power. Countdown to Iraq*. London: Hutchinson.
Chitty, C. (2001). *Understanding Schools and Schooling*. Abingdon: Routledge.
Clark, L. (2008). 'Now desperate parents hire lawyers to give them head start in battle for school places'. MailOnline, 24 October. www.dailymail.co.uk/news/article-1080040/Now-desperate-parents-hire-lawyers-head-start-battle-school-places.html (accessed 23 May 2013).
Coffield, F. (1999). 'Breaking the Consensus: Lifelong Learning as Social Control'. *British Educational Research Journal* 25(4): 479–99. http://www.tulipnetwork.org.uk/Website%20linked%20docs/Linked%20bibliog%20articles/UK%20pdfs/Bib_Coffield.pdf (accessed 23 May 2013).
Cohen, D. (2011). 'Secrets of the superheads: the teachers that are saving London's schools'. *London Evening Standard*, 31 January. www.standard.co.uk/lifestyle/secrets-of-the-superheads-the-teachers-that-are-saving-londons-schools-6561578.html (accessed 22 May 2013).
Collini, S. (2011). 'From Robbins to McKinsey' (Review of *Higher Education: Students at the Heart of the System*, Department of Business, Innovation and Skills, June 2011'. *London Review of Books* 33(16) 25 (August 2011): 9–14. www.lrb.co.uk/v33/n16/stefan-collini/from-robbins-to-mckinsey (accessed 13 May 2013).
Commission of the European Communities. (1995). 'Teaching and Learning: Towards the Learning Society' (White Paper). Brussels: Commission of the European Communities.
Cooper, C. (2013). 'Phillips launches "Brand Melanie" as she tries to become the darling of the American right'. *The Independent*, 6 May, p. 3.

Cummings, D. (2013). 'Some thoughts on education and political priorities'. http://s3.documentcloud.org/documents/804396/some-thoughts-on-education-and-political.pdf (accessed 18 November 2013).

Cusick, J. (2013). 'Were MPs misled? Gove recalled to committee over "bullying case"'. *The Independent*, 28 February, p. 20.

Cusick, James (2013) 'Dump f***ing everyone': the inside story of how Michael Gove's vicious attack dogs are terrorising the DfE' *The Independent* 15th February (available at: http://www.independent.co.uk/news/education/education-news/dump-fingeveryone-the-inside-story-of-how-michael-goves-vicious-attack-dogs-are-terrorising-the-dfe-8497626.html Access: 18th November 2013)

Edwards, A. (2013). '"Genetics outweighs teaching": Michael Gove's right hand man says it is IQ, not education, which determines child's future'. *MailOnline*, 12 October. http://www.dailymail.co.uk/news/article-2455623/Michael-Gove-advisor-Dominic-Cummings-claims-Genetics-outweighs-teaching.html (accessed 30 January 2014).

Finlayson, A. (1998). 'Tony Blair and the Jargon of Modernisation'. *Soundings* 10 (Autumn). http://www.academia.edu/2750847/Tony_Blair_and_the_jargon_of_modernisation (accessed 21 May 2013).

Foot, T. (2011). 'Student fee protests – kettle cops "had flawed intelligence"'. *Camden New Journal* 8 July. http://www.camdennewjournal.com/news/2011/jul/student-fee-protests-kettle-cops-%E2%80%98had-flawed-intelligence%E2%80%99 (accessed 25 May 2013).

Gamble, A. (1974). *The Conservative Nation*. London: Routledge & Kegan Paul.

Garner, R. (2013a). 'Gove and his "gang of arm-twisters" are ruining education, says teachers' union'. *The Independent*, 25 March, p. 30.

Garner, R. (2013b). 'Headteachers plan to set up Ofsted alternative'. *The Independent*, 17 May, p. 27.

Giddens, A. (1998). *The Third Way: The Renewal of Social Democracy*. Cambridge: Polity Press.

Grant, N. (2013). 'Michael Gove: Doing the Right Thing'. *International Socialism* 140 (Autumn): 131–54.

Guardian. (2006). 'Tony Blair's speech to Labour's spring conference'. 10 February. www.guardian.co.uk/politics/2006/feb/10/labour.tonyblair (accessed 20 May 2013).

Helm, T. (2013). 'Michael Gove urged to reject "chilling views" of his special advisor'. *The Observer*, 12 October. www.theguardian.com/politics/2013/oct/12/michael-gove-special-adviser (accessed 30 January 2014).

Herrnstein, R. J. and Murray, C. (1994). *The Bell Curve: Intelligence and Class Structure in American Life*. New York: Free Press.

Helm, Toby (2013) 'Michael Gove urged to reject 'chilling views' of his special adviser' *The Observer* 12th October Available at: http://www.theguardian.com/politics/2013/oct/12/michael-gove-special-adviser Access: 18th November

Herrnstein, Richard J. And Charles Murray (1994) *The Bell Curve: Intelligence and Class Structure in American Life* New York: Simon and Schuster

Hunter, J. D. (1991). *Culture Wars: The Struggle to Define America*. New York: Basic Books.

Husen, T. (1974). *The Learning Society*. London: Methuen.

Hutchins, R. (1970). *The Learning Society*. Harmondsworth: Penguin.

Huxley, T. H. (1874). *Science and Education*. Chapter 7: 'Universities: Actual and Ideal': http://ebooks.adelaide.edu.au/h/huxley/thomas_henry/science-and-education/chapter7.html (accessed 14 March 2013).

Jessop, B. (2002). *The Future of the Capitalist State*. Cambridge: Polity Press.

Judd, J. (1996). '"Super heads" to rescue schools'. *The Independent*, 16 December. www.independent.co.uk/news/super-heads-to-rescue-schools-1314808.html (accessed 22 May 2013).
Kozol, J. (2005). *The Shame of the Nation: The Restoration of Apartheid Schooling in America*. New York: Three Rivers Press.
Leavis, F. R. (1948). *The Great Tradition*. London: Chatto and Windus.
Levy, A. and Chapman, J. (2013). 'Revealed: Socialist links of academics trying to sabotage Gove's reforms of the school curriculum'. *MailOnline*, 21 March. www.dailymail.co.uk/news/article-2296420/Revealed-Socialist-links-academics-trying-sabotage-Goves-reforms-school-curriculum.html (accessed 24 May 2013).
Major, J. (2000). *The Autobiography*. London: Harper Collins Publishers.
Nunn, A. (2002). 'The Knowledge Economy Cacophony'. *Information for Social Change* 14 (Winter). http://www.libr.org/isc/articles/14-Nunn.html (accessed 21 May 2013).
Odone, C. (2011). 'Katharine Birbalsingh: The fearless woman who told the truth about teaching'. *The Telegraph*, 31 January. http://blogs.telegraph.co.uk/news/cristinaodone/100074105/katharine-birbalsingh-the-fearless-woman-who-told-the-truth-about-teaching/ (accessed 23 May 2013).
Radnedge, A. (2011). 'Children lose Met "kettling" lawsuit'. *Metro*, 8 September. http://metro.co.uk/2011/09/08/schoolchildren-sam-eaton-adam-and-rosie-castle-lose-met-kettling-lawsuit-143911/ (accessed 24 May 2013).
Ranson, S. (ed.). (1998). *Inside the Learning Society*. London: Cassell.
Richardson, H. (2010). 'Firms and charities line up to run free schools'. www.bbc.co.uk/news/education-10967859 (accessed 15 June 2013).
Schofield, K. (2012.) 'Ofsted chief: Teachers today don't know what stress is'. *The Sun*, 11 May. www.thesun.co.uk/sol/homepage/news/politics/4309855/Ofsted-chief-Sir-Michael-Wilshaw-says-teachers-dont-know-what-stress-is.html (accessed 25 May 2013).
Schon, D. (1973). *Beyond the Stable State. Public and Private Learning in a Changing Society*. Harmondsworth: Penguin.
School Without Walls. (1978). *Lunatic Ideas: How Newspapers Treated Education in 1977*. London: Corner House Bookshop.
Sparks, C. (1997). 'The Tories, Labour and the Education Crisis'. *International Socialism* 74 (March): 3–40. http://pubs.socialistreviewindex.org.uk/isj74/sparks.htm (accessed 23 May 2013).
Tisdall, E. K. M. (2010). 'Governance and Participation'. In B. Percy-Smith and N. Thomas (eds), *A Handbook of Young People's Participation: Perspectives from Theory and Practice*. Abingdon: Routledge.
Tomlinson, S. (2005). *Education in a Post-Welfare Society*. Maidenhead: Open University Press.
Wagg, S. (1996). '"Don't Try to Understand Them": Politics, Childhood and the New Education Market'. In J. Pilcher and S. Wagg (eds), *Thatcher's Children? Politics Childhood and Society in the 1980s and 90s*. London: Falmer Press, pp. 8–28.
Wakefield, M. (2013). 'Revealed: how exam results owe more to genes than teaching'. *The Spectator*, 27 July. www.spectator.co.uk/features/8970941/sorry-but-intelligence-really-is-in-the-genes/ (accessed 18 November 2013).
Warrell, H. (2013). 'Michael Gove attacks "low expectations in schools'. *Financial Times*, 9 May. http://www.ft.com/cms/s/0/96234454-b8c5-11e2-a6ae-00144feabdc0.html#axzz2U9iahTCe (accessed 23 May 2013).
Woodhead, C. (2002). *Class War: The State of Education*. London: Little, Brown.

Woodhead, C. (2009). *A Desolation of Learning: Is This the Education Our Children Deserve?* Stroud: Pencil-Sharp Publishing.
Wright, O. (2013). 'Tories "deleted broken promises from website"'. *The Independent*, 14 November, p. 7.
Wrigley, T. (2006). *Another School Is Possible*. London: Bookmarks.

11
Troubling Families
Parenting and the Politics of Early Intervention

Val Gillies

The election of the Thatcher government in 1979 is broadly acknowledged as marking a pivotal moment in social and economic history. As most theorists acknowledge, this rise to power was instrumental in ushering in and cementing a neoliberal regime that over the course of 30 years transformed global politics and society. Thatcher's infamous proclamation, 'there is no such thing as society ... only the individual and his family', heralded a new age in which economic liberalism came to infuse, shape and contain all aspects of life, including our most intimate spheres of existence. 'Neoliberalism' as a term has been put to promiscuous and often reductive use (Clarke 2008; Hall 2011) but few can question the radical assault on social values it is intended to describe. Principles of individual freedom, independence and personal responsibility, stressed alongside a valorisation of the market as the optimal site for maximising human well-being, have become ingrained in everyday common sense (Harvey 2007; Couldry 2011).

The political consequences of the neoliberal project have been well documented alongside sophisticated analyses of social and cultural impact. However, the extent to which neoliberal ideals have penetrated deep into the arena of family relationships is more rarely examined. A critical look back across the decades reveals a series of dramatic changes in conceptualisations of children and parents, highlighting how a particular kind of individualism and economic reasoning have come to reconstitute understandings of personhood and personal relations. At the centre of these profound shifts is a veneration of the ideal capitalist subject as not only self-serving but also self-producing, with everyday practices and even intimate relationships reducible to venture, speculation and investment. At the level of government, socially embedded lives have become reimagined as disaggregated individual projects to be managed along entrepreneurial lines (Rose 1999), with infant development acquiring a new central significance in the production of competent neoliberal selves.

This chapter examines how such individualist modes of thinking came to be superimposed on the essentially social experience of family as part of a concerted programme to promote childhood investment as an alternative to the welfare state. I begin by considering the longstanding politicisation of family relations, highlighting the division that opened up between traditional conservatives and economic liberals over representations and prescriptions. I then explore how neoliberal values came to permeate and colonise the apparently radical, progressive critiques and policies pursued through the New Labour years. Bearing testament to this process is the extent to which relational bonds of love and care are now routinely rendered as simply technical through the instrumental language of parenting skills and proficiencies. In particular I show how related themes of children's well-being and protection have been appropriated to justify a highly regulatory approach to family policy, eventually morphing into a distinct doctrine of 'early intervention' under the auspices of the current Conservative-led Coalition government.

Turning to examine early intervention in particular, I explore and detail its emergence as new orthodoxy and a political rallying point. Founded on the notion that individual parenting practices can be held accountable for children's future life chances, early intervention programmes target the family relationships of the poor ostensibly to prevent a transmission of deprivation. In practice, the attribution of limited life chances to 'suboptimal' parenting works to personalise and normalise inequality, while simultaneously conveying apparent concern for children's well-being. In cementing a broader shift away from state support towards a social investment model, the principle of early intervention marks an ideological convergence between traditional conservatism and economic liberalism, galvanising a cross-party political consensus in the process. But, as I demonstrate, the currently endorsed doctrine of early intervention is built on sand, propping up old and increasingly discredited ideas and policies.

The politics of family, old and new

Long cherished as the bedrock of society by politicians of all hues, family was articulated as a central theme by the Thatcher governments of the 1980s. Of particular concern was the changing structure and status of family in the wake of the so-called 'permissive sixties', which were portrayed as undermining the social fabric. But while the 'pro-family' rhetoric of Thatcher and successive Conservative governments railed against liberal views on sexuality, marriage and childrearing, the libertarian instincts of the party curbed meaningful policy incursions into what was regarded at the time as a private sphere lying beyond the boundaries of legitimate state intervention. By the 1990s, this tension in relation to the moral status of family had developed into an identifiable fault line among Conservatives, dividing those assuming a more reactionary position from those adopting a more liberal stance. The *Times* newspaper memorably characterised this in terms of 'Tory Mods and Rockers', with the former embracing change while the latter cling on to old sensibilities and standards.[1] This surfacing rift in the Tory party reflected a much broader political and cultural dynamic operating through the 1970s and 1980s. The previously cherished ideal of the nuclear family came under sustained attack from feminists and others amidst rising rates of divorce, cohabitation and birth outside of marriage. A critical lexicon emerged to highlight the repression of personal freedom and individuality associated with traditional family ideology. Public/private distinctions depicting families as independent units separate from the state were powerfully challenged by feminists, ushering in a new appreciation of the 'personal as political'. While most on the political right fiercely opposed such critiques, regarding them as deeply threatening to civilised moral values, feminists found unlikely support in a concentrated strand of neoliberal thinking that was wielding increasing power and influence. Individualistic, economic-centric values began to be articulated through a strategic and opportunistic engagement with feminist and new left egalitarian critiques (Boltanski and Chiapello 2005; Fraser 2009). Family as collective, structured experience was problematised as belonging to an old order, paving the way for a new emphasis on the personal as the key constituent of social life.

Such ideas were echoed and to some extent crafted by prominent sociological theorists in the 1990s who hailed the emergence of a new social order of 'reflexive modernity' transforming the experience of family (Giddens 1991, 1992; Beck and Beck-Gernsheim 1995, 2002). A post-traditional society was posited in which men and women, progressively freed from the roles and constraints associated with traditional social ties, were compelled reflexively to create their selves through day-to-day decisions. According to Anthony Giddens, our fundamentally altered experience of love, sexuality and relationality rendered family a 'shell institution': 'The outer shell remains, but inside they [i.e., those constituent elements] have changed' (Giddens 1998: 19). Drawing on Giddens' work in the 1990s, New Labour politicians set about developing their 'third way' approach, aiming to balance individual rights with social responsibility through an emphasis on both moral tolerance and personal obligation. The primary role accorded to family as the protector of civilisation was preserved in this account, but significantly through a focus on children as its principal constituents. Definitions of family structure became more flexible and inclusive, crucially through a centring of childrearing as the primary moral concern.

A year after the election of the first New Labour government, Giddens famously proclaimed: 'There is only one story to tell about the family today, and that is of democracy (1998: 93). This somewhat optimistic proclamation obscured the process by which trenchant critiques of 'the family' had been co-opted to propagate an advancing neoliberal ethos (Boltanski and Chiapello 2005; Fraser 2009). As Nancy Fraser (2009) argues, feminist emancipatory ideals were appropriated and made mainstream, achieving very different political ends from those intended. The concept of the personal as political increasingly became articulated as the personal is the *only* political, enforced through promotion of the self-determining, networked individual, liberated from gendered and classed expectations and ties. Children came to assume a much greater significance within a market-based ethic, as human capital requiring extensive investment to secure their futures as productive citizens.

To be more explicit, under the remit of New Labour, the institution of family was actively reconstructed to embrace an ideology better suited to advanced capitalist values. In the modern 'democratised family' women are freed up to enter the labour market alongside men, replacing male breadwinner models of family with norms which assumed dual earning households. Articulated through a discourse of gender justice, flexible capitalism is promoted as the progressive solution to women's inequality. The reality was a concentration of women in low-wage, insecure employment, and an overall decline in living standards despite steep rises in hours worked per household (Fraser 2009). Meanwhile, the female-dominated practice of childcare was redrawn as a motor of meritocracy, moving conceptualisations of family away from any association with class-bound trajectories. The role of family background in determining or limiting an individual's place and standing in society is rejected. Instead family is hailed as the formative site through which competent personhood is cultivated, with well-parented children better able to navigate and capitalise on new post-industrial economic landscapes (Gillies 2005, 2012).

The 'child-centred' age

Thus, while the concept of family has retained its political purchase over the years, it is a distinctly different entity that is conjured up in rhetoric and policy today. Thatcher's preoccupation with 'family values' and strengthening the traditional nuclear family have largely been replaced by a focus on 'parenting' and the 'well-being' of the child. Family is now represented less as a haven in a heartless world and more as an individual project and an essential cipher through which moral responsibility must be seen to be exercised. A key feature of this new public politics of family is the way in which attention has moved away from concerns with family structure and function, towards an emphasis on knowledge and proficiency. More specifically, governments have come to see families in terms of their practices, with a particular focus on the minutiae of childrearing translating into an ideology of family competence (Gillies 2011). As part of this shift, parents are depicted as the architects of family while children occupy a new status and significance as its core subject.

Moreover, such changes are tied to a characteristically neoliberal individualisation and dismemberment of family as an inherently collective endeavour. Children, as the nucleus of family, are accorded general needs and rights which position their interests in isolation from their family members. As distinct, separately conceived beings, children are attached to families primarily through contingent relationships with their parents. In the process, family becomes construed as an intrinsically precarious location for children as vulnerable and less powerful individuals, and the issue of child abuse perpetrated by parents and carers takes on increased significance (Parton 2006). In particular, attention is deflected away from broader structural and economic risks facing families, with the principal source of threat to children's well-being associated with the conduct of relationships within families and communities.

In the 'democratised family' children are accorded much greater autonomy and standing than in the past, reflecting a significant shift in public understandings of children's capacities and welfare needs (Edwards and Gillies 2013). Over the course of the last three decades child-centred discourse has filtered into public policy, profoundly shaping legislation and practice. The Children Act 1989 was a particular landmark with its focus on supporting children's self-determination within legal frameworks and prioritising their welfare. Values emphasising autonomy, choice and democracy have been similarly embraced as part of a broad take-up of a discourse of 'children's rights'. Legislation enacted as part of the Children Act 2004 also saw the implementation of the Every Child Matters framework to protect and foster children's well-being. This included the introduction of a 'Children's Commissioner' to promote awareness of the views, voices and interests of children.

This child-centred shift coincided with broader concerns that the United Kingdom was witnessing a 'crisis' of childhood (Lee 2001; Parton 2006; Kehily 2010). Reports, books and even a newspaper campaign[2] appeared, alleging that British children were exceptionally troubled (Palmer 2006; UNICEF 2007; Gilbert et al. 2008; Layard and Dunn 2009). Anxiety has coalesced in particular around the state of children's mental health, with claims made that one in ten suffers from a diagnosable disorder (Mental Health Foundation 2005). As Harry Hendrick (2003) notes, policy constructions of children across the last hundred years have been characterised by a mind–body continuum, with particular historical periods emphasising one or the other. Hendrick cites a bodily preoccupation with health and hygiene in the early part of the last century, overtaken by a postwar concern with psychological attachment, which shifted to a focus on physical abuse and 'battered baby syndrome' in the 1970s. Arguably the 1990s saw another pendulum swing towards a relatively disembodied conception of children's emotional well-being (or perceived lack of it).

Despite its potentially extensive scope, children's well-being is addressed as a curiously self-contained state of mind in much current literature. For example, 'The Good Childhood Enquiry', a highly publicised series of reports by the Children's Society, seeks to centre notions of well-being and positivity through an account of the potential consequences of contemporary children's unhappiness. In attempting to 'describe the state of children's well-being in the UK today', the report reifies the concept, treating it as an indicator in its own right. Lack of well-being is framed as the principal cause of problems, rather than as a symptom of adverse circumstances. As the following quotation from the 2012 report demonstrates, well-being as a state of mind becomes the primary focus for change: 'Low well-being could be an important indicator of longer-term repercussions in people's lives. If this is the case then focusing on subjective well-being, and particularly on children who experience low well-being, offers opportunities for early intervention which could substantially improve these children's life chances' (Children's Society 2012: 6).

Defined as an entirely subjective experience, and routinely measured separately from other contextualising factors, well-being encompasses notions of resilience to adversity, ensuring that children who struggle with poverty and other life stressors can be viewed as psychologically troubled, rather than just poor or overburdened. Parenting is accorded the primary role in laying the foundations for this mental buoyancy, reflecting the central significance childrearing has come to occupy in the new politics of family.

The rise of parental determinism

As has been noted, traditional conceptions of 'the family' were characterised by a strongly bounded notion of privacy. The intimate features of family life, including parent–child relationships, were generally positioned as outside the remit of state involvement in all but extreme circumstances. The advent of the 'New' Labour government marked a very different approach, communicated through an emphasis on the importance of children and their development. Family, it was suggested, must be repositioned in the collective imagination as a public rather than a private concern. A powerful moral argument was fashioned on the grounds of promoting both social order and justice, with parenting portrayed as holding the key to a safer and fairer society. This relied on a common-sense framing of parenting as a 'skill' that must be learnt. Detached from any appreciation of structural context, culture or values, good parenting was presented as set of neutral and natural techniques. 'Upskilling' parents, it was claimed, could reduce crime, antisocial behaviour and poverty whilst increasing the social mobility and life chances of poor children. Following this reasoning, the state had a responsibility to regulate and enforce good parenting for the sake of the nation and its vulnerable children. New guiding policy principles of prevention and early intervention began to take shape.

As many have pointed out, deprivation has long been depicted as a condition inherited through family lines (Townsend 1979; Walker 1990;

Welshman 2006). Nikolas Rose (1989) has documented how nineteenth-century philanthropists identified the family as a potential prophylactic against a perceived dangerous immorality exhibited by the growing urban poor. By the twentieth century, evolutionary biology was inspiring genetic accounts of social ills, expressed through anxieties about dysfunctional households passing degeneracy down through the generations (Welshman 2006). Eugenic-inflected preoccupations with 'problem families' and their pathologies dominated welfare and public health agendas until the 1960s, when they were overtaken by socially deterministic explanations (Starkey 2000). Poor families remained in the frame, but were accused instead of sharing and reproducing lifestyles and values that set them apart from mainstream society, thereby perpetuating a 'cycle of deprivation'. Popular with successive Conservative governments, theorising about inherited disadvantage and the existence of an underclass eventually fell out of favour when, despite concerted efforts, research consistently failed to establish links between poverty and cultural deficit (Atkinson, Maynard and Trinder 1983; Morris 1994).

'New' Labour, however, set about repackaging the old and discredited preoccupation with transmitted deprivation, presenting it as a progressive, liberal concern with tackling inequality and supporting the poor. Partly this was achieved through coupling parenting interventions with tangible support like tax credits to address family hardship. New Labour's flagship nationwide policy initiative, Sure Start, provided subsidised childcare, toy libraries, cafes and drop-in groups alongside more didactic attempts to regulate parenting practice through classes and explicit advice. Much-needed practical and financial assistance for parents was delivered through an impassioned commitment to invest in children's future, papering over the moral and political objections provoked by previous cultural deficit models. The promise of identifying and immediately addressing family-based risks to children's future outcomes proved to be a deeply appealing idea, communicated through an almost evangelical faith in the power of good parenting to compensate for social disadvantage.

But far from representing a timeless, universal skill set, a very particular understanding of good parenting evolved to embody this highly politicised investment in children's development. Phillip Brown (1990) mapped the beginning of this process, coining the term 'parentocracy' to describe how in the arena of education an emerging commitment to the 'wealth and wishes of parents' was displacing more traditional concerns with children's abilities and potential. Introduced by a Conservative government in the 1980s, parental choice in education was promoted as a mechanism for better meeting needs and driving up standards, with little consideration given to the deeply uneven territory from which such 'choices' are made (Ball 2008). This consumerist framework expanded under the auspices of New Labour, extending deep into the arena of childrearing itself. Good parenting became associated with choosing, accessing and continuously evaluating products and services (food, toys, childcare, parenting advice etc.). The ideology of 'parentocracy' also imposes a distinct moral agenda that naturalises individualism, competition and self-interest. Good parents are expected to fight tooth and nail to ensure their children succeed, even if this is at the expense of others (Reay 2012). This competitive imperative is endorsed through a normative promotion of 'intensive parenting', most often expressed in the form of attentive, child-centred mothering (Hays 1996; Wall 2010). Deeply gendered and classed in terms of sanctioned values and practices, intensive parenting is closely aligned with attachment theory, proposing continuous emotional labour to maximise an infant's social, emotional and cognitive capital. Dependent on middle-class resources and values, 'cultivational' approaches are characterised by the active manipulation of social and financial assets to ensure that middle-class advantage is passed down through the generations (Lareau 2003). This intensive model of childrearing has been broadly embraced as 'gold standard' parenting, ensuring class-specific family practices are now regularly held to account for the social and structural positions they reflect.

Troubling families: troublesome evidence

Strategic deployment of simplistic but appealing social justice narratives helped reframe childrearing as a job with attached performance indicators. However, it was an apparent grounding in 'evidence' that provided a seemingly unassailable legitimacy to new directions in family policy. New Labour's approach to government was characterised by a commitment to base policy making on evidence rather than ideology. This focus was summed up in their 1997 manifesto phrase, 'what counts is what works'. Leaving aside the inherently problematic concept of removing ideology from politics, the application of this conviction to family policy built on and compounded technocratic definitions of parenting. The middle-class values underpinning sanctioned models of childrearing were enshrined as optimal practice. At a public level it became commonplace to view parenting through an evaluative lens as something you got either right or wrong. Increasingly startling claims about the transformative powers of particular parenting practices began to permeate policy documents and political rhetoric, often marked by the prefix 'research has shown'. For example, the following assertions were used and recycled in a wide variety of New Labour speeches, reviews and strategy papers:

> We know from all the research evidence ... good parenting in the home is more important than anything else in determining children's outcomes. (Margaret Hodge, speech to the Social Market Foundation, May 2004)

> Parents and the home environment they create are the single most important factor in shaping their children's well-being, achievements and prospects. (Alan Johnson, Department for Education and Skills, Foreword to *Every Parent Matters*, 2007)

> Parental interest in a child's education has four times more influence on attainment by age 16 than does socio-economic background. (Alan Milburn, *Unleashing Aspiration: Final Report from the Panel on Fair Access*, 2009, p. 30)

Although such claims were invariably coupled with authoritative-looking footnotes and references, the substance and quality of the evidence cited was either over-interpreted to the point of distortion or strikingly flimsy. Many of the attributions and citations link, Chinese whisper-style, from policy review to policy review until their final source becomes untraceable. For example, Alan Milburn's claim that parenting is 'four times more influential than socio-economic background' was reproduced on a far-reaching scale, and became a 'factoid' regularly drawn on by local and national policy makers. The stated source for the figure (another policy review) makes no mention of it and so the origins of this claim remain a mystery. Much emphasis was, and continues to be, placed on Leon Feinstein's (2003) secondary analysis of the 1970s birth cohort study, which implicates social class in determining the trajectory of children's test scores from the age of 22 to 42 months. While this finding highlights the formative significance of class from a very early age, any association with childrearing is purely speculative given that no measure of parenting was included in the data.

As part of a more general commitment to what was termed 'evidence-based policy', New Labour initiated and encouraged a large body of research with the explicit aim of establishing links between parenting interventions and improved child outcomes. These included evaluation studies of large initiatives like Sure Start, parenting programmes and specific services.[3] In addition, a range of new birth cohort studies were designed to include 'measures' of parenting in order to track and link them to children's future outcomes. The results of this sustained research effort have to date proved inconclusive and, for those advocating parenting interventions as a pathway out of poverty, distinctly unhelpful. The introduction of Sure Start in particular was tied to grandiose promises that it would reduce poverty and social exclusion. Extensive evaluations have provided clear evidence that Sure Start benefited poor (and not so poor) families (Churchill 2011), but chronic inequality and intergenerational disadvantage remained endemic. In the wake of this realisation, many branded Sure Start an expensive failure, blaming lack of engagement with the neediest parents rather than the impossibly unrealistic aims framing the scheme.[4]

Well-established and longstanding evaluations of US parenting programmes yielded equally disappointing results for those looking to family-based interventions to solve deep-rooted social problems. For instance, after four decades Head Start, a model programme for the UK Sure Start initiative, could only demonstrate modest and temporary differences in children's school performance (Ellsworth and Ames 1998). Similar, transitory boost effects have been a characteristic of a wide range of US interventions (see Bruer 1999 for a detailed analysis). In addition, British cohort studies have produced mixed and contradictory analyses of the impact of parenting practices on children's outcomes across time. While some studies have sought to associate 'favourable parenting practices' with more advanced development at ages 3 and 5 (Ermisch 2008; Kelly et al. 2011), others focusing on outcomes at age 7 demonstrate the overwhelming significance of income and maternal education above and beyond parenting styles (Hartas 2011, 2012a; Dickerson and Popli 2012). As Demitra Hartas (2012b) states, in stark contrast to prevailing policy claims:

> Parents, it seems, matter most for who they are (for example, educated, capable of accessing resources and services) rather than for what they do. This is not to suggest that they shouldn't bother supporting their children's learning. Their involvement does matter, but it cannot be seen as the way to level the playing field for deprived children. (Hartas 2012b: 3)

Early intervention and the scientisation of parenting

Despite the scant evidence, in Britain depiction of disadvantage as cultural inheritance has remained a central policy tenet through a change of government to the new Conservative-led Coalition. Attempts to portray poor families as personally responsible for their own hardship have reached new extremes in the context of unprecedented cuts to welfare and public spending pursued in the name of austerity. The Deputy Prime Minister, Nick Clegg, asserted that 'parenting not poverty shapes a child's destiny'.[5] The Prime Minister, David Cameron, expressed similar sentiments, claiming that 'what matters most to a child's life chances is not the wealth of their upbringing but the warmth of their parenting'.[6] Behind this overblown political rhetoric lay subtle yet significant shifts in family policy.

The spectacle of powerful, privileged, white males with public school backgrounds briskly dismissing the relevance of class in determining life chances stretched credibility and highlighted the need for a more robust hook to hang parental determinism on. More significantly, a continued troubling of families had to be articulated through the Coalition's ideological narrative stressing the need to shrink the state through increasing personal responsibility. New Labour's preoccupation with family relationships had underpinned a huge expansion of state and third sector services aiming to support parenting. The Coalition's rise to power was driven by a very different austerity agenda pursued under the pretext of a global financial crisis. Plans to slash welfare and state spending were announced immediately, and much of the previous government's investments were dismissed as wasteful, ineffective and symptomatic of a 'nanny state' degrading personal responsibility (Gillies 2012).

The Coalition government remained invested in attributing social ills to poor parenting, while simultaneously presiding over savage cuts to family services. To square this circle, policy makers looked to the United States and an increasingly influential body of literature promoting heavily scientised interpretations of child development. In particular, it was claimed that advances in neuroscience could provide incontrovertible evidence of the formative impact of parenting in the first years after birth. This concept facilitated and bolstered a very specific focus on early years intervention as an evidenced, boundaried and cost-limited policy approach. Reports and reviews set about detailing the apparent physical damage inadequate parenting inflicts on infant brains, with the poorest in society implicated as most at risk (Wastell and White 2012). UK policy makers and politicians seized on this literature as hard evidence of the need to target initiatives more effectively at very deprived mothers of young children.

A government-commissioned independent review into early childhood intervention conducted by Labour MP Graham Allen (2011a, 2011b) played a particularly formative role in fostering and promoting this biologised policy direction. In a series of two reports Allen details near miraculous social and economic benefits that he claims are achievable through targeting the families of socially disadvantaged under three-year-olds. Central to Allen's account is a claim that children develop faulty 'brain architecture' if they receive suboptimal nurturing. This point is conveyed graphically, with the front cover of both his reports featuring brain scan images of children. An image branded 'normal' is placed next to a smaller, atrophied brain that has been labelled 'extreme neglect'. The origins of this powerful visual statement betray the shaky grip on science displayed throughout the reports. The images, in fact, derive from an article in a journal with doubtful credentials,[7] which considered the severe physical neglect and sensory deprivation experienced by Romanian orphans after the fall of the communist government there in the late 1980s. The sampled article provides few details of the methodology pursued and no clinical histories of the children scanned (Wastell and White 2012).

Leaving aside Allen's reliance on unsubstantiated research, there is no explanation of where the continuity might lie between infants experiencing malnourishment, disease and minimal human contact, and mothers failing to properly 'attune' to children's emotional needs (Allen 2011a: 17). In their extensive critique of current policy directions Wastell and White (2012) carefully and systematically dismantle the claims about brain damage that pepper Allen's work, showing how he misunderstands and misrepresents the science. Nevertheless, enthusiastic endorsements of the role neuroscience can play in developing and targeting parenting interventions have had a profound impact on the public imagination. Politicians, policy makers, health practitioners and social commentators from across the political spectrum have drawn heavily on the notion that the first three years of life represent a critical period for brain development. As the following quotes demonstrate, the implications reach far beyond early years provision:

> We know that there are specific changes that occur in a child's brain in the earliest years of its life that have a disproportionate impact on that child's fate; on that child's capacity to be able to make the right choices and avoid the wrong temptations. (Michael Gove, 2011)[8]

> For far too many people in society crime began before they were born. ... neuroscience demonstrates that the damage that we start children with, is damage that they keep ... We now know that we can pretty much figure out where an 18-year-old will be at the time that they are two and a half or three years old ... there are of course physical signs, including the scale and size and capacity of their brains to be able to deal with challenges. (Iain Duncan Smith, 2010)[9]

> Research has for decades kept proving that, by the age of three, a child's destiny is all but sealed by how much affection, conversation, reading and explaining they have received. Getting no love and no language relegates them to a lesser life. Recent research from the University of Pennsylvania scanned children's brains over 20 years and found cognitive stimulation by the age of four was the key factor in developing the cortex, predicting cognitive ability 15 years later. That shows how brief is the window of opportunity for changing lives. (Polly Toynbee, 2012)[10]

> The sad part of the increased knowledge about baby brain development is that it is clear that the way hardwiring consolidates the connections makes it very hard to undo or 'rewire'. (NHS Parenting Programme, The Solihull Approach)[11]

The strident tone of these claims implies the existence of a clear-cut, robust body of scientific evidence, belying the altogether more troubling reality. In an illuminating and detailed study, John Bruer (1999, 2011) has documented the rise of such deterministic discourses in the United States, highlighting their divergence from neuroscience as an emerging discipline. As a high-profile cognitive scientist, Bruer described his increasing bemusement on hearing and reading about breakthroughs in brain science that promised to revolutionise childcare policy. In an effort to trace the sources of such apparent breakthroughs, he found no new science, just a selective, oversimplified and overgeneralised reappropriation of longstanding studies. Significantly, he reveals how such claims derived from policy and advocacy circles rather than the scientific community, largely driven by philanthropists in a well-meaning but misleading campaign to revalidate parenting support initiatives like Head Start. As Bruer notes: 'Neuroscience was chosen as the scientific vehicle for the public relations campaign to promote early childhood programs more for rhetorical, than scientific reasons' (Bruer 2011: 2).

The seductive allure that brain scans can exert over the general public has been well documented, particularly in terms of the capacity of brain images to authenticate explanations that would otherwise lack plausibility (McCabe and Castel 2008; Weisberg et al. 2008). This potent effect has not been lost on UK policy makers, think tanks and voluntary organisations, with such images liberally disseminated alongside impassioned entreaties to fund early intervention. As in the United States, UK neuroscientists themselves have had notably little engagement in the translation and interpretation of their work. In fact, in direct contrast to the early intervention message, advances in the field of neuroscience continue to highlight the enduring adaptability and plasticity of the brain (Rutter 2007; Royal Society 2011a, 2011b).

The retreat of contemporary policy makers into biological determinism, and the flagrant misuse of science that this entails, bears an uncomfortable but striking resemblance to the rise of eugenics in the twentieth century. In line with the eugenics movement in its time, the proponents of brain science and early intervention receive much of their funding from wealthy philanthropists, regard negative traits as weakness to be rooted out in the lower orders, and are exerting a powerful influence over welfare and public health agendas. While brain development has replaced the concept of genetic weakness, the alleged consequences of a lack of timely intervention are almost as immutable. The 'prime window' for development is estimated at 18 months (plus the prenatal period), beyond which deficits are portrayed as increasingly harder to overcome.

Yet, for the time being, a heavily biologised narrative of early intervention retains a progressive aura. Positive values of social investment and moral necessity are stressed, with early intervention portrayed as an unquestionable social good. As Brid Featherstone and colleagues (2014) point out, critical analysis is hindered by general apprehension about the survival of state services in the context of austerity. This silence is further bolstered by the emotionally potent vision of children as perceived victims of neglect, making early intervention difficult to question without appearing to position oneself against children's well-being. But while presented as a discrete, time-limited inoculation against the incubation of poverty, the ideological underpinning of early intervention obscures the worsening hardship framing the lives of poor families in the current climate. Disadvantaged mothers might now receive training in parenting skills, but their prospects of securing decent housing, an income sufficient to feed their children and access to desperately needed support services diminish by the day.

Responsibilising families and traditionalising mothers

Policy appeals to early intervention as a concept are largely conveyed through a rhetoric of social munificence and paternalistic concern. Deserving poor families are positioned as naturally inclined to self-improvement and eager to address their personal, emotional and cultural deficits. Any hint of resistance to this programme of 'responsibilisation' is met with a rapid descent into moral pronouncement and authoritarian threat. With the rise of family policy under New Labour came a creeping encroachment of a criminal justice agenda (Pitts 2003). Disadvantaged families were increasingly drawn into judicial systems through the design and expansion of a range of legislative acts. Most notoriously, Parenting Orders were introduced to force parents to attend classes and adhere to particular childrearing rules. In addition, record numbers of parents (mainly mothers) were prosecuted and jailed for failing to prevent their children from truanting.[12] A similar hard-line approach is to the fore of the Coalition government's concern with 'troubled families' as the wellspring of antisocial behaviour, with this agenda largely driven by the Centre for Social Justice, a right-wing think tank founded by Iain Duncan Smith, Work and Pensions Secretary in the Coalition government.

Repeated government pledges to 'turn around' the lives of the nation's most troubled families have seen the setting up of a Troubled Families Unit and a national network of 'Troubled Family Trouble-Shooters', overseeing and coordinating interventions on a payment-by-results system. Struggling families are approached as if they were business units requiring rationalisation, performance management and heavy-handed financial disincentives. In her first report as head of the Troubled Families Unit, Louise Casey peddled gratuitous case studies of welfare dependency and child sexual abuse as if representative of a wider 'dysfunctional' rump of troubled families, detailing immorality, incompetence, ignorance and lack of aspiration. Related policy proposals have included limiting child-related benefits to two children in order to ensure the poor 'cut their cloth in accordance with their capabilities and finances',[13] and welfare payments administered through cards that restrict purchases to so-called 'priority items', to guard against the spending of public money on alcohol or cigarettes.[14]

A discourse of early intervention to some extent sugar-coats this ruthless drive to regulate and responsibilise poor families. It goes beyond the harsh rhetoric associated with accounts of an amoral underclass to offer a government-sponsored road to redemption. Disadvantaged parents are pathologised and blamed but ostensibly in order to receive help for the sake of their children. From this perspective, only the morally reprehensible would eschew an opportunity to become a better parent and transform their children's lives. This appeal to self-discipline can also be seen as marking a crucial political pivot point, marrying neoliberal sensibilities with more traditional conservativism. Libertarian values intersect with moral authoritarianism through a shared commitment to discipline the poor so they become able to embrace and manage themselves appropriately. This approach exemplifies a form of 'neoliberal paternalism' (Soss, Fording and Schram 2011), with good citizenship reduced to self-care and individual responsibility. State involvement in the sphere of the personal is justified on the grounds of ensuring the production of competent neoliberal subjects capable of managing their freedom.

In this particular manifestation of neoliberal paternalism, longstanding conservative ideals are appeased through a reinscription of traditionalised and heavily gendered family roles. While couched in the gender-neutral terminology of 'parenting', early intervention is almost exclusively targeted at mothers as the core mediators of their children's development. Old and highly contentious tenets of attachment theory are reinvoked and embellished with brain science to emphasise the primacy of mother–child relationships in the early years. The gender encoding of early intervention policy has become increasingly explicit. Current initiatives are largely directed and delivered through pre- and postnatal care provision in poor communities via targeted parenting education for pregnant women and new mothers. The default language of parenting continues to frame policy literature, but now frequently gives way to female pronouns and references to mothers, while fathers feature in relation to concerns about discipline and financial maintenance (Gillies 2012).

This invocation of mothering through the gender-negating language of 'parenting' results in the worst of both worlds for targeted women. Implicitly held to account for their children's development, the particular challenges and disadvantages facing them as women and mothers go unrecognised. They are, to all intents and purposes, trapped in an empty policy ethic of sameness in a context of ingrained difference and inequality (Haney 2004). The Allen review highlights the consequences of this strategic and cynical use of genderless concepts of parenting in early intervention discourses. Most notably, domestic violence is listed as highly damaging to children's development, while recommended policy solutions centre exclusively on enhancing a 'parent's' sensitivity to the child. Meanwhile, funding for domestic violence services has been reduced by almost a third, ensuring that large numbers of women and children are now regularly turned away from refuges (Towers and Walby 2012).

Challenging orthodoxies: recalibrating the debate

This chapter has offered a critical analysis of family policy as a politicised project. Pursued as part of a wider programme of economic reform and sold on the ticket of individual freedom, democracy and personal empowerment, neoliberal strictures have permeated and reordered contemporary political thinking about families to better fit with market-based ethics. The profound implications of this for children and parents have been explored to show how an apparently enlightened child-centred discourse and associated championing of children's well-being have concealed narrow and politicised conceptions. Dominant developmental perspectives construct children as minds in the making, detachable from broader family and material circumstances, and acknowledged only through consideration of their future capacity to compete in the marketplace.

A doctrine of early intervention has grown out of this fixation with maximising human capital. Initially designed as a practical policy measure to shape and support the development of competent neoliberal subjects, early intervention has come to occupy an increasingly ideological role in the context of contemporary austerity politics. Its power operates largely through reverberation of rhetoric, stressed in almost inverse proportion to actual government investment in programmes and initiatives. Funding cuts and payment-by-results schemes have decimated a previously thriving sector of 'parenting professionals'. Early intervention as a practice is now targeted towards a very small minority of families, while the contentions and distorted science framing the doctrine are drawn on more broadly to lend credence to the responsibilisation of the poor.

This is not to underplay the significance of such approaches for those caught in the cross hairs. Punitive, almost vengeful policy approaches (fines, imprisonment, or even care proceedings) can be enacted, supposedly to protect a child's psychological well-being and development. Crucially, concern is directed at what children will become rather than what they might be experiencing in the here and now. A twisted logic that advocates the docking of family benefits for the sake of the child can be articulated through reference to future prospects and the spectre of transmitted deprivation. Similarly, policy debates around child poverty now focus not on the moral repugnance of such a vulnerable group's suffering, but on the effects deprivation will have on their later life chances. Emphasis on tackling the 'causes rather than the symptoms of poverty' ensure that commitments to reduce disadvantage are deferred to unspecified dates in the future, chiefly through the expressed intention of preventing children from making the same mistakes as their parents. The tendency to define children in relation to their futurity is not new (Lee 2002; Mayall 2002), but the conceptual dislocation of children from their existent material lives has intensified with the rise of the early intervention movement.

The automatic eliding of children's best interests with the best interests of neoliberal regimes has been particularly effective in masking the brutal impact on women and children. The last 30 years have seen levels of inequality and child poverty soar,[15] while the current ongoing austerity drive has targeted family benefits and children's services. In the face of a ruthless programme of cuts, families have suffered disproportionately, with lone mothers and their children estimated to lose more than any other household type (Green 2013). At the same time, the vast majority of Parenting Orders are discharged against mothers, thus ensuring women continue to bear the brunt of punitive sanctions designed to discipline irresponsible parents (Peters 2012). And while the language of children's rights and wellbeing decorate policy commitments, the criminalisation and incarceration of children and young people have reached staggering heights, with use of custody for 10- to 14-year-olds rising by 550 per cent since 1996 (Barnardo's 2008). At a more general level, children and young people are subjected to an extraordinary level of surveillance and regulation. This ranges from compulsory checks for two-year-olds to ensure they are developing to order, to the extensive and intrusive use of CCTV in schools.

As Stuart Hall (2011) notes, this is the neoliberal engine at full throttle, despite – and perhaps because of – the continuing global economic crisis and subsequent discrediting of the fundamental ideas propping up economic and political orthodoxies. In the context of growing doubts about market-based rationality as a governing ethic, ruling elites are increasingly blaming the faulty psychology of individuals and looking to mechanisms and technology that force people to better fit the market model (Davies 2012). Current family policy directions reflect this overextension of neoliberal apparatus to embrace highly illiberal, coercive ideals (Davies 2012; Parton 2014). An advancing capitalist ethos through the 1990s appropriated and apparently championed women's and children's rights, but the progressive rhetoric is fast wearing thin amid retraditionalisation narratives, authoritarian policies and iniquitous austerity measures. New opportunities are emerging to question taken-for-granted conceptual frameworks and moral sensibilities. Women and children must be at the very heart of this recalibration.

Notes

1. See *The Times*, leader 'Mods and Rockers', 6 July 1998.
2. See 'Daily Telegraph campaign to halt the "death of childhood"'. www.telegraph.co.uk/news/yourview/1528718/Daily-Telegraph-campaign-to-halt-death-of-childhood.html#.
3. For example, Family Nurse Partnerships and Family Intervention Projects.
4. See, for example, Jill Kirby, 'It's time for the Government to admit that Sure Start has been an expensive failure': http://conservativehome.blogs.com/thecolumnists/2012/07/ts-time-for-the-government-to-admit-that-sure-start-has-been-an-expensive-failure-.html.
5. Nick Clegg, speech on social mobility, 18 August 2010. Transcript available at: www.libdems.org.uk/press_releases_detail.aspx?title=Nick_Clegg_delivers_speech_on_social_mobility&pPK=38cf9a88-0577-403e-9dcb-50b8e30ed119.

6. David Cameron, speech on supporting families. http://www.conservatives.com/News/Speeches/2010/01/David_Cameron_Supporting_parents.aspx.
7. See Wastell and White (2012) for a more detailed discussion.
8. See speech by Michael Gove, 21 November 2011. http://www.education.gov.uk/inthenews/speeches/a00199946/michael-gove-speaks-to-the-london-early-years-foundation-about-the-importance-of-early-years.
9. See speech by Iain Duncan Smith to the Centre for Social Justice. www.guardian.co.uk/politics/2010/apr/09/iain-duncan-smith-childrens-brains.
10. See Polly Toynbee. www.guardian.co.uk/commentisfree/2012/oct/18/tory-dogma-cut-price-baby-farming.
11. Solihull NHS Care Trust (2011), The Solihull Approach Resource Pack. Cambridge: Jill Rogers Associates.
12. Figures released by the Ministry of Justice following a freedom of information request in 2011: see 'Truancy laws caught 12,000 parents last year', *The Guardian*, 8 November 2011. www.guardian.co.uk/education/2011/nov/08/truancy-parents-12000-prosecutions.
13. See 'Iain Duncan Smith suggests two-child limit for benefits', *The Telegraph*, 25 October 2012. www.telegraph.co.uk/news/politics/9632688/Iain-Duncan-Smith-suggests-two-child-limit-for-benefits.html.
14. '"No booze" smart cards for benefit claimants who spend their handouts on drugs and alcohol', *Daily Mail*, 13 October 2012. http://js.dailymail.co.uk/news/article-2217101/Iain-Duncan-Smith-No-booze-smart-cards-benefit-claimants-spend-handouts-drugs-alcohol.html.
15. See Joseph Rowntree Foundation, Child Poverty in the UK. www.jrf.org.uk/work/workarea/child-poverty.

References

Allen, G. (2011a). *Early Intervention: The Next Step*. London: HMSO.
Allen, G. (2011b). *Early Intervention: Smart Investment, Massive Savings*. London: HMSO.
Atkinson, A. B., Maynard, A. K. and Trinder, C. G. (1983). *Parents and Children: Incomes in Two Generations*. London: Heinemann.
Ball, S. (2008). *The Education Debate*. Bristol: Polity Press.
Barnardo's. (2008). *Locking up or giving up – is custody for children always the right answer?* http://www.barnardos.org.uk/locking-up-or-giving-up--is-custody-for-children-always-the-right-answer/publication-view.jsp?pid=PUB-1461.
Beck, U. and Beck-Gernsheim, E. (1995). *The Normal Chaos of Love*. Cambridge: Polity Press.
Beck, U. and Beck-Gernsheim E. (2002). *Individualization*. London: Sage.
Boltanski, L. and Chiapello, E. (2005). *The New Spirit of Capitalism*. London: Verso.
Brown, P. (1990). 'The "Third Wave": Education and the Ideology of Parentocracy'. *British Journal of Sociology of Education* 11(1): 65–86.
Bruer, J. (1999). *The Myth of the First Three Years: A New Understanding of Early Brain Development and Lifelong Learning*. New York: Free Press.
Bruer, J. (2011). *Revisiting 'The Myth of the First Three Years'*. Special Briefing for Monitoring Parents: Science, Evidence, Experts and the New Parenting Culture. http://blogs.kent.ac.uk/parentingculturestudies/files/2011/09/Special-briefing-on-The-Myth.pdf.
Children's Society. (2012). *The Good Childhood Report 2012*. London: The Children's Society.

Churchill, H. (2011). *Parental Rights and Responsibilities: Analysing Policy and Service User Perspectives*. Bristol: Policy Press.

Clarke, J. (2008). 'Living With/in and Without Neo-liberalism'. *Focaal – European Journal of Anthropology* 51: 135–47.

Couldry, N. (2011). *Why Voice Matters. Culture and Politics After Neoliberalism*. London: Sage.

Davies, W. (2012). 'The Emerging Neocommunitarianism'. *Political Quarterly* 83(4): 767–76.

Dickerson, A. and Popli, G. (2012). *Persistent Poverty and Children's Cognitive Development: Evidence from the UK Millennium Cohort Study*. CLS Cohort Studies Working Paper, Centre for Longitudinal Studies.

Edwards, R. and Gillies, V. (2013). 'Where Are the Parents? Parental Responsibility in the 1960s and 2010s'. In C. Faircloth, D. Hoffman and L. Layne (eds), *Parenting in Global Perspective: Negotiating Ideologies of Kinship, Self and Politics*. Abingdon: Routledge.

Ellsworth, J. and Ames, L. J. (eds). (1998). *Critical Perspectives on Project Head Start: Revisioning the Hope and Challenge*. New York: State University of New York Press.

Ermisch, J. (2008). 'Origins of Social Immobility and Inequality: Parenting and Early Child Development'. *National Institute Economic Review* 205(1): 62–71.

Featherstone, B., White, S. and Morris, S. (2014). *Re-imagining Child Protection: Towards Humane Social Work with Families*. Bristol: Policy Press.

Feinstein, L. (2003). 'Inequality in the Early Cognitive Development of British Children in the 1970 Cohort'. *Economica* 70: 73–97.

Fraser, N. (2009). 'Feminism, Capitalism and the Cunning of History'. *New Left Review* 56: 97–117.

Giddens, A. (1991). *Modernity and Self-identity: Self and Society in the Late Modern Age*. Cambridge: Polity Press.

Giddens, A. (1992). *The Transformation of Intimacy: Sexuality, Love and Eroticism in Modern Societies*. Cambridge: Polity Press.

Giddens, A. (1998). *The Third Way*. Cambridge: Polity Press.

Gilbert, R., Spatz Widom, C., Browne, K., Fergusson, D., Webb, E. and Janson, S. (2008). 'Burden and Consequences of Child Maltreatment in High-income Countries'. *The Lancet* 373(9657): 68–81.

Gillies, V. (2005). 'Raising the Meritocracy: Parenting and the Individualisation of Social Class'. *Sociology* 39(5): 835–53.

Gillies, V. (2011). 'From Function to Competence: Engaging with the New Politics of Family'. *Sociological Research Online* 16(4). http://www.socresonline.org.uk/16/4/11.html.

Gillies, V. (2012). 'Personalising Poverty: Parental Determinism and the Big Society Agenda'. In W. Atkinson, S. Roberts and M. Savage (eds), *Class Inequality in Austerity Britain: Power, Difference and Suffering*. Basingstoke: Palgrave Macmillan.

Green, K. (2013). 'Lone parents are hit the hardest yet again'. *Huffington Post*. www.huffingtonpost.co.uk/kate-green-mp/lone-parents-are-hit-the-hardest-again_b_2426894.html?ncid=edlinkusaolp00000003&ir=UK.

Hall, S. (2011). 'The Neoliberal Revolution'. *Soundings* 48: 9–27.

Haney, L. (2004). 'Introduction: Gender, Welfare, and States of Punishment'. *Social Politics* 11(3): 333–62.

Hartas, D. (2011). 'Families' Social Backgrounds Matter: Socio-economic Factors, Home Learning and Young Children's Language, Literacy and Social Outcomes'. *British Educational Research Journal* 37(6).

Hartas, D. (2012a). 'Inequality and the Home Learning Environment: Predictions about Seven-year olds' Language and Literacy'. *British Educational Research Journal* 38(5): 859–79.

Hartas, D. (2012b). 'The Achievement Gap: Are Parents or Politicians Responsible'. *British Educational Research Association Insights* (2): 1–4.

Harvey, D. (2007). *A Brief History of Neoliberalism*. Oxford: Oxford University Press.

Hays, S. (1996). *The Cultural Contradictions of Motherhood*. New Haven, CT: Yale University Press.

Hendrick, H. (2003). *Child Welfare: Historical Dimensions, Contemporary Debate*. Bristol: Policy Press.

Kehily, M. J. (2010). 'Childhood in Crisis? Tracing the Contours of 'Crisis' and Its Impact upon Contemporary Parenting Practices'. *Media, Culture & Society* 32(2): 171–85.

Kelly, Y., Sacker, A., Del Bono, E., Francesconi, M. and Marmot, M. (2011). 'What Role for the Home Learning Environment and Parenting in Reducing the Socioeconomic Gradient in Child Development? Findings from the Millennium Cohort Study'. *Archives of Disease in Childhood* 96: 832–7.

Lareau, A. (2003). *Unequal Childhoods, Class, Race and Family Life*. Berkeley: University of California Press.

Layard, R. and Dunn, J. (2009). *A Good Childhood: Searching for Values in a Competitive Age*. London: The Children's Society.

Lee, N. (2001). *Childhood and Society: Growing Up in an Age of Uncertainty*. Buckingham: Open University Press.

Mayall, B. (2002). *Towards a Sociology for Childhood: Thinking from Children's Lives*. Buckingham: Open University Press.

McCabe, D. P. and Castel, A. D. (2008). 'Seeing Is Believing: the Effect of Brain Images on Judgements of Scientific Reasoning'. *Cognition* 107(1): 343–52.

Mental Health Foundation. (2005). *Lifetime Impacts: Childhood and Adolescent Mental Health*. London: Mental Health Foundation.

Morris, L. (1994). *Dangerous Classes. The Underclass and Social Citizenship*. London: Routledge.

Palmer, S. (2006). *Toxic Childhood: How the Modern World Is Damaging Our Children and What We Can Do About It*. London: Orion.

Parton, N. (2006). *Safeguarding Childhood. Early Intervention and Surveillance in a Late Modern Society*. Basingstoke: Palgrave Macmillan.

Parton, N. (2014). *The Contemporary Politics of Child Protection: From the Third Way to the Authoritarian Neo Liberal State*. Basingstoke: Palgrave Macmillan.

Peters, E. (2012). '"I blame the mother": Educating Parents and the Gendered Nature of Parenting Orders'. *Gender and Education* 24(1): 119–30.

Pitts, J. (2003). 'Youth Justice in England and Wales'. In R. Matthews and J. Young (eds), *The New Politics of Crime and Punishment*. Devon: Willan.

Reay, D. (2012). 'What Would a Socially Just Education System Look Like? Saving the Minnows from the Pike'. *Journal of Education Policy* 27(5): 587–99.

Reay, D., Crozier, G. and James D. (2001). *White Middle Class Identities and Urban Schooling*. Basingstoke: Palgrave Macmillan.

Rose, N. (1989). *Governing the Soul. The Shaping of the Private Self*. London: Routledge.

Rose, N. (1999). *Powers of Freedom: Reframing Political Thought*. Cambridge: Cambridge University Press.

Royal Society. (2011a). Brain Waves. Module 1: Neuroscience, society and policy. http://royalsociety.org/.

Royal Society. (2011b). Brain Waves. Module 2: Neuroscience: implications for education and lifelong learning. http://royalsociety.org/.

Rutter, M. (2007). 'Sure Start Local Programmes: an Outsider's Perspective'. In J. Belsky, J. Barnes and E. Melhuish (eds), *The National Evaluation of Sure Start: Does Area Based Early Intervention Work?* Bristol: Policy Press.

Soss, J., Fording, R. and Schram S. (2011). *Disciplining the Poor: Neoliberal Paternalism and the Persistent Power of Race.* Chicago: University of Chicago Press.

Starkey, P. (2000). *Families and Social Workers: The Work of Family Service Units 1940–1985.* Liverpool: Liverpool University Press.

Towers, J. and Walby, S. (2012). *Measuring the Impact of Cuts in Public Expenditure on the Provision of Services to Prevent Violence against Women and Girls.* Northern Rock Foundation and Trust for London. www.trustforlondon.org.uk/VAWG%20Full%20 report.pdf.

Townsend, P. (1979). *Poverty in the United Kingdom: A Survey of Household Resources and Standards.* London: Penguin.

UNICEF. (2007). *Report Card on Child Well-being in Rich Countries.* www.unicef-irc.org/publications/pdf/rc7_eng.pdf.

Walker, A. (1990). 'Blaming the Victims'. In C. Murray (ed.), *The Emerging British Underclass.* London: Institute of Economic Affairs, pp. 66–75.

Wall, G. (2010). 'Mothers' Experiences with Intensive Parenting and Brain Development Discourse'. *Women's Studies International Forum* 33(3): 253–63.

Wastell, D. and White, S. (2012). 'Blinded by Neuroscience: Social Policy, the Family and the Infant Brain'. *Families, Relationships and Societies* 1(3): 397–415.

Welshman, J. (2006). *Underclass: A History of the Excluded, 1880–2000.* London: Hambledon Continuum.

Weisberg, D. S., Keil, F. C., Goodstein, J., Rowson, E. and Gray, J. R. (2008). 'The Seductive Allure of Neuroscientific Explanations'. *Journal of Cognitive Science* 20(3): 470–7.

12
Recolonising the Digital Natives
The Politics of Childhood and Technology from Blair to Gove

Keri Facer

Introduction

In the late 1990s, as the World Wide Web was being presented as heralding a new 'Information Society', children's reportedly intuitive capacity to use new technologies began to provide a new set of metaphors for talking about adult–child relationships. In this context, the now familiar ideas of the 'digital native' and the 'digital immigrant' were born, which presented children as natural citizens of a new world order and adults as analogue trespassers, trying to keep up. Even shiny new Prime-Ministers-In-Waiting professed themselves daunted by children's capacity to enter into this new world:

> Ask me my three main priorities for Government, and I tell you: education, education and education. The first wonder of the world is the mind of a child. I sometimes sit reading a paper or watching TV, and look up to see my children at a computer, and marvel at what they can do; using that computer as easily as we read a book. (Tony Blair, speech to Labour Party Annual conference, 1996)

For those with an interest in children's rights and children's agency, it is instructive to trace how these ideas of the child as at the vanguard of a new revolution have played out in the politics of the last two decades. This chapter will seek to do just that and to examine the potential implications of these trajectories for future relations between adults and children; in particular as we are beginning to witness the emergence of a set of new technologies likely to play as transformative a role over the next 20 years as the Web has played over the last twenty.

There are many stories to tell about politics, childhood and technology in the years following Blair's famous conference speech. One important story would describe the continuing battle to make visible the banal materiality of children's so-called 'natural' ability to use digital technologies; to highlight that such abilities are dependent on existing material, economic and social resources in order to gain access to machines, to Internet connections, to support and advice and inspiration. This story continues to be important given that 300,000 children still have no access to the Internet at home (ONS 2012; OFCOM 2012), that types of use remain highly variable even amongst those with access, and that such inequalities in access and participation bring demonstrable inequities in relation to educational opportunities and social engagement (Davies and Enyon 2013). If the last 20 years of research into children's uses of digital technologies has taught us nothing else, it is that there is nothing magical about children's participation in digital culture – it remains highly dependent upon and supported by wider social, economic and cultural practices in homes and in schools (e.g., Facer et al. 2003; Ito et al. 2009; Davies and Enyon 2013).

This chapter, however, will take a different focus. Its aim is not to document the way in which the digital remains a site through which existing inequities are reproduced, nor to seek to challenge representations of children's technological cultures by presenting the 'reality' of children's lived experiences. Instead, it explores how political and media representations of the social implications of digital culture have been an important site for contesting and renegotiating the relationship between adults and children over the last two decades.

In particular, it argues that the conditions for the working out of adult–child relations in the digital age have been deeply shaped by a dialogic relationship between media representations (often spectacular) and policy responses over the last two decades. In this way, digital cultures follow in the long line of 'moral panics', which bring together media, political, religious and judicial spheres to manage a potential disruption to the status quo. The moral panic, in particular, is a familiar and recurring social response to children's use of new leisure technologies (cinema and comics, for example) (Barker 1989). These sudden flurries of concern can be understood as the 'front line' of an ongoing ideological debate in which newspapers are engaged in what McRobbie describes as an 'ongoing daily process of reaching out to win consent through endlessly defining and redefining social questions' (McRobbie and Thornton 1995: 565). This relationship between media and policy is particularly important when we consider the changing relationships between policy and media fields characterised by the rise of New Labour in the 1990s. Over this period, as Fairclough argues, 'there is no clear line between finding policies that work and policies that win consent' (2000). The new politics of spin have transformed the relationship between 'political' and 'media' spheres from one of recontextualisation (in Bernstein's terms) to a dialectical relationship between the two fields. Indeed, McRobbie now makes the case that 'most political strategies *are* media strategies. The contest to determine the news agenda is the first and last battle of the political campaign' (McRobbie and Thornton 1995: 571).

The chapter explores how adult–child relations are being constructed in media and political discourses in two key fields: first, in the debates over children's online safety; and second, in the use of digital technologies in schools. It then argues that the strategies of surveillance and control that are emerging to sustain traditional adult–child relations in both fields may pose significant risks to children's rights in the era of rich personal data. The chapter concludes by arguing that attempts to understand and to intervene in the politics of childhood and technology over the *next* two decades will therefore need to take account of the wider politics of the marketisation of human life through personal and biodata.

Constructing adult–child relations in online spaces: media, legal and policy debates, 1990s–2000s

In 1997 the United Kingdom witnessed a General Election that brought the Labour Party, now rebranded as 'New Labour', to power after 18 years of opposition. The media coverage of that year reports the Tamagotchi craze beginning to take hold; new smart cards being introduced for school dinners; and, in the United States, the Supreme Court was about to rule on the limits of free speech (and pornography) on the Internet. In UK politics, this was the year when the National Grid for Learning was launched as a flagship government policy, an initiative presented as the development of a massive information resource where children can 'access all of the world's riches' from home and school (Selwyn 1999; Facer et al. 2001). The marketing departments of the computing industry were also busy constructing the home computer as the 'must have' educational device for children, and newspapers were happily preparing to assist their readers to deal with this newfangled technology. Indeed, by Christmas 1997, more than half a million people had spent £700 million on the purchase of home computers. By the following year, one survey put home ownership of computers amongst a sample of 1,800 school-aged children at 69 per cent (Facer et al. 2003).

An important tactic in promoting parental purchasing of computers was the construction of a natural articulation between children and technology. Children were repeatedly presented as both innately capable of using new technologies and as at risk of being profoundly disadvantaged by not having access to the Internet. By the turn of the century, this idea of children as experts was increasingly being mirrored by ideas of adults as naive incompetents. The idea of the 'digital native' was being presented as the defining metaphor for contemporary youth, in contrast to the image of the faltering, struggling adult as 'digital immigrant' (Tapscott 1997; Prensky 2001). These narratives of digital childhood constructed adults as anxious, uncertain about how to manage new technologies:

> 'the rapid change the Internet can generate leaves adults floundering. It is "an uncivilising force in life. To have something that discredits you as you get older ..." He shakes his head. "A lot of our mental infrastructure is built on the belief that experience matters. When that falls away, all is

lost"' (Michael Lewis, speaking in a books interview for the *Independent*; Arthur 2001).

One logical conclusion of such accounts of children's 'natural' ability with digital technologies might have been to construct the Web as a new sort of digital space where one would naturally expect to find young people participating, playing and learning. Such an expectation, however, was clearly at odds with the spatial and social arrangements that underpinned the twentieth-century standard model of childhood (Prout 2005), which depended upon the idea of childhood as a space and time of sequestration from encounters with non-familial adults.

An important first legal and media battleground for the debate over the meaning of the Internet for adult–child relations was the US Cyberporn case. This case (which because of the structure of the Internet has implications internationally) was concerned with whether pornographic materials should be allowed to be presented on the Web; and many of the counter-arguments to online pornography were couched in relation to the potential harm to children. One article of the period summed up the debate as *'should kids be forced into an adult world, or should adults be forced into a kids world?'*(No Byline 1997). Unsurprisingly, for a debate formulated in these terms, the decision of the court was to uphold First Amendment rights to free speech on the Internet and to leave the decision about how to manage children's access to the Internet to parents.

The popular debate around childhood and technology in the late 1990s and early 2000s, therefore, was characterised by two powerful narratives: first, the powerful marketing narrative of the demanding and competent child, computer using, needing access to digital technologies in order to liberate their 'natural' capabilities; and second, the construction of the Internet as a new Wild West of 'anything goes' freedom of speech: there would be no concessions to children's participation in these spaces. From these two conditions emerged an increasing public anxiety about how children's participation in online spaces was to be policed and protected. This anxiety fuelled an explosion of discourse surrounding children and the Internet at the turn of the century as the news media identified a potential source of endless concerns with which they might attract and retain their readers. This anxiety reached a peak in 2000–1, with the convergence of three significant media events. The first was the murder of the young girl Sarah Payne by a paedophile who had accessed child pornography on the Internet (but who notably did not identify or target his victim via the Internet). The second was an 'investigation', reported in the press and on television by TV presenter Carol Vorderman,[1] of the grooming practices of paedophiles using the Internet. The third event was the arrest of the 'Wonderland' gang of child pornographers and their conviction and sentencing in January 2001. These events formed the backdrop for a series of articles throughout 2001 that were addressed directly to parents.

The first characteristic of these articles was their construction of the Internet not only as an adult space, but as a space in which other adults (in contrast to the naive parent) were expert in seeking out children to cause them harm. The articles employed a form of direct address that positioned the issue of children's safety in online spaces as a matter of the reading parent's immediate and urgent concern. Carol Vorderman's first article on this issue, for example, started with the phrase 'your child is just three clicks away from a paedophile'. That this was the parents' responsibility to resolve alone, that there was no collective care or concern for children online, was an argument made explicitly by another article: 'nobody will watch out for your child unless you do' (Wroe 2001). The scale of coverage of these issues should not be underestimated. We can see a large increase in the number of newspaper articles related to both pornography and paedophilia on the Internet between 1997 and 2001 (Facer 2012a). This results in a perfect storm of outrage and concern surrounding children's access to the 'dangerous adult' spaces of the Internet in 2001 and begins to lead to calls for new political and social structures (Facer 2012a; Hope 2013).

This perfect storm led to a number of policy interventions: the UK and the European Union subsequently invested significant funds in the establishment of high-tech crime units dedicated to tracking down online pornographers, and bills to prevent online grooming were presented in the House of Commons, bringing together the Home Office, the Education Department and both the government and opposition parties. Proposals from a new task force included the establishment of 'kite mark' systems for online content, effectively giving age ratings to different parts of the Internet; and the establishment of new 'children-only' online spaces. Notably, children's opinions, experiences and attitudes towards the use of the Internet were almost wholly absent from these debates. It was a public debate *about* children in which they had no opportunity to participate.

The settlements that resulted from these policy interventions sought, in many ways, to render children invisible in online spaces and to increasingly monitor and impede their navigation of such spaces, in order to ensure their 'protection'. With the exception of the increased efforts to identify and convict a limited number of criminal abusers, these strategies for child protection placed no limitations on adult behaviour online and, instead, sought to manage risk by significantly delimiting children's participation in digital spaces. If children were the 'digital natives' of the Internet, the adults had effectively exercised their power to colonise it. This settlement, however, relied for its success on children's compliance with the requirement to participate only in children-only spaces, and with parents' competence and acceptance of the role of monitoring and managing their children's online activity.

By 2007, a decade later, the fragility of this settlement was clearly visible. Parental anxiety remained, children clearly insisted on escaping from children-only online holding pens, and newspaper reports periodically reported online grooming and abuse. At this point, the new Prime Minister, Gordon Brown, commissioned Dr Tanya Byron, child psychologist and presenter of TV programme *The House of Tiny Tearaways*, to carry out an independent review of the risks to children from the Internet and computer games. Published in March 2008, the review clearly stated that it was the unsettling of the standard model of adult–child relations triggered by the different technological cultures of different generations that was the cause of the problem.

> For adults to educate, empower and protect children about issues they are less familiar with, have less experience, understanding and knowledge of, makes for an *uncomfortable dynamic* between the adult and child (DCSF 2008, emphasis added).

The aim of the report was therefore explicitly framed as one of working out how to reduce parental anxiety by reinstating the standard model of childhood, even in the context of technological change.

Byron's response to this 'uncomfortable dynamic' was to draw parallels between parents' roles in online and offline space: in particular, she suggested that there were simple similarities between helping children to learn to cross the road and helping them learn to participate in online space. This simile provides a comforting account of a return to confidence in adults' capacity to manage and enable childhood expertise in collaboration with supportive structures in online environments. The review also makes the case for children to be allowed to navigate online spaces and for such spaces to adapt to young people. Rather than implying a strategy of managing risk by excluding children from digital spaces, the report recommends building young people's capacity to 'keep themselves safe' and to develop resilience in response to difficult situations, in a context in which the wider environment would be responsive to their rights to participate in these spaces.

The tabloid press responded to this report by delighting in the opportunity to present images of young women wearing very few clothes alongside stories of young people who didn't fit the model of the well-behaved online child. Welcoming the chance to demonstrate concern for young people, as well as a prurient interest in young women's sexuality, these articles typically represent young women in particular as inevitably putting themselves at risk online:

> Last night the Daily Mail discovered some of the shocking content youngsters are putting up on these sites. This includes a 14 year old girl whose profile picture, which can be viewed by anyone, focuses on her breasts. Another 15 year old is smirking at the camera as she grabs her breasts. She has listed her date of birth, her home town and name of school. (Revoir, 2008, *Daily Mail*)

These reports undermine the idea of the child as compliant with a strategy of limiting their behaviour to 'child-appropriate' ways and places; they undermine, in other words, the idea that all children are willing to play a role 'as child' in online space.

In the political arena, the most visible test of the Byron report's proposals came in the *Digital Britain* report of the following year. It is probably important to note that the Byron report was commissioned as a collaboration between the Department for Children, Schools and Families and the Department for Media, Culture and Society (DMCS), with support from the Home Office for its subsequent policy proposals. In contrast, the *Digital Britain* report was led by the Department for Business, Innovation and Skills in collaboration with DCMS, and emerged at a time in which the economic impacts of the 2007–8 banking crisis were beginning to be felt.

Unsurprisingly, then, other than proposing a very limited set of optional rules for social media sites, *Digital Britain*, put simply, practically ignored Byron's implication that the Internet should be seen as a space in which children's rights and interests should be taken into account. Instead, it makes an uncompromising assertion of the unquestionable importance of complete online freedom: 'we should take the internet pioneers' assumptions of freedom, entrepreneurialism and untrammelled innovation as the base model' (BIS/DCMS 2009). In particular, the report constructed children not as individuals with rights to participate in the important public spaces of the Web, but as dependants with needs for which parents rather than the environment were both responsible and able to meet.

Over a decade after Blair's conference speech and the Cyberporn case, after the spectacular moral panics surrounding the Sarah Payne case and the Wonderland trials, after multiple inquiries and reports, the relationship between adults and children in online spaces therefore remains unresolved. The Internet continues to be publicly constructed as a site of untrammelled freedom of speech, ostensibly free from ideological constraints (other than the ideology that sees complete freedom as an unquestionable good). Parents are almost exclusively responsible for children's safety in those spaces, with limited publicly enforced social signposts and supports to assist that responsibility. And young people continue to resist their participation in the spaces confined to activities and places that are subject to parental and social approval. Indeed, as Davies and Eynon (2013) have demonstrated, the digital culture continues to be a site in which young people and adolescents in particular will inevitably seek to test and to extend parental and adult boundaries, as they work out what it means to move into adulthood.

As with child protection in other arenas, this situation can bring significant negative consequences for some young people. A public space that refuses to take account of children's participation within it, combined with young people who may not conform to 'safe' models of child behaviour, tends to bring ever closer adult scrutiny and control of such 'deviant' children 'for their own sake' (Walkerdine 1997; Chadderton 2012). The deviant teenager showing her breasts online must become the subject of increased scrutiny, approbation and punishment. If these children won't be shepherded, their behaviour must be ever more closely monitored and controlled, tracked and commented upon.

If the goal, however, is child safety, such an approach brings significant risks. As Dowty argues, high levels of surveillance and monitoring of children's activities can constitute an invasion of privacy that potentially has significant implications for child safety in the long run:

> Allowing children to control access to themselves is essential for the development of a healthy ego, and a vital means of enabling them to protect themselves. If we are to enable children to grow into confident, self-aware adults, and empower them to develop the kind of clear personal boundaries they need in order to recognise and withstand abusive behaviour, we have to be scrupulous about maintaining unambiguous boundaries ourselves. Uninvited intrusion into their personal space or conflicting messages about their privacy rights are counterproductive to good child protection. They may yet have unintended consequences for children's sense of personal integrity, and for the kind of society that they will create in future. (Dowty 2008: 398)

At a time when the UK has enshrined in law (Education Act 2011, Part 2, section 2) the rights of teachers to confiscate mobiles phones, look at their contents and delete material they dislike, Dowty's argument that we need to respect children's privacy becomes even more urgent. At a time when civil liberties are being challenged from all sides by governments claiming that they need to restrict our freedom for our own safety, we need to ask ourselves whether such an approach to child safety will be the best guarantee of the greatly prized values of Internet 'freedom' in the long term.

The year 1997 saw a set of adult–child relations beginning to be constructed around ideas of adult respect for children's new capabilities; by 2007, the narration of children's online digital cultures as a focus for surveillance and control was in the ascendancy.

The politics of childhood in the digital classroom

In contrast with children's participation in online spaces in their leisure time, children's use of digital technologies in schools has been almost uniformly presented as desirable by policy makers over the last three decades. Indeed, the modernisation of the classroom through the introduction of digital technologies has frequently been presented as a symbol of aggressive government action to adapt society to rapid technological and global change. This is true both of New Labour and of the recent proposals by the Conservative–Liberal Democrat Coalition government that took office in 2010 to create a 'wiki-curriculum' that reframes Information and

Communications Technology as 'Computer Science' in order to develop a new generation of eager programmers able to lead a fresh wave of economically lucrative innovation.

It is worth noting, however, that children's interactions with digital technologies might be very different today in schools were it not for the media and political furore over online child safety that I have already discussed. Consider, for example, the Stevenson Report, produced in 1996–7 for New Labour with the help, amongst others, of Stephen Heppell, a leading educational technology evangelist. At the heart of these proposals were suggestions that young people should use the Web as active online citizens, that they should have email accounts and that they might come together to work online and converse online freely as part of a model of active online, collaborative learning.

After 2001, and in direct response to the lobbying by newspapers and celebrities following the Sarah Payne murder, a radical brake was put on the idea of the child as an active digital citizen. Indeed, in the education field, the results were instant and wide ranging: the initial proposals in the National Grid for Learning to offer email accounts to individual children to participate in online discussions and exchange were definitively shelved. And along with this came new guidelines for schools preventing them from putting children's photographs on school websites or allowing children to be named in public websites. Not only should children not navigate online space, but they should not be visible in that space. At the same time, a new industry of children-only spaces was created on the Web. Rather than offering access to the complex spaces of the online world, filtering systems and so-called 'walled gardens' in education were designed to ensure that children only accessed those sites that were pre-approved by adults and where they would only encounter other children or adults vetted as suitable for interaction with children. Today, children's access to the Internet in most schools remains highly constrained and the early reports of digital technologies' transformative power in education remain largely unfulfilled (Selwyn 2011). In place of student-led change, investment focused in the main on tools for teachers, such as interactive whiteboards, and on large-scale capital investments in school infrastructure rather than student-owned technologies.

From one perspective, then, it might be possible to argue that the policies of the last 30 years have led to little discernable change in adult–child relations in the education arena, notwithstanding the potentially radical disruption to geographies of childhood afforded by networked technologies. To argue this, however, would be to ignore the implications of another too-often overlooked area of digital technology in education over the last two decades.

While much political and media attention has been turned to the question of children's access to online spaces, a much more mundane set of technologies have been instrumental in reframing adult–child relations in the school setting. These are the technologies of linked databases and spreadsheets that have become the structural underpinning for the target-setting culture of contemporary teaching and learning, as well as for the marketisation of education and its dependence on the illusions of school league tables (Leckie and Goldstein 2011).

Over the last decade, data technologies have come to provide the infrastructure that underpins a new global education discourse of international metrics, comparisons and performance assessment (Novoa and Yariv-Mashal 2003; Martens 2007; Grek 2009, 2012; Grek and Ozga 2010; Ozga 2012). Such technologies are the carrier mechanisms of what Levin (1998) calls the 'epidemic' of education reform; they are the foundation for producing league tables for 'parental choice' and serve as the warrant for political interference in education, whether in closing down schools or in demanding that they have new leadership.

While the gathering of data about young people and teachers has been a part of education for years, the intensification of such processes and their internationalisation has been significantly facilitated by data technologies (Ball 2003). These tools facilitate micro-level record keeping; they allow the rapid collation and analysis of massive amounts of data; they allow modelling and projection of 'ideal' trajectories; and they allow comparisons between schools, students and countries, all on an ongoing basis. Without networked data technologies, the system of international performance management, scrutiny and micro-surveillance would arguably be impossible in schools. What is noticeable is that although such technologies have, today, become so pervasive as to be almost invisible in schools, they have been treated as banal and unremarkable, the subject of no newspaper articles or press releases in themselves.

That this should be the case should not be a surprise. Since the large-scale promotion of technology in education, ministers of education have sought to mobilise digital technologies to make the child increasingly visible to teachers as a site for intervention and development. Consider David Blunkett's approving observation in 2001 that these technologies would: 'Allow ... teachers to monitor progress more precisely and push pupils on to more challenging topics as soon as they are ready' (Blunkett 2001, quoted in Selwyn 2003: 43). Or, more recently, Coalition Education Minister Michael Gove's approving comment that digital technologies can enable 'each pupil's strengths and weaknesses [to] be closely monitored without stigmatizing those who are struggling or embarrassing those who are streaking ahead. Teachers can adjust lesson plans to target areas where pupils are weakest, and identify gaps in knowledge quickly and reliably' (Gove 2012). These data technologies can be easily and seamlessly incorporated within the familiar narrative of childhood as a time and a site for scrutiny, attention and observation for the protection and development of the child.

What do the technologies of spreadsheet, of record keeping and linked databases, do to adult–child relations? Arguably, nothing. And yet when we look at the database as a mode of representation of children to adults, there are significant implications. The technology of the database, through its instantiation in league tables and school information management systems over the last 20 years, has radically fragmented the idea of the child. The student becomes visible to the school manager increasingly through the units of data that are captured about her and, in turn, the student becomes known through these tools as a collation of these discrete interconnected fragments; in them she is the red mark on the spreadsheet, the 'borderline case' in the C/D boundary. While such data have always been gathered about children in schools, the widespread adoption of these tools over the last two decades allows for the statistical comparison of the individual child to their ideal fictional Other in similar schools or different locations. This comparator is, therefore, no longer their colleague in the classroom, but an international standardised globalised schoolchild, the PISA[2] victorious Finnish, Singaporean or Canadian child (Grek 2009, 2012).

These processes tend to decontextualise the child, extracting them from their relationships to the extent that researchers and policy makers have tried to 'add back in' such information through remedial strategies such as 'value-added' test scores designed to make visible various indices of human relationships (Goldstein 2001). The database presents the child as an autonomous *figure*, as separate from rather than as fundamentally dependent upon and interdependent with the other students and people that surround her. These technologies encourage the child to inhabit the description of themselves offered by the spreadsheet. As Reay and Wiliam have documented, the child comes to know themselves as a 'six' or a 'nothing' (Reay and Wiliam 1999).

The symbolic fallout of these data technologies is to reconstruct the student as a system made up of discrete functioning parts – capacities in science, capacities in maths, capacities in English at ages 11, 14 and 16. The child is no longer an embodied person, but a cybernetic system that results from inputs (teaching strategies/school factors) and which generates outputs (results). In the development field others have argued that the symbolic fallout from such technologies of measurement and comparison has resulted in the conception of the individual no longer as a person, but as a set of disaggregated requirements (the person as system) (Illich 1992: 168). As a consequence, the primary problematic for the field shifts from a concern with the hungry person to a concern with 'providing sufficient calories' for populations. In education, this is reflected in a parallel shift away from the education of the child, to the 'raising of standards', a context in which the recognition and respect for the whole child becomes of less importance than the technical challenge of closing a disembodied 'attainment gap' between populations. In this context, the teacher becomes technician, tweaking discrete elements of the child to effect changes in the data that will provide the ultimate indicator of success or failure of the school as system.

The next two decades? Intervening in the politics of childhood and technology

The last two decades have seen the politics of childhood and technology, particularly in education, shift strongly in the direction of acceptance of surveillance and monitoring of children's use of technologies and *of* children *by* technologies. This has been achieved through a persistent set of references to children's 'needs' – whether for safety or for educational development – and a persistent obscuring of children's rights as participants in digital cultures. Such a shift has effectively reversed the narrative that ushered in the 'Internet era' which constructed children as the natives and pioneers of this new world. The adults have, effectively, sought to recolonise the terrain, and where they have failed, they have sought to constrain children's freedoms in that space.

Does this matter? After all, the scrutiny of children and attention to their behaviour and development can be understood as a sign of care; indeed, neglect offers very little to recommend it as an alternative. I would like to argue that the unquestioned acceptance of the discourse of necessary surveillance via digital technologies does matter, for two reasons.

First, it matters because surveillance and subsequent punishment for deviance from normal behaviour tends to be unevenly distributed across different groups of young people (Chadderton 2012, 2013). The punitive consequences of an intensified culture of surveillance are not likely to be equally felt, therefore, by all young people. Indeed, in education (in the United States in particular) we have seen the way in which the reframing of educational care as detailed measurement of progress against a standardised set of non-negotiable goals too often results in an impoverished educational offer for children of colour and poorer socio-economic groups (Anyon 2005; Haas Dyson 2010).

The second reason that this routine acceptance of the digital as a means of detailed scrutiny of children matters is because the next two decades are likely to see a whole-scale proliferation of data technologies in all areas of human life. The expectations that we establish around rights to privacy, to access to data and to control of data will be important not only for young people but for everyone. It is to this issue that I want to turn to conclude the chapter, as it implies the need for researchers to begin to pay attention to a new set of issues in the field of childhood and digital culture in order to proactively intervene in the political debates in this area.

In 2011, the World Economic Forum announced the emergence of a new 'economic asset class' that promised new opportunities in terms of the development of goods and services. Those countries and companies who were able to exploit it would be in a leading position to make significant profits. This new economic asset class is *us*. In other words, it is the massive proliferation of data that is being produced by our participation in online spaces; our use of mobile technologies; our medical, health and educational data; our movements in public spaces and via transport systems; our conversations online with friends; and the emails and records we keep in the new spaces of cloud computing. The ability to mine this data, identify patterns and use it to generate new insights and new products will be key to the creation of new economic value over the next two decades (Cliff et al. 2007; Lanier 2013).

This development, in many ways, depends on us all becoming active and complicit partners in the creation of this new asset class. Consider, for example, the range of ways in which personal mobile devices are becoming tools for monitoring and surveillance of the self. First, the body itself is being transformed into a site of 'data collection'. There are now commercially available 'tracking devices' in the form of bracelets that keep a record of an individual's sleep patterns, movement, activity, pulse, heart rate, sweat responses and so forth.[3] Second, commercial and academic research organisations are working hard to develop means of documenting daily lives in ever more detail, from people's energy consumption to their social media use, to their interactions in the home.[4] Third, we are seeing the development of sensor technologies that begin to make it practically feasible to gather rich biological and environmental data on an ongoing basis.[5] At the same time, sensors embedded in city streets are already beginning gather information on everything from levels of particulates in the atmosphere to the movement of mobile phones around the city.[6] There are also now those, such as the 'quantified self' movement, who are welcoming such self-scrutiny by producing detailed, often witty, representations of the self in visual 'Annual Reports' that detail everything from calories consumed to films watched.

The potential for large-scale economic benefits to be gained from encouraging large-scale data generation about behaviour and biology, interactions and preferences, suggests that there will be increasing tools and social incentives to participate in such personal data collection. Just as the uses of Internet technologies have produced new anxieties and new forms of social practice, so will data technologies bring new anxieties and practices.

What might this mean for children and young people and for the politics of childhood over the next two decades? One trajectory, and the likely trajectory on the evidence of the last two decades, is that the era of Big Data will only serve to intensify the scrutiny and self-scrutiny of children and young people. The development of personal digital sensor tools to enable constant bodily and environmental scrutiny potentially allows for the radical amplification of this process. These tools make it possible to monitor, tweak and work on the self to adapt to changing conditions and comply with the latest standards. The child becomes Popkewitz's 'unfinished cosmopolitan' (Popkewitz, Olsson and Petersson 2006) with bio-digital bells on, constantly challenged to scrutinise the self for changes and (required to?) seek digital and bio-augmentations to competitively adapt to the environment. Imagine, for example, the standardisation of tools that keep records of physical activity, nutrition, brain wave activity, digestive processes and media consumption and associate these activities with recommended levels of activity or content for children of their age. Teachers and parents, in this context, may have ongoing access to these data and use them to inform judgements about the child's daily activities. This may not, however, be something that adults 'do to' children. Consider, for example, the growing popularity of personal devices such as Jawbone, that track physical activity, and the relish with which individuals connect these to social media sites to provide constant updates on reading, sports and location to their friends (and indeed, anyone else who reads their page). This opens up the possibility that such constant self-scrutiny might come to form part of the 'gamification' of everyday life, a competitive activity engaged in willingly in the name of pleasurable competitive play but in which the rules of the game are determined by adaptation to norms and aspirations set by the game designers.

An alternative trajectory, and one that might form the basis for a new politics of childhood and technology, can also be imagined. This trajectory would be premised upon a reversal of the logic of a centralised standardised model of childhood identity and behaviour and that seeks out and punishes deviance from the norm – whether the teenager pushing boundaries in online spaces or the child who fails to meet expected standards for her age. Instead, it would recast the young person as having the right to be considered the primary holder of data about themselves and the primary author of the narratives about themselves that are produced from those data. Rich data would be harnessed and used in pursuit of respect for and representation of the distinctive experiences, interests and capabilities of the unique person.

Given these possible trajectories, the politics of childhood and technology over the next two decades should not be allowed to be reduced to an impoverished debate about the relative needs of adults versus children, or equated simply with protecting children from the threat of online marauders or failing grades. Instead, common cause may need to be made between adults and children. After all, the question of what rights the person has to authoring the narrative of themselves, of maintaining control over how their behaviours and actions are scrutinised and made visible, is not age specific. It may be time to reach a settlement between the digital natives and the digital immigrants that recognises that we are interdependent in this sort of digital environment. After all, the rights to personal ownership and use of data that are waived for children today may be the rights that are waived for the generation of adults who will be cared for by them in future.

Notes

1. Carol Vorderman was, at the time, the popular 'resident mathematician' on the Channel 4 TV programme *Countdown*. Her ability to do rapid mental arithmetic and to put a series of vowels and numbers on a board for contestants to choose from had, in the context of the current debasement of mathematical skills in the UK, given her something of the identity of a trusted public intellectual.
2. Programme for International Student Assessment.
3. See, for example, https://jawbone.com/up/international.
4. See, for example, www.homenetworks.ac.uk/, http://wegov-project.eu/ and www.ted.com/talks/deb_roy_the_birth_of_a_word.html.
5. See, for example, www.bodymedia.com/ and www.media.mit.edu/galvactivator/.
6. See, for example, http://www.sensaris.com/smartcities/ and http://cityware.org.uk.

References

Anyon, J. (2005). *Radical Possibilities: Public Policy, Urban Education, and a New Social Movement*. New York: Routledge.

Arthur, C. (2001). 'The books interview: The teens who took over the net'. *Independent*, 21 July.

Ball, S. (2003). 'The Teacher's Soul and the Terrors of Performativity'. *Journal of Education Policy* 18(2): 215–28.

Barker, M. (1989). *Comics: Ideology, Power and the Critics*. Manchester: Manchester University Press.

BIS/DCMS (Department for Business Innovation Skills/Department for Culture Media and Sport). (2009). *Digital Britain*. Norwich: The Stationery Office. Retrieved from www.tsoshop.co.uk.

Chadderton, C. (2012). 'UK Secondary Schools under Surveillance: the Implications for Race. A Critical Race and Butlerian Analysis'. *Journal of Critical Education Policy Studies* 10(1). http://www.jceps.com/PDFs/10-1-06.pdf.

Chadderton, C. (2013). 'Secondary Schools under Surveillance: Young People "as" Risk in the UK. An Exploration of the Neoliberal Shift from Compassion to Repression'. In E. Cudworth, P. Senker and K. Walker (eds), *Technology, Society and Inequality: New Horizons and Contested Futures*. Peter Lang.

Cliff, D. et al. (2007). *Technology Trends, Horizon Scan Paper for Beyond Current Horizons*. Bristol: Futurelab.

Davies, C. and Eynon, R. (2013). *Teenagers and Technology*. London: Routledge.

DCSF (Department for Children, Schools and Families). (2008a). *Safer Children in a Digital World: The Byron Review*. Nottingham: DCSF. Retrieved from www.dcsf.gov.uk/byronreview.

DCSF (Department for Children, Schools and Families). (2008b). *Byron Review Action Plan*. London: DCSF.

DCSF (Department for Children, Schools and Families). (2010). *Do We Have Safer Children in a Digital World? A Review of Progress since the 2008 Byron Review*. Nottingham: DCSF. Retrieved from www.teachernet.gov.uk/publications.

Dowty, T. (2008). 'Pixie-dust and Privacy: What's Happening to Children's Rights in England?' *Children and Society* 22: 393–9.

Facer, K. (2012a). 'After the Moral Panic? Reframing the Debate about Child Safety Online'. *Discourse: Studies in the Cultural Politics of Education* 33(3): 397–413.

Facer, K. (2012b). 'Personal, Relational and Beautiful: Education, Technologies and John Macmurray's Philosophy'. *Oxford Review of Education* 38(6): 709–25.

Facer, K., Furlong, J., Furlong, R. and Sutherland, R. (2003). *Screenplay: Children and Computers in the Home*. London: Routledge.

Facer, K., Sutherland, R., Furlong, R. and Furlong, J. (2001). 'Constructing the Child Computer User: From Public Policy to Private Practice'. *British Journal of Sociology of Education* 4(4): 91–108.

Fairclough, N. (2000). *New Labour, New Language?* London and New York: Routledge.

Goldstein, H. (2001). 'Using Pupil Performance Data for Judging Schools and Teachers: Scope and Limitations'. *British Educational Research Journal* 27(4): 433–42.

Gove, M. (2012). Keynote Speech, BETT Show, London, January 2012.

Grek, S. (2009). 'Governing by Numbers: the PISA 'Effect' in Europe'. *Journal of Education Policy* 24(1): 23–37.

Grek, S. (2012). 'What PISA Knows and Can Do: Studying the Role of National Actors in the Making of PISA'. *European Educational Research Journal* 11(2): 243–54.

Grek, S. and Ozga, J. (2010). 'Governing Education through Data: Scotland, England and the European Education Policy Space'. *British Educational Research Journal* 36(6): 937–52.

Haas Dyson, A. (2010). 'Where Are the Childhoods in Childhood Literacy?' *Journal of Early Childhood Literacy* 1(1): 9–39.

Hope, A. (2013). 'The Politics of Online Risk and the Discursive Construction of School 'e-safety'. In N. Selwyn and K. Facer (eds), *The Politics of Education and Technology: Conflicts, Controversies and Connections*. New York: Palgrave Macmillan.

Illich, I. (1992). *Ivan Illich in conversation*, ed. D. Cayley. Toronto: House of Anansi Press.

Ito, M. et al. (2009). *Living and Learning with New Media: Summary of Findings from the Digital Youth Project*. Boston: MIT Press.

Lanier, J. (2013). *Who Owns the Future?* New York: Penguin.

Leckie, G. and Goldstein, H. (2011). 'A Note on "the Limitations of School League Tables to Inform School Choice"'. *Journal of the Royal Statistical Society A*, 174: 833–6.

Levin, B. (1998). 'An Epidemic of Education Policy: What Can We Learn from Each Other?'. *Comparative Education* 34(2): 131–42.

Martens, K. (2007). 'How to Become an Influential Actor – the 'Comparative Turn' in OECD Education Policy'. In K. Martens, A. Rusconi and K. Lutz (eds), *Transformations of the State and Global Governance*. London: Routledge, PP. 40–56.

McRobbie, A. and Thornton, S. (1995). 'Rethinking 'Moral Panic' for Multi-mediated Social Worlds'. *British Journal of Sociology* 46(4): 559–74.

National Grid for Learning. (1997). *The Government's Consultation Paper*. London: DfEE.

No Byline. (1997). '£100m to get kids on the net'. *Daily Mirror*, 7 October, p. 5.

Novoa, A. and Yariv-Mashal, T. (2003). 'Comparative Research in Education: a Mode of Governance or a Historical Journey?' *Comparative Education* 39(4): 423–38.

OFCOM. (2012). *Children and Parents: Media Use and Attitudes Report*. London: OFCOM. http://stakeholders.ofcom.org.uk/binaries/research/media-literacy/oct2012/main.pdf.

ONS. (2012). *Statistical Bulletin: Internet Access – Households and Individuals, 2012*.

Ozga, J. (2012). 'Assessing PISA'. *European Educational Research Journal* 11(2): 166–71.

Popkewitz, T., Olsson, U. and Petersson, K. (2006). 'The Learning Society, the Unfinished Cosmopolitan, and Governing Education, Public Health and Crime Prevention at the Beginning of the Twenty-first Century'. *Educational Philosophy and Theory* 38(4): 431–49.

Prensky, M. (2001). *Digital Game-Based Learning*. New York: McGraw-Hill.
Prout, A. (2005). *The Future of Childhood*. Abingdon: Routledge Falmer.
Reay, D. and Wiliam, D. (1999). 'I'll be a nothing': Structure, Agency and the Construction of Identity through Assessment'. *British Educational Research Journal* 25(3): 343–54.
Revoir, P. (2008). 'Millions of girls "are at risk online"'. *Daily Mail*, 1 April.
Selwyn, N. (1999). 'Gilding the Grid: The Marketing of the National Grid for Learning'. *British Journal of Sociology of Education* 20(1): 55–68.
Selwyn, N. (2003). *Telling Tales on Technology*. Cardiff: Ashgate.
Selwyn, N. (2011). *Schools and Schooling in the Digital Age: A Critical Analysis*. Abingdon: Routledge.
Tapscott, D. (1997). *Growing Up Digital: The Rise of the Net Generation*. New York: McGraw-Hill.
Walkerdine, V. (1997). *Daddy's Girl: Young Girls and Popular Culture*. Cambridge, MA: Harvard University Press.
World Economic Forum. (2011). *Personal Data: The Emergence of a New Asset Class*. Geneva: World Economic Forum. http://www.weforum.org/reports/personal-dataemergence- new-asset-class.
Wroe, M. (2001). 'We want your help'. *Sunday Times*, 14 October.

13
Kids for Sale?
Childhood and Consumer Culture

David Buckingham

Commercial marketing to children is by no means a new phenomenon. Indeed, historical studies show that children have been a key target for marketers since as far back as the mid-nineteenth century (e.g., Cross 1997; Cook 2004; Jacobson 2004; Denisoff 2008). Nevertheless, in recent years children have become increasingly important both as a market in their own right and as a means to reach adult markets. Companies are seeking to engage with children more directly and at an ever-younger age; and they are using a much wider range of techniques that go well beyond conventional advertising.

Marketers often claim that children are becoming 'empowered' in this new commercial environment: the market is seen to be responding to needs and desires on the part of children that have hitherto been largely ignored or marginalised, not least because of the social dominance of adults. However, critics have expressed growing concern about the apparent 'commercialisation' of childhood. Popular publications, press reports and campaigns have addressed what are seen to be the damaging effects of commercial influences on children's physical and mental health – or indeed, much broader consequences for their loss of 'childhood innocence'. Far from being 'empowered', children are typically seen here as victims of a powerful, highly manipulative form of consumer culture that is almost impossible for them to escape or resist.

In this chapter, I argue that we need to look beyond this rather polarised debate. In particular, I suggest that these views of children as consumers fail to address the ways in which consumer culture itself is currently changing. As I shall indicate, the more ubiquitous and 'participatory' techniques that are now being used by commercial companies reflect a new construction of the child consumer. This new construction in turn requires us to rethink the terms of the debate, and some of the basic assumptions we make about childhood and consumer culture.

Constructing the child consumer: campaigners, marketers and academics

In the wake of Naomi Klein's influential *No Logo* (2001), there has been a flurry of popular campaigning publications about children and consumer culture: prominent examples include Juliet Schor's *Born to Buy* (2004), Susan Linn's *Consuming Children* (2004), Ed Mayo and Agnes Nairn's *Consumer Kids* (2009) and Joel Balkan's *Childhood Under Siege* (2011). Other popular books in this vein include discussions of children's consumption alongside broader arguments about the apparent demise of traditional notions of childhood – as in the case of Sue Palmer's *Toxic Childhood* (2006), Richard Layard and Judy Dunn's *A Good Childhood* (2009) and Jay Griffiths' *Kith: The Riddle of the Childscape* (2013). The arguments in these publications are, by and large, far from new. One can look back to similar arguments being made in the 1970s, for example by groups like Action for Children's Television in the United States (Hendershot 1998); or to announcements of the 'death of childhood' that have regularly recurred throughout the past two centuries (e.g., Postman 1983). Even so, there now seems to be a renewed sense of urgency in these claims.

Such campaigners typically presume that children used to live in an essentially non-commercial world, or a kind of idyllic 'golden age'. Many of them link the issue of consumerism with other well-known concerns about media and childhood: as well as turning children into premature consumers, the media are accused of promoting sex and violence, obesity, drugs and alcohol, gender stereotypes and false values, and taking children away from other activities that are deemed to be more worthwhile. Of course, this is a familiar litany, which tends to conflate very different kinds of effects and influences. It constructs the child as innocent, helpless, and unable to resist the power of the media. These texts describe children as being bombarded, assaulted, barraged, even subjected to 'saturation bombing' by the media: they are being seduced, manipulated, exploited, brainwashed, programmed and branded. And the predictable solution here is for parents to engage in counter-propaganda, to censor their children's use of media, or simply keep them locked away from corrupting commercial influences. These books rarely include the voices of children, or try to take account of their perspectives: this is essentially a discourse generated by parents *on behalf of* children.

Meanwhile, there has been a parallel growth in marketing discourse specifically focused on children. Again, there is a long history of this kind of material. As Dan Cook (2004) and Lisa Jacobson (2004) have shown, the early decades of the twentieth century saw marketers increasingly addressing children directly, rather than their parents. In the process, they made efforts to understand the child's perspective, and began to construct the child as a kind of authority, not least by means of market research. In recent years, however, this kind of marketing discourse has proliferated, most notably in relation to the category of the 'tween' – a particular segment of the child market that has become especially prominent in the past two decades (see Mitchell and Reid-Walsh 2005). More recent examples would include Gene Del Vecchio's *Creating Ever-Cool* (1997) and Anne Sutherland and Beth Thompson's *Kidfluence* (2003); although perhaps the most influential account is Martin Lindstrom's *Brandchild* (2003), which is the basis of a major consultancy business that has effectively become a brand in its own right.

The most striking contrast between these accounts and those of the critics of consumer culture is the very different construction of the child consumer. The child is seen here as sophisticated, demanding and hard to please. Children, we are told, are not easily manipulated: they are an elusive, even fickle market, sceptical about the claims of advertisers, and discerning when it comes to getting value for money – and they need considerable effort to understand and to capture. Of course, given the political pressure that currently surrounds the issue of marketing to children (most notably around so-called 'junk food'), marketers are bound to argue that advertising has very little effect, and that children are 'wise consumers'. Yet this idea of the child as sovereign consumer often elides with the idea of the child as a citizen, or an autonomous social actor, and with the notion of children's rights; and it is often accompanied by a kind of 'anti-adultism' – an approach that is very apparent, for example, in the marketing of the global children's television channel Nickelodeon (Banet-Weiser 2007). To use one of Nickelodeon's key marketing slogans, in the new world of children's consumer culture, *kids rule*.

These contrasting views of consumption are also played out in academic theories and debates. On the one hand, we have accounts that see consumption as a kind of betrayal of fundamental human values. From this point of view, the pleasure of consumption is something to be suspected, a matter of inauthentic, short-term gratification – unlike the apparently authentic pleasures of human interaction, true culture or spontaneous feeling. This argument stands in a long tradition of critical theory, from Adorno and Marcuse (and indeed more conservative critics like F. R. Leavis and Ortega y Gasset) through to contemporary authors such as Zygmunt Bauman (2007) and Benjamin Barber (2007). For such critics it is generally *other people's* consumption that is regarded as problematic: the argument is informed by a kind of elitism, whereby largely white, male, middle-class critics have stigmatised the consumption practices of others – women, the working classes and now children (Seiter 1993).

On the other hand, there are accounts that emphasise the agency of consumers – that is, their ability to define their own meanings and pleasures, and to exercise power and control. Such accounts were particularly prominent in 'postmodernist' cultural studies at the beginning of the 1990s (e.g., Fiske 1990; Featherstone 1991), although they have arguably resurfaced with some more celebratory accounts of fandom and so-called 'participatory culture' (Jenkins 2006). Far from being passive dupes of the market, consumers are regarded here as active and autonomous; and commodities are seen to have multiple possible meanings, which consumers can select, use and rework for their own purposes. In appropriating the 'symbolic resources' they find in the marketplace, consumers are engaging in a productive and self-conscious process of creating an individual 'lifestyle' and constructing or 'fashioning' their identities. In the process, they are seen to be evading or resisting the control of what Fiske (1990) calls 'the power bloc'.

I have admittedly sketched these debates in somewhat stark and exaggerated terms here. Nevertheless, there is a clear polarisation in accounts of consumer culture – and specifically of children as consumers – that replays a much wider polarisation within the human sciences more broadly, between structure and agency. In relation to children, this typically results in a standoff between two diametrically opposed views: the child as innocent victim versus the child as competent social actor. On the one hand, we have the call to protect children from exploitation and manipulation; and on the other, the call to extend their rights to self-determination and autonomy. In relation to children's consumption, this leads to a series of binary oppositions that tend to dominate the debate. Are children active or passive consumers? Are they knowledgeable or innocent, competent or incompetent, powerful or powerless?

Later in this chapter, I will discuss some of the broader problems with this debate, and point to some possible means of moving beyond what has become a kind of conceptual impasse. First of all, however, I want to describe some of the ways in which the children's market itself is changing. In my view, these changes represent a different way of conceiving of, or constructing, the child consumer. These developments seem to make redundant the binary oppositions I have outlined above, and require us to ask some new questions.

Children: a growing but uncertain market

Estimates of the size of the children's market are somewhat variable, and occasionally seem quite hyperbolic. Child marketing guru Martin Lindstrom (2003), for instance, suggests that children aged 8–14 in the United States spend around $150 billion annually, 'control' another $150 billion of their parents' money, and influence family spending of up to $600 billion a year. He asserts that children may be responsible for almost two *trillion* dollars of annual global expenditure. Figures for Europe tend to be more modest. In the UK, one annual survey of children's pocket money suggests that children aged 7–16 receive an average of €35 per month, making a total of almost €80 million – a figure that has increased by 600 per cent over the past 20 years (HBOS 2007). The cost of bringing up a child from birth to the age of 21 is estimated to be in excess of €220,000, a figure that is rising significantly faster than inflation (Liverpool Victoria Friendly Society 2010). From a marketing perspective, children are generally seen to play three main roles. They are an increasingly significant market in their own right, through spending their own disposable income, gained from gifts and part-time work as well as regular allowances. However, they are also an important means of reaching adults: the influence that children exert on adults' purchases is more economically significant than what they buy themselves, and can include choices of holidays, cars, new technology and other expensive goods. Thirdly, they are seen as a future market – a 'market potential' – with whom companies wish to establish relationships and loyalties that they hope will be carried through into adulthood (McNeal 1999).

Nevertheless, the children's market is significantly more volatile and uncertain than adult markets. The failure rate for new products is much higher here than in the adult market (McNeal 1999); and while enormous amounts of money can undoubtedly be made from successful brands and product ranges, there is also a high degree of risk. The history of children's 'crazes' (such as Pokémon or Ninja Turtles) shows recurring patterns of rise and fall, which companies have significant difficulties in predicting or managing (Tobin 2004). At the peak of a craze, desperate parents may queue for hours in toyshops to buy scarce merchandise; while a few months down the line, vast quantities of the same goods may be on their way to landfill. Even very well-established brands are not immune from competitive challenge, as the 'doll wars' between Barbie and the Bratz range have recently shown (Clark 2007).

One approach that marketers have used in attempting to manage risk in the children's market is segmentation, most notably in terms of gender and age differences. However, this approach has some ambivalent consequences. On the one hand, segmentation provides a means for marketers to manage risk – to know and perhaps exercise greater control over potential markets; but the more segmented markets are, the smaller they become. The logic then points towards globalisation: smaller national markets can be amassed into much larger markets if they are targeted on a global scale – although this in turn requires products to be produced for global rather than national consumption, which itself requires difficult calculations about cultural specificity (Buckingham 2007).

Thus, gender differentiation is a key factor, particularly for younger children, where the market is heavily polarised into 'pink and blue'. There are significant risks for marketers here in trying to cross the line, in order to appeal to both groups. It used to be the received wisdom among marketers that the way to succeed was to appeal to boys first – girls were quite likely to buy boy-oriented products, although boys were less comfortable with products they perceived as too 'girly' (Schneider 1987). More recent analyses of contemporary toy advertising would suggest that this polarisation has been maintained (Griffiths 2002); and some products (and indeed entire television channels) are sometimes developed in distinct 'boy' and 'girl' versions. Yet while critics argue that the market actively produces or at least reinforces these gender distinctions and identities, it would clearly be in the commercial interest of marketers to minimise such differences (and hence to maximise the size of the market) rather than to accentuate them.

Likewise, age differences are also highly significant, but complex to manage. Dividing children into a series of niche markets defined by age means that new products can be sold at different stages, while others are cast off or 'outgrown'; and the history of children's marketing has seen the ongoing construction of new age-defined categories such as 'toddlers', 'teenagers' and, most recently, 'tweens' (Cook 2004). Yet children do not always 'act their age'. While younger children may well aspire to consume products that appear to be designed for those who are older than them, older children are unlikely to wish to be associated with items that are seen as too 'childish'. Commercial goods serve as powerful but often very ambivalent markers of 'age identities' – although here again, it is often very difficult for marketers to manage and control the meanings that children produce.

New marketing techniques

Another way in which marketers have sought to manage risk in the children's market is through the use of new media and new techniques. Pre-eminent amongst these has been the rise of integrated, cross-media marketing – sometimes variously termed '360 degree marketing' or 'synergistic marketing'. This practice has been especially apparent in most of the leading children's 'crazes' and product ranges of the past 30 years: examples of current successes would include Disney's *High School Musical* and *Hannah Montana* and Warner Brothers' *Harry Potter*, as well as franchised characters aimed at younger children such as Bob the Builder and Thomas the Tank Engine. In each case, the core text or product provides the basis for an ever-expanding range of ancillary products and merchandise.

Of course, this is far from being a recent development. Disney is the best-known example of this phenomenon: right from the early days of the Mickey Mouse clubs (which began in cinemas in the 1930s, and came to television in the mid-1950s), merchandising has been an indispensible aspect of the enterprise, and has even sometimes served to keep the media production operation afloat (see de Cordova 1994; Bryman 1995; Wasko 2001). Yet following the advent of so-called 'program-length commercials' on US television in the late 1970s – cartoons produced or commissioned by toy companies as 'shop windows' for their products – media and merchandising have become inextricably connected. The presence of such branded merchandise in so many media and market sectors – including not just toys, but also clothing, food, gifts and other paraphernalia – effectively makes them impossible to avoid, generating a 'virtuous circle' of ubiquitous mutual promotion.

In this context, traditional advertising (for example on television or in print media) is gradually becoming redundant – and indeed goods such as Pokémon products were never advertised as such. Traditional advertising is now in decline, and an increasing proportion of marketing budgets is now spent on other forms of promotion, public relations and branding. Marketers are also developing a range of new techniques, many of which are particularly prevalent in the children's and youth markets (see Montgomery 2007). These include the following:

- *Product placement*: not in itself a new strategy, but nevertheless a practice that is becoming more widespread in a range of media, and has recently been legalised at a European level (albeit not in children's programmes).
- *'Embedded' marketing*, for example through the use of commercial messages in computer sports games or online social worlds.
- *Advergaming*, that is games (most obviously on company websites) using commercial or branded imagery or content.
- *Viral marketing*, whereby commercial messages (in the form of emails or SMS texts or images) are forwarded from one user to another.
- *'Immersive' marketing* and the gathering of personal data in online social worlds, both subscription sites and 'free' branded ones.
- *Social networking* – in particular, the use of 'applications' that involve users in competitions featuring branded products and services, the use of branded materials (such as 'skins' or backgrounds), and the ways in which users are invited to define and construct their personal profiles in terms of preferences for consumer goods.
- *Sponsorship*: again, a well-established strategy but one that appears to be becoming more widespread, not least as part of the wider privatisation of public institutions, events and services (for instance in education).
- *Peer-to-peer marketing*, whereby opinion leaders are recruited and paid as 'brand champions' or 'ambassadors' who will actively display and advocate the use of particular products within their contact group.
- The commercial cultivation of forms of *'fan culture'* that involve collecting commodities (often those with a market-induced 'rarity' value), or creating forms of fan 'art' (for example, creating and circulating re-edited video material).
- So-called *user-generated content*, in which companies recruit consumers to create blogs or online videos (or alternatively masquerade as ordinary consumers to do so) promoting particular brands or products.

These new techniques are fairly diverse, and some may ultimately prove much more successful than others – although the expenditure on such approaches is undoubtedly increasing quite significantly at present.

However, they have certain qualities in common. For the most part, they are about *branding* – creating a set of values or emotions associated with the brand – rather than the marketing of specific products. Many of them depend to a large extent on the use of *digital media*, with its immediacy of access, its networking capacity, and its apparent 'youth' appeal, as well as its capacity for surveillance of consumer behaviour. Many are *'personalised'*, in the sense that they seem to appeal and respond to the individual's wants and needs, rather than addressing them as a member of a mass market. They are often potentially *deceptive* or 'stealthy', in the sense that their persuasive intentions are not made apparent – for example through commercial messages being embedded in other content, rather than clearly identifiable, as is the case with television commercials or banner advertising online. Finally, many of them are *'participatory'* or 'interactive', in that they require the positive engagement of the consumer, who may be called upon to engage actively with the communication, to pass it on to others, or even to help create the message.

In all these respects, these new techniques reflect much broader trends in contemporary consumer culture, which apply to adults as well as children. Rather than adopting aggressive 'hard sell' techniques, marketers increasingly have to take account of consumers' scepticism and potential resistance. The consumer is defined and addressed not as vulnerable and open to manipulation, but as 'savvy', sophisticated and discriminating. Again, there is a long history of this approach, dating back at least to the late 1950s (see Frank 1997), but it has become increasingly *de rigueur* in the business. The aim here is not so much to sell specific products but rather to engage with consumers' sense of personal agency, and to create more intense forms of intimacy and 'bonding' in the relations between consumers and brands (Arvidsson 2006).

Knowing consumers?

The increasing risks and uncertainties of the children's market also place a new premium on knowledge. Marketers can never be sure that they can fully 'know' children or predict their behaviour. As a result, a thriving research business has grown up, which now seeks to access children's perspectives directly, rather than merely those of their parents. These 'commercial epistemologies' (Cook 2000) often draw on the creative and ethnographic tools for accessing children's 'voice' developed within academic disciplines such as anthropology and Cultural Studies. For instance, researchers may visit children repeatedly in their homes, spending extended periods with them in their most private spaces, such as bedrooms and bathrooms. They film children playing with toys and engaged in other mundane tasks such as eating, using these methods because interviews do not always reveal behaviour which children are reluctant to admit (such as playing with toys they claim to have grown out of). In this way, researchers access new information that can be used commercially: for instance, seeing children playing with empty bubble bath containers inspired the redesign of packaging (Schor 2004). Likewise, in the practice known as 'cool hunting', young people may be recruited as 'consultants' to supply their own views on products and advertisements, or employed to track trends among their peer groups. For example, Dubit, a UK-based youth research company, has a website aimed at young people that pays them to answer surveys about new ad campaigns, technologies or products, alongside chat and games. Digital media also provide new means of gathering and accessing data about consumer behaviour. The practice of 'data mining' involves the gathering, aggregation and analysis of data about consumers, either based on their responses to online requests or questionnaires or (more covertly) through the use of 'cookies' that track their movements online. Such practices are widely used in social networking sites and online worlds, not only in online shopping or commercially branded sites. In these ways, the media that are often celebrated for their ability to 'empower' consumers also provide powerful means of surveillance.

Companies operating in this market typically claim to offer privileged insights into the views and perspectives of young people. Their research is often aligned with the rhetoric of 'empowerment' identified above: young people are frequently described as self-determining, autonomous and innately 'savvy' in their dealings with the commercial world. Children, we are told, want to be in control, to be 'listened to, heard, respected and understood': they must not be patronised. They can recognise when advertisers are trying to manipulate them; and while they are quick to adopt new trends, they are also quick to move on. As such, they are extremely powerful and influential consumers: 'they get what they want when they want it' (Sutherland and Thompson 2001). This new rhetoric of the competent child consumer is also aligned with a familiar discourse about young people and technology. Children are represented as 'digital natives', who are 'born with a mouse in their hands', as Lindstrom (2003) puts it. As such, they can best be reached through the kinds of 'participatory' techniques I have identified above. While campaigners frequently express alarm about the deceptive and invasive nature of such approaches, for marketers they are a means to empowerment: they provide children with the means to register their needs, find their voices, build their self-esteem, define their own values, and develop independence and autonomy.

Ethics and theories: beyond the binaries

These new practices undoubtedly raise new ethical questions, yet they are ones that policy makers have struggled to address. In the UK, for example, the symptomatically titled government report *Letting Children Be Children*, authored by the Chief Executive of the Mothers' Union, Reg Bailey (2011), proposed a series of measures to address practices such as peer-to-peer marketing, although these have proven hard to define, let alone implement. Regulations that apply to conventional advertising (for example, on television) are difficult to apply online, or to these more pervasive forms of marketing. Many new marketing techniques blur the boundaries between promotional messages and other content, making it possible to embed advertising in contexts where it is less likely to be recognised as such. They often entail the gathering, aggregation and use of personal data about consumers without them necessarily being aware that this is taking place; and children may also be encouraged or required to provide personal information about others, for example parents or friends, without their knowledge, raising significant concerns about privacy (see Livingstone 2006; Buckingham et al. 2007; Nairn and Monkgol 2007). 'Peer-to-peer' and viral marketing represent a modern form of 'word of mouth', although they also depend on a degree of deception, whereby users (rather than companies) are seen as the authors or at least the distributors of commercial messages. There are also justified concerns that children are being recruited for market research at an ever-younger age, and that the aims of such research are not always clearly explained. There may be further violations of privacy here, as such researchers are increasingly keen on studying children in their 'natural habitat' of the home or the peer group.

However, these developments also raise broader questions about children's understanding of commercial motivations and practices, and more broadly about their competence as consumers. Research has only recently begun to explore how children engage with these new practices (Montgomery 2007) – although there may be little reason to expect that children are any less knowledgeable about them, or indeed more vulnerable to deception, than adults. Children (or indeed adults) may be more or less knowledgeable about such techniques, but that knowledge in itself does not necessarily confer the power to resist them. Furthermore, the fact that children are now increasingly addressed and engaged as 'active' participants does not necessarily mean that they have greater agency or power. As I have suggested, these developments can be seen to represent a much more general paradigm shift in the nature of consumer culture, away from a 'mass marketing' model towards one that is significantly more pervasive, more personalised and more participatory. In this context, consumers' agency itself is being produced and engaged in new ways. Easy oppositions of the kind with which we began – between active and passive, knowledgeable and innocent, competent and incompetent, powerful and powerless – no longer apply. We need to look beyond such binary thinking, towards a more complex understanding of children's consumer practices.

Ultimately, the limitations of much of the debate in this area derive from the broader assumptions about childhood on which it is based. It seems to be assumed that there is a natural state of childhood that has been destroyed or corrupted by marketers – or, alternatively, that children's 'real' innate needs are somehow being acknowledged and addressed, even for the first time. It is also believed that there is something particular to the condition of childhood that makes children necessarily more vulnerable – or indeed spontaneously more wise and sophisticated, for example in their dealings with technology; and that adults are somehow exempted from these arguments.

Aside from the sentimentality of these assumptions, this kind of polarisation fails to acknowledge some of the paradoxes here. For example, it is entirely possible that children (or indeed adults) might be active and sophisticated readers of media, but might nevertheless still be influenced – or indeed that an *illusion* of autonomy and choice might be one of the prerequisites of contemporary consumer culture. *Activity* is not necessarily the same thing as *agency*. At the same time, we need to acknowledge the genuine difficulties, risks and uncertainties that are entailed for marketers in actually targeting children – and that the power of the marketers may also be more limited than is often assumed. The paradox of contemporary marketing is that it is bound to construct children as active, desiring and autonomous, and in some respects as resisting the imperatives of adults, while simultaneously seeking to make them behave in particular ways.

Consumption in context

The other recurring problem with this polarised debate is its tendency to displace attention away from other possible causes of the phenomena that are at stake. Politically, this kind of approach feeds into a familiar game of 'blaming the media'. For example, there is a growing tendency in many countries to blame marketers and advertisers for the rise in childhood obesity; and this is an issue that is also becoming an increasing preoccupation for researchers (see Buckingham 2009a, 2009b). Yet there may be many other complex reasons for this phenomenon. In fact, poor people are most at risk of obesity – and this clearly has something to do with the availability and price of fresh food, and the time that is available to people to shop and prepare their own meals. The rise of obesity might also be related to the rise of 'car culture', the fact that children (at least in some countries) are now much less independently mobile, and the increasing privatisation of public leisure facilities. Research suggests that advertising is a relatively insignificant influence on food choice (Buckingham 2011); yet, as with debates about media violence, blaming the media allows politicians to displace attention away from other potential causes, while also being seen to be 'doing something' about the problem.

The key point here is that it makes little sense to abstract children's relationship with advertising, or their consumer behaviour, from the broader social and historical context. Indeed, the distinction between consumption and the 'context' in which it occurs may itself be misleading: it might be more appropriate to regard consumption as a form of *social practice*, and as a dimension of other social practices, which collectively *construct* 'contexts' (see Johansson 2010; Pilcher 2013). In a capitalist society, almost all our social activities and relationships are embedded within economic relations. The children's market works through and with the family, the peer group and – increasingly – the school. We need to address how consumption practices are carried out in these different settings, how they help to define the settings themselves, and how they are implicated in the management of power, time and space. In the process, we need to move beyond the notion of the consumer as a self-contained individual, and beyond individualistic notions of desire, identity and lifestyle, to focus instead on relationships and reciprocity.

Anthropological and sociological studies of childhood have begun to address these dynamics in other areas of children's lives (see Qvortrup, Corsaro and Sebastian-Honig 2009); and in some recent studies, this approach has begun to be applied to children and parents' everyday consumption practices as well (see Martens, Southerton and Scott 2004). This work addresses central questions to do with the construction of childhood identities and the wider 'generational order', drawing on the Sociology of Childhood as well as on Cultural Studies and on anthropological studies of 'material culture' (see Buckingham and Tingstad 2010; Buckingham 2011).

One particular focus of interest here is how consumption produces and sustains hierarchies of status and authority in children's peer groups. Thus, some research shows how children's clothing purchases can be a site of anxiety about status and belonging as well as of play and creativity (Boden et al. 2004; Pilcher 2011). To what extent does knowledge of consumer culture function as a kind of cultural (or subcultural) capital for children? How do the hierarchies of taste and 'cool' within the peer group relate to the hierarchies within adult culture (for example, of class, ethnicity or gender)? How might such hierarchies work with or against the imperatives of consumer culture (for example, by rendering the 'cool' uncool overnight)? How do we interpret the anti-consumerist rhetoric of some forms of youth culture – and the ways in which it been appropriated for so-called 'ethical' consumption?

Another focus here is the changing role of parenting, and the social expectations that surround it. Gary Cross (2004) has identified the symbolic tension here between parents' desire to shelter the child, to use childhood as a place for pedagogic nurturing, and their desire to allow the child a space for expression, to indulge the freedom they themselves have lost. As parents spend less and less time with their children, they may be more inclined to compensate by providing them with consumer goods. As such, contemporary parenting is now increasingly implicated with the operations of the market – and yet parents often regard this with considerable ambivalence (Pugh 2009).

Other studies have addressed the experience of young people who are excluded from peer group culture because of their lack of access to consumer goods (e.g., Chin 2001; Croghan et al. 2006). Not all consumers are equally able to participate, since participation depends not just on one's creativity but also on one's access to material resources: the market is not a neutral mechanism, and the marketised provision of goods and services (not least in the media and in education) may exacerbate existing inequalities. In this context, it is particularly important to understand the consumption practices of children in disadvantaged communities, for whom 'consumer choice' may be a fraught and complex matter. While many children may be able to access some aspects of the goods that become the *lingua franca* of children's culture – for instance, by being part of the audience for the advertising that surrounds them – their experience of the actual products is likely to vary widely with material purchasing power. Elizabeth Chin's work (2001) on poor African American children usefully challenges the idea that less wealthy children are somehow more at risk from the seductions of consumer culture, exploring how their strikingly altruistic consumption practices – during a shopping trip she arranged as part of the research – are embedded within their social and familial relationships.

Conclusion

Children's involvement in consumer culture is a profoundly ambivalent phenomenon. Of course, there is always an economic 'bottom line': the global child market is a significant source of commercial profit – although, as I have argued, profit is by no means easy or straightforward to secure. On the other hand, the meanings and pleasures that consumer culture affords children – and the roles that it can play in the formation of childhood identities – are significantly more difficult to predict. The market clearly does have a considerable power to determine the meanings and pleasures that are available; but children themselves also play a key role in creating those meanings and pleasures, and they may define and appropriate them in very diverse ways. Seeing this in terms of a simple opposition between structure and agency is inadequate, especially in the changing context of contemporary consumer culture. We undoubtedly need more adequate theoretical approaches; but we also need to account for the specificity of children's consumption practices in relation to the social contexts and circumstances of their daily lives.

The real problem here, I would suggest, is not primarily to do with the 'commercialisation' of some imaginary pre-commercial or non-commercial 'essence' of childhood. Rather, it is to do with the much broader processes of marketisation and privatisation. As other contributors to this book have shown, commercial forces now play an increasingly important role, not just in children's leisure and play, but also in education, in the provision of welfare and social services, and in resources and support for parenting. Despite the often melodramatic claims of campaigners and the generalised optimism of the marketers, the outcomes of children's increasing immersion in consumer culture are by no means the same for all. The logic of the market is such that it is bound to serve those who offer the most lucrative means of generating profit: and as such, it must inevitably contribute to growing inequalities. Advertising and marketing to children may provide convenient and even therapeutic targets for campaigners; but the marketisation and privatisation of public services have much more far-reaching consequences for children's lives. The more significant problem here is not so much that markets produce 'commercialism' or 'materialism', but rather that they inevitably accentuate inequality.

References

Arvidsson, A. (2006). *Brands: Meaning and Value in Media Culture*. London: Routledge.
Bailey, R. (2011). *Letting Children Be Children: Report of an Independent Review of the Commercialization and Sexualization of Childhood*. London: Department for Education.
Balkan, J. (2011). *Childhood Under Siege: How Big Business Ruthlessly Targets Children*. London: Bodley Head.
Banet-Weiser, S. (2007). *Kids Rule! Nickelodeon and Consumer-Citizenship*. Durham, NC: Duke University Press.
Barber, B. (2007). *Consumed: How Markets Corrupt Children, Infantilize Adults, and Swallow Citizens Whole*. New York: Norton.
Bauman, Z. (2007). *Consuming Life*. Cambridge: Polity Press.
Boden, S., Pole, C., Pilcher, J., and Edwards, T. (2004). 'New Consumers: the Social and Cultural Significance of Children's Fashion Consumption'. *Working Papers: Cultures of Consumption Series* 16.
Bryman, A. (1995). *Disney and His Worlds*. London: Routledge.
Buckingham, D. (2007). 'Childhood in the age of global media', *Children's Geographies* 5(1-2): 43–54.
Buckingham, D. (2009a). 'The Appliance of Science: the Role of Research in the Making of Regulatory Policy on Children and Food Advertising in the UK'. *International Journal of Cultural Policy* 15(2): 201–15.
Buckingham, D. (2009b). 'Beyond the Competent Consumer: the Role of Media Literacy in the Making of Regulatory Policy on Children and Food Advertising in the UK'. *International Journal of Cultural Policy* 15(2): 217–30.
Buckingham, D. (2011). *The Material Child: Growing Up in Consumer Culture*. Cambridge: Polity Press.
Buckingham, D. et al. (2007). *The Impact of the Media on Children and Young People*. Review of the literature prepared for the DCSF Byron Review. http://www.dcsf.gov.uk/byronreview/ (Annex G).
Buckingham, D. and Tingstad, V. (eds). (2010). *Childhood and Consumer Culture*. London: Palgrave Macmillan.
Chin, E. (2001). *Purchasing Power: Black Kids and American Consumer Culture*. Minnesota: University of Minnesota Press.

Clark, E. (2007). *The Real Toy Story: Inside the Ruthless Battle for Britain's Youngest Consumers*. London: Black Swan.

Cook, D. T. (2000). 'The Other "Child Study": Figuring Children as Consumers in Market Research, 1910s–1990s'. *Sociological Quarterly* 41(3): 487–507.

Cook, D. T. (2004). *The Commodification of Childhood: The Children's Clothing Industry and the Rise of the Child Consumer*. Durham, NC: Duke University Press.

Croghan, R., Griffin, C., Hunter, J. and Phoenix, A. (2006). 'Style Failure: Consumption, Identity and Social Exclusion'. *Journal of Youth Studies* 9(4): 463–78.

Cross, G. (1997). *Kids' Stuff: Toys and the Changing World of American Childhood*. Cambridge, MA: Harvard University Press.

Cross, G. (2004). *The Cute and the Cool*. New York: Oxford University Press.

de Cordova, R. (1994). 'The Mickey in Macy's Window: Childhood, Consumerism and Disney'. In E. Smoodin (ed.), *Disney Discourse*. London: British Film Institute.

Del Vecchio, G. (1997). *Creating Ever-Cool*. Gretna, LA: Pelican.

Denisoff, C. (ed.). (2008). *The Nineteenth-Century Child and Consumer Culture*. Aldershot: Ashgate.

Featherstone, M. (1991). *Consumer Culture and Postmodernism*. London: Sage.

Fiske, J. (1990). *Understanding Popular Culture*. London: Unwin Hyman.

Frank, T. (1997). *The Conquest of Cool*. Chicago: University of Chicago.

Griffiths, J. (2013). *Kith: The Riddle of the Childscape*. London: Hamish Hamilton.

Griffiths, M. (2002). 'Pink Worlds and Blue Worlds: a Portrait of Infinite Polarity'. In D. Buckingham (ed.), *Small Screens: Television for Children*. London: Leicester University Press.

HBOS. (2007). 'Pocket Money Rises 600% in 20 Years'. Press Release. http://www.hbosplc.com/media/pressreleases/articles/halifax/2007-07-21-Pocketmone.asp?section=halifax.

Hendershot, H. (1998). *Saturday Morning Censors: Television Regulation Before the V-Chip*. Durham, NC: Duke University Press.

Jacobson, L. (2004). *Raising Consumers: Children and the American Mass Market in the Early Twentieth Century*. New York: Columbia University Press.

Jenkins. H. (2006). *Convergence Culture*. New York: New York University.

Johansson, B. (2010). 'Subjectivities of the Child Consumer: Beings and Becomings'. In D. Buckingham and V. Tingstad (eds), *Childhood and Consumer Culture*. London: Palgrave Macmillan.

Klein, N. (2001). *No Logo*. London: Flamingo.

Layard, R. and Dunn, J. (2009). *A Good Childhood: Searching for Values in a Competitive Age*. London: Penguin.

Lindstrom, M. with Seybould, E. (2003). *BrandChild*. London and Sterling VA: Kogan Page.

Linn, S. (2004). *Consuming Kids*. New York: Anchor Books.

Liverpool Victoria Friendly Society. (2010). 'The Cost of Raising a Child Tops £200,000'. Press Release, 23 February. http://www.lv.com/media_centre/press_releases/.

Livingstone, S. (2006). 'Children's Privacy Online'. In R. Kraut, M. Brynin and S. Kiesler (eds), *Computers, Phones and the Internet*. New York: Oxford University Press.

Martens, L., Southerton, D. and Scott, S. (2004). 'Bringing Children (and Parents) into the Sociology of Consumption'. *Journal of Consumer Culture* 4(2): 155–82.

Mayo, E. and Nairn, A. (2009). *Consumer Kids: How Big Business Is Grooming Our Children for Profit*. London: Constable.

McNeal, J. U. (1999). *The Kids' Market: Myths and Realities*. New York: Paramount.

Mitchell, C. and Reid-Walsh, J. (eds). (2005). *Seven Going on Seventeen: Tween Studies in the Culture of Girlhood*. New York: Peter Lang.
Montgomery, K. (2007). *Generation Digital*. Cambridge, MA: MIT Press.
Nairn, A. and Monkgol, D. (2007). 'Children and Privacy Online'. *Journal of Direct Data and Digital Marketing Practice* 8: 294–308.
Palmer, S. (2006). *Toxic Childhood*. London: Orion.
Pilcher, J. (2011). 'No logo? Children's Consumption of Fashion'. *Childhood* 18(1): 128–41.
Pilcher, J. (2013). '"Small, but very determined": a Novel Theorization of Children's Consumption of Clothing'. *Cultural Sociology* 7(1): 86–100.
Postman, N. (1983). *The Disappearance of Childhood*. London: W. H. Allen.
Pugh, G. (2009). *Longing and Belonging: Parents, Children and Consumer Cultur*. Berkeley: University of California Press.
Qvortrup, J., Corsaro, W. and Sebastian-Honig, M. (eds). (2009). *The Palgrave Handbook of Childhood Studies*. London: Palgrave Macmillan.
Schneider, C. (1987). *Children's Television: The Art, the Business and How it Works*. Lincolnwood, IL: NTC Business Books.
Schor, J. (2004). *Born to Buy: The Commercialised Child and the New Consumer Culture*. New York: Scribner.
Seiter, E. (1993). *Sold Separately: Children and Parents in Consumer Culture*. New Brunswick, NJ: Rutgers University Press.
Sutherland, A. and Thompson, B. (2001). *Kidfluence: The Marketer's Guide to Understanding and Reaching Generation Y*. New York: McGraw-Hill.
Tobin, J. (ed.). (2004). *Pikachu's Global Adventure: The Rise and Fall of Pokémon*. Durham, NC: Duke University Press.
Wasko, J. (2001). *Understanding Disney*. Cambridge: Polity Press.

14
The Politics of Children's Clothing
Jane Pilcher

Age-related altercations about clothing are a longstanding phenomenon; the fashion choices of 'the young' have not always been to the taste or enjoyed the wholehearted approval of the 'not young'. Commonly recognisable flash points between young people and their parents, teachers or employers include the shape of shoes, the knot of a tie, the length of a hem, the cut of trousers or the depth of a neck line. Disagreements about clothes – and where, when and how they are worn, and by whom – can be understood as an expression of differences in values, identities and interests between younger and older age groups. Typically, age-related conflicts over clothing fashions have tended to be between teenagers and adults, and worked out in the context of familial rules, or the localised uniform policies or 'dress codes' of schools and workplaces. Public and media interest in the issue has been only sporadic, arising especially in relation to the more 'spectacular' fashions of youth cultures like Mods, Rockers or Punks (Hebdige 1979; Bennett 2001; Hall and Jefferson 2005; Cohen 2011).

In this chapter, I argue that developments in the politics of children's clothing since the 1990s represent a significant shift in the longstanding phenomenon of adult concern over what young people wear. I show that, rather than teenagers, the principal focus of age-related tension, disagreement and controversy over clothing since the 1990s has instead been the fashions of children, and particularly girls. Moreover, rather than the clothing of the young being largely a concern of parents or teachers, resolved through family rules or school uniform codes, what children (especially girls) wear on their bodies has also become a prominent issue of public debate and one to be resolved through government intervention, at least in part. In the chapter, I address this politics of children's clothing from different perspectives, including via public discourses and formal governance in several Western countries, and data on pre-teenage girls' experiences of negotiations with their mothers as to what gets bought, worn and where. My focus throughout is what these various iterations of the politics of children's clothing reveal about childhood in relation to generational interests and identities in contemporary consumer societies. In particular, I suggest that, in focusing on the 'troublesome' bodies (Smart 1995) of girls as emblematic of the 'crisis' of childhood, dominant discourses in the politics of children's clothing have failed to recognise a broader set of issues about childhood, fashion and consumer culture.

Public and policy discourses

Just as expressions of age-related tensions about the meanings of clothing fashions in terms of values, identities and interests have a long history, so too do associations made between clothing styles, gender and sexuality. In particular, women's clothing styles have long been read as a code for their receptivity to sexual interest from men (Craik 1994; Entwhistle 2000; Wade 2013); hence the archetypal response of a father to a daughter's choice of clothing – 'You are *not* going out dressed like that, young lady!' As I will now show, both age and gendered/sexualised elements of the symbolic value of clothing were invoked in the politics of children's clothing from the 1990s onwards.

Around the 1990s, and in the context of underlying anxieties about the 'crisis' of childhood in consumer societies, public discourses in a number of Western countries began to make links between clothing fashions and the 'sexualisation of children' and specifically, girls (Duschinsky 2013). For example, in the UK, articles appeared in the *Independent* newspaper in the early 1990s discussing threats to childhood innocence in the form of children's exposure and access to 'sexy' clothes and images. Consequently, in the UK press, 'sexualisation' was increasingly used to infer children's social and moral corruption, and specifically that of girls (Duschinsky and Barker 2013). For some commentators at least, aspects of such trends in children's fashion were encapsulated by the marketing term 'tweenager',[1] used to describe children about 8 to 12 years old and which depicts them as knowing, active consumers of fashion (e.g., BBC 2000, 2003). Tweenagers are seen in these accounts as problematical because, in being knowing, active consumers who use fashion as a symbolic means of constructing and presenting self-identity, these children are less like 'children' and more like teenagers and adults. 'Childhood', it is suggested, is eroded as a result.

In the United States, evidence of an increased public voicing of concerns about the 'crisis' of childhood through its sexualisation, and the role of girls' clothing in it, can be found in the publication of a rash of populist books with titles like *So Sexy So Soon* (Levin and Kilbourne 2008). These books typically appealed to worried parents and educators and proposed plans of action to counter the unwelcome social and cultural trends perceived to be corrupting childhood (see also, for example, Lamb and Brown 2006; Durham 2008; Reist 2009; Orenstein 2011). In the publisher's blurb for *So Sexy So Soon*, it is girls' clothing which is highlighted as a manifestation of the sexualisation of childhood via examples of 'thong panties, padded bras, and risqué Halloween costumes for young girls' and 'hot young female pop stars wearing provocative clothing' (Levin and Kilbourne 2008). Also in the United States, the American Psychological Association (APA) reported on the 'sexualisation of girls', citing examples of girls' clothing, and received widespread media coverage (for example, BBC 2007; Weiner 2007). The authors of the report concluded that the process of sexualisation, indicated by trends in girls' clothing, was widespread, and that its prevalence may have had a range of negative effects on girls' mental and physical health, including eating disorders, low self-esteem and depression (APA 2007).

Parliamentarians, governments, think tanks and campaigning groups in several Western countries have also contributed to the politics of children's clothing in relation to the sexualisation of childhood, within which girls' clothing is positioned to be so central. For example, in Norway, the Minister of Family Affairs urged retailers to withdraw 'sexualising' garments from their shops, such as small bras, string briefs and baby bikinis (Rysst 2010), whilst the Dutch government proposed a policy against the sexualisation of girls and young women in its Emancipation Strategy of 2008–11 (Duits and Van Zoonen 2011). In Australia in 2006, sexualised clothing for girls featured in reports published by the Australia Institute, a think tank (Rush and La Nauze 2006a, 2006b). These reports influenced a subsequent Australian parliamentary inquiry into the issue of the sexualisation of children in the contemporary media environment (Australian Senate 2007). In 2010, the Scottish parliament published a report into sexualised goods aimed at children which also considered the issue of sexualised clothing for girls (Buckingham et al. 2010). Elsewhere in Europe, a parliamentary report entitled *Against Hyper-Sexualisation* was published in France in 2012 (Jouanno 2012). Amongst other things, it called for a ban on child-sized but adult-styled clothing and the outlawing of child models in advertising (Willsher 2012).

In the UK, the politics of children's clothing in relation to sexualisation and consumer culture, and girls' role in it, have been equally prominent. By the mid to late 2000s, the state of childhood was on the agenda of the Labour government via the Children's Plan drawn up by the Children's Minister, Ed Balls (BBC 2010), and the commissioning of independent reports on the impact of the commercial world on children's well-being (Buckingham 2009) and on the links between sexualisation and violence against girls and women (Papadopolous 2010). In its contribution to the 2007 consultation process on the impact of the commercial world on children's well-being, the UK charity the National Society for the Prevention of Cruelty to Children (NSPCC) pointed to the ways in which sexualisation is evident through 'children's fashion mimicking adult women's clothing' (NSPCC 2008: 11). Other contributors to the debate about the commercialisation and sexualisation of childhood in the UK during this period included the National Union of Teachers. In 2007, the union was reported to be concerned that children's education and their 'enjoyment of childhood' were being undermined by the sexualisation of girls through 'inappropriate' clothing such as lingerie and T-shirts (Meikle 2007).

Meanwhile, as concerns about the 'crisis' of childhood through its sexualisation became firmly embedded in public discourses, a series of media reports and features in the UK criticised retailers who had been marketing 'inappropriate' styles of clothing for children or, more specifically, girls (for example, Williams 2010; Hamilton 2011). In 2010, the influential UK parenting website Mumsnet launched its own campaign against the sexualisation of children, notably called 'Let Girls Be Girls' (Mumsnet 2012). Amongst other activities, Mumsnet campaigners contacted retailers with specific examples of 'inappropriate products', and requested that they stop selling items which 'exploit, emphasise or play upon children's sexuality'. Mumsnet reported that many high street retailers subsequently signed up to this pledge (Mumsnet 2012).

Amongst UK parliamentarians it is David Cameron who has, as Leader of the Conservative Party and, later, Prime Minister, been at the forefront of public discourse in the UK about the 'crisis' of childhood through sexualisation, the part played in it by children's (girls') fashions, and the need to re-establish proper generational boundaries in order to counter these trends (Duschinsky and Barker 2013). In his speech to the 2009 Conservative Party conference, Cameron argued that, 'We've got to stop treating our children like adults and adults like children' (Cameron 2009). In a later newspaper article in 2010, he highlighted the ways that 'Children are being pushed into grown-up territory well before their time' and how 'girls are encouraged to dress like women, [and] wear lingerie' (Cameron 2010). As argued by Duschinsky and Barker (2013), the sexualisation of childhood was subsequently presented as core to the programme of the UK's Conservative–Liberal Democrat Coalition government from 2010, as part of their centring of families as the keystone of a strong and stable society. The commissioning of the Bailey Report (Department for Education [DFE] 2011) is further evidence of the centrality of these concerns for Cameron and for the Coalition government. The report was led by Reg Bailey (the Chief Executive of the Christian organisation, the Mothers' Union), and received high-profile encouragement by the Prime Minister, David Cameron (Number 10 2012).

The Bailey Report is revealing as to the meanings, values, interests and identities articulated and contested in the politics of children's clothing more broadly. For example, throughout the report, children's (specifically, girls') clothing is invoked as emblematic of the commercialisation and sexualisation of childhood: 'bras (padded or not), bikinis, short skirts, high-heeled shoes, garments with suggestive slogans, or the use of fabrics and designs that have connotations of adult sexuality' (DFE 2011: 42). Both the title of the report ('Letting Children Be Children') and its content emphasise the responsibility of parents 'to be parents', and the need for consumer culture to be 'family-friendly' so that children are not forced to 'grow up too quickly'. The emphasis is on the protection of children from the 'seamier' side of society (DFE 2011: 2), especially sexuality. The implication here is that it is in children's interests to defer sexuality (including that signified by 'inappropriate' clothing styles), to its proper place in their adult futures, not least because premature exposure may make children vulnerable to sexual exploitation and abuse by adults in the here and now. The articulations of children, childhood, generational relations and sexuality made within the Bailey Report echo socially conservative fears and concerns from the 1980s. At this time, the political new right in the UK presented school sex education and also the provision of contraception for under-16s as emblematic of the moral deterioration of British society, and of the breakdown of traditional generational relationships and statuses (Abbott and Wallace 1992; Pilcher 1996, 1997, 2005; Duschinsky and Barker 2013).

Throughout, the authorial voice of the Bailey Report presents itself as an engagement with expressed parental concerns about the commercialised and sexualised culture children encounter: one of its key themes is 'making parents' voices heard' (DFE 2011: 18). The voices of children themselves, in contrast, are almost wholly absent from the Bailey Report. Moreover, there is a tendency within the report to refer to 'children' as if they are ungendered, even when discussing bras and bikinis and other items of specifically girls' fashion. Despite a brief acknowledgement of perspectives which position children as differentiated subjective agents (DFE 2011: 10), it is clear that the authorial voice of the Bailey Report prefers to infer children's interests and/or substitute them with the interests of parents and also to attribute to children a collective, unitary identity.

In these ways, the Bailey Report identifies traditional familial generational relations of authority as the key to protecting children's immaturity, innocence and vulnerability, qualities which are themselves assumed to be inherently desirable in childhood. In short, the Bailey Report's articulations of children, childhood and generational relations can be recognised as being comfortably in keeping with conventional, normative ideas about the interests, identities and generational status of children, especially in relation to sexuality, apparent in much of public discourses and formal governance on childhood, both within the UK and beyond.

On the basis of its findings, one of the Bailey Report's recommendations was that retailers should develop and comply with a voluntary code of good practice for all aspects of children-related retailing (DFE 2011: 16). Subsequently, in September 2011, the British Retail Consortium published its guidelines for 'responsible retailing' in clothing for the under-12s in order to preserve 'the innocence of our children' (British Retail Consortium 2011). Another recommendation of the Bailey Report, accepted by Prime Minister David Cameron, was that a website should be developed to facilitate complaints and concerns from the public about sexualisation. As Duschinsky and Barker (2013) suggest, these kinds of outcomes indicate that public and policy discourses on sexualisation in childhood, and with it the part played by children's clothing fashions, looks set to continue (see for example, Arnold 2013; Coughlan 2013).

Let's hear it from the girls: clothing, meanings and negotiations

Public discourses and formal governance relating to the commercialisation and sexualisation of childhood have, then, positioned children's (girls') clothing as central, both within the UK and elsewhere. The 'Letting Children Be Children' report by Reg Bailey (DFE 2011) is, I have argued, representative in many ways of high-profile discourses in this politics of children's clothing. These discourses, in 'retreating into an invocation of childhood innocence', tend only to connect loosely with the social and cultural world of children and, specifically, girls (Kehily 2012: 13). Typically, public and policy discourses within the politics of children's clothing articulate the views and concerns of adults, and especially, parents. For example, and as noted above, the Bailey Report has 'making parents' voices heard' as one of its key themes (DFE 2011). Whilst the extent to which public and policy discourses accurately represent the views of parents on the sexualisation of children's clothing is subject to debate (for example, see Bragg et al. 2011; Bragg and Buckingham 2012; Barker and Duschinsky 2013), it's true to say that parents' voices predominate. In contrast, almost completely absent from public and policy discourses are the voices of children themselves, including those of girls, whose clothing consumption has so often been presented as emblematic of the broader 'crisis of childhood' and of intergenerational relations of authority in contemporary societies. To further analyse the politics of children's clothing, I turn next to evidence on girls' experiences of and perspectives on the 'what, why and where' of their own clothing consumption. I draw on fieldwork from a year-long ethnographic study of children's clothing consumption,[2] and focus particularly on the complexities of the meanings, values, interests and identities articulated by girls aged 5 to 12 in relation to their own clothing, and on negotiations between mothers and daughters as to what girls wear, and where.

Parents are ever present within the politics of children's clothing, alternately constituted as the source of and the solution to the problem of what children (girls) come to wear (Bragg et al. 2011; Bragg and Buckingham 2012). In our study, we found evidence of parenting practices in relation to the management of tensions between clothing fashions and children's interests. These are crystallised within instances of intergenerational altercations and negotiations involving mothers and daughters as to what gets bought, worn and where. For example, Katy (aged 7) said that her mother did not really like her to have clothes with glitter or sparkle on them and that they often argued about the purchase and wearing of tops without any sleeves. Katy's mother pointed to the 'tarty' and 'revealing' styling of the clothing: 'The only time I give in a little bit is the school disco'. Similarly, in the following data extract, Hayley (aged 8) and her mother Janet are discussing a particular top which has caused a disagreement between them because it was too 'revealing':

Hayley: I don't even wear it.
Janet: No, well that was 'cos I didn't really agree with that one.

Hayley went on to explain that she wore the top for 'dressing up ... just at home' because due to her mother's disapproval, 'I'm not allowed to go out, am I?'. For both Hayley and Katy, their consumption of 'revealing' clothing was constrained by their mothers' ideas of what was acceptable for them to wear, and where, in the context of the cultural regulation of childhood and of feminine sexuality. These mothers were concerned about the moral danger that arises from the ways in which clothes revealed the bare skin of the girls' bodies. Clearly, though, the revealing tops at issue *were* purchased and used, even though they were coded by the mothers as 'restricted' – that is, to be worn only in certain contexts. In Hayley's case, this meant only for 'dressing up' inside the house. For Katy's mother, Amanda, the school was an acceptable and known (safe) interior space/place and the disco an acceptable occasion for such restricted clothing to be worn, not least because 'other girls' there would also be wearing them. In alluding to the 'other girls', Amanda was also conceding the significance of feminine culture within the peer group for her daughter, of securing acceptance and a sense of belonging from wearing the 'right' clothes, a point that was also referred to by Katy in relation to her desire for high-heeled shoes. For Hayley, too, fitting in with feminine peers was important in her liking for a crop-top: 'I just kind of like it because everyone else has got one, so I kind of get one to fit in.'

Girls in our study both desired and actually wore the types of contested and controversial clothing, shoes and accessories which have featured in the politics of children's clothing and are generally associated, at least in Britain, with 'emphasised', or 'excessively' sexualised adult femininity (Connell 1995; Cook and Kaiser 2004; McRobbie 2007). These included high-heeled shoes and fashion garments such as crop-tops, halter-neck tops and miniskirts. What our data show about these contested and controversial items, though, is that the girls understood and gave meaning to these items in ways that are different from adults' predominant construction of them as 'sexualising'. For example, in her photo project, Megan (aged 8) had a photo taken of herself wearing camouflage-style trousers and a cropped, gypsy-style top which displayed her belly. She described them as her 'dressing-up clothes, my night out, going out night clothes, very, very trendy'. Clearly, for Megan, the fashionable 'trendiness' of the clothes was important, in keeping with a 'tweenager'-style valuing of fashion amongst girls under 12 years old (Cook and Kaiser 2004). Similarly, in her project work, Katy (aged 7) chose a picture of a 'one-shoulder' top as an item of clothes she would like because 'I like the style and I like the pattern'. Hayley (aged 8) also had a gypsy-style top, which she explained was 'like elasticated and you can pull it over [off] your shoulder'. For Hayley, though, this style of clothing was not suitable for wearing out to her church: the implication here is that this is because of the 'bare shoulder' effect of the top. In fact, none of the girls in our study spoke directly about the effect of revealing skin as an explicit reason for their liking, wanting or wearing such items of clothing. Emma (aged 5) said she had an off-the-shoulder dress in pink, 'sort of see-through' material with 'a lot of sparkle'. For Emma, the attraction of the dress was more to do with the fabric and the embellishments than the bare skin the styling of the dress revealed. Susie (aged 10, and Katy's older sister) discussed her liking of halter-neck tops, which she had 'a lot of', and also a mini-skirt, liked because of its elastic waist feature. Again, the baring of skin through these favoured styles was not the appealing feature; instead, it was the hyper-feminine styling and/or the embellishments of the garments (see also Russell and Tyler 2002). Amongst the girls in our study, then, there is evidence of a desire for and active wearing of clothes that revealed bare flesh, including shoulders and upper chest areas, midriffs or bellies and the leg above the knee. Yet it is the styling of the clothes that was emphasised by the girls, not the revealing of the body they enabled. Nor, in the girls' accounts of their preferences, was it suggested that the deliberate 'smallness' of the clothing style was used in order to 'age up' their bodies (Hockey and James 1993; Wright 1993).

In contrast, when the girls spoke about their clothing dislikes, it was the very effect of revealing skin that they mostly objected to. The study sample included two girls (sisters) of Pakistani heritage and whose religious affiliation was Muslim. In accordance with their Muslim culture, Saima (aged 12) and Yasmeen (aged 7) expressed strongly disapproving views on 'revealing clothing', with mini-skirts, shorts, cropped jackets, bikinis and strappy vest tops being singled out for critique. Although neither Katy (aged 7) nor Megan (aged 8) expressed disapproval or rejection of revealing clothing styles, other girls in our study also reported their dislike and in some cases strong disapproval of 'showing' one's body via clothing. For Hayley (aged 8), it was revealing clothes (such as crop-tops) that 'show too much bare skin' that were especially problematical; her preference was for styles that she described as 'more covered'. The brevity of clothing was also a continuing theme in Hayley's project work. In a discussion of a crop-top style T-shirt, she came the nearest of all the girls to explicitly identifying the sexual meanings of such clothing styles. For Hayley, the T-shirt in question was 'Yuk ... awful', due to a combination of its bright colour and it being 'too short': 'It's just a bit tarty and a bit showy'. It is clear from the project work and interview data presented here that the girls' reasons for disliking 'revealing' clothing in relation to their own bodies centred on the unwanted effect of showing their skin or underwear. Although not clearly articulated by the girls, with the possible exception of Hayley, I suggest that their objections stemmed from a nascent concern with sexual modesty, documented in other contexts by Lees (1986).

In the girls' discussions of clothing fashions worn by others, especially celebrities they had encountered through magazines or television, issues of sexual modesty were addressed more clearly. Susie (aged 10) drew a picture of the singer Beyoncé wearing high heels, short skirt and a string or halter-neck top. For Susie, Beyoncé is someone who 'sometimes the things she wears are a bit too skimpy../. Short and a bit too ... erm ... (*Interviewer: You wouldn't go out in it?*). Yeah (laughs)'. Elsewhere in her project, Susie included a picture of an off-the-shoulder crop-top as an item she disliked because 'I can't really wear it out anywhere because it's a bit ... (*Interviewer: Like something Beyoncé would wear?*) Yes'. Like Beyoncé, singer Kylie Minogue was another celebrity anti-role model for the girls in our study due to the styling of her clothing and the sexually immodest bodily display it entailed. For Hattie (aged 12), Kylie 'wears too many short dresses and shows off too much of her legs'. Similarly, Saima (aged 12) cut out a picture of actress and singer Jennifer Lopez wearing short, tight shorts and wrote her own caption: 'Now, there's no need for that'.

Our data suggest that the meanings the girls in the study gave to 'revealing' clothing were marked by ambivalence, an ambivalence rarely acknowledged in the politics of children's clothing. In relation to their own bodies, the girls stressed the styling and embellishments, the trendiness and fashion of clothing which helped cement relationships with their peers. These meanings won out, over and above the effect of revealing their skin. When this effect was discussed, it was, in most cases, unwanted and the cause of anxiety about being subjected to the sexual gaze of unspecified others and in violation of a girl's sense of modesty in relation to her own body. In relation to the bodies of celebrities encountered through media culture, an understanding of the sexually symbolic value of current fashions in terms of modesty and morality emerged strongly, over and above the styling, embellishment and 'trendiness' of the clothing itself. The small, short clothes (Wright 1993) may have been functional in that they were sufficient to cover the crucial areas of the celebrity women's bodies and prevent nakedness. Nonetheless, such clothes were coded by the girls as symbolically immodest, as 'not nice'. This points to the girls' knowledge and understanding of the symbolic value of clothing in relation to femininity, even if they did not clearly articulate its gendered, sexualised component – especially in relation to themselves (see also Russell and Tyler 2002; Cook and Kaiser 2004).

My earlier review of the politics of children's clothing clearly showed that it is girls and their 'troublesome' bodies (Smart 1995; Pilcher 2007, 2012) who have been subjected to close surveillance and negative evaluation. At the same time, the lived experience of girlhood, including in relation to sexuality, has been overlooked (Jackson and Scott 2010; Kehily 2012). Although the girls in our study had not acquired the competencies and discourses necessary fully to articulate bodies and clothing as sexual (Jackson and Scott 2010), they did evaluate clothing styles in terms of a nascent sense of sexual modesty. Moreover, through negotiations with their mothers as to what got bought, worn and where, the girls were also acquiring competency in sexual self-surveillance and self-deployment of the gaze of the generalised, patriarchal other. From the perspective of the social conservatives who have campaigned so vociferously on the issue of children's (girls') clothing, this competency in girls under 12 is likely to be interpreted as evidence to support claims made about the sexualisation of childhood and the destruction of childhood 'innocence'. From other, more liberal perspectives, evidence of ambivalence in girls' feelings about 'controversial' clothing styles and of their evaluative competencies in this respect could be interpreted more positively as a sign of agency and subjectivity, of engagement with the lived reality and enduring presence (Kehily 2012) of sexual cultures which children, and perhaps especially girls, have never really been separated from.

Contexts and consequences

I began this chapter with a suggestion that, whilst disagreements over fashion are a long-established feature of age relations, the recent wave of controversy about pre-teenage children's clothing styles is unprecedented: the clothing consumption practices of an age group have never before generated such widespread public discourses, formal inquiries and policy interventions. This is because the politics of children's clothing is at root about the values, interests and identities bound up with, on the one hand, constructions of childhood and, on the other, sexuality – and public and policy concerns about childhood and sexuality are both deeply embedded and highly ambivalent features of social relations.

Childhood, and the children who serially and temporarily occupy this generational space in the age structure, have long carried a burden of responsibility both for the current condition of society and for its future, progressive reproduction (Pilcher 2012). For example, during the early years of the twentieth century, working-class children (especially girls) emerged as a pre-eminent group of individuals through whose unfinished, and therefore malleable, bodies the future health and progress of 'the Nation' would be secured; hence, the expansion of 'mothercraft', and health and physical education in the UK school curriculum (Cooter 1992; Hendrick 1997; Pilcher 2007). To this generic burden of responsibility placed on childhood for social and cultural reproduction, the recent politics of children's clothing adds the profoundly problematical element of sexuality. Sexuality has disrupted ideas about the proper character and status of children from at least Rousseau onwards because of the dual construction of children as 'innocent' and yet simultaneously susceptible to sexual knowingness (Jackson and Scott 2010; Egan and Hawkes 2012). In the UK in the 1980s, the anxieties of social conservatives about childhood and sexuality, and much else, found expression through the issues of sex education in schools and the provision of contraception to girls under the age of 16 (Pilcher 1996, 2005). Since then, childhood and children have been burdened with responsibility for concerns arising from the commercialisation and sexualisation of the cultural landscape, alongside the more established anxieties about changing family formations and intergenerational relationships. The politics of children's clothing is, in this sense, merely the latest iteration of centuries-old moralising about and interventions in childhood, in which childhood is a 'code' for other social issues (Jenkins 2004), drawn upon as a moral resource (Wyness 2006), by moral entrepreneurs (Cohen 2011), to try and shape, amongst other things, parenting practices, and sexuality.

Contemporary discourses about what current cohorts of children wear have, then, foregrounded sexuality and its display through clothing fashions, and (once again) have overly focused attention on the 'problematical' bodies of girls. Meanwhile, others parties involved in the politics of children's clothing, especially the designers, manufacturers and retailers of 'inappropriate' children's clothing, have largely escaped this kind of close and sustained surveillance. For sure, there have been media 'naming and shaming' exposés, pleas by campaign groups like Mumsnet in the UK and by politicians in countries like Norway and France to stop selling sexualising clothing for children, and recommendations for voluntary codes of good retailing practice, such as arose from the Bailey Report (DFE 2011). These may have had some impact, at least in the short term, on the designers, manufacturers and retailers of children's clothing.[3] However, and as Buckingham suggests in his contribution to this book, these kinds of interventions to stem the marketing of thongs and innuendo-laden T-shirts for pre-teen girls leave untouched the much broader, pernicious processes of neoliberal marketisation and privatisation affecting children's lives, where profit is king.

A further consequence of the close-up focus on girls and what they wear on their bodies is that the latent social classism of the politics of children's clothing has been overlooked. Arguably, the subjects of concerns about trends in children's clothing are especially girls in working-class families (most likely, perhaps, to shop at Primark, a budget UK retailer widely vilified in the media as a purveyor of sexualised clothing for girls). 'Low culture', implicit in the contemporary notion of 'chav' fashion (Bragg et al. 2011; Bragg and Buckingham 2012; Jones 2012), has long been regarded as lacking in parenting skills and in sexual morality (Mort 2000), and therefore as a potential contaminant of idealised, middle-class childhood innocence. In the predominant discourses within the recent politics of children's clothing, then, 'sexualised [working class] girls reject innocence in favour of sexuality and in so doing fissure bourgeois conceptions of the child' (Egan and Hawkes 2012: 278).

In these various ways, the key discourses within the politics of children's clothing have served to replicate and reinvigorate both a narrow, conservative sexual morality and a hegemonic neoliberal market philosophy. The close-up focus on girls and their clothing as emblematic of the 'crisis' of childhood and of intergenerational relations more broadly has also led to the eclipsing of other perspectives in the politics of children's clothing. For example, a more broadly conceived politics of children's clothing might include the manufacture and distribution of children's clothing through sweatshops and the use of child labour (McDougall 2007; *Daily Mail*, 23 June 2008), along with the close relationship between media products such as television programmes, films and books and the marketing and merchandising of children's clothing, typified through 'Disneyfication' (Wasko 2001). Here, children's bodies effectively become mobile advertisements through their clothing, a phenomenon which is also evident in the high-end designer children's wear market (Philby 2013).

Above all else, the overly attentive focus on girls and what they wear on their bodies has meant that the significant problem of gender inequality and the wider dominant sexist culture of feminine commodified sexuality has been left virtually uncontested.[4] Following on from my earlier points about media product merchandising, the 'Disneyfication' of children's fashion might, in a more broadly conceived politics of children's clothing, also raise questions about gender stereotyping and the socialisation of girls into hetero-normative scripts, especially through the ubiquitous (pink) Princess narratives (Giroux 1995; Orenstein 2011). Although voiced alongside worries about sexualisation, parental concerns about gender stereotyping of clothing (and other products) were noted almost in passing in the Bailey Report (see also Barker and Duschinsky 2012), and did not feature in any of its policy recommendations (DFE 2011). In keeping with the sidelining of the issue within the Bailey Report, the links between gender stereotyping and the problematising of the sexuality of girls have not been central in the dominant discourses about children's clothing trends. Instead, the issue has been left to the preserve of more peripheral participants, such as the feminist campaign group Pink Stinks (www.pinkstinks.co.uk).

As Penny (2010a) has suggested, socially conservative contributors to debates about trends in children's fashion have tended to regard the dominant culture of feminine commodified sexuality as perfectly acceptable per se; their concern is children's (girls') *premature* engagement with it. Within the politics of children's clothing, the values and interests underpinning mainstream concerns about girls' fashions have meant a narrow focus on re-establishing traditional generational relations of authority as a means of protecting childhood innocence. Meanwhile, as shown in this chapter, pre-teenage girls like Hayley, Susie and Hattie are not growing through childhood in a context of a more socially progressive, healthy and educative sexuality, but are instead (already) developing competencies in individualised sexual self-surveillance under the restricting terms of a gendered and sexist dominant sexual culture. To paraphrase Penny (2010b), the problem is not that girls are 'growing up too fast', as the moral conservatives' rhetoric within the politics of children's clothing claims. Instead, it's that the lived reality of sexual cultures for girls means that they are growing up to understand that they should be ashamed if they express preferences for some clothing styles over others, and that they should regard their own sexual bodies as problematical. However, for the present at least, the gender values and interests underpinning sexualised fashions in relation to 'emphasised' (Connell 1995) or 'excessive' (McRobbie 2007) femininity and their role in perpetuating and accentuating gender inequality remain largely outside the terms of debate within the politics of children's clothing.

Notes

1. In fact, the terms 'tween' and 'tweenager' have a relatively long and somewhat variable history in the consumer market (Mitchell and Reid-Walsh 2005, for example).
2. Data presented in this chapter draw on ethnographic fieldwork (Hammersley and Atkinson 1995) undertaken in England in 2003–4 with eight families. Each family contained at least one child between the ages of 6 and 11, whose consumption of children's clothing was tracked over a calendar year. The families were selected to be illustrative of key social variables, including income level, gender and ethnicity, urban and rural location. Data collection methods sought to place children at the centre of the research (Pole, Mizen and Bolton 1999) via deploying a range of participatory methods, including drawings, writing and photography. Along with focus groups of parents, and semi-structured interviews with and diary-work by parents, the methods collectively aimed to provide insight into the role of children as consumers of clothing within the context of different kinds of families across a full year. In order to provide an insight into the interconnected nature of children's consumption of clothing with its production, interviews were held with personnel in the children's wear industry, including store buyers and other executive decision makers. The research was funded by the ESRC/AHRB under the 'Cultures of Consumption' research programme and was conducted by myself and my colleagues: Sharon Boden, Tim Edwards and Christopher Pole.
3. Our own study of the children's wear industry certainly revealed a concern for company image and reputation of the brand. See Pilcher (2013).
4. Recent campaigns by peripheral groups against mainstream constructions of sexualisation include the SPARK (Sexualization Protest: Action, Resistance, Knowledge)

movement in the United States (www.sparksummit.com); the Object organisation in the UK (www.object.org.uk); and, arguably, the global Slut Walk movement (Valenti 2011; Ringrose and Renold 2012).

References

Abbott, P. and Wallace, C. (1992). *The Family and the New Right*. London: Pluto Press.
APA (American Psychological Association). (2007). *Report of the APA Task Force on the Sexualization of Girls*. Washington, DC: American Psychological Association. http://www.apa.org/pi/women/programs/girls/report.aspx.
Arnold, B. (2013). 'Paltrow criticised over girls bikinis on her website'. *Yahoo UK Movie News*. http://uk.movies.yahoo.com/paltrow-criticised-over-girls-bikinis-on-her-website-071949951.html.
Australian Senate. (2007). *Inquiry into the Sexualisation of Children in the Contemporary Media Environment*. Parliament of Australia. http://www.aph.gov.au/Senate/committee/eca_ctte/sexualisation_of_children/tor.htm.
BBC (British Broadcasting Company). (2000). 'Tweenagers rule the High Street'. BBC News. http://news.bbc.co.uk/1/hi/business/882606.stm.
BBC. (2003). 'How tweenagers are taking over'. BBC News. http://newsvote.bbc.co.uk/mpapps/pagetools/print/news.bbc.co.uk/1/hi/uk/2863819.stm.
BBC. (2007). 'Sexualisation "harms" young girls'. BBC News, 20 February. http://news.bbc.co.uk/1/hi/health/6376421.stm.
BBC. (2010). 'Stop sexualising children, says David Cameron'. BBC News, 18 February. http://news.bbc.co.uk/1/hi/8521403.stm.
Bennett, A. (2001). *Cultures of Popular Music*. Milton Keynes: Open University Press.
Bragg, S. and Buckingham, D. (2012). 'Global Concerns, Local Negotiations and Moral Selves: Contemporary Parenting and the "Sexualization of Childhood" Debate'. *Feminist Media Studies* 13(4): 643–59.
Bragg, S., Buckingham, D., Russell, R. and Willett, R. (2011). 'Too Much, Too Soon? Children, "Sexualization" and Consumer Culture'. *Sex Education: Sexuality, Society and Learning* 11(3): 279–92.
British Retail Consortium. (2011). *Responsible Retailing: BRC Childrenswear Guidelines*. London: BRC.
Buckingham, D. (2009). *The Impact of the Commercial World on Children's Wellbeing*. Report of an Independent Assessment for the Department of Children, Schools and Families and the Department of Culture, Media and Sport. Annesley: Department for Children, Schools and Families.
Buckingham, D., Bragg, S., Russell, R. and Willett, R. (2010). *Sexualised Goods Aimed at Children*. Report for the Scottish Parliament Equal Opportunities Committee. The Scottish Parliament.
Cameron, D. (2009). 'Putting Britain Back on Her Feet'. Speech to the Conservative Party Conference, 8 October. http://www.conservatives.com/News/Speeches/2009/10/David_Cameron_Putting_Britain_back_on_her_feet.aspx.
Cameron, D. (2010). 'Too much too young'. *Daily Mail*, 19 February. http://www.dailymail.co.uk/debate/article-1252156/DAVID-CAMERON-Sexualisation-children-too-young.html#ixzz2CNyUvb4a.
Cohen, S. (2011). *Folk Devils and Moral Panics*. London: Routledge. First published 1972.
Connell R. (1995). *Masculinities*. Cambridge: Polity Press.
Cook, D. and Kaiser, S. (2004). 'Betwixt and Be Tween. Age Ambiguity and the Sexualisation of the Female Consuming Subject'. *Journal of Consumer Culture* 4: 203–27.

Cooter, R. (ed.). (1992). *In the Name of the Child. Health and Welfare 1880–1940*. London: Routledge.
Coughlan, S. (2013). 'Modern childhood "ends at age 12"'. BBC News, 6 March. http://www.bbc.co.uk/news/education-21670962.
Craik, J. (1994). *The Face of Fashion*. London: Routledge.
Daily Mail. (2008). 'Exposed. Primark's sweatshops that pay children just 20p a day'. *Mail Online*, 23 June.
DFE (Department for Education). (2011). *Letting Children Be Children*. Bailey Review of the Commercialisation and Sexualisation of Childhood. London: Department for Education.
Duits, L. and Van Zoonen, L. (2011). 'Coming to Terms with Sexualisation'. *European Journal of Cultural Studies* 14(5): 491–506.
Durham, M. G. (2008). *The Lolita Effect: The Media Sexualization of Young Girls and What You Can Do about It*. New York: Overlook.
Duschinsky, R. (2013). 'The Emergence of Discourses on Sexualization: 1981–2010'. *Social Politics* 20(1): 137–56.
Duschinsky, R. and Barker, M. (2013). 'Doing the Mobius Strip'. *Sexualities* 16(5–6): 730–42.
Egan, R. D. and Hawkes, G. (2012). 'Sexuality, Youth and the Perils of Endangered Innocence: How History Can Help Us Get Past the Panic'. *Gender and Education* 24(3): 269–84.
Entwhistle, J. (2000). *The Fashioned Body*. Cambridge: Polity Press.
Giroux, H. (1995). 'Animating Youth: the Disnification of Children's Culture'. *Socialist Review* 24(3): 23–55.
Hall, S. and Jefferson, T. (eds). (2005). *Resistance Through Rituals* (2nd edn). London: Routledge.
Hamilton, J. (2011). 'Paedo bikini banned'. *The Sun*, 12 January. http://www.thesun.co.uk/sol/homepage/news/2931327/Primarks-padded-bikini-tops-for-kids-condemned.html.
Hammersley, M. and Atkinson, P. (1995). *Ethnography: Principles in Practice*. London: Routledge.
Hebdige, D. (1979). *Subculture: The Meaning of Style*. London: Routledge.
Hendrick, H. (1997). 'Constructions and Reconstructions of British Childhood'. In A. James and A. Prout (eds), *Constructing and Reconstructing Childhood* (2nd edn). London: Falmer Press.
Hockey, J. and James, A. (1993). *Growing Up and Growing Old*. London: Sage.
Jackson, S. and Scott, S. (2010). *Theorizing Sexuality*. Milton Keynes: Open University Press.
Jenkins, P. (2004). *Moral Panic: Changing Concepts of the Child Molester in Modern America*. New Haven, CT: Yale University Press.
Jones, O. (2011). *Chavs: The Demonization of the Working Class*. London: Verso.
Jouanno, C. (2012). *Contre l'hypersexualisation, Un nouveau combat pour l'ègalite*. Rapport parlementaire. Sènatrice de Paris, 5 March. http://www.social-sante.gouv.fr/IMG/pdf/rapport_hypersexualisation2012.pdf.
Kehily, M. J. (2012). 'Contextualising the Sexualisation of Girls Debate: Innocence, Experience and Young Female Sexuality'. *Gender and Education* 24(3): 255–68.
Lamb, S. and Brown, L. M. (2006). *Packaging Girlhood: Rescuing Our Daughters from Marketers' Schemes*. New York: St. Martins Griffin.
Lees S. (1986). *Losing Out. Sexuality and Adolescent Girls*. London: Hutchinson.
Levin, D. and Kilbourne, J. (2008). *So Sexy So Soon: The New Sexualized Childhood and What Parents Can Do to Protect Their Kids*. New York: Ballantine.

McDougall, D. (2007). 'Child sweatshop shame threatens Gap's ethical image'. *The Observer*, 28 October.
McRobbie, A. (2007). 'Top Girls?'. *Cultural Studies* 21(4–5): 718–37.
Meikle, J. (2007). 'Teachers union attacks stores for "sexualisation" of children'. *The Guardian*, 7 April. www.guardian.co.uk/business/2007/apr/07/retail.advertising.
Mitchell, C. and Reid-Walsh, J. (2005). *Seven Going on Seventeen*. London: Peter Lang.
Mort, F. (2000). *Dangerous Sexualities: Medico-Moral Politics in England since 1830*. London: Routledge.
Mumsnet. (2012). 'Let Girls Be Girls campaign'. www.mumsnet.com/campaigns/let-girls-be-girls.
NSPCC. (2008). *The NSCPP's Response to the Impact of the Commercial World on Children's Wellbeing*. London: NSPCC. http://www.nspcc.org.uk/inform/policyandpublicaffairs/consultations/2008/impactofthecommercialworld_wdf58611.pdf.
Number 10. (2012). 'PM: let children behave like children'. http://www.number10.gov.uk/news/child-internet-safety/.
Orenstein, P. (2011). *Cinderella Ate My Daughter*. New York: HarperCollins.
Papadopoulos, L. (2010). *Sexualisation of Young People Review*. London: Home Office.
Penny, L. (2010a). 'Let girls wear Primark's padded bikinis'. *The Guardian*, 18 April.
Penny, L. (2010b). 'Stop this slut-shaming'. *The Guardian*, 9 August.
Philby, C. (2013). 'Kid couture'. *The Independent*, 22 March.
Pilcher, J. (1996). 'Gillick and After: Children and Sex in the 1980s and 1990s'. In J. Pilcher and S. Wagg (eds), *Thatcher's Children? Childhood, Politics and Society in the 1980s and 1990s*. London: Falmer Press.
Pilcher, J. (1997). 'Contrary to Gillick: British Children's Sexual Rights Since 1985'. *International Journal of Children's Rights* 5(3).
Pilcher, J. (2005). 'School Sex Education: Policy and Practice in England 1870–2000'. *Sex Education* 5(2): 153–70.
Pilcher, J. (2007). 'Body Work: Childhood, Gender and School Health Education in England, 1870 to 1977'. *Childhood* 14(2): 215–33.
Pilcher, J. (2012). 'Girl Power ... and Responsibility'. Leicester Exchanges. http://leicesterexchanges.com/2012/10/11/girl-power/.
Pilcher, J. (2013). '"Small But Very Determined": A Novel Theorization of Children's Consumption of Clothing'. *Cultural Sociology* 7(1): 86–100.
Pole, C., Mizen, P. and Bolton, A. (1999). 'Realising Children's Agency in Research'. *International Journal of Social Research Methodology, Theory and Practice* 2(1): 33–54.
Reist, M. T. (2009). *Getting Real: Challenging the Sexualization of Girls*. Canberra: Spinifex Press.
Ringrose, J. and Renold, E. (2012). 'Slut-Shaming, Girl Power and "Sexualisation": Thinking through the Politics of the International SlutWalks with Teen Girls'. *Gender and Education* 24(3): 333–43.
Rush, E. and La Nauze, A. (2006a). *Corporate Paedophilia: Sexualisation of Children in the Media*. Australia Institute, Discussion Paper 90, October.
Rush, E. and La Nauze, A. (2006b). *Letting Children Be Children: Stopping the Sexualisation of Children in Australia*. Discussion Paper 93, December.
Russell, R. and Tyler, M. (2002). 'Thank Heaven for Little Girls: "Girl Heaven", and the Commercial Context of Feminine Childhood'. *Sociology* 36: 619–37.
Rysst, M. (2010). '"I am only 10 years old": Femininities, Clothing-Fashion Codes and the Intergenerational Gap of Interpretation of Young Girls' Clothes'. *Childhood* 17(1): 76–93.
Smart, C. (1995). *Law, Crime and Sexuality*. London: Sage.

Valenti, J. (2011). 'Slut walks and the future of feminism'. *The Washington Post*, 3 June. http://www.washingtonpost.com/opinions/slutwalks-and-the-future-of-feminism/2011/06/01/AGjB9LIH_story.html.

Wade, L. (2013). 'The Balancing Act of Being Female; Or, Why We Have So Many Clothes'. *Sociological Images*. http://thesocietypages.org/socimages/2013/01/22/the-balancing-act-of-being-female-or-why-we-have-so-many-clothes.

Wasko, J. (2001). *Understanding Disney*. Cambridge: Polity Press.

Weiner, S. (2007). 'Goodbye to Girlhood'. *The Washington Post*, 20 February. www.washingtonpost.com.

Williams, R. (2010). 'Padded bikinis unleash a storm over sexualised clothing for kids'. *The Guardian*, 17 April. www.guardian.co.uk/society/2010/apr/16/children-clothing-survey-bikini-heels.

Willsher, K. (2012). 'French report calls for end to sexualisation of children'. *The Guardian*, 6 March.

Wright L. (1993). 'Outgrown Clothes for Grown-up People'. In J. Ash and E. Wilson (eds), *Chic Thrills. A Fashion Reader*. Berkeley: University of California Press.

Wyness, M. (2006). *Childhood and Society*. Basingstoke: Palgrave Macmillan.

15
Children's Rights or Employers' Rights?
The 'Destigmatisation' of Child Labour

Steve Cunningham and Michael Lavalette

The extent and nature of child labour

Estimating the extent of child labour has never been an easy task. For obvious reasons, governments in countries characterised by high levels of child labour are notoriously reluctant to seek reliable data, or to publish it where it does exist. Doing so would be to advertise their failure to abide by international child labour conventions, which many have ratified but, for whatever reasons, have failed to enforce. Also, by its nature, much child labour, particularly its more hazardous and exploitative variants – such as child prostitution, child armed combatants, trafficked children – is illegal, 'hidden' and difficult to quantify.

Nonetheless, since the mid-1990s, a wider recognition of the extent and problematic nature of child labour has led to calls from the International Labour Organisation (ILO) and the United Nations (UN) for concerted international action to address the problem. Consequently, various formal targets and initiatives designed to eradicate child labour, or significantly reduce its incidence, have been adopted. These include the Millennium Development Goals, ILO Convention 182 (1999), and the ILO's 2006 Global Action Plan to eliminate the worst forms of child labour by 2016. However, as the ILO and the UN have recently acknowledged, the targets set by these initiatives have not been achieved, and it is now estimated that 306 million children aged 5–17 are working. Some of these are engaged in what the ILO conventions categorise as 'light, permissible forms' of work, but 215 million are what the ILO classifies as 'child labourers'. These are children who are 'under the minimum age legally specified for that kind of work, or work which, because of its detrimental nature or conditions, is considered unacceptable for children and is prohibited' (ILO 2012: 12). Of these, 115 million are occupied in 'hazardous' forms of labour, and some 76.5 million of this group are aged between 5 and 14 (ILO 2011). Nor has there been much progress on tackling even the 'worst' forms of child labour, despite a formal international consensus over the need to eliminate them. These include 'occupations' such as slavery, bondage, drug trafficking, forced recruitment of children for armed combat, and child prostitution. As the US Department of Labor's (USDL) 2012 report, *2011: Findings on the Worst Forms of Child Labor* showed, international moral opprobrium has failed to translate into significant improvements. In 56 of the 144 countries covered by the report there had been only a 'minimal' level of advancement towards addressing the worst forms of child labour, and no advancement at all was identified in a further 27 countries (USDL 2012).

Whilst raw statistical data of this kind serves to highlight the intractable nature of the incidence of child labour, it cannot convey the suffering and loss of human potential experienced by child labourers themselves. Since the inception of the ILO's International Programme on the Elimination of Child Labour (IPEC) in 1992, the scale of this suffering has been well documented. The ILO's 2011 report, *Children in Hazardous Work*, is a recent example of this, as is the report on child labour recently published by the UK's former Prime Minister, Gordon Brown, now the UN's Special Envoy for Global Education. As he argues:

> even the hardened social reformers in Britain of the 1840s would have been shocked by the conditions facing children today in the world's poorest countries. In West Africa, children as young as 12 are working in narrow tunnels down the shifts of artisanal gold mines. In India, children are trafficked and traded as bonded labourers to work in agriculture, manufacture and domestic services. In Bolivia, young children are working long hours with machetes to cut sugar cane on commercial farming estates. Meanwhile, an untold number are trapped in the worst forms of child labour, including child prostitution and forced recruitment into armed groups. (Brown 2012: 4)

Evidence provided by this and countless other studies contradicts the common-sense notion that the vast majority of children working in developing countries are employed in 'stable' and 'nurturing' environments, where their labour constitutes a valuable form of informal 'education' and 'training'. On the contrary, the primary motive for employing children is, as the ILO acknowledge, frequently sheer exploitation. Often children work because they are 'much less costly' than adults, are 'less aware of their rights, less troublesome and more willing to take orders and to do monotonous work without complaining'. They are 'prepared to engage in work activities which are considered too menial by adults', and are considered to be 'more trustworthy' and 'less likely to be absent from work' (ILO 1996: 13).

Claims that child labour is a 'culturally determined' practice, focused upon meeting domestic consumption needs, have also been undermined by studies which show that the commodities produced using child labour are frequently bound for international, rather than domestic consumption.

The USDL 1995 report, *By the Sweat and Toil of Children*, was one of the first major studies documenting the extent to which goods imported into developed countries were tainted with child labour (USDL 1995). Since then, non-governmental organisations (NGOs), the anti-globalisation and corporate-watch movements have done much to draw attention to the links between child labour and *specific* transnational corporations (TNCs). (See, for example, Christian Aid & SACCS 1997; Human Rights Watch 2002; Venkateswarlu 2003; Thomas 2009.) Sadly, scandals over the use of exploitative child labour in the manufacturing chains of TNCs are now commonplace. For example, in the 12 months prior to the writing of this chapter, the electronics giants Samsung, Apple and Nintendo, the multi-billion-pound commodities corporation Glencore, the clothing retailer H&M and the chocolate corporation Nestlé, which produces brands like KitKat, Aero and Smarties, were all implicated in child labour 'scandals'. Even Britain's much revered National Health Service, a public service that lay at the heart of the celebrations at the London Olympics opening ceremony, was found to have procured surgical instruments that were tainted with child labour (China Labor Watch 2012; Doward 2012; Fair Labor Association 2012; Moore 2012; Thomas 2012; Walker 2012; Garside 2013). These scandals continue to arise, despite the existence of grandiose, but essentially meaningless codes of conduct, which rhetorically commit TNCs to promoting 'ethical' labour standards and business practices. As a recent UNICEF report acknowledged, these are all too frequently not worth the paper they are written on, invariably glossing over 'endemic child labour in the area of operations, or ... in a company's supply chain' (Umlas 2012).

The ILO and UN seem perplexed and dismayed at the failure of the international community to significantly reduce the incidence of child labour. The ILO states that 'the persistence of child labour is one of the biggest failures of development efforts' (ILO 2010), whilst the UN argues that efforts to eradicate child labour 'are failing in the face of inertia, indifference and an indefensible willingness on the part of too many governments, international agencies, and aid donors to turn a blind eye' (Brown 2012: 4). The remainder of this chapter provides some suggestions as to why, despite the multitude of targets, goals and initiatives agreed since the mid-1990s, child labour remains such an intractable problem. We argue that in order to understand the persistence of the phenomenon, there is a need to appreciate the importance of the 'paradigm shift' that has occurred in the way child labour is portrayed and explained. This new, 'destigmatised' view of child labour is based upon the following key assumptions:

1. Child labour is embedded in the historical and cultural 'traditions' of developing countries. Any attempts to restrict it are based upon a Eurocentric understanding of the phenomenon, failing to appreciate the realities of life in developing countries.

2. Efforts to reduce or eradicate child labour through the imposition of Western-determined labour standards, arbitrary prohibitions, or via international trade sanctions will create more harm than good. In the absence of compensatory measures, children removed from the workplace will be plunged into poverty and forced into even worse, more exploitative situations.
3. Children themselves must be consulted about any interventions that might impact upon their well-being. The international community must acknowledge that in certain contexts and situations children should be afforded the 'right to work'.
4. The most effective – indeed the only – way to eliminate child labour is through a gradual process of economic growth. In this chapter, we refer to this as 'developmentalism', since one of its key premises is that all countries must inevitably go through the same, at times painful, stages of growth in order to progress economically. Just as European countries and the United States went through their 'child labour' stages of economic development, so too must today's developing nations. As was the case with today's 'rich' countries, 'poor' nations will themselves eventually reach a stage of economic development that deems child labour unnecessary and even undesirable.

Some of these assumptions may seem less contentious than others, but together they constitute a 'potent cocktail', which has served the interests of those who wish to 'detoxify' child labour very well. Our aim with this chapter is to challenge the basis of some of the assumptions that underpin this 'alternative' paradigm and to highlight some of the risks associated with any uncritical embrace of its key tenets.

The neoliberal, 'developmentalist' approach to child labour

At the heart of this 'new' approach to child labour is what we refer to as neoliberal 'developmentalism', which sees the practice as essentially a problem of pre-capitalist social relations of undevelopment. Those who embrace this position maintain that the eradication of child labour in the 'advanced' countries offers the model for newly industrialising countries to follow. It is suggested that economic growth, the democratising process and development of modern society gradually contributed to the elimination of child labour and that this pattern will be repeated in the newly developing world. This is essentially the line of argument presented by free-market liberals within the financial institutions emanating from the Bretton Woods conference of Western powers in 1944 – the IMF (International Monetary Fund) and the World Bank, and, more recently, the WTO (World Trade Organization). The belief is that the spread of an integrated capitalism will increase wealth, which will trickle down to improve the lives of the poor and gradually eradicate child labour.

We will examine World Bank and IMF 'developmentalist' approaches to child labour in more detail later. It is, though, important to point out that this perspective links into a long tradition of historical child labour research that is based on similar premises. This 'conservative' historiography, which, since the mid-1990s, has been frequently cited in policy documents on child labour published by the Bretton Woods institutions, has produced a broadly uncritical history of child labour eradication, which focuses on the 'civilising' tendencies of capitalist economic growth and industrialisation. Key examples are drawn from a particular reading of the history of child labour exploitation and its 'demise' in the advanced economies. In Britain, for example, it is argued that child labour exploitation was at its most extreme during the 'proto-industrial' period and that the worst exploiters of children's labour were their parents. Thus, according to Clark Nardinelli, a strong and often cited advocate of this position, 'rather than increasing the exploitation of children, the industrial revolution – if anything – decreased it. The new employment created by industrialization created opportunities for children to escape exploitation ... and ... created alternatives to parental control' (Nardinelli 1990: 98). For Nardinelli then, capitalist industrialisation was a 'liberating' force for children. Not only did it ameliorate the conditions of their employment, heralding an end to the 'abuses' and 'tyranny' that took place under the domestic system, it also ultimately secured the economic growth and prosperity required to ensure the demise of child labour:

> The general perception is that the Factory Acts, by reducing child labor, began an improvement in the condition of children, an improvement that has continued to this day ... [However] rising income, not factory legislation, was chiefly responsible for the long-term reduction in child labor. As income rises in any economy, child labor declines and the general condition of children improves. As the industrial revolution increased income in Britain (and elsewhere), changing opportunities enabled the typical family to reduce its reliance on child labor. (Nardinelli 1990: 8)

Indeed, according to Nardinelli, the Factory Acts probably harmed rather than enhanced the well-being of children. Their earnings, he argues, often meant the difference between a tolerable standard of living and utter destitution, and the prohibition of children's labour in factories may simply have forced parents to seek work for their children in other, more exploitative or harmful occupations. Whilst he offers little concrete evidence to support his analysis, he concludes that 'many, perhaps most, of the children forced out of factories found their way into occupations less desirable in every respect' (Nardinelli 1990: 156). Moreover, Nardinelli suggests that none of today's major industrial countries enacted effective laws during their formative stages of industrialisation. All acknowledged that child labour legislation would seriously hamper economic performance, and all postponed such intervention until 'the take-off into sustained growth had been completed' (Nardinelli 1990: 130). In summary, Nardinelli considers that 'children will remain an important source of labor in developing nations for many generations to come' (Nardinelli 1990: 153).

From this perspective, then, the development of modern capitalism – and with it a democratising polity – was part of the process of protecting rather than exploiting children, and stopping instead of increasing child labour. The assumption is that all developing countries should be left to follow the same laissez faire-inspired progression through the various 'stages' of economic growth, and that once a particular phase of development is attained child labour will decline in importance. This approach is evident in a paper written by J. A. Dorn, then Vice President of Academic Affairs at the US-based right-wing think tank, the Cato Institute. 'Only a short time ago in the United States,' he argued, 'it was not uncommon for 12-year-olds to work long hours on a farm or in a factory to help their families survive.' Should the United States 'now prevent such children from working in poor countries to improve living standards?' (Dorn 2002). For these writers, the demand for child labour is a consequence of the 'undercapitalised' state of developing world economies, and the only effective way of eliminating it is through globalisation, trade liberalisation and economic growth. The resulting economic progress, it is argued, will generate real improvements in working conditions and material living standards, and dependence on child labour will diminish as a result. Child labour, then, is 'a necessary evil' that all Western capitalist nations have been through and, inevitably, all industrialising countries will have to go, or are currently going through. The following comments, made by David Lindauer, a World Bank consultant, epitomise this approach:

> If [children] were not in the factory, they might be separated from their mothers and working as maids, or at home on consignment, or in local [non-exporting] carpet factories. Even worse, they might be begging or scavenging ... [We] cannot solve the problem of child labor in a poor country by prohibiting ... contractors from hiring anyone under the age of 14 ... It will not change the fundamental circumstances of the ... labor market ... When wages and household incomes rise, families can afford not to require their children to work (or accompany their mothers to work) ... With rising wages, companies also will be less likely to employ children ... We know of no case where a nation developed a modern manufacturing sector without first going through a 'sweat shop' phase. How long ago was it that children could be found working in the textile factories of Lowell, Massachusetts, of Manchester, England, or of Osaka, Japan? Should the developing countries of today be any different? (Cited in Rothstein 1994: 54)

This perspective proliferates, particularly amongst neoliberal economists and political scientists, who seek to promote an orthodox, deregulatory approach to development (see, for instance, Powell and Zwolinski 2012). The current global crisis may have dented the reputation of orthodox, neoliberal approaches to economic development, but the commentators, academics, politicians and financial institutions that have been responsible for promoting it are undaunted. Indeed, they appear to have emerged from the crisis emboldened, convinced that what is needed is a more 'pure' variant of neoliberal developmentalism, one that is completely untainted by the sentimental 'imperfections' of 'traditional' routes to development.

Of course, there are a number of problems with this approach to child labour. First, although there was a decline in the level of child labour exploitation in Britain in the second half of the nineteenth century, this was the consequence of a number of specific features. Amongst the most important were changing economic technologies, the development of a more organised form of capitalism, the need for an educated workforce, the development of state social policy to control and shape family life, concern over the future of the 'British race' and the 'problem of order' in the expanding urban areas. The combination of these factors, at a particular historical juncture, reshaped children's labour market activities, pushing them into part-time jobs that could be combined with schooling. However, the part-time jobs did not stop being exploitative, they just stopped being the object of the concerns of social commentators and the 'child labour problem' disappeared from view (Lavalette 1994, 1999; Cunningham 2000). Second, as Pat Hudson argues, 'before making unequivocal statements about the liberating effects of industrialisation, it should not be ignored that the decline in child labour in western societies was part of a larger global process which did much to advance the exploitation of labour, including child labour, in other parts of the world' (Hudson 1992: 427). Third, the evidence suggests that neoliberal-inspired economic growth has often been accompanied by an increase rather than a decline in child labour in many countries. Finally, as has been shown elsewhere, child labour in advanced, economically 'developed' capitalist nations is far from being eradicated, and this contradicts the 'developmentalist' perspective. The continuing widespread use and exploitation of child labour in 'developed' nations shows that the practice is not destined to disappear in the transition from a more 'savage' to a more 'advanced' form of capitalist accumulation.

The World Bank, the IMF and child labour

There can be little doubt that neoliberal developmentalism has shaped the approach adopted by the Bretton Woods institutions towards child labour. Nowhere was this more evident than in an influential report produced by the World Bank's Faraaz Siddiqi and Harry Anthony Patrinos, just a couple of years before *Thatcher's Children?* was published. This frequently cited document declared that child labour 'augments national economic development' and represents 'a fundamental evolutionary stage in the development of a country'. Children's contributions to family income in the developing world, it argued, mirror those of late eighteenth-century England, and, as was the case in England, once a certain level of development is reached, reliance on child labour will decline and children in these countries, like their earlier English counterparts, will be removed from the workplace. From this perspective, therefore, attempts to prohibit child labour through, for example, trade restrictions based on labour standards are counterproductive:

> The problem with such a stance is that (i) not all forms of child labor are exploitive or cruel; (ii) the age deemed 'child' labor is not clear; (iii) poor countries cannot necessarily afford such measures; (iv) levels of poverty would increase; and (v) school attendance would decline. Furthermore, free trade is probably part of the solution to eradicating child labor. This is because a free trade regime promotes development worldwide. And as countries develop, the incidence of child labor decreases substantially.
> (Siddiqi and Patrinos 1994)

Another World Bank working paper, published in 1995, made much the same point. Significantly, this paper also called for the World Bank to seek to initiate an attitudinal change in the way child labour is perceived, calling for the institution to spearhead the development of 'a less stigmatized view of child labour' (Grootaert and Kanbur 1995).

As we will show later, the World Bank has since engaged in just such a project, becoming more adept at disguising its crude developmentalist vision for 'managing' child labour. However, the message remains largely the same: the solution to child labour lies not in universal labour standards, but in trade liberalisation and economic growth. In this respect, the abolition of child labour, and the 'right' for children not to be exploited, are legitimate aspirations, but ones that can only be achieved in the long term through the promotion of negative, liberal freedoms: neoliberal 'globalisation' alone can provide developing countries with the means of achieving the rapid growth necessary to achieve marked reductions in absolute levels of poverty and the incidence of child labour. The World Bank's appointment of Kaushik Basu as its Chief Economist in October 2012 will doubtless help further cement this approach towards child labour into its development agenda. As *Newsweek* acknowledged, Basu's most influential work, published in 1998, constituted a forthright ideological defence of child labour, pointing to the 'risks' posed by 'unnecessary', 'ill-thought out' child labour regulation (Zeitlin 2012: 9). Basu, like Nardinelli, whom he quotes extensively, sees child labour as an inevitable stage in economic development. It is also possible to detect in his work a clear attempt to move forward the World Bank's strategy to promote a 'less stigmatised view of child labour':

> In the popular mind child labor is very often equated with child abuse ... The phenomenon is taken to be a product of avaricious entrepreneurs seeking cheap labor ... The popular instinct among most sections of our society is to support ideas such as those outlined in Senator Harkin's bill in the United States, which seeks to ban the import of child-labor-tainted products. ... As stated in the introduction, we reject this view ... And indeed there is over-whelming support for this rejection. (Basu 1998: 412–13)

This neoliberal model of development has, for many years, been imposed on developing nations via World Bank and IMF Structural Adjustment Programmes (SAPs), the sole aims of which are to promote economic liberalisation and trade. Not surprisingly, given the ideological orientation of these institutions, economic rather than social objectives dominate. At the time that the first edition of this book was published, the World Bank barely tried to disguise its indifference to the social damage caused by its initiatives, but it now devotes more resources to 'detoxifying' its image. However, the ideological influences underpinning its initiatives remain much the same, as does their impact. The World Bank's loans to developing countries have profoundly ideological conditions attached, such as labour market deregulation, the abolition of government subsidies, reduced levels of taxation and cuts in government expenditure. These represent a de facto dictation of both economic and social policy to countries seeking assistance. The same is true of IMF-sponsored interventions in developing countries. As a United States General Accounting Office (USGAO) Report acknowledged, the 'negotiation procedure' over SAP conditionalities has been reduced to a process of form filling whereby 'the Fund brings uniform drafts (with spaces to be filled) from Washington, in which even matters of language and form are cast in colorless stone' (USGAO 2001: 29). In effect, 'Debtor nations forego economic sovereignty and control over fiscal and monetary policy ... state institutions are undone and "economic tutelage" is installed'. (Chossudovsky 2003a: 35). Thus, the Bretton Woods institutions seek to impose a form of 'market colonialism', which subordinates the needs and desires of people and governments in developing nations to those of international creditors and multinational corporations.

The devastating social impact of SAPs on developing nations has been well documented (Geo-Jaja and MacLeans 2001; Chossudovsky 2003b). Wherever they have been implemented, they have typically been associated with declining incomes, increased inequality and falling levels of funding for public services such as education, which invariably has led to an increased rather than a reduced incidence of child labour. Thus, as we saw earlier, not only does child labour continue in many forms, it shows signs of increase in an alarming number of countries. Not surprisingly, it is in those nations which have been most exposed to SAPs, attacks on organised labour and trade liberalisation policies of the sort advocated by organisations such as the World Bank that the situation appears to have deteriorated the most. In short, the 'developmentalist' claim – that low levels of labour market regulation will ultimately promote economic growth in developing countries and hence deliver lower levels of child labour – has proven to be false. Such strategies appear to have led to more, not fewer, children in the workplace. In other words, structural adjustment programmes and market liberalisation and deregulation increase inequality and the vulnerability of the very poorest. As Bhaskaran et al. (2013) argue:

> The key point is that child labour needs to be understood not simply (as it often is) as a kind of cultural remnant or the consequences of poverty, but rather also as a direct result of the ways in which contemporary production networks are organized and governed. Arguments that see economic development as the means to ending child labour are therefore entirely misplaced. It is, of course, true that child labour has deep roots in poverty and deprivation … but it does not follow that the solutions lie in economic growth. Indeed, it has been widely acknowledged child labour does not correlate in any straightforward or predictable sense to patterns of growth, levels of gross domestic product. (2013: 9)

How do advocates of trade liberalisation and SAPs respond to their critics? Even when the demands of neoliberal globalisation lead to the sort of consequences outlined above, its promoters and sponsors remain reluctant to make the connection between the inconvenient facts and their economic prescriptions. Critics are told that the small sacrifices of the present, although unfortunate, are by far outweighed by the positive 'aspirations' for the future. In this regard, 'the high transition costs are seen as an acceptable price to be borne stoically by the living in the name of future generations' (Evans 2002: 202–3) Thus, World Bank, IMF and WTO policies that deprive families of the means of achieving subsistence and of educating their children free of charge, and that lead to increased incidences of child labour, are not seen as human rights violations, but as inevitable and necessary forms of 'structural adjustment'. These are short-term difficulties that will be overcome via the longer-term process of economic growth. At best, the Bretton Woods institutions interpret worsening socio-economic trends as a need to refine their approach rather than a failure of neoliberal economic policy.

The 'detoxification' of structural adjustment

Recent attempts by the major global financial institutions to allay concern about such findings and portray a 'social dimension' to their actions remain unconvincing. These efforts are epitomised by the IMF's formal commitment to broaden the objectives of its SAPs to include an explicit focus on poverty reduction. The main aspect of this new 'pro-poor' strategy has been the replacement of the Enhanced Structural Adjustment Facility (ESAF), the most common form of credit granted under SAPs, with the Poverty Reduction and Growth Facility (PRGF), and more recently the Extended Credit Facility. (For a discussion of the different credit facilities offered by the IMF, see Lenisink 1996.) Countries seeking funding under both these programmes have been expected to submit Poverty Reduction Strategy Papers (PRSPs), which are supposed to outline, after a broad consultative process with a vaguely defined 'civil society', a country's poverty-reduction priorities and the economic policies needed to achieve them. However, although the names of these programmes have changed, the conditions attached to them remain much the same. The PRSPs, for instance, frequently represent little more than nationally rubber-stamped IMF-produced templates, 'which although produced by highly indebted countries from across the world are in essentials all the same and reflect neoliberal orthodoxies' (Laird 2008: 380). Commenting on the PRGF, the USGAO admits that the PRGF did 'not differ from its [the IMFs] previous program' and that it signified a mere 'shift in emphasis rather than a change in the fund's stated philosophy' (USGAO 2001: 7, 24). In fact, the IMF's new 'ethical focus' represents little more than an attempt by the institution to provide itself with a cloak of respectability, in the face of a growing acknowledgment of the profoundly damaging consequences of its policies. Its economic prescriptions remain the same, and the requirements of PRGF loans have proven to be just as harmful to developing countries as those attached to the ESAF. As the International Trade Union Confederation (ITUC) argues: 'With few exceptions, PRSPs simply replicate the privatisation and liberalization policies that have long been at the heart of the IMF and World Bank programmes, even though governments, not the IFIs, are supposed to be responsible for formulating their own poverty reduction strategies' (ITUC 2008). Loan conditions focus solely on macroeconomic targets and objectives, and countries that fail to promote the neoliberal policy prescriptions favoured by the IMF have their borrowing rights suspended.

The World Bank's efforts to promote itself as a 'pro-poor' institution are no more convincing than those of the IMF. Like the IMF, it has sought to legitimise its interventions and policies by presenting itself as an organisation committed to fighting poverty and its consequences (Bello and Guttal 2006). Nowhere is this more apparent than in its World Development Report for 2000/2001, *Attacking Poverty*:

> Poverty amid plenty is the world's greatest challenge. We at the bank have made it our mission to fight poverty with professionalism, putting it at the centre of all the work we do ... This report seeks to expand the

understanding of poverty and its causes and sets out actions to create a world free from poverty in all its dimensions. (World Bank 2001: v)

However, there is little to distinguish the proposals set out in *Attacking Poverty* from the orthodox, damaging strategies that the World Bank has traditionally adopted. Of course, the language appears more benign and conciliatory than previous policy documents, and the bank even accepts that market reforms may 'have unintended consequences for poor people' (it could hardly deny it). The 'medicine', though, is essentially the same – more trade liberalisation, more privatisation and more deregulation. Nothing, the bank argues, not even the 'unintended casualties' of liberalisation, should allow developing nations to stray from the free market path laid out for them. 'It is critical,' the report insists, 'that the difficulty of reform and the impossibility of compensating every loser [should] not lead to policy paralysis' (World Bank 2001: 76).

In 2006, the World Bank announced that it would make an adherence to core labour standards, including Conventions 138 and 182 on child labour, a requirement for its lending. This ostensibly progressive initiative followed on from the 2003 World Bank report, *Unions and Collective Bargaining: Economic Effects in a Global Environment*, which appeared to represent an almost Damascene conversion on the part of the bank to the potential of labour regulation to enhance economic and social development (World Bank 2003). There is, however, little evidence to suggest that this 'commitment' has translated into loan conditions that might permit improvements in core labour standards. Indeed, on the contrary, not only is the bank's so-called 'commitment' to core labour standards conspicuously absent from its wider policy agenda, it is actually positively undermined by a number of its 'flagship' pro-business policies.

The influential *Doing Business* initiative is a good example of this. *Doing Business* (2009) is a major World Bank strategy, aimed at 'ranking' developing countries according to the extent to which government regulation impacts upon business 'friendliness'. In part, the aim is to provide potential investors with a reference guide of 'investment friendly' nations, but, importantly, its findings and recommendations are also used to shape the conditions attached to both World Bank and the IMF loans. Put simply, the general rule is that the better a country's labour standards are, the lower its *Doing Business* investment ranking will be. Conversely, nations that make strenuous efforts to deregulate labour markets and remove social protection are rewarded with higher investment rankings. Its ranking system is clearly at variance with the bank's rhetorical concern for core labour standards. As the International Trade Union Confederation points out: 'Countries can only improve their ... overall *Doing Business* ranking, by eliminating worker protection regulations. Despite the fact that many World Bank Group loans now include CLS requirements, no points are given for abiding by these standards' (ITUC 2007: 7).

Just to reiterate, *Doing Business* is not simply a reference guide for potential investors – its judgements on particular nations feed into the conditions attached to World Bank and IMF loans. Indeed in 2008, the ITUC identified 16 instances where *Doing Business* recommendations were used to pressurise nation states to weaken labour market regulation, once again undermining the World Bank's claims to be interested in core labour standards: 'By discouraging countries from maintaining anything above the bare minimum level of labour market regulation, *Doing Business* actually undermines development goals promoted by the World Bank and other international organizations' (ITUC/Global Unions (2008).

Burkina Faso is one country where *Doing Business* rankings have been used to pressure the national government to cut social provision, and following its 'reform' of a number of its social programmes it is now cited by the World Bank as an example for others to follow. In fact, it was ranked as one of the top ten '*Doing Business* reformers' in 2009 (World Bank 2009). Clearly, bank officials were not perturbed by the country's UN Development Programme 'Human Development' ranking of 176th out of 177 nations (UNDP 2007: 232). Nor, apparently, were they concerned by the country's widely acknowledged poor record in child trafficking and child labour exploitation. The following comments, made by a UN special rapporteur on human rights after a visit to the country, certainly bring into question the World Bank's choice of it as a 'beacon' nation for economic development:

> Authorities such as the Ministry of the Interior [of Burkina Faso] and representatives of civil society interviewed by the Special Rapporteur mentioned child trafficking as one of the major problems affecting Burkina Faso ... These children work mainly in the primary sector (agriculture) and secondary sector (domestic service in the case of girls) ... Many girls give accounts of being subjected to physical, psychological or sexual abuse. Besides the children's physical integrity, some of their fundamental rights are also disregarded, on account of being made to work too early, being exposed to harsh living conditions, etc. The problem of education is ever-present too; in the towns, children who work do not attend school. (UNCHR 2006: 16)

What this illustrates is the incongruence between the bank's stated commitment to core labour standards and the messages it sends out to developing countries about the best ways to promote economic development. Its lending policies, as well as its 'flagship' initiatives such as *Doing Business*, rarely devote any serious consideration to core labour standards, and they invariably continue to be based upon unreconstructed neoliberal orthodoxies. As with other aspects of the World Bank's initiatives, recent years have seen attempts to 'detoxify' *Doing Business*, and in 2009 it claimed that it would incorporate more progressive indicators, such as labour rights, into the

Employing Workers Index of its *Doing Business* strategy. Little evidence of this has emerged. As Kang argues, 'the World Bank's new rhetoric is best understood as a cosmetic change brought about by the possible crisis of legitimacy stemming from the global financial crisis' (Kang 2009: 484).

Dealing with the 'casualties' of structural adjustment

Elsewhere, the bank has set out its proposals for dealing with the 'unintended casualties' who inadvertently fail to benefit from its neoliberal prescriptions, including children. Its Early Childhood Development Programme (ECDP), which sets out the bank's strategy for dealing with ill health, malnutrition, high mortality rates, and educational waste among poor children in developing countries, is indicative of its approach towards the social problems these nations face. As Penn notes, the ECDP sees them not as evidence of the failure of neoliberal economic policy, but as 'technical failures of adjustment which can be remedied by suitably targeted investments in health, education and welfare' (Penn 2002: 122). Thus, rather than acknowledging their structural causes, and the bank's own culpability in exacerbating the profound difficulties developing countries face, problems such as childhood malnutrition, illness and indeed child labour are attributed to poor parenting and inappropriate childrearing techniques. Mary Eming Young, the bank's senior public health specialist, summarises succinctly the assumptions underpinning its ECDP: 'Lack of proper handling and affection has been shown to cause children's growth to falter just as much as lack of proper food ... Parents, especially those who are young and inexperienced, are too often unaware of the fundamental needs of a young child and of the many simple ways available to meet them' (Eming Young 1999).

A more recent World Bank analysis of ECDP initiatives serves to highlight the continuing emphasis the organisation seeks to place on their value: 'the failure of low-income children to develop to their full cognitive and emotional capacity is a major obstacle to their economic well-being, as well as to their contributions to future economic growth ... These early developmental shortfalls contribute substantially to the intergenerational transmission of poverty through reduced employability, productivity, and overall well-being later in life' (World Bank 2001). The solution to the problems faced by children in the developing world, therefore, lies not in a fundamental transformation of the global economic system that creates and perpetuates underdevelopment and its attendant problems of child poverty, infant mortality and child labour, but in targeted interventions (mainly of girls and young mothers) that 'show parents and caregivers how to improve their interaction with young children and how to improve the quality of care these children receive, enriching their environment and thereby enhancing their development' (Eming Young 1999). Through such initiatives, it is argued, the 'intergenerational transmission of poverty' can be solved.

Of course many of the initiatives supported by the Bank's ECDP, particularly food programmes, have no doubt helped alleviate some of the difficulties poor communities in developing countries face. However, these programmes deal merely with the symptoms of the problems they purport to solve, and ultimately serve to divert attention away their fundamental structural causes. Thus, rather than linking problems like child malnutrition and child labour to the wider socio-economic environment that families in developing countries find themselves in – that is, one characterised increasingly by declining wages, unemployment, job insecurity and reduced levels of social support – and seeking to change it, ECDPs take this environment as given, instead focusing on the way families, particularly mothers, can mitigate its worst effects. Indeed, in examining the rationale for ECDPs, one is reminded of the explanations advanced by Victorian philanthropists and policy makers to account for high levels of child mortality, malnutrition and physical deterioration in late nineteenth-century Britain. Then, by pathologising the poor, and blaming them for circumstances that were clearly beyond their control, bourgeois politicians were able to affect an interest in the working class, whilst at the same time promoting a socio-economic environment which made their condition worse (Davin 1978; Dyehouse 1983). The same, it could be argued, is true of initiatives introduced under the World Bank's ECDP. As Penn argues, 'Their main, if not deliberate function is to legitimise the claim of the World Bank to be concerned about the welfare of children, despite [its promotion of] macroeconomic policies which make their condition worse' (Penn 2002). A secondary and equally important function is the role they play in refocusing debates about child labour, poverty and malnutrition, by suggesting that they are 'the result of inappropriate child care practices and not of income, famine, or preventable health problems' (Sridhar 2008: 150).

The ECDP has indeed served to legitimise the activities of the World Bank, and there are now many within the academic and NGO communities who appear genuinely to believe that early intervention programmes aimed at stimulating young children and improving childrearing techniques are the most effective way of combating the problems developing countries face. The bank's 'international partners' on early childhood development programmes include not only bourgeois research institutes such as the Aga Khan and Soros Foundations, but also mainstream NGOs such as CARE International and Save the Children Alliance, and international bodies such as UNICEF and the World Health Organization. Each of these organisations participates in the World Bank's ECDP, and, together with development academics, they are responsible for generating and publishing a plethora of research on the effectiveness of particular initiatives. Through its encouragement and funding of such research, the bank has very skilfully shifted the development agenda away from the consequences for the world's children of the destructive neoliberal economic policies it imposes on developing countries, and reinforced the hold of its own dominant development discourse in academic and research institutions throughout the world. At the same time, it has created what Chossudovsky describes as its own 'counter-paradigm', which has generated a semblance of critical debate without addressing the social and political foundations of the market system (Chossudovsky 1997). This 'counter-paradigm' rarely challenges the bank's neoliberal dogma, focusing instead on the impact of its supposedly altruistically motivated interventions at a micro level.

In this sense, we should not underestimate the important role research into problems such as child labour can play in reinforcing what has been referred to as 'paradigm maintenance'. As Broad argues, through funding, privileging and promoting the work of researchers who embrace (or at least do not threaten) their neoliberal worldview, global financial institutions 'skew' the research agenda. Critical, dissonant research is discouraged 'in a way that undermines debate and nuanced research conclusions, instead encouraging the confirmation of *a priori* neoliberal hypotheses' (Broad 2006: 388).

Children's 'right to work'?

In the context that we have just described, the growing interest the World Bank and the other Bretton Woods institutions have taken in the recent shift in emphasis in child labour research towards a concern for children's rights should also be viewed with caution. As we noted earlier, recent decades have not witnessed any significant fall in the levels of intensity of child labour exploitation. However, rather than this coinciding with increasing efforts to draw attention to the global, structural causes of its growth, and to promote measures that would lead to its abolition, it has occurred at a time when increasing numbers of academics, NGO activists and politicians have adopted elements of the 'children's rights agenda'. Central to this change in emphasis was the introduction of the UN Convention on the Rights of the Child (UNCRC) that was formally adopted by the UN General Assembly in 1989. As William Myers points out, 'No observer of the history of child labour thought and action can fail to be impressed by the rather sudden and dramatic changes of perspective attributed to the influence of the United Nations Convention on the Rights of the Child' (Myers 1999: 14) The Convention asserts some basic values regarding the treatment, participation and protection of children within society. It contains a number of contradictions within it, but some advocates have described it as 'akin to a manifesto for the children's rights movement' (Franklin and Franklin 1996: 2). It has led some to argue that the 'protectionist paradigms' traditionally advocated by child labour activists are inappropriate. On the one hand, those who denounce child labour and pursue protectionist campaigns stand accused of promoting peculiarly Western values that have little relevance to the lives of children in the developing world. They are, according to Ben White, 'out of tune with the realities of life in the countries of the South today' (White 1996: 832). On the other hand, traditional approaches to child labour are seen as denying children's agency and locking them into a restricting life stage, 'childhood', where their lives are devalued and rights restricted or denied. Thus, Olga Nieuwenhuys argues that the 'moral condemnation of child labor assumes that children's place in society must perforce be one of dependency and passivity' (Nieuwenhuys 1996: 238). Some activists have gone so far as to argue for children's right to work. Per Miljeteig, for example, states: 'It can no longer be single-handedly stated that *work as such* is bad or harmful for children':

> There is a growing understanding that work might have beneficial effects on children, in terms of teaching them important skills, giving them a sense of self-esteem and of being productive. Through their work, children can contribute to their own material wellbeing as well as that of their families. There is a growing understanding that working children are ... not always victims of evil influences or exploitation. (Miljeteig 2000: 7)

Much of the literature generated within this new paradigm seems motivated by a genuine concern that protectionist policies can do more damage than good, ultimately depriving children and their families of much needed income (Myers 1991; Nieuwenhuys 1994; Boyden, Ling and Myers 1998). Those who embrace the paradigm often cite instances where the removal of children from certain forms of manufacturing employment is said to have led to negative outcomes for the children concerned. One frequently cited example is the aftermath of the 1995 CBS television channel child labour investigation into the use of child labour in soccer ball production in Sialkot, Pakistan. Following the scandal, children were largely withdrawn from the production chain. According to Farzad Khan (2007), the 'moral probity and self-righteous passion' associated with this campaign had 'unintended consequences': family incomes, he argues, fell and children were prevented from undertaking valuable work that they enjoyed. The work, he states, had 'provided them [the children] with dignity and a sense of soldiering solidarity with their household, by helping to bear its cost of living' (Khan, Munir and Willmott 2007: 1067). Another often cited case is the reaction of the Bangladeshi garment industry to the threat of the enactment of the Harkin Bill in the United States, which would have prohibited the import of minerals and goods produced with child labour. It is claimed that the mere threat of sanctions led to the dismissal of thousands of children (mainly girls), who, in the absence of any other means of earning a living, were forced to take up even worse jobs as brick-breakers, domestic servants or even sex workers. The 'lessons of Bangladesh' have now become a key component of the narrative that shapes mainstream child labour debates, the assumption being that threats of economic coercion, in the form of trade sanctions or 'social clauses', should be avoided at all costs. Children, it is argued, must be consulted on decisions that affect them before any attempt is made to withdraw them from the workplace.

Obviously, nobody would want to recommend a strategy that would reduce the incomes of children to starvation levels or expose them to destitution or even more severe forms of exploitation. However, the arguments presented by those who champion 'children's right to work' have not remained uncontested. First, the 'children's rights' advocates have been accused of failing to appreciate the exploitative nature of many of the labour practices they seek to defend. For instance, Nielsen argues that critics of the Harkin Bill have presented an idealistic interpretation of the conditions experienced by child workers in the Bangladeshi garment industry prior to their removal. This often involved children working 14-hour days, where they were subject to 'harsh forms of discipline and supervision'. Nielsen also points out that the existence of readily available child labour was one of the principal reasons for the notoriously low levels of pay in the sector, and for the poverty which itself forced parents to allow their children to work in the first place (Nielsen 2005). Others, such as Mohina Gulrajani, criticise the failure of the children's rights paradigm to acknowledge the unjust nature of the world economic order as the root cause of child labour (Gulrajani 2000: 39). Indeed, in its more extreme forms this position can sometimes translate into little more than an uncritical acceptance of the neoliberal developmentalist position, thus providing a powerful ideological justification for child labour (see, for example, Liebel 2000). In this respect it can inadvertently 'serve to redefine the problem, to narrow the agenda and/or to transfer moral culpability from corporations to critics' (Nielsen 2005: 580).

We feel that this 'reorientation of culpability' in child labour debates is an important, but increasingly neglected issue, and it is one that those who defend children's 'right to work' do not fully address. One particularly unfortunate consequence of the 'reframing' of child labour debates is that it can, in some instances, serve to vindicate the exploitative practices of the principal beneficiaries of child labour exploitation – global transnational companies. It is no coincidence that representatives of TNCs, many of whom have themselves been implicated in child labour scandals, have also enthusiastically embraced the notion of children's 'right to work'. Hence, the International Organisation of Employers (IOE), which represents major corporations, insists that attempts to link the issue of working children with international trade and to impose trade sanctions on countries where the problem of child labour exists 'are counter-productive and jeopardize the welfare of children' (IOE 1996a): 'The fact of employing children has, in a number of contexts, been understood to be positive since, through work, children can acquire marketable skills and earn indispensable income for themselves and their families, which can be a necessity in poor families and in developing economies' (IOE 2013).

The IOE's *Resolution on Child Labour*, adopted in 1996 (and still operative), maintains that only neoliberal-influenced open trading and investment can create the rising standards of living that will ultimately lead to improved labour standards and the abolition of child labour (IOE 1996a). In fact, the IOE goes further, condemning what it sees as the ILO's 'over-extensive interpretation' of certain already existing labour-related Conventions. The ILO, it argues, should cease 'criticizing minor deviations from obligations under ratified Conventions' and should accept 'the fact that ILO Conventions are not "set in stone" and are not the solution to all the problems of the world of work' (IOE 2000). What is needed, then, is less – not more – regulation. So instead of contemplating more stringent international labour legislation, the ILO should 'work towards greater flexibility in national policies and labour markets and correspondingly greater flexibility in the international labour standards' (IOE 1996b).

We are therefore beginning to see a coincidence of interests between, on the one hand, well-meaning activists, many of whom are genuinely concerned about the potentially negative impact of arbitrary prohibitions on child labour, and, on the other hand, TNCs and the Bretton Woods institutions who are keen to promote, in the World Bank's words, a 'less stigmatizing view of child labour'. Ultimately, advocates of 'children's right to work' – whatever their ideological motivations – need to address some fundamental questions. As Tsogas puts it:

> Taking this argument to its logical extreme we can argue that no laws would have helped abolish slavery, since slaves and the economies of the societies they lived in were too poor to sustain 'free' labour, or any human rights for that matter. The question therefore is: where do we actually draw the line? Are there any human rights and values below which, as human kind, regardless of political or level of economic development, we are not prepared to go? (Tsogas 1999: 362)

According to the ILO, the answer to this final question is unequivocally yes, and among the eight Conventions it deems 'as being fundamental to the rights of human beings at work, *irrespective of levels of development of individual member States*' is Convention 138, which calls for 'the effective abolition of child labour' (ILO 2002, emphasis added). However, as with TNCs, Convention 138 has always sat uncomfortably with the Bretton Woods institutions. Indeed, the World Bank sees 138 as tainted with 'developed-country bias' and of 'promoting a Euro-American view of children'. The Convention, it argues, is based upon the concept of an 'ideal childhood' and fails to acknowledge the realities of life in developing countries, where the 'vast majority of child workers are involved in agricultural work, typically in family-run farms' (Betcherman et al. 2004: 6).

What is clear then, is that neither the World Bank, nor TNCs, will support proposals that might lead to the 'effective abolition' of child labour in instances where they claim that children's work has 'positive effects on the income of poor families' and where it 'may also be a factor in the ability of these countries to compete internationally' (Shihata 1996: 395). Traditionally, this has set the World Bank and TNCs at odds with child labour campaigners and activists who have demanded an end to child exploitation. However, with the emergence and consolidation of the 'children's rights paradigm', this is no longer the case. The bank, its partner institutions, and TNCs are effectively 'let off the hook' and provided with a solution to a problem that has bedevilled them for years – that is, how to reconcile their ideological opposition to child labour regulation with their claim to support children's interests worldwide. It is hardly surprising, then, that the World Bank and the IOE now regularly invoke children's rights discourse in their policy documents on child labour. Thus, according to Zafiris Tzannatos, the then head of the World Bank's Global Child Labor Program, any international effort to tackle the problem must 'include the perspective of working children and youth as well as that of their families'. Children, he insists, are 'partners and stakeholders' and the international community needs to 'develop ways to include them – whenever appropriate – in programming, planning, policies, advocacy and research concerning child labor' (Miljeteig 2000). 'Rights-based approaches' to child labour, we are told, 'expand development objectives beyond physical assets and income growth' allowing 'for complexity in understanding the phenomenon of child labor as it varies by location, cultural context, and sector' (Betcherman et al. 2004: 7).

More recently, the IOE's Secretary General, Brent Wilton, utilised similar language when defending the use of trafficked child labour in unregulated 'rathole' coal mining in Meghalaya, India. He was responding to an article in the *International Herald Tribune*, which reported that as many as 70,000 children, some as young as five, were toiling in the most appalling conditions, in mines where workplace-related deaths were virtually a daily occurrence:

> In areas of extreme poverty, where any job done by anyone can make the difference between survival and death, where alternatives to child work are thin on the ground, or absent ... child labour becomes a necessity ... Business alone should not bear the brunt of the blame. Shutting down a business in the circumstances described ... shifts the problem; such action does not solve it ... As the child quoted in the last sentence of this article asks: 'How can we not work, we have to eat?' (Wilton 2013)

Wilton's willingness to defend children's labour in such plainly appalling conditions should remind us of the dangers associated with any uncritical 'celebration' of children's right to work. As one of the mine managers questioned by the *Tribune* investigators admitted, 'People [here] die all the time ...

You have breakfast in the morning, go to work and never come back. Many have died this way' (Harris, Gottipati and Mandhana 2013: 2).

Whilst not wanting to devalue the good intentions of academics and NGOs calling for working children's participation in decisions that affect them, we do question the motives underpinning the sudden concern expressed by the World Bank and TNCs to ensure child labourers have a 'right to work' and are 'adequately consulted'. As Jeremy Seabrook argues, 'It is ... no coincidence that international institutions at the forefront of the demands for children's "right to choose" are those same institutions that are pursuing the logic of "no alternative" to market liberalisation and neo-liberalism' (Seabrook 2001: 65) – that is, those institutions that have for decades insisted that protectionist policies hurt children and that the only solution to child labour is neoliberal-inspired economic growth. The World Bank's newfound desire to consult those affected by its policies would, as he points out, 'be more convincing if it did not coincide with a global program of privatisations and cuts in government spending on nutrition and health', which itself is responsible for many of the difficulties children in developing countries face (Seabrook 1997: 22). In this respect, the 'children's rights' debate is in danger of affirming, rather than countering, IMF, World Bank and TNC interpretations of child labour. Even where such research has a 'discordant' or 'dissenting' edge or tone, it can be 'functional' in that it constitutes a 'safe', 'contained' critique. To cite Ralph Miliband, it is in danger of developing into a form of 'radicalism without teeth', which has the potential to distract attention from the greatest problem of all – the profoundly unjust nature of the world economic order and exploitative business practices (Miliband 1969: 195). Instead, the focus turns towards micro-level initiatives that deal only with its symptoms, and the 'bigger picture', of dealing with poverty in what is now a world of enormous plenty, is lost. Important as these initiatives may be in mitigating the worst aspects of child labour in some communities, this shift in emphasis ultimately serves to legitimise the activities of those who profit from exploitative child labour and the Bretton Woods institutions. It allows the latter to fund, engage with and support purportedly 'cutting edge' research developments, and provides them with a semblance of commitment to the social and economic well-being of children in developing countries. Once again, we do not wish to denigrate the motives of well-meaning academics and activists who seek to place children's rights at the forefront of the development agenda. However, as Seabrook insists, 'it is of not lesser importance to understand the context that may well undermine, if not cancel, them' (2001: 66).

There is therefore a danger that the debate over children's rights 'stylises' the policy issues pertaining to child labour, and diverts resources and attention from what should be a central focus – that is, the exposure of the global structures and institutions that force millions of the world's poor to rely on their children's earnings for subsistence. As Dunu Roy argues, 'The issue of rights cannot be resolved as long as wrongs continue to be the basis for the production and reproduction of human life.' For Roy, the 'predatory, rapacious, capitalist system' is at the root of the problem of child labour, and debates over 'illusory rights' for children merely act as an ideological smokescreen, disguising the way current economic arrangements reinforce the conditions that create and sustain children's exploitation (Roy 1998).

References

Basu, K. (1998). *Child Labor: Cause, Consequence and Cure, with Remarks on International Labor Standards*. Washington, DC: World Bank.
Basu, K. and Pham Hoang, V. (1998). 'The Economics of Child Labor'. *The American Economic Review* 88(3): 412–27.
Bello, W. and Guttal, S. (2006). 'The Limits of Reform: the Wolfensohn Era at the World Bank'. *Race & Class* 47(3): 68–81.
Betcherman, G., Fares, J. Linstra, A. and Prouty, R. (2004). *Child Labor, Education and Children's Rights*. Washington, DC: World Bank Social Protection Unit.
Bhaskaran, R., Nathan, D., Phillips, N. and Upendranadh, C. (2013). 'Vulnerable Workers and Labour Standards (Non) Compliance in Global Production Networks: Home Based Child Labour in Delhi's Garment Sector'. DfID Working Paper 16. www.dfid.gov.uk/r4d/PDF/Outputs/tradepolicy/ctg-wp-2013-16.pdf.
Boyden, J., Ling, B. and Myers, W. E. (1998). *What Works for Working Children*, Stockholm: RaddaBarnen/UNICEF.
Broad, R. (2006). 'Research, Knowledge, and the Art of 'paradigm maintenance': the World Bank's Development Economics Vice-Presidency (DEC)'. *Review of International Political Economy* 13(3): 387–419.
Brown, G. (2012). *Child Labour and Educational Disadvantage: Breaking the Link, Building Opportunity*. Office of the UN Special Envoy for Education. http://educationenvoy.org/child_labor_and_education_US.pdf.
China Labor Watch. (2012). *An Investigation of Eight Samsung Factories in China*. http://www.chinalaborwatch.org/pdf/Samsung%20Report%200904-v3.pdf.
Chossudovsky, M. (2003a). *The Globalisation of Poverty: Impacts of IMF and World Bank Reforms*. Panang, Malaysia: Third World Network.
Chossudovsky, M. (2003b). *The Globalization of Poverty and the New World Order*. Canada: Global Research.
Christian Aid & SACCS. (1997). *A Sporting Chance: Tackling Child Labour in India's Sports Goods Industry*. Christian Aid & SACCS.
Cunningham, S. (2000). 'Child Labour in Britain, 1900–1970'. Unpublished PhD, University of Central Lancashire.
Davin, A. (1978). 'Imperialism and Motherhood'. In *History Workshop Journal* 5(1): 9–66.
Dorn, J. A. (2002). *Trade and Human Rights: The Case of China*. Washington, DC: Cato Institute. http://www.freetrade.org/pubs/freetrade/chap8.html (accessed 24 April 2002).
Doward, J. (2012). 'H&M comes under pressure to act on child labour cotton'. *The Observer*, 16 December.
Dyehouse, C. (1983). 'Working Class Mothers and Infant Mortality in England 1895–1914'. *Journal of Social History II*.

Eming Young, M. (1999). *Early Childhood Development: Investing in the Future.* Washington, DC: World Bank.
Evans, T. (2002). 'A Human Right to Health?' *Third World Quarterly* 23(2): 197–215.
Fair Labor Association. (2012). *Sustainable Management of Nestle's Supply Chain in the Ivory Coast – Focus on Labor Standards.* http://www.fairlabor.org/sites/default/files/documents/reports/cocoa-report-final_0.pdf.
Franklin, A. and Franklin, B. (1996). 'The Developing Children's Rights Movement in the UK'. In J. Pilcher and S. Wagg, S. (eds), *Thatcher's Children?* Bristol: Falmer Press.
Garside, J. (2013). 'Investigators uncover child labour at Apple suppliers'. *The Guardian*, 26 January.
Geo-Jaja, A. and MacLeans, A. (2001). 'Structural Adjustment as an Inadvertent Enemy of Human Development in Africa'. *Journal of Black Studies* 32(1): 30–49.
Grootaert, C. and Kanbur, R. (1995). *Child Labor: A Review: Background Report for the World Development Report.* Office of the Vice President. http://www.gdsnet.org/Child-Labor-aReview.PDF.
Gulrajani, M. (2000). 'Children's Work and Children's Education: Issues in Development Economics'. Paper given at the international conference, Rethinking Childhood: Working Children's Challenge to the Social Sciences, Bondy (France) 15–17 November 2000.
Harris, G., Gottipati, S. and Mandhana, N. (2013). 'Toiling in India's "ratholes"'. *International Herald Tribune*, 27 February, p. 2.
Hudson, P. (1992). 'Clark Nardinelli, Child Labour and the Industrial Revolution, Review'. *Economic History Review* 45: 426–7.
Human Rights Watch. (2002). *Child Labor and Obstacles to Organizing on Ecuador's Banana Plantations.* Human Rights Watch.
ILO (International Labour Organisation). (1996). *Child Labour: Targeting the Intolerable.* Geneva: International Labour Organisation.
ILO. (2002). *Fundamental ILO Conventions.* http://www.ilo.org/public/english/standards/norm/whatare/fundam/index.htm.
ILO. (2010). *Accelerating Action Against Child Labour: Global Report to the follow-up to the ILO Declaration on Fundamental Principles and Rights of Work.* Geneva: ILO. http://www.google.co.uk/url?sa=t&rct=j&q=ilo+global+report+on+child+labour&source=web&cd=2&ved=0CD0QFjAB&url=http%3A%2F%2Fwww.ilo.org%2Fipecinfo%2Fproduct%2Fdownload.do%3Ftype%3Ddocument%26id%3D13853&ei=5xc3UfuMFoOSOOrfgMgL&usg=AFQjCNEBgtrn43hZa3u9bXh1g2FfM8UtJQ.
ILO. (2011). *Children in Hazardous Work: What We Know, What We Need to Do.* Geneva, ILO. http://www.ilo.org/ipecinfo/product/download.do?type=document&id=17035.
ILO. (2012). *Tackling Child Labour: From Commitment to Action.* Geneva: ILO. http://www.ilo.org/ipecinfo/product/download.do?type=document&id=20136.
IOE (International Organisation of Employers). (1996a). *General Council of the International Organisation of Employers: Resolution on Child Labour* (adopted on 3 June 1996). Geneva: IOE.
IOE. (1996b). *Policy Statement on the Social Clause.* Geneva: General Council of the IOE.
IOE. (2000). *ILO Standards: Position Paper of the IOE* (adopted by the IOE General Council on 9 June 2000). Geneva: IOE.
IOE. (2013). *The Elimination of Child labour: An Important Issue for Employers.* http://www.ioe-emp.org/index.php?id=150.
ITUC (International Trade Union Confederation). (2007). *The Role of IFIs in Supporting Decent Work and Countering the Risks of Financial Globalisation: Statement by Global*

Unions to the 2007 Annual Meetings of the IMF and World Bank. http://www.ituc-csi.org/IMG/pdf/statement.imfwb.1007.pdf (accessed 17 January 2008).

ITUC. (2008). *Challenging the IFI: Practical Information and Strategies for Trade Union Engagement with International Financial Institutions*. http://www.ituc-csi.org/IMG/pdf/Challenging_IFI_EN-PDF.pdf (accessed 15 April 2009).

ITUC/Global Unions. (2008). *The IFIs' Use of Doing Business to Eliminate Worker Protection: Analysis of Doing Business 2008 and New Country Evidence*. http://www.ituc-csi.org/IMG/pdf/doing_business.pdf (accessed 2 April 2009).

Kang, S. L. (2009). 'Labor and the Bank: Investigating the Politics of the World Bank's Employing Workers Index'. *Journal of Workplace Rights* 14(4): 481–501.

Khan, F. R., Munir, K. A. and Willmott, H. (2007). 'A Dark Side of Institutional Entrepreneurship: Soccer Balls, Child Labour and Postcolonial Impoverishment'. *Organization Studies* 28(7): 1055–77.

Laird, S. E. (2008). 'African Social Services in Peril: A Study of the Department of Social Welfare in Ghana under the Highly Indebted Poor Countries Initiative'. *Journal of Social Work* 8(4): 377–98.

Lavalette, M. (1994). *Child Labour in the Capitalist Labour Market*. Aldershot: Avebury.

Lavalette, M. (ed.). (1999). *A Thing of the Past? Child Labour in Britain in the Nineteenth and Twentieth Centuries*. Liverpool: Liverpool University Press.

Lenisink, R. (1996). *Structural Adjustment in Sub-Saharan Africa*. London: Longman.

Liebel, M. (2000). 'Social Transformations by Working Children's Organisations? Experiences From Africa and Latin America'. Paper given at the international conference, Rethinking Childhood: Working Children's Challenge to the Social Sciences, Bondy (France) 15–17 November 2000.

Miliband, R. (1969). *The State in Capitalist Society: An Analysis of the Western System of Power*. New York: Basic Books.

Miljeteig, P. (2000). *Creating Partnerships With Working Youth*. World Bank.

Moore, M. (2012). 'Nintendo parts factory uses child labour'. *The Daily Telegraph*, 18 October.

Myers, W. E. (1991). *Protecting Working Children*. London: Zed Books.

Myers, W. E. (1999). 'Considering Child Labour: Changing Terms, Issues and Actors at the International Level'. *Childhood* 6(1): 13–26.

Nardinelli, C. (1990). *Child Labor and the Industrial Revolution*. Bloomington and Indianapolis: Indiana University Press.

Nielsen, M. E. (2005). 'The Politics of Corporate Responsibility and Child Labour in the Bangladeshi Garment Industry'. *International Affairs* 81(3): 559–80.

Nieuwenhuys, O. (1994). *Children's Lifeworlds: Gender, Welfare and Labour in the Developing World*. London: Routledge.

Nieuwenhuys, O. (1996). 'The Paradox of Child Labor and Anthropology'. *Annual Review of Anthropology* 25: 237–51.

Penn, H. (2002). 'The World Bank's View of Early Childhood'. *Childhood* 9(1).

Powell, B. and Zwolinski, M. (2012). 'The Ethical and Economic Case Against Sweatshop Labour: A Critical Assessment'. *Journal of Business Ethics* 107: 449–72.

Rothstein, R. (1994). *The Global Hiring Hall: Why We Need Worldwide Labor Standards*. The American Prospect. http://prospect.org/article/global-hiring-hall-why-we-need-worldwide-labor-standards.

Roy, D. (1998). 'Rights of Child Labour: Ethics, Production and Nation State'. *Economic and Political Weekly*, 31 January.

Seabrook, J. (1997). 'Reform and transformation'. *New Internationalist*, November, p. 22.

Seabrook, J. (2001). *Children of Other Worlds: Exploitation in the Global Market*. London: Pluto Press.
Shihata, I. F. I. (1996). 'The World Bank's Protection and Promotion of Children's Rights'. *International Journal of Children's Rights* 4: 383–405.
Siddiqi, F. and Patrinos, H. A. (1994). *Child Labor Issues Causes and Interventions*. World Bank, Human Resources and Operations Policy Department and Education and Social Policy Department.
Sridhar, D. (2008). 'Hungry for Change: the World Bank in India'. *South Asia Research* 28(2): 147–68.
Thomas, M. (2009). *Belching Out the Devil: Global Adventures With Coca Cola*. Reading: Random House.
Thomas, N. (2012). 'Glencore accused of child labour'. *The Daily Telegraph*, 16 April.
Tsogas, G. (1999). 'Labour Standards in International Trade Agreements: An Assessment of the Arguments'. *International Journal of Human Resource Management* 10(2): 351–75.
Umlas, E. (2012). *Corporate Social Responsibility Working Paper: Sustainability Reporting on Children's Rights*. New York: UNICEF.
UNCHR (United Nations Commission on Human Rights). (2006). *Report on Burkino Faso submitted by Ms. Gabriela Rodríguez Pizarro, Special Rapporteur to the UN*, E/CN.4/2006/73/Add.2. http://daccessdds.un.org/doc/UNDOC/GEN/G06/100/47/PDF/G0610047.pdf?OpenElement (accessed 2 February 2007).
UNDP (United Nations Development Programme). (2007). Human Development Report, 2007/08: Fighting Climate Change, Human Solidarity in a Divided World, Hampshire, Palgrave Macmillan. Internet Reference: http://hdr.undp.org/en/media/HDR_20072008_EN_Complete.pdf (accessed 3 May 2008).
USDL (United States Department of Labor). (1995). *By the Sweat and Toil of Children, Volume II: The Use of Child Labor in US Agricultural Imports and Forced and Bonded Child Labor*. Washington, DC: Bureau of International Labor Affairs.
USDL. (2012). *2011, Findings on the Worst Forms of Child Labor*. Washington: US Department of Labor.
USGAO (United States General Accounting Office). (2001). *Report to the Chairman, Committee on Foreign Relations, U.S. Senate: The International Monetary Fund – Few Changes Evident in New Landing Program for Poor Countries*. Washington, DC: USGAO.
Venkateswarlu, D. (2003). *Child Labour and Trans-National Seed Companies in Hybrid Cottonseed Production in Andhra Pradesh*. Glocal Research and Consultancy Services, Hyderabad. http://www.indianet.nl/Cotton_seeds.doc.
Walker, N. (2012). 'Outcry and child labour behind surgical tools'. *Scotland on Sunday*, 30 June.
White, B. (1996). 'Globalization and the Child Labour Problem'. *Journal of International Development* 8(6): 829–39.
Wilton, B. (2013). 'How Can we Truly Eliminate the Scourge of the Worst Forms of Child Labour?' IOE Press Statement, 28 February. http://www.ioe-emp.org/fileadmin/ioe_documents/publications/Policy%20Areas/child_labour/EN/_2013-02-28__G-168_IOE_Secretary-General_on_eliminating_the_scourge_of_the_worst_forms_of_child_labour.pdf.
World Bank. (2001). *World Development Report for 2000/2001: Attacking Poverty*. New York: Oxford University Press.
World Bank. (2003). 'Labor standards and their role in economic development'. Press Release, 12 February. http://web.worldbank.org/WBSITE/EXTERNAL/NEWS/0,,contentMDK:20091472~menuPK:34457~pagePK:34370~piPK:34424~theSitePK:4607,00.html (accessed 2 August 2004).

World Bank. (2009). *Doing Business: Comparing Regulation in 181 Economies*. Washington, DC: Palgrave Macmillan. http://www.doingbusiness.org/Documents/FullReport/2009/DB_2009_English.pdf (accessed 14 July 2009).

World Bank. (2011). *No Small Matter: The Impact of Poverty, Shocks, and Human Capital Investments in Early Childhood Development*. Washington, DC: World Bank. http://siteresources.worldbank.org/EDUCATION/Resources/278200-1298568319076/nosmallmatter.pdf.

Zeitlin, M. (2012). 'Kaushik Basu: A Renegade Thinker Arrives at the World Bank'. *Newsweek* (International edition), 260(13): 24 September.

16
Saving the Children?
Pornography, Childhood and the Internet

David Buckingham and Despina Chronaki

In May 2013, the Office of the Children's Commissioner for England published a report entitled *'Basically ... porn is everywhere': A Rapid Evidence Assessment on the Effect that Access and Exposure to Pornography has on Children and Young People* (Horvath et al. 2013). Produced by a team of psychologists from three English universities, the report was accompanied by a press release that began as follows:

> The Office of the Children's Commissioner for England is calling for urgent action to develop children's resilience to pornography following a research report it commissioned which found that: a significant number of children access pornography; it influences their attitudes towards relationships and sex; it is linked to risky behaviour such as having sex at a younger age; and there is a correlation between holding violent attitudes and accessing more violent media.
>
> The report ... also found that:
>
> - Children and young people's exposure and access to pornography occurs both on and offline but in recent years the most common method of access is via internet enabled technology
> - Exposure and access to pornography increases with age
> - Accidental exposure to pornography is more prevalent than deliberate access
> - There are gender differences in exposure and access to pornography with boys more likely to be exposed to and deliberately access, seek or use pornography than girls.
>
> It concludes that there are still many unanswered questions about the affect [*sic*] exposure to pornography has on children: a situation the Office of the Children's Commissioner considers requires urgent action in an age where extreme violent and sadistic imagery is two clicks away.[1]

Predictably, the report received extensive media coverage. While much of this simply filleted the press release, it also tended to accentuate the interpretation that was placed on the report by the Children's Commissioner, Maggie Atkinson: her identification of pornography with 'extreme violent and sadistic imagery' and her assertion that young people were being 'raised on a diet of pornography' were headlined in several newspapers, although neither of these claims is made in the report itself. Such stories were often accompanied by pictures of fresh-faced young children – typically aged around seven or eight – gazing into computer screens. Reading this coverage, and listening to radio phone-ins and workplace discussions later that day, it appeared that definitive evidence had finally been obtained: pornography was indisputably harmful to children, and now something would have to be done about it.

Over the ensuing weeks, the issue of children and pornography recurred on the news agenda in several forms. The murders of five-year-old April Jones in Wales and 12-year-old Tia Sharp in London were both linked to the killers' use of child pornography. Google was berated for launching a 'porn app' for its new Glass device, and promptly withdrew it. Teachers were issued with a guide on how to curb the new craze of 'sexting' – the sharing of explicit images (often of one's own body) through mobile phones and the Internet. John Carr, the government's leading adviser on Internet safety, called for search engines to proactively block child pornography, and was supported by the Business Secretary, Vince Cable. Newspaper columnists and editorial writers – from the ultra-conservative Melanie Phillips of the *Daily Mail* to the traditionally liberal *Guardian* – called unanimously for Internet pornography (and not only child pornography) to be banned forthwith.

These stories mark another flare-up in what has been a growing concern about these issues in public debate in Britain over the past several years. Following the last Labour government's review of research on 'the sexualisation of young people' (Home Office 2010), the incoming Coalition government commissioned the Chief Executive of the Mother's Union, Reg Bailey, to produce a report entitled *Letting Children Be Children* (Department for Education 2011). In addition to proposing curbs on 'sexualised' clothing (as discussed by Jane Pilcher elsewhere in this volume), it also presented a set of policy recommendations designed to restrict children's exposure to sexual content in media such as music videos and men's magazines. Meanwhile, the Christian group SaferMedia has waged a highly successful 'Block Porn Campaign' focusing on children's access to pornography; and it has been supported by the influential voice of the *Daily Mail*, with headlines like 'Online porn is turning children into sex attackers' (13 June 2012) and 'Children grow up addicted to online porn sites' (18 April 2012), as well as 'confessionals' such as 'How internet porn turned my beautiful boy into a hollow, self-hating shell' (19 April 2012). Just as this chapter was being written, the *Mail* was reporting on a proposed 'summit' at which the Culture Secretary, Maria Miller, would be calling Internet service providers to account. Its front-page headline quoted from an interview with Prime Minister David Cameron: 'PORN: PM'S FEAR FOR HIS CHILDREN. I worry they'll see online filth, he says. So NOW will he act?' (17 June 2013). And lurking in the background of this increasingly febrile debate is the figure of the predatory paedophile, most spectacularly in the form of a whole series of children's entertainers – starting with the late DJ and presenter Jimmy Savile – whose abuse of children in the 1960s and 1970s came to light over several months in 2012 and 2013.

What's the problem?

The intensity of these debates clearly reflects the broader issues that are at stake here. The combination of childhood and sexuality is always especially inflammatory (as David Rudd suggests elsewhere in this volume in relation to children's literature). At least since the time of the Romantics, children have been assumed to be necessarily and inherently asexual: childhood innocence is premised on the notion that children are ignorant of sex, and do not experience sexual feelings or desires. As Stevi Jackson (1982) and others note, sexuality is a key dimension of the distinction between childhood and adulthood: despite Freud's 'discovery' of infantile sexuality, the image of the sexual (or 'sexualised') child fundamentally threatens our sense of what children should be. Representations of children that seem to suggest otherwise are especially scandalous (Higonnet 1998). James Kincaid's work on images of children in nineteenth-century art and literature (Kincaid 1992) is particularly troubling in this respect: it implies that the post-Romantic construction of the innocent child is itself a manifestation of an unspoken (and unspeakable) adult desire.

Anxieties around this issue have a long history. Danielle Egan and Gail Hawkes (2007, 2010; Hawkes and Egan 2008) have traced the history of concerns about childhood sexuality, for example in campaigns around 'child purity' in the late nineteenth century, the 'social hygiene' movement of the early twentieth century and the childrearing manuals of the 1930s and 1940s. There is an extensive body of literature on the prevention of masturbation, the need for regimes of bodily privation that will curb young people's sensuality, and especially the need to restrain the sexual agency and expression of working-class girls. As Egan and Hawkes suggest, these concerns have been reinforced by the medicalisation of childhood sexuality: the authority and expertise of developmental psychologists, physicians and sexologists are drawn upon to justify the close supervision and regulation of children's sexual instincts. Egan and Hawkes argue that such concerns reflect a strange ambivalence about childhood sexuality: it is both denied (because children are deemed to be innocent) and yet seen as a potentially unstoppable force once it is 'released' by external corrupting influences. And of course, as Foucault (1978) argues, all this discourse about children and sexuality merely serves to inflame the desires that it seeks to repress.

This well-established set of concerns seems to have taken a distinctively modern turn with the emergence of new concerns about risk. Again, there are much broader issues at stake here, expressed in Ulrich Beck's widely cited notion of the 'risk society' (Beck 1992), or in Anthony Giddens's claim that discourse about risk has become much more prevalent as modern societies have become more uncertain about the future (Giddens 1991). This growing preoccupation with risk can be seen as a manifestation of what Foucault terms 'governmentality' (Lupton 1999). New technologies and strategies for risk management and risk avoidance are developed in order to encourage people to regulate their own behaviour, and to become self-policing. People are apparently empowered to make their own choices, but they are also required to take responsibility for the consequences of those choices – although in the case of children, it is largely parents who are required to exercise choice and responsibility on behalf of children themselves.

Inevitably, children have come to occupy a special place in these discourses about risk and safety. As Allison James and Adrian James (2008) suggest, the prominence of this issue is symptomatic of the changing cultural politics of childhood, at least in the UK: it can be seen to reflect a kind of backlash against the assertion of the child as a social actor. Here, children are seen to be 'at risk', but also as 'risky', as a threat to others, especially as they get older. This framing of childhood in terms of risk is apparent in a whole range of areas, including criminal justice, welfare policy, health and safety, the regulation of public space, education – and the media. As Stevi Jackson and Sue Scott suggest: 'Childhood is increasingly being constructed as a precious realm under siege from those who would rob children of their childhoods, and as being subverted from within by children who refuse to remain childlike' (1999: 86).

Again, these broad issues have been widely addressed elsewhere – not least by other contributors to this book. Our suggestion here is that the concern about children and pornography can be seen in similar terms. As is so often the case in such debates, children's own voices and perspectives are conspicuous by their absence. In the second half of this chapter, we seek to make good some of this absence by drawing on our own research about children's and young people's interpretations of sexual content in media, and specifically of pornography. Yet we need to begin by considering how the issue is typically framed within the public debate. How is the 'problem' of children-and-pornography socially and discursively constructed? And what evidence do we actually have about it?

As will already be apparent, this is a debate in which inflated rhetoric tends to take the place of careful analysis. Despite the cautious conclusions of the Children's Commissioner's report, it was her repeated line about children 'raised on a diet of porn' that made the headlines. The suggestion that young children are bombarded, depraved and corrupted by a relentless tide of electronic filth has become an axiom of public debate. Even so, it is too easy – and actually quite misleading – to dismiss this as merely another 'moral panic' (see Buckingham and Jensen 2012). The concern about children and pornography is not an irrational fuss about nothing: it is a response to social, cultural and technological change that deserves to be taken seriously. However, taking it seriously entails a clear and rigorous definition of the issues, and a hard look at the evidence. It is to these that we now turn.

Defining (and not defining) terms

The first difficulty here is to do with the lack of clarity about the foci of concern: 'pornography' and 'children'. Obviously, 'pornography' can be defined in various ways: one person's erotica is another person's pornography. In this case, however, there is another, more specific confusion in the wider debate, between *child* pornography – that is, pornography designed for adult consumption, featuring the sexual abuse of children – and children's consumption of mainstream 'adult' pornography. Child pornography is, of course, illegal; pornography featuring adults, and designed for (and consumed by) them, is not. In mainstream media (television, film/video, computer games etc.), there are age-based classification systems backed up by various forms of regulation and legislation designed to prevent children's access to such material (although such systems do not generally operate online).

A further confusion here is between pornography and violence. We would not deny that some pornography features representations of violence – although 'violence' is another somewhat ill-defined term in these debates. However, to blur the distinction – as the Children's Commissioner does in her press release – is highly problematic. The common implication here is that all – or at least a large proportion – of pornography is 'violent and sadistic' or that it contains (as the Deputy Children's Commissioner suggests in her preface to the report) significant amounts of 'rape, bestiality [and] the use of pain and humiliation'. We do not know of any research that establishes this, and the Children's Commissioner's report does not cite any; indeed there are some large-scale analyses of pornographic content that directly show otherwise (Williams 1999). Of course, there are some feminists who believe that all acts of heterosexual sex in real life must necessarily entail violence and coercion, since heterosexual sex is *by definition* a manifestation of patriarchal oppression (e.g., MacKinnon 1989). We do not take this view, and we find the implication that pornography is inherently or predominantly 'violent and sadistic' highly improbable. It should also be noted that the possession of so-called 'extreme' pornography depicting rape or 'life-threatening injury' is illegal in the UK.

A further confusion here is around the term 'children' or 'young people'. It is a very different matter for, let's say, a five-year-old or a 15-year-old to be exposed to pornography, although both are legally 'children'. A five-year-old is only likely to do so accidentally; a 15-year-old might well actively seek it out. Children of different ages will obviously have different levels of knowledge and experience of sex, which they will have gleaned from various sources. As we shall see below, there is little evidence that very young children are accessing online pornography to any significant extent – although the more adults talk about the issue, the more their curiosity might be aroused. Equally, most parents are likely to respond to their children's exposure to pornography in very different ways depending on the age of the children. Here again, there is a need for much greater precision about the exact nature of the concern.

Yet whether or not they are deliberate, these confusions serve strategic purposes for those who seek to restrict children's access to the Internet, and who wish to ban pornography in general. Associating children's access to mainstream pornography with *child* pornography – a practice that is illegal and undeniably harmful to the children involved – significantly raises the stakes in favour of greater regulation. Asserting that pornography predominantly involves sadistic violence also makes it much harder to resist the call for censorship – again despite the fact that such material is already proscribed. And focusing the discussion on children – when the main audience for pornography is adults – equally serves to make the case significantly more persuasive. We are not implying that there is any kind of deliberate deception being practised here, let alone that there is no cause for concern: we are simply suggesting that we need to be much clearer as regards what it is that we should be concerned *about*.

A body of evidence?

The second key issue here is to do with evidence. Press reporting – and the Children's Commissioner's press release itself – gives the impression of a substantial weight of evidence all pointing in the same direction. In fact, there has been hardly any research on the effects of pornography on children. For obvious ethical reasons, almost all the research has been conducted with adults (especially, for some strange reason, college students from Midwestern American universities). Given that we might expect significant differences between adults and children – in terms of knowledge and experience, as well as understanding – in this field, there are significant limitations in the extent to which we can generalise from research with adults and apply it to children. While some recent European studies have focused on teenagers (e.g., Peter and Valkenburg 2008), we would also argue that there are problems in extending these findings to children in general.

There is some evidence about children's *self-reported access* to pornography; and some evidence from questionnaires about how they feel about this. We will consider this below, but it should be emphasised that this research tells us nothing at all about *effects*, whether harmful or otherwise. Some of these surveys (albeit mainly those with adults) report evidence of *associations* between access to pornography and particular sexual attitudes, beliefs or behaviours, but they do not establish any *causal relationships*. It is surely not outlandish to suggest that people who are particularly interested in sex are more likely to seek out pornographic content; but it is clearly absurd to infer from this that it is porn that *makes* them more likely to be 'promiscuous' or to have 'permissive' attitudes.

To be fair, the authors of the Children's Commissioner's report are quite clear about this – and they are especially cautious about the claims relating to the effects of media violence. In this respect, they are in line with earlier reviews, such as those produced by Ofcom in 2005 and 2011, which found no clear or conclusive evidence that sexually explicit material 'impairs the development of minors' (Ofcom 2005, 2011). However, these distinctions are almost entirely obscured in the Commissioner's own statements and in the ensuing media coverage, where the issue is framed very strongly in terms of 'influence'. Indeed, we would argue that this basic confusion between correlation and causality is a persistent characteristic of media reporting of social science research – and this is perhaps especially the case in relation to the effects of media violence. As a result, the issue comes to be framed in terms of a simplistic cause-and-effect logic: it is porn that *makes* children do or think bad things.

When we look at the research that *does* explore children's access to pornography, we find a picture that is rather at odds with that dominating the public debate. The key study here is the *EU Kids Online* research, a massive 25-country project funded by the European Commission's Safer Internet programme (Livingstone et al. 2011). We have some significant reservations about the conceptual biases of this research – and particularly its framing of the topic in terms of a binary of 'risk' versus 'opportunity'. The study starts from an assumption that pornography is *by definition* 'risky' (Hasebrink et al. 2009) – which would seem to imply that it necessarily carries the potential of causing harm. Yet the research itself tells us nothing at all about effects or influence (whether harmful or beneficial), and does not seek to do so. The only harm that is identified is the possibility that children might be offended or upset by what they see – not that it might inform their attitudes or behaviour.

There is a further caveat here, to do with methodology. In common with all the other research in this field, this research relies on self-reporting – and there are all sorts of reasons why, in this area in particular, self-reporting may not be reliable. While the analysis of qualitative interviews has yet to be published (as of the writing of this chapter), the quantitative studies have involved administering questionnaires in which children are interrogated by adults at enormous length (77 pages of questions) about their experience of sexual content online. Children cannot fail to gain a strong impression that there is a problem here, and this seems likely to result in over-reporting, both of negative responses to such content and perhaps also of the degree of exposure to it. Unfortunately, there is no differentiation here between different types of sexual content, so it is hard to know whether the respondents' definitions of 'pornography' coincide with those of the researchers.

As such, this is research that appears – both conceptually and methodologically – inclined to feed the concern about harmful influence. Yet what we find here is rather different. Only 23 per cent of the sample (aged 9–16) reported having seen pornography (in any medium) in the past year; and only 2 per cent had seen anything that combined sex with violence. These figures were higher for older children: the numbers of younger children who reported having done so are very low. Fourteen per cent of the sample claimed they had seen sexual content online (only slightly more than had done so offline, in other media); and only 4 per cent (and 3 per cent in UK) said they had seen it and been 'bothered' by it, with younger children in the majority here. (The term 'bothered' is a rather inclusive and strange term in this context; but it is worth noting again that children were repeatedly asked whether such material 'bothers' them, rather than if they found it funny or educational or informative, for example – or indeed asked *why* they were 'bothered'.) Of the small minority who said they were 'bothered', the large majority said that they 'got over it straight away'; and participants reported a range of strategies for dealing with such material, including deleting it, reporting it, blocking the person who sent it, and changing their filter settings.

Where does this leave us? We would agree with the Children's Commissioner's report that some children do see pornography, both online and offline; that this tends to begin in the early teenage years, and increases with age; and that boys are generally more inclined to do so than girls, and to feel more positive about it. We would also agree that much of the exposure to pornography is accidental or unwanted rather than deliberate – although much of it might well be motivated by curiosity, or a wish to appear 'adult' or 'cool' for the benefit of peers. We do not know whether children's access to pornography has increased historically, but it seems entirely reasonable to assume that it has, both because of technological changes and because of the growth of the pornography industry.

However, what we do *not* know is whether and how pornography influences young people's sexual attitudes and behaviour. Of course, it is likely that young people *learn* from pornography, in both positive and negative ways: they might learn false beliefs or risky behaviour, but they might also learn useful information that is not so easily available elsewhere. Yet there is very little evidence about what they learn; about the relative significance of pornography as compared with other potential sources of learning; about how long-lasting or robust such learning might be; or more generally about how people make use of the *meanings* they derive from pornography in attempting to understand their real-life experiences.

The facts of life?

Some years ago, research by David Buckingham and Sara Bragg (2003, 2004) sought to develop a more child-centred perspective on these issues, albeit in relation to 'mainstream' sexual content (pre-watershed TV, teen magazines, advertising, music videos) rather than pornography as such. This research included a large-scale survey, as well as focus groups and creative approaches designed to enable children to explore the issues on their own terms. Three main points can be drawn from this work here.

First, we found that the media do not tell children a single, straightforward story about sex and relationships. Despite some of the more alarmist public commentary, children are not being confronted with endless incitements to promiscuity or unsafe sex: they are also seeing messages that warn them about the dangers of sex, that show a variety of different types of relationships, and that define what is sexy, or what being sexual is all about, in very diverse ways. In effect, the media are offering children mixed messages about sex, and children are having to make their own way through this material. In their efforts to make sense of these contradictory messages, they are also making decisions about how far they want to remain a child or to become an adult – and indeed what kind of an adult they want to be. While this might be seen as liberating in some respects, it could also be seen as a burden.

Second, children are not uncritically consuming this material. On the contrary, we found that they were making complex judgements – for example about what is realistic and what isn't, or indeed what they should trust and what they shouldn't. They are comparing what they see in the media with what they see in real life, including what parents and teachers tell them and what they see parents and teachers doing (which are not necessarily always the same thing). They are using their media literacy – their knowledge of how media work, of how television programmes (for example) are made, how stories and characters are constructed, and the conventions of particular media genres. They are not treating the media as a window on the world or an infallible guide to behaviour.

Third, it was found that children can have a variety of emotional responses to sexual content. They can find it exciting and fascinating, but they can also find it disgusting and shocking. Many of the children in our research claimed that they already knew all about sex – or at least much more than their parents thought they did; but they also often claimed that there were things they didn't want to see, even things that they felt they were not ready for. They also said they did not want to come across such things unexpectedly, or when they had not chosen to do so. As this implies, children learn to regulate their own emotional responses, and to talk about them (or not talk about them), in different ways in different settings. Yet ultimately, they do not perceive this in terms of risk: there might be a risk of seeing things that you don't like, or that you find gross or disgusting, but children develop ways of handling such experiences.

Learning about (and from) pornography

While Buckingham and Bragg's research relates primarily to 'mainstream' sexual content, at least some of the findings could well be extended to children's experiences with more explicit or pornographic material. Pornography is a media genre with its own rules and conventions. Here again, we might expect children to become more critical or 'media literate' consumers over time, and to find ways of coping with experiences that might prove shocking or upsetting.

Despina Chronaki's ongoing doctoral research is based on a qualitative study of how people account for their early experiences with sexual content. Twenty-seven young adults (aged 17-22) from three European countries have been asked to talk retrospectively about these experiences during in-depth, face-to-face interviews. Rather than gathering responses to predefined topics on a questionnaire, the research aims to explore how these young people perceive and define the issues at stake in their own terms – including what they themselves define as 'pornographic' in the first place. We start from the assumption that talking about sex in a social setting like that of a research interview is a social performance, where different identities and selves are constructed and projected via assertions of different types of knowledge. Beginning from a basic thematic analysis of the young people's accounts, the study moves on to look at the cultural, ethical and political discourses that they invoke in explaining their responses. Finally, it looks at how the young people define and represent the experience of pornography within a broader personal narrative about their upbringing, sexual development and sexual culture. This threefold analysis addresses key questions about how young people learn to govern their sexual and ethical conduct, which have largely been ignored in research thus far.

In relation to the aims of this chapter, we want to focus on the particular issue of 'literacy' – that is, how young people come to learn about pornography and about sexuality more broadly, by developing and combining different kinds of knowledge and competency. The issue of children's 'porn literacy' has arisen as one potential response to public concern about the issue: while regulation or censorship of the Internet is seen by many as a lost cause, it is argued that children need to be equipped with the means to understand their likely experience of pornography, to cope emotionally with it, and to regulate their own responses – and that schools and parents need to assist them with this (Burns 2013). So how much and what exactly do young people know about pornography? What does their assumed 'porn literacy' consist of, and how 'porn literate' are they?

Clearly, the media are not young people's only source of information about sex. Several participants in this study discussed how they learnt about sex at school, usually during sex education lessons:

I was taught all this at school – so we did have, like sexual health classes at school. So obviously we learn about sex, how to have safe sex and that. (George, 17)

As George's comment implies, sex is often framed in terms of health when discussed at school. Sexual health is a contested matter when it comes to pornography, where sexual activity is assumed to be casual, between people who are not engaged in a romantic relationship, and where people do not engage in sex with just one partner (Peter and Valkenburg 2008). It is also risky, because in the majority of representations people are having unprotected sex. In this sense, school provides a regulatory framework for understanding sexuality in terms of health. However, such knowledge is not imposed on young people: rather, it is presented in terms of a personal choice between a healthy sex life and an unhealthy one.

Knowledge about sex is also generated within the family. Even secrecy about sex is some sort of indication that affection, intimacy or romance may result in something complex and potentially problematic like sex, a kind of experience that only adults are assumed to have. In this context, pornography may help to fill gaps in knowledge – although this potentially educational function is typically ignored in mainstream psychological research:

Parents don't talk at all about it [sex], so you don't know even the basics if you don't watch sexual content [in media]. (Maria-Eleni, 19)

In other cases, however, parents do talk about sex and consider this process a necessary parental responsibility:

I have talked about it when I was younger, when we had that, 'obviously we need to talk to you before you go to bed with anybody, a talk about the flower and the bee', or whatever you call it. (Elisabeth, 19)

Parents and teachers are typically allocated the role of safeguarding children's well-being and morality; and in several cases in this sample, this was informed by religious beliefs. Religiosity is also a factor that psychological research has prioritised as an effective means to support young people's 'battle' against pornography (Hardy et al. 2013). However, religion can restrict young people's access to knowledge about sex:

> *I don't really hear discussions about porn, I think ... I guess for me that I'm from a more Christian environment and we rarely talk about that.* (Laura, 20)

The construction of sexuality as sinful – or more broadly as a moral issue, subject to confession – has a long history, and for many people religion continues to provide the most prominent discursive framework for understanding sex. Even where religious beliefs are not explicit, sexuality is still predominantly conceptualised in terms of ethics – as Trine (18) put it, 'it's something that you've always been taught, what's right and what isn't'. These arguments are also informed by dominant psychological assumptions about young people – the notion that their minds are particularly 'impressionable' and hence that their attitudes or behaviour are more likely to be influenced by external forces such as pornography.

However, pornography is a form of *mediated representation*: it operates according to particular codes and conventions, and it uses particular formal techniques and devices to guarantee (or to proclaim) its veracity. As with other media genres, viewers learn to make judgements about its authenticity and credibility, and hence its trustworthiness as a potential guide to behaviour in real life. Individuals make judgements about these matters based partly on their understanding of the process of representation itself, and partly on their understanding of reality and of their own experience; and they are informed in this respect by their education and upbringing. As John (18) suggests, in pornography:

> *... people always are playing towards a camera, if you know what I mean ... But it's like, I've always seen it as fake and I've been told by my mum and dad and stuff like that.*

This process of making judgements is learned gradually, from an early age:

> *I don't really remember, there was always a kind of knowledge you know. I mean, even when watching a kiss on TV you were thinking that something romantic or erotic was going on.* (Eva, 22)

As this implies, children do not come to the media as blank slates, without any knowledge of sex: rather, there is a continuing process of learning about intimacy, love and sexuality, in which children draw upon a range of sources both in mediated representations and in real life (for example, through observing the relationships of their parents, siblings and peers). Even from a young age, children are actively interpreting representations of intimacy such as kissing, hugging or implied sexual activity. At the same time, they also become aware of the moral debates that surround these representations:

There's always a massive debate whether it should be right or wrong, especially when there are young children or people that are vulnerable. (Ellie, 17)

As Ellie's comment implies, there is often a 'third person effect' that is characteristic of discussions of the influence of media communication (see Davison 1983): it is always *others* with 'more impressionable minds' than oneself who are deemed to be at risk. In distancing herself from these others, and in positioning herself as one who has moved beyond the problematic category of childhood, Ellie seeks to establish her own legitimacy in discussing the issue of pornography.

The participants here had encountered sexual content in a range of media, and were inclined to believe that it was more widely available today than in their own childhoods:

Like, even on TV during the day, you sometimes see that stuff. It's magazines in the drawer. (Nikolas, 19)

Among this sample of young people, who had grown up with access to the Internet at home, five respondents actually had their first experiences with sexual content in the form of photographs, while another five had later experiences with videos (mostly having deliberately sought them out), and two with short stories. Several had their first experiences with online advertisements for sex services, which they had mostly come across accidentally or been sent without having requested them:

They were proper emails, these are pictures of full-on hardcore porn, kind of like ... it'd be like, men inserting their penis into women, like pictures of them. (Kelly, 20)

I saw all the pictures he [my brother] had saved came up like Google, MSN pictures, and there was a naked lady. (Don, 21)

However, as several of these participants suggested, such representations could also be encountered offline, in other media (such as magazines or television). Some – particularly males – had seen 'violent' sadomasochistic and fetishistic material, although they also tended to reject it as 'weird'. Overall, their experience of such material was diverse, in terms of both media form and content; and while more explicit material (and the representation of particular kinds of practices) was defined as 'pornographic', this was a flexible and sometimes quite hazy category.

This research therefore suggests that young people's interpretations of pornography, and their judgements about it, entail several kinds of knowledge or 'literacy'. There are forms of socio-cultural literacy that help to define what is sexual in the first place, what counts as an appropriate form of sexuality or sexual expression, and what constitutes an appropriate sexual relationship (for example, in terms of ideas about romance, trust or commitment). Then there is a more specific form of sexual literacy that relates to biology and physical health, for example in relation to practising safe sex. Finally, as Buckingham and Bragg (2004) suggest, there is a form of media literacy at stake here, as young people mobilise their knowledge about how media texts are constructed and about the conventions of different media genres, and make judgements about realism, aesthetics and cultural value. These diverse forms of literacy provide the interpretative frameworks through which young people make sense of representations of sexuality, including pornography. However, these representations are themselves quite diverse: rather than assuming that 'pornography' is a single, agreed category, we find that young people perceive and understand the range of sexual representations they encounter in quite diverse ways, according to their different varieties of socio-cultural, sexual and media literacy. They also recognise that these representations can serve different functions for different people, and provide different opportunities for both pleasure and learning.

Seeking solutions

In this chapter, we have offered what we hope is a more considered and proportionate response to the public concern about children and pornography. We have emphasised the need to be clear about the actual focus of concern, and to take account of the available evidence – and to take seriously the experiences and perspectives of children and young people themselves. We have emphasised the fact that young people are not passive victims of such material, but that they interpret and evaluate it in diverse and complex ways. Yet, having considered all this, the key question remains: what is to be done?

We need to begin from the recognition that pornography (however defined) is a fact of life, and has always been so. After all, the original term, πορνεία (porneia), is ancient Greek. Explicit sexual representations have existed – or have had to be suppressed – in all recorded societies. However hard we might try to keep children away from the 'secrets' of the adult world, it is inevitable that they will encounter pornography sooner or later. Nevertheless, we would accept that there is a new issue here, or at least a significant shift in scale. The Internet and other digital media clearly do afford much easier access; and the production and distribution of pornography – in both professional and amateur forms – has grown significantly in recent years.

There are some good reasons for concern about pornography. Even if there is limited evidence about the harm that it causes to its *users*, it remains the case that – as in many other industries – people may be harmed and exploited in the course of its production. As with other cultural products, some pornography is likely to be seen by some people as offensive; and they have a right to be able to avoid it, or restrict their own access to it. Equally, there is evidence that some (although by no means all) sex criminals use pornography, perhaps as an outlet but perhaps also as fuel for their fantasies. Whether this causes them to commit crimes that they would otherwise not have committed is less clear: the incidence of child abuse and rape long predates the modern pornography industry, and both thrive in situations where pornography is barely available. Meanwhile, rapists and paedophiles may well be sexually aroused by material that none of us would meaningfully categorise as pornographic.

Even so, pornography is not going to go away, and it is misleading – even irresponsible – to suggest that it might do. It is certainly possible for governments to attempt to regulate the Internet, but it is unlikely that they will prove especially successful in doing so. At the time of writing (mid-2013), UK policy makers are actively exploring the possibility of blocking Internet content that they deem to be harmful to children. Claire Perry MP – appointed by the current Prime Minister David Cameron as his special adviser on 'preventing the sexualisation and commercialization of childhood' – has been a particularly vocal advocate of online filtering systems. A Bill designed to introduce automatic blocking of online pornography received its first reading in the House of Lords in May 2013, and was supported by the National Association of Headteachers; while in the same month, the government promised that public wifi would be 'porn free' by the end of the year.

In our view, such technological solutions are unlikely to prove effective. It is possible to block and to monitor access; but it is also relatively easy to evade such restrictions. Perhaps more significantly, there is no accepted definition of what should be banned, and it is unlikely that one will be agreed – or indeed that any such blocking software would respond in sufficiently sensitive ways to the diverse needs of users. It is worth emphasising again that child pornography and 'extreme' violent pornography are already banned: they exist, but there are significant penalties for those who are found to possess them. It is very unclear how and in what terms such legislation might be extended to pornography or sexual representations in general, even though there are some who would like this. The notion that anything deemed potentially harmful to children might be banned for the entire adult population is unlikely to win general support.

In this context, we are left with the classic liberal response: education. Despite the alarmist spin placed upon the Children's Commissioner's report, its recommendations in this respect are for the most part eminently pedagogical. The Department for Education is urged to promote the integration of discussions of pornography (and of Internet safety) into sex and relationships education 'as a means of building young people's resilience', alongside a wider national awareness-raising campaign. If such educational initiatives are designed in a way that allows for open debate, that avoids moralistic panics, and that takes account of the range of 'literacies' children are likely to possess, they should undoubtedly command support – although they would take us well beyond much of what passes for sex and relationships education in schools today.

However, the obvious problem with such an educational approach is that it appears to pass the buck to teachers. In the days following the publication of the Children's Commissioner's report, there was much public alarm about the possibility of teachers discussing pornography with young children. Without adequate training and support for teachers, and amid a climate of growing public hysteria, this educational response seems unlikely to resolve the controversy. We fully expect that calls to control the Internet in the name of children will continue to intensify in the coming years.

Note

1. http://www.childrenscommissioner.gov.uk/content/press_release/content_505.

References

Beck, U. (1992). *Risk Society: Towards a New Modernity*. London: Sage.
Buckingham, D. and Bragg, S. (2003). *Young People, Media and Personal Relationships*. London: Broadcasting Standards Commission.
Buckingham, D. and Bragg, S. (2004). *Young People, Sex and the Media: The Facts of Life?* Basingstoke: Palgrave Macmillan.
Buckingham, D. and Jensen. H. (2012). 'Beyond "media panics": Reconceptualising Public Debates about Children and Media'. *Journal of Children and Media* 6(4): 413–29.
Burns, J. (2013). 'Schools "should teach how to view porn", sex forum says'. BBC News Online: www.bbc.co.uk/news/education-22308393 (accessed 17 June 2013).
Davison, W. P. (1983). 'The Third Person Effect in Communication'. *Public Opinion Quarterly* 47(1): 1–15.
Department for Education. (2011). *Letting Children Be Children*. London: Department for Education.
Egan, R. D. and Hawkes, G. L. (2007). 'Producing the Prurient through the Pedagogy of Purity: Childhood Sexuality and the Social Purity Movement'. *Journal of Historical Sociology* 20(4): 443–61.
Egan, R. D. and Hawkes, G. L. (2010). *Theorizing the Sexual Child in Modernity*. London: Palgrave Macmillan.
Foucault, M. (1978). *The History of Sexuality, Volume 1*. Harmondsworth: Penguin.
Giddens, A. (1991). *The Consequences of Modernity*. Cambridge: Polity Press.
Hardy, S. A., Steelman, M. A., Coyne, S. M. and Ridge, R. D. (2013). 'Adolescent Religiousness as a Protective Factor against Pornography Use'. *Journal of Applied Developmental Psychology* 34(3): 131–9.

Hasebrink, U., Livingstone, S., Haddon, L. and Ólafsson, K. (eds). (2009). *Comparing Children's Online Opportunities and Risks across Europe: Cross-national Comparisons for EU Kids Online* (2nd edn). London: London School of Economics.
Hawkes, G. L. and Egan, R. D. (2008). 'Developing the Sexual Child'. *Journal of Historical Sociology* 21(4): 443–65.
Higonnet, A. (1998). *Pictures of Innocence: The History and Crisis of Ideal Childhood.* London: Thames & Hudson.
Home Office. (2010). *The Sexualisation of Young People.* London: Home Office.
Horvath, M. A. H, Alys, L., Massey, K., Pina, A., Scally, M. and Adler, J. R. (2013). *'Basically, porn is everywhere': A Rapid Evidence Assessment on the Effect that Access and Exposure to Pornography has on Children and Young People.* London: Office of the Children's Commissioner.
Jackson, S. (1982). *Childhood and Sexuality.* Oxford: Blackwell.
Jackson, S. and Scott, S. (1999). 'Risk Anxiety and the Social Construction of Childhood'. In D. Lupton (ed.), *Risk and Sociocultural Theory: New Directions and Perspectives.* Cambridge: Cambridge University Press, pp. 86–107.
James, A. and James, A. (2008). 'Changing Childhood in the UK: Reconstructing Discourses of "Risk" and "Protection"'. In A. James and A. James (eds), *European Childhoods: Cultures, Politics and Childhoods in the European Union.* Basingstoke: Palgrave Macmillan, pp. 105–28.
Kincaid, J. (1992). *Child Loving: The Erotic Child and Victorian Culture.* London: Routledge.
Livingstone, S., Haddon, L., Görizig, A. and Ólafsson, K. (2011). *Risk and Safety on the Internet: The Perspective of European Children.* London: London School of Economics.
Lupton, D. (1999). 'Introduction: Risk and Sociocultural Theory'. In D. Lupton (ed.), *Risk and Sociocultural Theory: New Directions and Perspectives.* Cambridge: Cambridge University Press, pp. 1–11.
MacKinnon, C. A. (1989). 'Sexuality, Pornography, and Method: "Pleasure under Patriarchy"'. *Ethics* 99(2): 314–46.
Ofcom. (2005). *R18 Material: Its Potential Impact on People Under 18: An Overview of the Available Literature.* London: Ofcom.
Ofcom. (2011). *Sexually Explicit Material and Video on Demand Services.* London: Ofcom.
Peter, J. and Valkenburg, P. M. (2008). 'Adolescents' Exposure to Sexually Explicit Internet Material, Sexual Uncertainty, and Attitudes Toward Uncommitted Sexual Exploration: Is There a Link?'. *Communication Research* 35: 579.
Williams, L. (1999). *Hardcore: Power, Pleasure and the 'Frenzy of the Visible'.* Berkeley: University of California Press.

Index

2011: Findings on the Worst Forms of Child Labor (US Dept. of Labor report, 2012) 276

Abraham Moss High School, Manchester 187
Abu Ghraib (prison, Baghdad) 70
Action for Children's Television (pressure group) 243
Adorno, Theodor 244
Advergaming 248
Aga Khan Foundation 289
Against Hyper-sexualisation (book) 260
Alanen, Leena x
Aliens Love Underpants (book) 130
All Must Have Prizes (book) 192, 194
Allen, Graham 214–15, 218
Almond, David 127–8
American Psychological Association 260
Amis, Martin 131
Anderson, M.T. 133
Angel (song) 35
Anti-Academies Alliance 192
Anti-Defamation League 42
Anti-Social Behaviour Act (2003) 148
Anti-Social Behaviour Orders ('ASBOs') 4, 125, 142–3, 148–9, 155
Apple (electronics corporation) 277
The Apprentice (TV programme) 112
Association of Teachers and Lecturers 187, 196
At Swim, Two Boys (book) 130
Atkinson, Maggie 195, 302
Attacking Poverty (World Bank World Development report for 2000-1) 285–6
Audit Commission 141
Auld, Lord 11
Australia Institute 260
Axon, Mrs Sue 167–9

Bad Boyz series 124
Baggini, Julian 93

Bailey, Reg/ report for Dept. for Education (2011) 251, 261–3, 268–9, 302
Balkan, Joel 243
Ball, Stephen J. 181–5
Balls, Ed 260
Barber, Benjamin 244
Barbie dolls 246
Barker, Steven 35–6
Barnado, Dr Thomas 102
Barnado's 61, 111, 168
Barnes, Julian 131
Barthes, Roland 179, 190
Basically...porn is everywhere (report by Office of the Children's Commissioner, 2013) 301
Basu, Kaushik 282
Bauman, Zygmunt 110, 244
Beck, Ulrich 119, 304
Beckford, Jasmine 29
The Bell Curve (book) 197
Benn, Melissa 184, 192
Bernstein, Basil 226
Best, Joel 70
Beveridge, William 90
Beyonce (singer) 266
Bhaskaran, Resmi 284
Big Brother (TV programme) 112, 134
Big Society, The (government slogan) 59
Billy Elliot (film) 128, 130
Bingham, Lord 10–12
Birbalsingh, Katharine 192
Bishop, John 107
Blackman, Marjorie 129
Blair, Cherie 128
Blair, Leo 128
Blair, Tony xii, xiii, 2, 3, 89–91, 93, 106, 109, 110, 114, 119, 121–3, 128, 140, 148, 179–80, 183–9, 191, 225
Block Porn Campaign 302
Blume, Judy 131
Blunkett, David 22, 184, 187–90, 234
Blyton, Enid 122
Bob the Builder (franchise) 247

The Book Thief (book)　129
Bono (singer)　102, 109, 111, 112, 113
Boomtown Rats, The (band)　108
Born to Buy (book)　243
Bousted, Mary　187
Boy Meets Boy (book)　130
The Boy in the Striped Pyjamas (book)　129
Boyce, Frank Cottrell　124
Boyne, John　129
Bragg, Sara　172, 263, 269, 309–10, 314
Brandchild (book)　244
Brandt Report (1980)　110
Brat Camp (TV programme)　120
Bratz dolls　246
Brave New World (book)　132
Breadline Britain in the 1990s (TV series, 1991)　103
Bretton Woods conference (1944)　278–9, 281, 283, 293, 295
Bridget Jones' Diary (book)　131
Brighouse, Tim　183, 188
British Retail Consortium　262
Broad, Robin　290
Broken Windows thesis　142
Brown, Gordon　xiii, 89–90, 109, 180, 230, 276
Brown, Philip　210
Browne Wilkinson, Lord　5–6
Bruer, John　215–16
Bruns, Axel　28
Buckingham, David　172, 263, 268, 269, 309–10, 314
Bulger, Denise　1
Bulger, James (murder case)　xiii, 1–25, 120, 141
Bulger, Ralph　1, 17–19
Burchill, Julie　130
Burgess, Melvin　131
Bush, George W.　72
Butler, Judith　80
Butler-Sloss, Dame Elizabeth　13–15
By the Sweat and Toil of Children (US Dept. of Labor report, 1995)　277
By The Time You Read This, I'll Be Dead (book)　132
Byatt, A.S.　124
Byron, Tanya　230–1

Cable, Vince　302
Callaghan, James　182
Camara, Dom Helder　101, 108
Cameron, David　303, 315
Cameron, David　xii, 90, 103, 196, 213, 261, 262
Campaign for State Education　192
Campbell, Alastair　179, 189, 190
Captain Underpants (book)　130
CARE International　289
Carey, Peter　124
Carlile Report (on physical restraint in custodial institutions, 2006)　147
Carlisle, Kimberley　29
Carr, A.P.　167
Carr, John　302
Casey, Louise　217
The Casual Vacancy (book)　131
The Catcher in the Rye (book)　126
Cato Institute　280
Celebrity Big Brother (TV programme)　112
Centre for Policy Studies　181
Centre for Social Justice　217
Changing Schools (pressure group)　192
Chernobyl (nuclear disaster, 1986)　119
child labour　275–96
child poverty　89–99, 101–14
Child Poverty Action Group　97
Child Poverty in Perspective (UNICEF report, 2007)　170
childhood/ adulthood (debate over blurred distinction between)　119–20, 228, 243, 259–63, 304, 315
Children Act (1978)　163
Children Act (1989)　58, 163, 167, 208
Children Act (2004)　163, 195
Children and Family Court Advisory and Support Service　54
Children in Hazardous work (ILO report, 2011)　276
Children in Need appeal　101
Children Under Siege (book)　243
children's literature　118–135
Children's Ombudsmen　169
Children's Plan (2007)　163
Children's Rights Alliance　168
Children's Society　209
Chin, Elizabeth　254
Chossudovsky, Michel　290

Christophe's Story (book)   129
Chronaki, Despina   310
Citizens Charter   182
Clapton, Eric (singer/guitarist)   35
Clarke, Ken   156–7
Clay (book)   128
Clegg, Nick   213
Cleveland (child abuse case)   29, 32
Climbie, Victoria (death of)   29, 31, 48, 53, 168
Cock & Bull (book)   131
Coffield, Frank   191
Cole, Babette   130
Collini, Stefan   179
Collins, Suzanne   134
Colwell, Maria (death of)   27–29, 31, 40
Comic Relief appeal   101, 112–13
commercial sexual exploitation of children (CSEC)   71–2
Common Assessment Framework (for children and young people)   51
competition states   181
Comprehensive Future (pressure group)   192
Connelly, Tracey   28, 35
Connolly, Peter ('Baby P', case of)   xii, xiii, 27–42, 45, 52–7, 60, 62, 168
Conservative Party   196, 261
Conservative-Liberal Democrat Coalition (2010)   45, 57–9, 107, 148, 180, 193, 195, 205, 213–14, 217, 232
Consumer Kids (book)   243
Consuming Children (book)   243
ContactPoint (government database)   51, 56–7
Cook, Daniel   xi, 243
Coram Boy (book)   133
Cosmic (book)   124
Couldry, Nick   112
Counting Stars (short stories)   127
Court Services Bill (2000)   11
Creating Ever-Cool (book)   243
Crime and Disorder Act (1998)   4, 141–2, 155
Crime Survey of England and Wales   144
Criminal Justice Act (2003)   143
Criminal Justice and Court Services Act (2000)   148

Criminal Justice and Police Act (2001)   148
Criminal Justice and Public Order Act (1994)   4
Criminal Justice Bill (2000)   11
Cross, Gary   253
Cummings, Dominic   196–7
Cunningham, Hugh   80
The Curious Incident of the Dog in the Night-Time (book)   125–6, 133–4
Curtis, Richard   113
Cyberporn case (in USA)   228, 231

Dahl, Roald   130
Danesi, Marcel   125
Davies, Chris   231
Davies, Nick   32
Davies, Stevie   124
The Day My Bum Went Psycho (book)   124
De Vries, Jantina   172
Declaration of the Rights of the Child (1959)   161
Del Vecchio, Gene   244
Deliver Us From Evie (book)   130
Detention and Training Orders   143
Diary of a Wimpy Kid (book)   130
Digital Britain (government report, 20009)   231
Disneyfication   269
Do They Know It's Christmas? (song)   107
Doing Business (initiative of World Bank)   286–8
Doing It (book)   131–2
doli incapax (incapable of forming the intent to commit a crime or tort)   140
Donaldson, Lord   2, 5, 166
Donnelly, Jack   171
Dorn, J.A.   280
Downes, Daragh   122
Dowty, Terri   232
Dragon's Den (TV programme)   112
Dubit (youth research company)   250
Duggan, Mark   153
Duncan Smith, Iain   215, 217
Dunn, Judy   243
Durant, Alan   124

Early Childhood Development Programme (of the World Bank)   288–9
Eccleshare, Julia   124

Education Act (1993) 185
Education Action Zones 184, 186
Education for Citizenship and the Teaching of Democracy in School (report, 1998) 184
Education Reform Act (1988) 182
Education, education, education (speech by Tony Blair, 1996) 180, 225
Egan, Danielle 303
Eleven Plus examination 184, 189
Eliot, George 193
Embedded marketing 248
Erlbruch, Wolf 130
EU Kids Online research 307
European Commission on Human Rights 6–8
European Commissioner's Safer Internet programme 307
European Convention on Human Rights (ECHR) 2, 7, 9, 14–15
European Court of Human Rights 6–10, 12
Every Child Matters agenda/framework 163, 208
Every Child Matters: Change for Children in Social Care (2004) 55
Every Child Matters: Change for Children programme (2004) 48–52, 55, 59, 61–2
Every Parent Matters (Dept. for Education and Skills, 2007) 212
Excellence in Schools (White Paper, 1997) 184
Eynon, Rebecca 231

Factory Acts (nineteenth century) 279
Fairclough, Norman 226
Family and Parenting Institute 60
Family Law Reform Act (1969) 164
Famous, Rich and in the Slums (TV documentary, 2011) 110–13
Farepak (Christmas savings club, collapse of, 2006) 95–6
Farrington, David, 50
Fathallah, Judith 132
Fear of Flying (book) 131
Featherstone, Brid 216
Feed (book) 133
Feinstein, Leon 212
Feltz, Vanessa 112
Fettes College 122

Fielding, Helen 131
Fine, Anne 119, 131
First Love, Last Rites (book) 131
Fiske, John 245
Fitzgerald, Edward QC 4
Flanagan, Sir Ronnie 149–50
The Fold (book) 132
Forever (book) 131
Foucault, Michel 304
Framework for the Assessment of Children in Need and Their Families (2000) 47, 61
Franzen, Jonathan 124
Fraser, Lord 165, 168
Fraser, Nancy 206
Freeman, Claire 130
Freud, Sigmund 303
Friend, Natasha 132
The Full Monty (film) 128

Gamble, Andrew 183
Gasset, Ortega y 244
Gavin, Jamila 133
Geldof, Sir Bob 102, 108, 109, 112, 113
Geneva Declaration (1924) 161
German Medical Association 173
Giddens, Anthony 119, 121, 123, 133–4, 206, 304
Gillick v. West Norfolk and Wisbech Area Health Authority 176
Gillick, Victoria/ Gillick ruling 163–9
Gillies, Val 197
Gillmoor, Dan 27–8
Girls Under Pressure (book) 132
Glaser, Sheri R. 77
Gleitzman, Morris 129
Golding, Peter xi, 103
Goldson and Coles Report (on child deaths in custody, 2005) 147
The Good Child Enquiry 208
A Good Childhood (book) 243
Good Childhood Inquiry (2009) 169
Google (search engine) 302
Google Glass device 302
Gove, Michael xii, 61, 180, 193, 196, 215, 234
Greenslade, Roy 13, 16, 24
Grieve, Dominic 25
Griffiths, Andy 124
Griffiths, Jay 243
Gulrajani, Mohina 292

Haddon, Mark   125, 133–4
Hall, Lee   128
Hall, Stuart   220
Hannah Montana (product range)   247
Hard Pressed (report on press coverage of social work, social services)   30–3
Harkin Bill (US Child Labor Deterrence Act, 1999)   291–2
Harkins, Neil   25
The Harmonica (book)   129
Harry Potter (product range)   247
Harry Potter books   120–5
Hartas, Demitra   213
Hattersley, Roy   188
Hawkes, Gail   303
Head Start programme (in USA)   213, 216
Hendrick, Harry   208
Hengst, Heinz   134
Henry, Lenny   113, 189
Henry, Tyra (death of)   29
Heppell, Stephen   233
Herrnstein, Richard J.   197
High School Musical (product range)   247
Hillgate Group   181
Hindley, Myra   15, 17
His Dark Materials (trilogy)   123, 133
Hodge, Margaret   211
Hoestlandt, Jo   129
Holes (book/film)   128
Holzwarth, Werner   130
Hope and Glory (TV drama series)   189
Hope, Lord   6
House of Commons Children, Schools and Families Committee   54
The House of Tiny Tearaways (TV programme)   120, 230
Households Below Average Income (HBAI) report   97–8
How I Live Now (book)   132
How to Lose Friends and Alienate People (book/film)   193
Howard, Michael   1–6, 8, 12, 140–1, 151
Howarth, Gerald   2
Hudson, Pat   281
Human Rights Act   168
The Hunger Games (book)   134
Hussain, Abed   7
Huxley, Aldous   132
Huxley, Thomas Henry   179

ILO Convention   138 293
ILO Convention   182 (1999) 275
ILO Global Action plan (2006)   275
ILO International Programme on the Elimination of Child Labour (1992)   276
IMF Enhanced Structural Adjustment Facilities   285
IMF Extended Credit Facility   285
IMF Poverty Reduction and Growth Facility   285
IMF Structural Adjustment Programmes   283–5
Immersive marketing   248
The Impoverishment of the UK (PSE report, 2013)   92
Information Society   225
Institute of Economic Affairs   181
Institute of Fiscal Studies   60, 98
Institute of Ideas   105
Integrated Children's System   51, 56
International Labour Organization (ILO)   81, 275–7, 293
International Monetary Fund   108, 278–9, 281–8
International Organisation of Employers (IOE)   292–4
International Trade Union Confederation (ITUC)   285, 286
International Year of the Child (1919)   161
IOE *Resolution on Child Labour* (1996)   293

Jackson, Stevi   303, 304
Jacobson, Lisa   243
James, Adrian   x, xi, 304
James, Allison   x, xi, 304
Jawbone (tracking device)   238
Jenkins, Simon   12
Jenks, Chris   74
Jessop, Bob   181
Johnson, Alan   212
Johnston, Tony   129
Jones, April (murder of)   302
Jong, Erica   131

Kang, Susan   288
Kaslik, Ibi   132
Kay, Ellen   118

Kehily, Mary Jane 169
Kelling, George L. 142
Kellner, Douglas 108
Kennedy, Julia 33–5
Kenrick, Joanna 132
Kerr, M.E. 130
Khan, Farzad 291
Kibera (slum district, Nairobi) 110–13
Kidfluence (book) 244
Kim, Gooyong 108
Kincaid, James 71, 72, 303
Kinney, Jeff 130
Kippers (Kids In Parents' Pockets Eroding Retirement Savings) 121
Kith: The Riddle of the Childscape (book) 243
Klein, Naomi 243
Knowledge Economy 188
Kozol, Jonathan 191
Kristeva, Julia 126

Labour Party 121, 141
Lady Chatterley's Lover (book) 131
Lady: My Life as a Bitch (book) 131
Laming Report (on death of Victoria Climbie, 2003) 53
Laming Report (*The Protection of Children in England*, 2009) 54–6
Larkin, Philip 29, 131
The Last Book in the Universe (book) 132
Lawrence, D.H. 131
Layard, Richard 243
Le Guin, Ursula 121
League of Nations 161
Leavis, F.R. 244
Lennon, John 109
Let Girls Be Girls (Mumsnet campaign) 261
Letting Children be Children (report by Mothers' Union, 2011) 250, 261–3, 268–9, 302
Leveson Inquiry (into phone-hacking by newspapers, 2011–12) 113
Levin, Benjamin 234
Levithan, David 130
Levy, Alan QC 7
Lewis, C.S. 121
Lewis, Michael 228
Liddle, Dean 25
Lindauer, David 280

Lindstrom, Martin 244, 245, 250
Linn, Susan 243
Little Ted's Nursery, Plymouth xii
Live 8 (concerts, 2005) 108, 110
Live Aid (concerts, 1985) xiii, 107, 108, 113
Living Marxism (magazine) 105
Lloyd, Dominic 6–7
Local Safeguarding Children Boards 58
Local Schools Network 192
Loughton, Tim 36
Lowe Bell (PR firm) 190
Lowe, Nigel 167

Major, John 3, 59, 121–2, 182, 183
Mandelson, Peter 96
Manzoor, Sarfraz 108–9
Marcuse, Herbert 244
Marr, Andrew 41
Marrin, Minette 10
Marx, Karl 108, 194
May, Theresa 149
Mayall, Berry 171
Mayo, Ed 243
McAra, Lesley 151
McCann, Madeleine 33, 35
McCartney, Paul 109
McEwan, Ian 131
McEwan, Leon 20–1
McGuinness, Paul 109
McKinsey (management consultants) 181
McLachlan, Sarah 35
McRobbie, Angela 226
McShane, Denis 73
McVie, Susan 151
Mellor, David 18–20, 23
Metroland (book) 131
Meyer, Stephenie 123
Mickey Mouse Clubs 247
Middlemarch (book) 193
Middleton, Sue 103
Milburn, Alan 212
Miliband, Ed 94, 99
Miliband, Ralph 295
Miljeteig, Per 291
Millenium Development Goals (ILO initiative) 275
Miller, Maria 303
Minogue, Kylie (singer) 266
Mitchell, Andrew 107

Index 323

Mitchell, David   124
Monkey Taming (book)   132
Monty Python (comedy troupe)   89
Moravcsik, Julius   75
Morland, Mr Justice   1
Morley, Ben   129
Morrow, Virginia   171
Mortal Engines (book)   133
Mothers' Union   251, 261, 302
Mountjoie, Edward de   102
Mr Men (books)   193
Mumsnet (website)   261, 268
Munro, Eileen (chair, review of child protection, 2011)   36, 57
Murdoch, Rupert   185
Murray, Charles   156, 197
My Son Is An Alien (book)   125
Myers, William   290
Myracle, Lauren   131

Na, An   132
Naipaul, V.S.   124
Nairn, Agnes   243
Nardinelli, Clark   279–80, 282
Narey, Martin   61
National Association for the Prevention of Cruelty to Children (NSPCC)   60, 102, 260
National Association of Head Teachers   188
National Association of Local Government Officers (NALGO)   103
National Children's Home   102
National College of School Leadership   189
National Curriculum   122, 125, 190, 192, 194
National Grid for Learning   227, 233
National Health Service (UK)   277
National Union of Teachers (NUT)   185, 196
neoliberalism   xi, 104, 112, 204, 220, 269, 275–96
New Labour   32, 52, 56, 59, 89–99, 128, 140–57, 183, 185–6, 188, 190–1, 205–7, 209–13, 217, 226–7, 232–3
New Labour, New Life for Britain (pamphlet, 1996)   183
Newcastle United FC   106
News Corporation   185

NHS Parenting Programme   215
Nicholson, William   132
Nickelodeon (children's TV channel)   244
Nielsen, Michael E.   292
Nieuwenhuys, Olga   291
Ninja Turtles (children's craze)   246
Nintendo (electronics corporation)   277
No Logo (book)   243
Noughts & Crosses (book)   129

O'Hagan, Andrew   4
O'Neill, Brendan   105–6
O'Neill, Jamie   130
Ofcom   307
offences brought to justice (OBTJs)   147, 149–50
Office for Standards in Education, Children's Services and Skills (OFSTED)   53, 195–6
Office of Standards in Education (OFSTED)   182–3, 190
One Direction (singing group)   113
Open Public Services White Paper (2011)   59
Operation Elveden (investigation of illegal newsgathering)   24
Organisation for Economic Cooperation and Development (OECD)   181–2
Orkneys (child abuse case)   29
Osborne, George   xii

paedophilia   229
Palmer, Sue   170, 243
Pannick, David QC   19
parens patriae (the power of the state to intervene against an abusive or negligent parent)   169
Parenting Orders   217
parentocracy   211
Parris, Matthew   3
Patrinos, Harry Anthony   281
Payne, Sarah/ 'Sarah's Law'   xii, 228, 231, 233
Peer-to-peer marketing   248, 251
penalty notices for disorder (PNDs)   147, 149–50, 155
Penn, Helen   288–9
Penny, Laurie   269–70
Perfect (book)   132
Perry, Claire   315

Peters, Julie Anne 132
Philbrick, Rodman 132–3
Phillips, Melanie 7, 190, 192, 194, 302
Pierson, John 4
Pilcher, Jane 302
Pilkey, Dav 130
Pill, Lord Justice 5
Pink Floyd, The (band) 110
Pink Stinks (pressure group) 269
Pithers, David 46
Plomin, Robert 197
Pokemon (children's craze) 246, 248
Police and Crime Commissioners (PCCs) 152
Police and Criminal Evidence Act (1984) 152, 154
Police Reform Act (2002) 148
Police Reform and Social Responsibility Act (2011) 152
Poor Kids (TV documentary, 2011) 104–7
Popkewitz, Thomas 237–8
pornography 229, 301–16
Portnoy's Complaint (book) 131
post-welfare society 181
Poverty and Social Exclusion (ESRC-funded report) 90
Poverty Reduction Strategy Papers 285
Power, Michael 57
Primark (store) 268
Product placement 248
Programme for International Student assessment (PISA) 181–2, 235
Protecting Children (Home Office guide, 1998) 46
Pullman, Philip 123–5, 127, 133

The Rachel Papers (book) 131
Rainbow Boys (trilogy) 130
Ramsbottom, Sir David 13
Reading the Riots (*Guardian*/LSE Report, 2011) 153
Red Nose Day 107, 112
Red Tears (book) 132
Rees, Erik 21
Reeve, Philip 133
Refugee Boy (book) 129
Rentoul, John 2
Rich and Mad (book) 132
Ridley, Philip 133

Rights of Children and Young Persons (Wales) Measure (2011) 164, 173
risk society 119, 304
Rizer, Arthur 77
The Road of Bones (book) 119
Rochdale (child abuse case) 29
Rock Against Racism 108
Rolling Stones, The (band) 125
Rose, Nikolas 210
Rosoff, Meg 132
Roth, Philip 131
Rowling, J.K. 121–4, 133
Roy, Dunu 295
Rudd, David 303
Rumsfeld, Donald xiii, 69–70
Rutter, Michael 51

Sachar, Louis 128
SaferMedia (Christian group) 302
Salinger, J.D. 126
Samsung (electronics corporation) 277
Sanchez, Alex 130
Santana, Arthur 42
The Savage (book) 128
Save the Children (Sweden) 173
Save the Children Alliance 289
Savile, Jimmy 303
Scarman, Lord 166
School Standards and Framework Bill (1997) 184
Schor, Judith 243
Scott, Sue 304
Scribbleboy (book) 133
Scruton, Roger 8
Seabrook, Jeremy 295
Secret Millionaire (TV series) 106
Secure Training Centres 143
Secure Training Orders 143
Self, Will 131
Shaftesbury, seventh Earl of 102
Sharp, Tia (murder of) 302
Shephard, Gillian 183
Shoesmith, Sharon 28, 33, 35, 37, 54
Siddiqi, Faraaz 281
Silber, Justice 168
The Silence of the Lambs (film) 20
The Silence Seeker (book) 129
Silent Hill (video game) 20
Singh, Prem 7
Skellig (book) 127–8

Skinny (book)   132
Smith, Ali   124
Smith, David James   1
Smith, Zadie   111
So Sexy So Soon (book)   259
Social Market Foundation   211
Social networking   248
Social Work Reform Board   58
Social Work Task Force   53, 55, 58
Socialist Educational Association   192
Society for Adolescent Medicine   124
Soros Foundation   289
Sparks, Colin   191
Spice Girls, The (singing group)   130
Sponsorship   248
Sport Relief appeal   107
Standards and Effectiveness Unit (Dept. for Education and Skills)   184
Star of Fear, Star of Hope (book)   129
Steel, Mark   108, 111
Stephenson, Thomas Bowman   102
Stevenson Report (1996–7)   233
Steyn, Lord   6
stop and search (police tactic)   154
The Story of the Little Mole Who Knew It Was None of His Business (book)   130
Straw, Jack   2, 3, 10–13, 19
Sugar Rush (book)   130
Sugar, Sir Alan   112
Supernanny (TV programme)   120, 134
Sure Start Children's Centres (closure of)   60
Sure Start pre-school programme   90, 184, 186, 197, 210, 212–13
Sutherland, Anne   244
Sutherland, Selina   102
Sutherland, Stewart   182
Swedish National Board of Health   173
Swedish Ombudsman for Children   173

Talbot, Brian   131
Tamagotchi ('digital pet') craze   227
The Tale of One Bad Rat (book)   131
Taylor, Lord (of Gosforth)   1
Tears in Heaven (song)   35
Thatcher, Margaret   xii, 59, 89, 121, 160, 164–5, 168, 172, 204–5, 207
Thatcher's Children?   x, 45, 180, 282
Thatcherism   32, 93, 98
Then (trilogy)   129

Thomas the Tank Engine (franchise)   247
Thompson, Beth   244
Thompson, Robert   xiii, 1–25
Time for a Fresh Start (report on youth justice, 2010)   151
Tisdall, Kay   194
Tolkein, J.R.R.   121
Tomlinson, Sally   181, 185, 191
Toxic Childhood (book)   170, 243
Toynbee, Polly   215
Troubled Families Unit   217
Trunkfield, Richard   24
ttfn (book)   131
ttyl (book)   131
Turner, Mr Justice   4
Twilight book series   123, 125, 132
Tzannatos, Zafiris   294

Uglies (book)   125, 132
UK Children's Commissioner   170, 195, 301–2, 304–8, 315
UK Deputy Children's Commissioner   305
UK Youth Parliament   169
UN Convention Against Transnational Organized Crime (2000)   75
UNICEF   170–1, 277, 289
Unions and Collective Bargaining (World Bank report, 2003)   286
United Nations Convention on the Rights of the Child (UNCRC, 1989)   xiv, 81, 160–4, 167, 170–1, 173, 290
United Nations Development Programme   97
United Nations Trafficking Protocol   82
United States General Accounting Office Report (2001)   283
US Criminal Alien Program   79
US Dept. of Health and Human Services   76, 83
US National Child Abuse and Neglect Data System   83
US Secure Communities Program   79
User generated content   248

Venables, Jon   xiii, 1–25
Viral marketing   248, 251
Vorderman, Carol   228–9

Index 327

Wall Street Journal 197
Walliams, David 107–8
Wallis, Neil 20
Wastell, David 214
Waters, Sarah 130
Waugh, Benjamin 102
The Weakest Link (TV programme) 112
West London Free School 193
Westerfield, Scott 125, 127, 132
White, Richard 167
White, Sue 214
Who, The (band) 125
Widdecombe, Ann 12
Wilson, Jacqueline 130, 132
Wilson, James Q. 142
Wilton, Brent 294
Winterson, Jeanette 130
Wishaw, Sir Michael 196
Wolf, Christopher 42
Wonderland trial (of child pornographers, 2001) 228, 231
Wonga.com (payday loan company) 106
Woodhead, Chris 182–4, 188, 190, 192
Woolf, Lord Chief Justice 13, 17–19, 23
Working Together (*Munro Review*, 2013) 59–61
Working Together (revised guide, 2010) 55, 58

Working Together to Safeguard Children (government guide, 1999) 47, 62
Working Together Under the Children Act 1989 (Home Office guide, 1991) 46–8
World Bank 108, 278–80, 281–8, 290, 293–4
World Bank Child Labor Programme 294
World Economic Forum 236
World Health Organisation 289
World Trade Organisation (WTO) 278, 284
Wrigley, Terry 194

Yelland, David 22
Young, Dumb and Living Off Mum (TV programme) 121
Young, Mary Eming 288
Young, Toby 193
Youth Inclusion Programmes 147
youth justice 140–57
Youth Justice and Criminal Evidence Act 1999 143
Youth Justice Board 142, 147
Youth Offender Panels 143

Zephaniah, Benjamin 129
Zizek, Slavoj 69–70
Zusak, Markus 129